# National Courts and the Standard of Review in Competition Law and Economic Regulation

Europa Law Publishing, Groningen 2009

# National Courts and the Standard of Review in Competition Law and Economic Regulation

Edited by Oda Essens, Anna Gerbrandy and Saskia Lavrijssen

Europa Law Publishing is a publishing company specializing in European Union law, international trade law, public international law, environmental law and comparative national law.
For further information please contact Europa Law Publishing via email: info@europalawpublishing.com or visit our website at: www.europalawpublishing.com.



Typeset in Scala and Scala Sans, Graphic design by G2K Designers, Groningen/Amsterdam

NUR 828; ISBN 978-90-8952-001-2

## Foreword

This book collects the papers that were presented during an international conference on judicial review in competition law and economic regulation that was successfully organised by the *Europa Institute* of Utrecht University in May 2008. One of the main aims of the conference was to explore the interaction between European and national law when national courts set the standards of review and standards of proof when reviewing decisions of national competition authorities and economic regulators that apply European law in a comparative setting.

Stimulating presentations from academics and practitioners from different Member States and EU institutions led to lively discussions. On the one hand, it was fascinating to see how the judicial review of the application of European substantive norms in the area of competition law and economic regulation is characterised by so much variety in legal systems. It would seem that until now the direct influence of European law on the standard of review and the standard of proof applied in the different Member States is limited. On the other hand, when taking a closer look at what the national courts in the different Member States actually do, one could argue that in practice the national courts tend to apply similar standards of review and proof when reviewing decisions of national competition authorities and economic regulators. This book does not only collect the conference papers, but also provides for an enlightening synthesis in which the editors provide some provisional conclusions and further food for thought.

The conference and the book can be seen as an example of the many projects in which the *Europa Institute* is involved. Analysing in a comparative way the interaction between European law and national law in a whole range of areas will continue to be high on the agenda of the *Europa Institute* for the coming years.

The editors are grateful for the editorial assistance provided by Wies Smit, Dorienke Kraak, Rieneke Knol and Margot Aelen.

Professor Sacha Prechal,
Professor of European law
Board Member *Europa Institute*, Utrecht University

CHAPTER I

# Introduction

This book collects the papers that were presented during the international conference 'Judicial Review in Competition Law and Economic Regulation' that was organized by the Europa Institute of Utrecht University on 22 and 23 May 2008. The topic of the conference and this book were chosen in reaction to a heated debate by practitioners and academics on the appropriate standards of review and proof to be applied by Community courts and national courts in reviewing decisions of the European Commission or national authorities (national competition authorities and national regulatory authorities) in competition law and economic regulation cases. At the European level this debate was stimulated by several judgments of the Court of First Instance annulling European Commission (hereinafter: Commission) decisions in merger cases after a thorough review of the Commission's facts, reasoning and assessment of the facts.[1]

The Commission appealed the *Tetra Laval* judgment of the Court of First Instance (hereinafter: CFI). The Commission argued that the CFI had overstepped the boundaries of the legality review on the basis of Article 230 EC by substituting the appraisal of economic data by the Commission and raising the requisite standard of proof. These arguments of the Commission were rejected by the European Court of Justice (hereinafter: ECJ).[2] Taking into account that Commission decisions in merger cases are based on complex economic and legal assessments with a margin of discretion for the Commission, the ECJ clarified the standard of review and the standard of proof to be applied to these Commission decisions.

As argued by the Commission, the ECJ indeed recognises that the Commission has a margin of discretion with regard to economic matters.[3] However, this margin does not mean that the Community Courts must refrain from reviewing the Commission's interpretation of information of an economic nature. Not only must the Community Courts, *inter alia*, establish whether the evidence relied on is factually accurate, reliable and consistent, but also whether that evidence contains all the information which must be taken into account in order to assess a complex situation and whether it is capable of substantiating the conclusions drawn from it. Such a review is all the more necessary in the case of a prospective analysis, such as is required when examining a proposed merger with conglomerate effects.[4] According to the ECJ, the CFI by no means added a condition relating to the requisite standard of proof but merely drew attention to the essential function of evidence, which is to establish convincingly the merits of an argument or, as in the present case, of a decision on a merger.[5]

---

1 Case T-342/99, *Airtours* v. *Commission* [2002] ECR II-2585, Case T-310/01, *Schneider Electric* v. *Commission* [2002] ECR-II 4071, Case T-5/02 and *Tetra Laval* v. *Commission* [2002] ECR II-4381.

2 Case C-12/03 P, *Commission* v. *Tetra Laval* [2005] ECR I-987, par. 39.

3 Joined Cases C-68/94 and C-30/95, *France and Others* v. *Commission* (*'Kali & Salz'*) [1998] ECR I-1375.

4 Case C-12/03 P, *Commission* v. *Tetra Laval* [2005] ECR I-987, par. 39.

5 Case C-12/03 P, *Commission* v. *Tetra Laval* [2005] ECR 1-987, par. 41.

The *Tetra Laval* judgment and other judgments relating to merger control, such as the judgments in *Airtours* and *Schneider Electric*, fed the debate at the national level. In the Netherlands, for instance, the Rotterdam District Court annulled several decisions of the Netherlands Competition Authority (*Nederlandse Mededingingsautoriteit*: NMa) after an intensive review of the facts, reasoning and assessment by the NMa.[6] On appeal against the judgment of the District Court in the *Nuon/Reliant* case, the NMa argued that the Rotterdam court applied a too strict standard of review and too high standard of proof, making the work of the NMa very difficult indeed.[7] On appeal these arguments were rejected by the Trade and Industry Appeals Tribunal (*College van Beroep voor het Bedrijfsleven*: CBB).[8] The CBB reiterated its previous case law regarding the standard of review in merger cases, once more stressing that the NMa had to make it sufficiently plausible that the conditions for the disapproval or the conditional approval of a merger of the Competition Act have been met. Although the CBB applied this standard already before the *Tetra Laval* case, and the *Tetra Laval* case is not explicitly mentioned, it is a matter of debate whether or not the CBB relied implicitly on the above-mentioned paragraphs of the *Tetra Laval* case in order to specify the standard it requires from the NMa. Furthermore, the CBB held that the District Court of Rotterdam had applied the correct test in the judgment under appeal, as it merely had examined whether the NMa had made it sufficiently plausible whether the legal conditions for the decision at hand were met. It was also this possibly decentralised application of a community standard of review or community standard of proof in Dutch merger control that fed our curiosity as to the influence of European case law on the standard of review in other areas of economic law, and in other countries as well. Hence our incentive for organising this conference.

*Central question and subquestions*

The above-mentioned cases illustrate clearly that there is an ongoing tension between the right of the market parties to effective legal protection against administrative decisions impinging upon the rights they derive from European law (or national competition and regulatory law) and the interest of the Commission and the national authorities in needing a degree of leeway to effectively exercise their powers. In *Tetra Laval* the ECJ has clarified how it will deal with this tension when assessing Commission decisions implying complex economic appraisals at the European level. The central question of this book evolves around the impact of this judgment: what is the impact of the *Tetra Laval* standard on the standards of review and standards of proof applied by the national

6 See contribution of Lavrijssen in this book.

7 District Court of Rotterdam, MEDED 04/135-WILD, NUON v. NMa, LJN: AT6440. Kalbfleisch, 'Intensiteit van rechterlijke toetsing van marktautoriteiten', speech on the occasion of the fiftieth anniversary of the Trade and Industry Appeals Tribunal (College van Beroep voor het Bedrijfsleven: CBB), www.nmanet.nl.

8 CBB, AWB 05/440, *NUON* vs *NMa*, LJN: ZA3274.

courts in competition law and economic regulation cases at the national level? This central question leads to eight subquestions that were the subject of debate during the conference and that are analysed in the contributions of this book:

- How should the *Tetra Laval* standard of the ECJ be interpreted?
- Is this standard binding on the national courts?
- What are the standards of review and standards of proof applied by national courts when reviewing decisions of national competition authorities and national regulatory authorities?
- What is the influence of European law on the national standards of review and the national standards of proof? Have the national courts applied the *Tetra Laval* standard or a similar standard in practice?
- What are the reasons for the presence or absence of a European legal influence on the national standards of review and standards of proof?
- Are there many differences between the standards of review and standards of proof applied by the national courts of the different Member States?
- Should there be more convergence between the standards of review and the standards of proof applied by the national courts of the different Member States and should there be more convergence between the European and national standards?
- Should the *Tetra Laval* standard play a role in the convergence of national and European standards of review and standards of proof in competition law and economic regulation cases and if so, what role?

*Structure of this book*

The contributions in this book will reflect on the above-mentioned central question and subquestions.

The second chapter of this book is written by Judge Arjen Meij of the Court of First Instance. In this chapter judicial review by the EC Courts in competition law cases and beyond is highlighted from the perspective of the Community Judiciary. In the third chapter of this book Tom Zwart approaches the scope of review of administrative action from a more general constitutional and comparative perspective, including the US, Canada, EU, Germany and the UK. The fourth chapter of this book is written by Annetje Ottow. This contribution deals with the growing importance of economic analysis in competition law and economic regulation. Also the impact of economisation on the standards of review and standards of proof applied by the European and national courts when reviewing decisions of the European Commission or of the national authorities is discussed. In the fifth chapter Mathieu Schimmel and Rob Widdershoven provide, from a general administrative law perspective, some analytical observations on the meaning and the practical application of the *Tetra Laval* standard by the European courts in competition law cases and beyond as well as on the possible consequences for the national courts of the EU Member States.

After these general contributions seven country reports deal with the standards of review and the standards of proof applied by the national courts in competition law and economic regulation cases and the (possible) impact of European law in these cases. For a good understanding of the functioning of the systems of legal review by the courts in the separate Member States, each of the contributions sets out the relevant constitutional and legal context of the country discussed. This includes a discussion of the main legal concepts that are linked to the legal review by the national courts, such as the concepts of 'judicial review', 'discretion' and 'standards of review'.

Jörg Terhechte deals with judicial review in competition law and economic regulation cases in Germany. Nicolas Petit and Louise Rabeux analyse judicial review by the national courts in French competition law and economic regulation. Kati Cseres and Jurian Langer discuss judicial review in competition law and economic regulation cases in Hungary. Roberto Caranta and Barbara Marchetti examine the judicial review of regulatory decisions by the Italian courts. Saskia Lavrijssen explores judicial review of decisions by national competition authorities and national regulatory authorities in the Netherlands. Iñigo del Guayo provides an analysis of the judicial review in competition law and economic regulation by the Spanish courts. Following these contributions, Eva Edwardsson discusses judicial review in competition law and economic regulation in Sweden. The final contribution contains a report on the United Kingdom; an analysis undertaken by Cosmo Graham.

On the basis of these contributions and the discussions during the conference, the final chapter contains the concluding synthesis, which aims to formulate some answers and suggestions concerning the subquestions and the central question of this book.

CHAPTER 2

# Judicial Review in the EC Courts: *Tetra Laval* and Beyond

A. Meij

## 1 Introduction*

The theme of this conference is timely chosen, as the application of European competition law by national authorities and courts is full swing under way and the national regimes are largely set up after the European model. This is not to suggest that this contribution will represent a model for the conference debate, far from it. The purpose of this contribution is not even to present a more or less detailed analysis of the subject matter, but rather to give a flavour of it from the perspective of the Community judicature.[1] To that effect, it may be a good idea to highlight a few cases which, apparently, have contributed to incite the organisers to convene this conference.

First of all, however, it is appropriate to outline briefly the jurisdictional setting in which judicial review has developed within the EC. Then, I will very summarily go through some competition cases in order to find out which are the typical approaches, notions and distinctions as regards judicial review in this area of the law. I also intend to make a brief excursion to adjacent areas of case law, which give rise to similar questions, such as state aid and marketing authorisations for pharmaceuticals. Finally we may have a closer look to find out whether it is possible to identify more precisely the areas of administrative discretion and inherently limited judicial review.

## 2 The jurisdictional setting

As I understand it, this conference is concerned with judicial control of administrative decisions, rather than judicial decisions on the merits of a case. Judicial control of administrative decisions may be organised in rather different ways, some of which will probably be highlighted during this conference. It is no news to tell that the main venue in the Community Courts against Commission decisions, the action under Article 230 EC, was initially modelled after the *'recours pour excès de pouvoir'* before the French *Conseil d'État*.[2] This is, also in the EC Courts, conceived as a *'recours objectif'*, the main purpose of which is to review the legality of the act undertaken (hence *'contentieux de la légalité'*), in order to either uphold this act or remove it wholly or partially, but altogether from what is called the objective legal order through its annulment *erga omnes*. I call this to mind as this particular conception of judicial protection of private persons as against administrative action presumably serving the public interest, is characterised by a refined system of modalities concerning, on

* The views expressed herein are entirely personal and do not have any bearing on any pending cases before the Court. The author would like to thank Tristan Baumé, legal secretary at the CFI, for his assistance in preparing some parts of this paper.

1 A great number of articles have been published on the subject. To mention but two of those, reference may be made to Bailey (2004) p. 1327, and to Sibony (2007) p. 205.

2 See Donnat (2008) p. 6, and for a detailed study of the French system, Chapus (2008).

the one hand, limited access to court and limited grounds of appeal and, on the other hand, far-reaching powers for the Court to remove the contested act from the legal order. Indeed, as is well known, access to court under Article 230 EC is governed by strict standing conditions. The grounds of appeal listed in this provision – lack of competence, infringement of an essential procedural requirement, infringement of the Treaty or of any rule of law relating to its application, and misuse of powers – are framed according to early conceptions at the *Conseil d'Etat*.[3] Even if these grounds are limited in number, in the EC context, infringement of the Treaty or of any rule relating to its application virtually encloses any plea in law one can think of. On the other hand, the power to remove an administrative act altogether from the legal order may seem far-reaching, but it is restricted at the same time; as its task is limited to controlling the legality of the administrative act on points raised by the applicant,[4] it is not for the Court to pronounce itself on the merits of a case, and even less to take over the role of the administration by adopting a new decision, but for the administration in the event of an annulment to proceed to a fresh decision complying with the judgment of the Court.[5]

Basically, this conception of judicial review seems to aim at striking a balance between private and public interests in order to protect the objective legal order in which the *'pouvoir public'* acts on the basis of the constitutional principle of legality, rather than to protect the position of the private individual involved in all its, also subjective, aspects. This is of no surprise for those familiar with French administrative and legal thinking and it may be interesting in this respect to hear more about the French system of judicial review later at this conference.

Typically, against this background, the Community Courts from the outset have paid careful attention to apply various standards of review (in French *'degrés de contrôle'*), according, on the one hand, to the room of manoeuvre left to the administration by Treaty or legislative provisions and, on the other hand, to its concern not to substitute its own opinion to that of the administrative body where the latter's conclusions are not deprived of ground. Perhaps this is not an appropriate moment to go further into notions of legality and legitimacy of administrative action, or, for that matter, into considerations of balance of power and rule of law, but I would insist that these are all part of the background against which techniques of judicial review in the framework of the *'recours pour excès de pouvoir'* have been cultivated in the Community Courts. For the purpose of this presentation it suffices to say that the judicial review exerted by the Court stems directly from the principle governing the institutional balance established by the Treaty, i.e. it is for the courts to say what the law is and which are the

3 See Donnat (2008) p. 127.

4 Although the Court is bound by the pleas put forward by parties in controlling the legality of administrative acts, such is not the case in the event of grounds of public order, which may – and must – be raised by the Court *motu proprio*.

5 Cf. Articles 231, 233 EC.

limits it imposes on administrative action, but not to substitute their appraisal to that of the administration and to adopt the required administrative act in its place. This is a distinctive feature of the *'contentieux de la légalité'* as opposed to the *'contentieux de pleine juridiction'*, which indeed allows the Court to take over from the administration and replace the administrative decision by its own.[6] Consequently, where the broad nature of the provision to be applied or the analytical process required to subsume the facts of the case under such provision, leave room for manoeuvre or for policy considerations, the question arises which extent of judicial review is appropriate to safeguard the legality of the administrative act at stake, without the Court taking up a role properly pertaining to the administration.

At this stage, let me turn to a few flowers in EC case law, in order to illustrate – admittedly, in a somewhat selective way – what is presently happening there.

## 3 Some competition cases

It seems only natural to begin with a few words on the much discussed *Tetra Laval* case,[7] in which the CFI annulled a Commission decision declaring the concentration of *Tetra Laval* and *Sidel* incompatible with the common market, on the ground that on several points the Commission failed to sufficiently establish the anti-competitive effects it expected to result from the operation. As requested by the Commission on appeal, the ECJ examined in particular the standard of review applied by the CFI and the requirements it imposed on the Commission as regards the quality of the evidence the latter may rely upon. The CFI had assimilated the requirements to which the analysis of a merger producing a conglomerate effect as in *Tetra Laval*, is subject to those defined by the Court in case *Kali & Salz*[8] with regard to the creation of a situation of collective dominance. Since the effects of a conglomerate-type of merger are generally considered to be neutral or even beneficial for competition the CFI closely examined the proof of the anti-competitive effects of the merger, alleged by the Commission, and required such proof to be supported by convincing evidence.[9] On appeal the Commission closely linked up the standard of proof and the scope of review, submitting that the required standard of convincing evidence transforms the role of the Courts to that of a body which is competent

6 See Article 229 EC, according to which unlimited jurisdiction may be conferred to the EC Courts in relation to fines.

7 Case T-5/02 *Tetra Laval* v. *Commission* [2002] ECR II-4381, para. 155, confirmed by the Court in appeal in Case C-12/03 P *Commission* v. *Tetra Laval* [2005] ECR I-987.

8 Joined Cases C-68/94 and C-30/95 *France and Others* v. *Commission ('Kali & Salz')* [1998] ECR I-1375, para. 222.

9 Case T-5/02 *Tetra Laval* v. *Commission* [2002] ECR II-4381, para. 155.

to rule on the matter in all its complexity and which is entitled to substitute its views for those of the Commission.[10]

The ECJ first pointed out that as regards the tests to be applied when carrying out judicial review of a Commission decision on a concentration, the CFI was right to rely on the judgment in case *Kali & Salz*, where the Court stated that the basic provisions in question confer on the Commission a certain discretion, especially with respect to assessments of an economic nature, and that, consequently, review by the Community Courts of the exercise of that discretion must take account of the margin of discretion implicit in the provisions of an economic nature which form part of the rules on concentration. However, according to the ECJ, this does not mean that the Community Courts must refrain from reviewing the Commission's interpretation of information of an economic nature. Thus distinguishing the scope of review from the standard of proof, the ECJ required with regard to the latter that the Community Courts establish firstly, whether the evidence relied on is factually accurate, reliable and consistent, secondly, whether the evidence contains all the information which must be taken into account in order to assess a complex situation and, thirdly, whether it is capable of substantiating the conclusions drawn from it. The ECJ also considered that where the CFI required a precise examination, supported by convincing evidence, of the anti-competitive effects, it did not add a supplementary condition relating to the requisite standard of proof but merely drew attention to the essential function of evidence. More precisely, in this case which involved prospective analysis of market developments, the purpose of thorough examination of the available evidence was qualified as establishing the plausibility of the economic development envisaged by the contested decision.[11]

This approach, meticulously distinguishing between the establishment of the factual substrate and the discretionary appraisal thereof, is also followed, albeit with a different result, in the *General Electric* case,[12] which is concerned with a Commission decision prohibiting a merger between General Electric and Honeywell in the commercial jet aircraft industry. The Commission considered this merger would entail horizontal, vertical and conglomerate effects which were to strengthen GE's dominant position on related markets. In this case, the CFI started to draw attention to the essential difference between factual matters and findings, on the one hand, which may be found to be inaccurate by the Court in the light of the arguments and evidence brought before it, and, on the other hand, appraisals of an economic nature, referring to this effect to the *Tetra Laval* case. Among many other issues, the Court examined closely the findings of the Commission according to which GE had a dominant position on the market for large commercial jet aircraft engines, as it considered that this pre-merger dominant position was a cornerstone of the Commission's analysis, since a number of the limbs of the reasoning in the contested

10 Case C-12/03 P *Commission* v. *Tetra Laval* [2005] ECR I-987, para. 27.

11 Case C-12/03 P *Commission* v. *Tetra Laval* [2005] ECR I-987, paras 38-45.

12 Case T-210/01 *General Electric Company* v. *Commission* [2005] ECR II-5575.

decision were based on it. It concluded, on the one hand, that the facts relied upon by the Commission in its analysis of the applicant's market share were in essence established, and, on the other, that the Commission did not make a manifest error of assessment in holding that the applicant's market share could, in the circumstances of this case, be indicative of pre-merger dominance on the market for large commercial jet aircraft engines. Similarly, it closely scrutinised the Commission's findings on vertical integration, based on evidence to the effect that GE pursued the commercial policy of using the commercial means at its disposal to increase its strength on the relevant market. However, for its review of the Commission's appraisal of the dominance issue, it had recourse to the classic criterion of whether the latter made a manifest error of assessment in concluding that prior to the merger GE held a dominant position on this market.[13]

From these examples it may be inferred, at least in the area of merger control, that the measure of judicial review is clearly to be distinguished from the verification of evidence required to meet the applicable standard of proof. Indeed, this line of case law allows for only remotely reviewed discretion on the part of the Commission as regards the appraisal of the economic data of the case and the conclusions to be drawn from those data. However, it would not allow such appraisal and the resulting conclusions to be based on inaccurate, incomplete or inappropriate evidence. Contrary to what the Commission seemed to suggest, the discretionary power of appraisal for the administration does not imply that it is not accountable for the soundness of the foundation the appraisal is based on. In case of prospective market analysis the required standard of proof is to establish the plausibility of the expected development. Where the alleged prognosis is contrary to usual theoretical assumptions, as in the case of anti-competitive effects of a conglomerate merger, the examination of the evidence will be all the more thorough.

Would all this be different in cases under Articles 81 and 82 EC? The first case in point on this matter is *Remia*,[14] where the Court distinguished comprehensive review of the question whether or not the conditions are met for the application of, then, Article 85(1) EC, from limited review of the Commission's appraisal of complex economic matters. According to a classic formula the latter review is limited to verifying whether the relevant procedural rules have been complied with, whether the statement of the reasons for the decision is adequate, whether the facts have been accurately stated and whether there has been any manifest error of appraisal or a misuse of powers.[15] This limited review is often referred to as marginal review.[16] It may be noted at once that virtually all elements of this formula require full review, with the exception only of the

[13] Case T-210/01 *General Electric Company* v. *Commission* [2005] ECR II-5575, paras 62-63, 181, 241 and 280.

[14] Case 42/84 *Remia* [1985] ECR 2545.

[15] Case 42/84 *Remia* [1985] ECR 2545, para. 34.

[16] See e.g. Tiili (1999) p. 889.

review of the appraisal itself that has determined the result embedded in the contested act. Apparently, the idea that only a manifest error of appraisal is capable of affecting the legality of the contested act reflects the marginal nature of the review. In *Remia* no such error was found in the Commission's appraisal to the effect that a four year period for a non-competition clause in an agreement for the transfer of an undertaking, rather than the ten year period proposed, was appropriate in order to remain outside the scope of Article 81(1) EC.

In a similar case, *Métropole television,*[17] the Commission accepted various non-compete and exclusivity clauses as ancillary restrictions to the creation of a joint venture in the television industry, provided that such clauses would not last for more than three years. In that case, the CFI considered that the assessment of whether these clauses were objectively necessary for the implementation of the main operation, the joint venture, and proportionate to it, entailed complex economic assessments which were only subject to limited review.[18] As regards the conditions for an exemption under Article 81(3) EC, the CFI followed a similar approach in *GlaxoSmithKline,*[19] referring inter alia to *Remia* and *Tetra Laval.* It noted, in particular, the Commission's margin of discretion, subject to restricted judicial review, consisting of weighing up the advantages expected from the implementation of the exempted agreement and the disadvantages which it entailed for the final consumer. For the Court, this operation takes the form of a balancing exercise carried out in the light of the general interest appraised at Community level. In this context, it underlined in particular that it is not for the Court to substitute its own economic assessment for that of the Commission.[20]

The approach to judicial control of Commission decisions on abuse of dominant position under Article 82 EC is not dissimilar. A perspicuous recent illustration in that respect is provided by the well-known *Microsoft* case,[21] where the CFI summarised the scope of review exerted by it by reference to virtually all elements discussed above and developed in cases such as *Remia* and *Tetra*

---

17 Case T-112/99 *Métropole télévision and others* v. *Commission* [2001] ECR II-2459.

18 Case T-112/99 *Métropole télévision and others* v. *Commission* [2001] ECR II-2459, paras. 114 et seq.

19 Case T-168/01 *GlaxoSmithKline* v. *Commission* [2006] ECR II-2969.

20 Case T-168/01 *GlaxoSmithKline* v. *Commission* [2006] ECR II-2969, paras. 241-244. For a more detailed analysis, see Bailey (2004) p. 1355, who suggests that the judicial self-restraint shown by the practice of limited review as regards the Commission's margin of appreciation, is not required by the Treaty. It would appear, however, that the conception of judicial control of legality in Article 230 precisely implies this approach of judicial review. Moreover, the wording of Article 81 EC, in which the words 'shall be' and 'may be' are respectively employed at paragraphs 1 and 3, implies that once an agreement is held to be restrictive of competition, there is in principle no room for policy consideration at the level of Article 81(1) EC while there is such room at the level of Article 81(3) EC. It should be emphasised, nonetheless, that the appraisal of the restrictive nature or effect of an agreement, which is undertaken when applying Article 81(1) EC, may involve in itself choices of competition policy which, by their very nature, lend themselves to marginal review from the part of the Court.

21 Case T-201/04 *Microsoft* [2007] ECR II-3601.

*Laval*. It also underlined that the Community Courts cannot substitute their own assessment of matters of fact for the Commission's.[22] Among numerous exercises of the appropriate degrees of review throughout the judgment, one example suffices to illustrate the constant and meticulous variation in the standards of review applied in the course of such review process. As regards the duty for the Commission to establish that the refusal to supply information allowing for interoperability entailed a risk for elimination of competition on the work group server operating systems market, the applicant contended inter alia that the criterion applied by the Commission was not sufficiently strict. As this point concerned the conditions for the application of Article 82 EC, it is not surprising that the Court comprehensively determined that in order for Article 82 EC to be applied, it was not required that competition was already eliminated from the market, neither that its elimination was imminent, nor that all competition would be eliminated. What mattered, according to the CFI, was that the refusal was liable or likely to eliminate all effective competition. To that effect, a marginal presence of competitors in certain niches on the market did not suffice to substantiate the existence of effective competition. Subsequently, the Court closely scrutinised whether the evidence relied on by the Commission did indeed substantiate its findings, in order, finally, to leave the conclusion that the evolution of the market revealed a risk that competition would be eliminated on account of the Commission, while finding no manifest error in the assessment leading to that conclusion.[23]

The provisional upshot is that in the area of Articles 81 and 82 EC the Community Courts comprehensively review whether or not the legal conditions for their application are met. Full review is also exercised as to procedural requirements and to the establishment of the facts, their accuracy as well as their adequacy to substantiate the conclusions drawn from them. On the other hand, limited or marginal review is exerted, first, where the nature of the legal provision applied allows for some policy discretion on the part of the administrative body and, second, where the administrative body is faced with a 'complex' factual setting, be it of an economic or otherwise scientific nature, the appraisal of which may lead to different but equally justified conclusions. In that respect, the expression 'manifest error of assessment' reflects the idea that the Court will strike down the act only when the conclusion adopted by the administrative body cannot be supported at the requisite level by the data which are at its disposal. In any case, the Courts refrain from substituting their own assessment for the Commission's. The burden of proof and the standards of review may vary according to whether the decision establishes an infringement or responds to a request for authorisation and to whether it concerns past behaviour or a prognosis of expected developments.

It should also be noted that where a legal provision uses open-ended notions the content of which still needs to be clarified, the Court may adopt two seem-

[22] Case T-201/04 *Microsoft* [2007] ECR II-3601, paras. 87-89.

[23] Case T-201/04 *Microsoft* [2007] ECR II-3601, paras. 560-618.

ingly opposite approaches. On the one hand, it may well consider that this legal provision leaves discretion to the administrative body as to the policy to be developed on its basis. On the other hand, however, since this provision is subject to legal interpretation, the Court, which is ultimately responsible, by virtue of Article 220 EC, to interpret the Treaty and the law derived from it, will be led, as the case law advances, to progressively set out the precise legal content of that provision. Hence, the role of the Community judge will necessarily increase. Such is, for instance, remarkably the case as regards Article 82 EC, with respect to which one may safely state that an abuse of a dominant position is what the Court says it is. Since the notion of abuse of dominant position is within the realm of legal interpretation, defining the conditions under which behaviour is or is not, in principle, covered by this notion is a matter of law and not of policy discretion on the part of the Commission.

## 4 Other areas of administrative regulation

The differentiation of judicial review found so far is by no means a phenomenon exclusively pertaining to competition law. It is rather inherent to the conception of review of legality enshrined in Article 230 EC. The practice of limited judicial review has been extensively applied and developed in cases where the Treaty provides broad discretionary powers for the Community legislator in areas of common policies such as agriculture. Although neither the method of review nor the commonly used terminology to define the process appear very different, for the purpose of the present contribution the focus is rather on review of the application of opaque norms in respect of complex factual situations requiring an appraisal which leaves room for policy choices or different opinions in balancing diverging interests at stake. Many other areas of administrative intervention show approaches to judicial review largely similar to competition cases.

It may not be surprising that the exercise by the Commission of its powers in the area of state aid, similarly concerned with ensuring undistorted competition, frequently requires the assessment of complex economic data. In a recent case, *SIDE* v. *Commission,*[24] the CFI recognised a wide discretion for the Commission, under Article 87(3) EC, to assess the compatibility of certain types of aid with the common market. As the exercise of this discretion involves complex economic and social assessments, here again judicial review is confined to establishing 'that the rules of procedure and the rules relating to the duty to give reasons have been complied with and to verifying the accuracy of the facts relied on and that there has been no error of law, manifest error in the assessment of the facts or misuse of powers'.[25] The object of the contested aid was to disseminate French language and literature by means of a mechanism offsetting the

24 Case T-348/04 *SIDE* v. *Commission* [2008] ECR II-625.

25 Case T-348/04 *SIDE* v. *Commission* [2008] ECR II-625, para. 96.

extra costs of handling small orders. It had been declared compatible with the common market, under Article 87(3)(d) EC, which provides that aid to promote culture and heritage conservation may be considered to be compatible with the common market where such aid does not affect trading conditions and competition in the Community to an extent that is contrary to the common interest. The CFI investigated thoroughly whether, as the applicant sustained, the Commission had overestimated the extra costs, with the effect that the amount of aid paid clearly exceeded the cost of processing small orders and, therefore, went beyond the pursuit of the sole cultural objective covered by the derogation in Article 87(3)(d) EC. Finding manifest inconsistencies and mistakes in the calculations on which the decision was based, the CFI concluded that the applicant was justified in claiming that the Commission overestimated the costs of processing small orders which were actually incurred by the beneficiary of the aid and which were supposed to be strictly and proportionately offset by the contested aid. In this case, the contested decision was annulled for manifest error of assessment, but, apparently, the source of this error was an inaccurate establishment of the facts underlying the assessment.[26]

A case concerning the withdrawal of marketing authorisations of medicinal products, *Artegodan* v. *Commission*,[27] gave the CFI the opportunity to specify its approach to judicial review of non-economic, scientific assessments. The Community Code on medicinal products provides that the competent authorities are to suspend or revoke the marketing authorisation of a medicinal product where, on the basis of the progress of scientific knowledge and new data collected, in particular in the context of pharmaco-vigilance, that product proves to be harmful in the normal conditions of use or where its therapeutic efficacy is lacking. In this context, the CFI exercised judicial review by reference to two principles identified in case law, i.e. the conditions for (withdrawal of an) authorisation must be interpreted and applied in accordance with, on the one hand, the principle that protection of public health must take precedence over economic considerations and, on the other, the precautionary principle, according to which, in case of uncertainty as to the existence or extent of risks to human health, the institutions may take precautionary measures. The Code on medicinal products foresees mandatory consultation of a scientific committee (Committee for Proprietary Medicinal Products, hereafter 'CPMP') providing the Commission with scientific evidence enabling the latter to assess in full knowledge whether the medicinal product under consideration still has a favourable benefit/risk balance. As regards the legality of the CPMP's scientific opinion, the CFI held that it could not substitute its own assessment for that of the committee's. Only the proper functioning of the CPMP, the internal consistency of the opinion and the statement of reasons contained therein were subject to judicial review. As regards the latter aspect, the Court could only examine

[26] Case T-348/04 *SIDE* v. *Commission* [2008] ECR II-625, para. 136.

[27] Joined Cases T-74/00, T-76/00, T-83/00, T-84/00, T-85/00, T-132/00, T-137/00 and T-141/00 *Artegodan GmbH a.o.* v. *Commission* [2002] ECR II-4945.

whether the opinion contained a statement of reasons from which it was possible to ascertain the considerations on which the opinion was based and whether it established a comprehensive link between the medical and scientific findings and its conclusions.

It follows that the Court will not control the scientific assessment itself. However, it exercises a full control, not only over the regularity of the procedure followed by the committee, but also over the internal coherence of the statement of reasons contained in the scientific opinion. In this respect, the Court verifies in particular whether the pharmaceutical substance in question has undergone a detailed, objective and transparent scientific assessment, based on a comparison of the most representative scientific reports put forward by the pharmaceutical laboratories concerned. As regards the Commission's exercise of its discretion, while drawing conclusions from the committee's opinion, the CFI recalled first that judicial review is restricted to verifying that the measure in question is not vitiated by a manifest error or a misuse of power and that the competent authority did not clearly exceed the bounds of its discretion. Then it stated that in case of an advised withdrawal, where scientific evolution does not make it possible to determine the existence of a risk with sufficient certainty, the margin of discretion which the Commission enjoys when choosing the level of protection is limited by two elements. First, there must be new data giving rise to serious doubts as to the safety or the efficacy of the medicinal product in question. Second, the decision of the Commission must comply with the general principle that precedence must be given to the protection of public health over economic considerations. Subsequently, the Court exercised a quasi-full review of the existence of new scientific data. It observed that neither the scientific committee, nor the Commission, in the contested decisions, claimed to have relied on an assessment of the acceptable risk in respect of the short-term therapeutic effects of the medicinal products in question. To justify the contested decisions, the Commission solely relied on application of the scientific criterion of long-term efficacy of the medicinal products in question. The reference to this criterion of long-term efficacy, in opposition with the criterion of short-term efficacy upon which the Commission had relied earlier, was not based on new scientific data. Against that background, the Court found that even if they are based on a consensus in the medical community, mere changes in good clinical practices, that is to say, in the therapeutic practices considered to be the most appropriate in the light of current scientific knowledge, could not on their own justify the withdrawal of a marketing authorisation, where those changes are not based on new scientific data or information. Strikingly, where hardly any review of the substance of a scientific appraisal seems possible or appropriate, consistency of reasoning is all the more thoroughly reviewed.

## 5 Standard of review; some food for thought

By way of concluding remarks three elements catch the eye. Firstly, in order to carry out their task of guaranteeing that the law is observed in the interpretation and application of the Treaty within the framework of the action for annulment, the EC Courts have at their disposal an impressive set of tools which has been well defined in *Tetra Laval*. When looking at the approaches in various areas of the case law, it is to be noted that the essential elements of the toolkit reappear, albeit in varying terminology. The approaches are particularly homogeneous in the different areas of competition law. Apart from full or comprehensive review of the interpretation of the conditions for application of the relevant provisions, it is conspicuous that accuracy and reliability of the facts, their consistency and completeness, as well as their capability to substantiate the conclusions drawn from them, are in principle subject to comprehensive review. The area of limited or marginal review is indeed relatively small and essentially confined to appraisal of complex issues requiring scientific analysis, be it of an economic or otherwise scientific nature.

A second consideration may indeed be that there is no difference as regards review of economic assessments or assessments based on other scientific evidence. The core of administrative discretion seems to result, first, from the applied provision itself, which may allow for different solutions and, second, from the complexity of the appraisal involved. If in the case law presented above, discretion seems to relate mainly to the appraisal following consistent analysis, it follows that in the end such discretion also extends to the final subsumption of facts under the relevant provision.

Thirdly, it is important to bear in mind that discretion, and its correlative marginal review by the Court, does not allow the administrative body to be less scrupulous concerning evidences and their consistency. *Tetra Laval* shows in particular that lower intensity of review does not imply lower standard of proof. Rather than intensifying judicial review of the Commission's economic assessments, the judgments in *Tetra Laval* only tend to specify the standard of proof and its actual application.

Finally, it may be useful to recall the different stages through which the Court may have to go when reviewing an administrative act, since each of those stages may entail a different standard of review. First, as regards the facts as established by evidences, the Court exercises comprehensive review in relation to their accuracy and reliability, consistency and completeness, as well as their capability to substantiate the conclusions drawn from them. Second, as concerning the appraisal of those facts, the Court will apply a marginal review when this assessment involves complex considerations from which different conclusions may be drawn. Marginal review is applied in such cases as the Court would otherwise be at risk of substituting its own views to that of the administrative body. Third, the appraisal of facts may lead immediately to their qualification in law, which in principle is subject to comprehensive review from the part of the Court.

In that respect it is also noteworthy that although margin of appreciation and margin of discretion both involve marginal review from the part of the Courts, these notions should not be confused. While the former refers to the margin which the administrative body enjoys because of the complexity of the appraisal involved, the latter refers to the policy discretion granted by a given provision. It is indeed often the case that the Commission enjoys a margin of appreciation (in assessing, for instance, the anticompetitive effects of a given agreement) but does not in principle enjoy any policy discretion as to the legal consequence to be drawn from the conclusion of the assessment (Article 81(1) prohibits agreements having anticompetitive effects).

That being so, distinguishing the notions discussed above may be difficult, as they may sometimes be inextricably intertwined. It will be noted, first, that the appraisal of facts and their qualification in law may be difficult to distinguish as they are intimately linked to each other and somehow represent two faces of the same coin. Second, policy discretion and margin of appreciation are both involved when the Commission decides on the maximum length a non-compete clause may have in order to be held as ancillary restraint.[28] On the one hand, such an assessment raises complex issues which entail some margin of appreciation to the benefit of the Commission. On the other hand, by its very nature this assessment also pertains to the development of competition policy, which in turn entails some policy discretion to the benefit of the Commission. Third, the case law in relation to Article 82 EC offers striking examples of the difficulty to distinguish competition policy and the interpretation of a legal provision.

[28] See Case T-112/99 *Métropole télévision and others* v. *Commission* [2001] ECR II-2459.

## Bibliography

BAILEY (2004)

D. Bailey, 'Scope of Judicial Review under Article 81 EC' [2004/5] *Common Market Law Review* p. 1327- 1360

CHAPUS (2008)

R. Chapus, *Droit du contentieux administratif* (Paris 2008)

DONNAT (2008)

F. Donnat, *Contentieux communautaire de l'annulation* (Paris 2008)

SIBONY (2007)

A. Sibony & E. Barbier de La Serre, 'Charge de la prevue et théorie du contrôle en droit communautaire de la concurrence: pour un changement de perspective' [2007/2] *Revue Trimestrielle de Droit Européen* p. 205-252

TIILI (1999)

V. Tiili & J. Vanhamme, 'The "Power of Appraisal" (Pouvoir d'appréciation) of the Commission of the European Communities vis-à-vis the Powers of Judicial Review of the Communities' Court of Justice and the Court of First Instance' [1999/3] *Fordham International Law Journal* p. 885-901

CHAPTER 3

# The Scope of Review of Administrative Action From a Comparative Perspective

T. Zwart

## 1 Introduction[1]

The *Tetra Laval* judgment of the Court of First Instance (hereafter: 'CFI') has caused a stir because of its novel approach towards judicial review in competition cases.[2] In its decision in the case the CFI has subjected the factual assessments made by the Commission to a more rigorous examination than before.[3] This paper approaches the scope of review of administrative action, which was highlighted by *Tetra Laval*, from a comparative perspective, which includes the U.S., Germany and Canada.

To this end, section 2 will describe the principles that underlie this concept, which, to a certain extent, are contradictory and pull the courts into opposing directions. Sections 3 and 4 will illustrate this contradiction by discussing two tests, applied by courts to review administrative action, which are on opposite sides of the spectrum, *i.e.* comprehensive and limited review.

As the *Tetra Laval* judgment demonstrates, the annulment of administrative decisions can create tensions and controversy. In order to enhance the acceptability of their decisions and their own legitimacy, it is important that the courts clarify and explain why they have chosen a particular test. Therefore section 5 will outline a model that guarantees the necessary transparency with regard to the determination of the appropriate test, the so-called 'pragmatic and functional approach' developed by the Canadian Supreme Court. Finally, section 6 contains some concluding observations.

The words 'tribunals', 'agencies' and 'authorities' will be used indiscriminately hereafter to describe entities charged with the implementation of law or policy or both.

## 2 The bipolar scheme created by the need for judicial review and agency autonomy

The controversy caused by the *Tetra Laval* judgment is neither new nor unique. In every jurisdiction, both national or international, courts and administrative authorities face great challenges to achieve harmonious co-operation and coexistence. This tension is caused by two aspects of the concept of separation of powers, or institutional balance,[4] which may conflict in any given case.[5]

---

1 I would like to thank Jack Connah, Cambridge 2008, Lobke Errens, Utrecht 2009, and Amy Zheng, Harvard 2009, for their invaluable assistance. Any defects are entirely my own responsibility.

2 Case T-5/02 *Tetra Laval BV* v. *Commision* [2002] ECR II-4381; See for an analysis of the case from a scope of review perspective Craig (2006) pp. 453-474.

3 Craig (2006) p. 470; Schwartze (2004) pp. 1001-101.

4 See Case T-68/89 *Società Italiana Vetro SpA* v. *Commission* [1992] ECR II-1403, at para 319.

5 The point that standards of review relate to the separation or balance of powers at the international level as well, is made convincingly in Ehlermann (2004) p. 491.

On the one hand, the concept of separation of powers implies that administrative authorities should remain within the territory assigned to them by law, in particular by the constitution. Consequently, courts have the duty to review the lawfulness of administrative acts to ensure that the authorities will not act *ultra vires* their constitutional remit. This approach corresponds with the Diceyan view, which used to dominate Anglo-Canadian administrative law, under which the courts' primary role is to constrain administrative power.[6] The idea was that if administrative tribunals would overstep their boundaries, for example by assuming legislative powers, the freedom of the individual would be jeopardised.[7] In this view courts are uniquely qualified to interpret democratically-enacted statutes; to protect the legislature's intentions from being watered down through the administrative process; and to protect the individual against an overpowering executive.[8]

On the other hand, the concept of separation of powers also guarantees the agency's freedom to act within the territory assigned to it by the constitution. This guarantee sets limits to what the courts can do when reviewing agency action. Thus, courts are not supposed to substitute their own decisions for those of the administrative authorities, nor second-guess their findings. This approach corresponds with the 'new Rule of Law' view that has emerged in Anglo-Canadian law, which urges courts to respect and advance the role of administrative tribunals.[9] This approach further acknowledges that as the role of the court is to interpret the intention of Parliament, the court must acknowledge that Parliament intends those administrative agencies that it has created to exercise their special functions, without undue interference by the courts.[10]

The bipolarity created by the seemingly contradictory need for review and the need for agency autonomy is evidenced by the two opposing tests that the courts have used in many jurisdictions, including Germany, England and the U.S., in approaching review of administrative action, *i.e.* comprehensive and limited review, which will be discussed in the following sections.[11]

## 3 Comprehensive review

The most rigorous test applied by courts in many jurisdictions, which is usually referred to as 'correctness', implies full intensity review. When it applies this test, a court considers itself to be in as good a position as the pri-

6 Dicey (1927); Dicey's views on courts and administrative tribunals are discussed in Burnett Harvey (1960-1961) p. 487; Arthurs (1979); and McLachlin (1998-1999) p. 175.

7 McLachlin (1998-1999) p. 175.

8 McLachlin (1998-1999) p. 176.

9 McLachlin (1998-1999) p. 175.

10 McLachlin (1998-1999) p. 177.

11 Between these opposite sides of the spectrum there are several shades of grey, like the sub and super *Wednesbury* tests, reasonableness *simpliciter* and proportionality.

mary decision-maker to weigh the factors involved. In common law jurisdictions the test was developed at a time when courts still considered administrative agencies and tribunals as inferior courts, the decisions of which could be subjected to full review as part of appeal proceedings. Although nowadays the test is mainly used to review issues of law, in some jurisdictions courts have been willing to apply it to other areas as well, especially if the challenged decision touches upon (human) rights.

This is the case in Germany, for example, as illustrated in the *Multiple Choice Exam* decision.[12] A medical student, who had failed a multiple-choice exam, challenged some of the questions before the administrative courts. These courts pointed out that, on the basis of existing case law, they were supposed to accord great deference to the experts that had composed the exam. The courts would only intervene if a question was manifestly wrong or had no foundation in science. Since neither could be said of the contested questions, review was denied.

The student subsequently filed a constitutional complaint with the Federal Constitutional Court, challenging the limited review exercised by the administrative courts. She claimed that her right laid down in Article 19, Section 4 of the German Constitution had been infringed. Under this provision any person whose rights have been violated, ought to have recourse to a court. The Constitutional Court felt that the applicant's complaint was well-founded. Since the administrative courts had been unwilling to look into her objections to the contested exam, they had denied her right to an effective remedy. According to the Court, Article 19 (4) does not only confer a right of access to a court, but it also implies that one is entitled to an effective review by that court. As a consequence, courts should undertake a thorough examination both of the law and the facts concerning the challenged decisions, and not simply rely upon the determinations made by the administrative authorities.

Consequently, according to the Court, the margin of discretion to be accorded to the authorities with regard to exams should be very limited, since otherwise it would be impossible to guarantee an effective review by the courts. The courts are expected to review whether the exam authorities have adhered to the prescribed standards. As far as medical exams were concerned, the courts should ascertain whether the questions were understandable, clear and not open to debate. A question which does not meet these standards is unlawful. It is the task of administrative courts to exercise this kind of review, if necessary with the help of experts.[13]

The application of the correctness-test in cases involving rights can be explained by reference to German history. As a result of the atrocities committed by the Nazi regime, the view which emerged in post-war Germany was that

12 BVerfGE 84, 59 (1991).

13 The German administrative courts are not altogether happy with this approach, because they feel caught between a rock and a hard place. While the Constitutional Court pushes for exacting review, administrative authorities complain about government by the judiciary, Niehues (1997) p. 557.

in a modern democratic state, public authorities are bound by the law even when they have discretionary powers.[14] There is a strong belief, therefore, that an individual should be compensated for harm caused by a public body, especially when constitutionally guaranteed rights are involved.

## 4 Limited review

### 4.1 Limited review of discretionary acts: the *Wednesbury* case

The most lenient test applied by courts in many jurisdictions, which is usually referred to as 'patent unreasonableness', is based on deference towards the original decision-maker. When it applies this test, a court will determine whether the challenged decision is outrageous. This test is mainly used to review the exercise of discretionary powers, decisions involving policy issues and factual assessments.

The limited review approach is exemplified by a 1948 case decided by the English Court of Appeal *per* Lord Greene, called *Associated Provincial Picture Houses* v. *Wednesbury Corporation* or *Wednesbury* for short.[15] Under the Sunday Entertainments Act 1932 the licensing authority had the power to issue licenses to cinemas to open on Sundays 'subject to such conditions as it thinks fit to impose'.

Associated Provincial Picture Houses Ltd. had applied for a Sunday license for its Gaumont Cinema in Wednesbury. The Wednesbury Corporation, the public licensing authority of the Borough of Wednesbury, had granted the license subject to the condition that no children under the age of fifteen would be admitted, even if they would be accompanied by an adult. Associated Provincial Picture Houses brought proceedings claiming this condition was illegal and unreasonable.

In the Court of Appeal, Lord Greene, M.R. made clear that since the applicable provision of the Sunday Entertainments Act was widely drawn, granting the licensing authority an absolute discretion to impose any conditions whatsoever, there was little to no room for judicial intervention. But interestingly, Associated had not only claimed that the condition was illegal, it also alleged it to be unreasonable. Initially it looked as though Lord Greene was going to equate 'unreasonableness' with illegality. But halfway into his judgment he changed course. He admitted that unreasonableness may be invoked as an independent ground for review, distinguishable from illegality. Thus, in his view, courts can interfere, if a decision 'is so unreasonable that no reasonable authority could ever have come to it'.[16]

---

14 Arai-Takahashi (2000) p. 70.

15 [1948] 1 KB 223.

16 [1948] 1 KB 230.

In *Wednesbury*, 'unreasonableness' has been used in a very restrictive sense. Lord Greene pointed out that something overwhelming is required to prove that a decision is Wednesbury-unreasonable,[17] 'something so absurd that no sensible person could ever dream that it lay within the powers of the authority'.[18] This restrictive formula is being applied in order to preserve the separation of powers. If judges were allowed to consider the mere reasonableness of administrative decisions, they would in fact be invited to substitute their own views for those of the administration. Manifest unreasonableness is more objective, because it is supposed to be more obvious.

The example set by Lord Greene in *Wednesbury* was soon followed by courts in other jurisdictions, both within and outside of the Commonwealth. In many jurisdictions, tests have been introduced allowing courts to review the patent unreasonableness of discretionary acts, like the standard called *erreur manifeste d'appreciation* employed by the French Council of State, the *willekeurverbod* in the Netherlands and 'patent unreasonableness' in Canada.

### 4.2 Limited review of facts and law: the U.S. approach

While *Wednesbury* is a good example of limited review of a discretionary act, similar deferential tests have been applied by courts to issues of fact and law, in particular by courts in the U.S.

In the U.S., courts usually have considerable regard for factual findings of administrative agencies. The Administrative Procedure Act (hereafter: 'APA') contains three standards of review applicable to agency fact finding. The most stringent standard allows the court to review the facts itself *de novo*, but this is seldom used.[19] In informal rulemaking procedures[20] the facts are reviewed under the very deferential 'arbitrary and capricious test'.[21] Courts apply the substantial evidence standard to facts found in formal adjudicatory agency proceedings.[22] A court using this deferential test will assess the reasonableness of the agency's fact-finding, while avoiding the question whether or not it would have reached the same conclusion on the basis of the evidence.

In *Consolo* v. *Federal Maritime Commission*, Justice White in expressing the unanimous view of the Supreme Court provided the following rationale for this deferential approach:[23]

---

17 [1948] 1 KB 230.

18 [1948] 1 KB 229.

19 §706 (2)(F) APA.

20 Under the APA, rules drafted by agencies can be submitted either to formal, trial-like, on-the-record proceedings or to more informal 'notice-and-comment' proceedings which allow for public participation by submission of written comments.

21 §706 (2)(A) APA; see Aman (2001) p. 463.

22 §706 (2)(E) APA.

23 383 U.S. 607 (1966) at 620.

> 'Congress was very deliberate in adopting this standard or review (*i.e.* the substantive evidence test, TZ). It frees the reviewing courts of the time-consuming and difficult task of weighing the evidence, it gives proper respect to the expertise of the administrative tribunal and it helps promote the uniform application of the statute.'

Consequently, apart from reasons of economy and practicality, this deferential attitude is justified out of respect for agency expertise.[24]

In *Florida Power Commission* v. *Florida Power & Light Company*, Justice White, delivering the opinion of the Court, again emphasised the need to respect the agency's expertise:[25]

> 'Particularly when we consider a purely factual question within the area of competence of an administrative agency created by Congress, and when resolution of that question depends on "engineering and scientific" considerations, we recognize the relevant agency's technical expertise and experience, and defer to its analysis unless it is without substantial basis in fact.'

This respectful attitude of U.S. courts towards agencies is not confined to fact-finding. In *Chevron* v. *Natural Resources Defense Council*, the Supreme Court has also adopted a deferential approach to agency interpretations of law.[26] As is the case elsewhere, courts in the U.S. often have to deal with statutes the language of which is ambiguous. Until 1984 the courts used to determine on a statute-by-statute basis how to deal with these ambiguities. If the court felt that the ambiguity was accidental, in the sense that Congress had aimed at a particular result but had failed to express this, the Court would consider itself best suited to clarify the issue. However, if the Court came to the conclusion that the ambiguity was intentional, in the sense that Congress had avoided having to make a political choice by delegating to the agency, it would show deference towards the agency interpretation.

The Supreme Court changed course in *Chevron*. The case concerned rules issued by the Environmental Protection Agency (hereafter: 'EPA') under the Clean Air Act. During the Carter Administration, the EPA had promulgated very strict regulations, which were environmentally friendly, but did not go down very well with the business community. When the Reagan Administration came into office, the EPA replaced the existing rules by regulations which gave companies more leeway. Not surprisingly, these rules were then challenged by the National Resources Defence Council, an environmental organisation. Since these different sets of rules were rooted in an interpretation of the same statutory language, the question before the Supreme Court was how courts should treat agency interpretations of Acts of Congress. Should judges rely upon their

---

24 See also Aman (2001) pp. 446- 457.

25 404 U.S. 453 (1972) at 463.

26 467 US 837 (1984).

own construction of the statute or should they respect the agency's interpretation?

The Supreme Court applied a two-step analysis which became known as the '*Chevron* two-step'. The first question is whether Congress has directly addressed the precise question. If the intent of Congress is clear, the agency and the court have to defer to the position of Congress; they cannot amend its views. If the court determines that Congress has not directly addressed the precise question, by being silent or ambiguous, the answer of the agency will be decisive. In such a case, a court may not substitute its own construction of a statutory provision for a reasonable interpretation made by the agency.

The outcome of *Chevron* is that courts should ordinarily yield to the agencies' interpretations of the statutes they administer, unless their construction was unreasonable. By this judgment the Court has replaced the statute-by-statute evaluation with an across-the-board presumption that, in the case of ambiguity, agency discretion is intended.[27] Courts must defer to the agencies to respect the fact that Congress has transferred regulatory responsibility to those agencies and to ensure that policy choices, which are a necessary element of interpreting statutes, are being made by persons answerable to the political branches rather than unelected judges. According to the Supreme Court in *Chevron*, it is the constitutional duty of the court to defer to agency interpretation of law, despite the fact that under that same Constitution it is the responsibility of the judicial branch to interpret the law.

## 5 The pragmatic and functional approach adopted by the Canadian Supreme Court

### 5.1 Introduction

Whether a court will apply limited or comprehensive review will usually depend on the weighing of the circumstances of the case. Since the annulment of administrative decisions can create tensions or outright controversy between the courts and administrative authorities, it is important that the courts clarify and explain why they choose a particular test. This will enhance the acceptability of the decision and the legitimacy of the court. The Canadian Supreme Court has developed a concept called the 'pragmatic and functional approach', which is a model of transparency. It will be discussed in this section.

### 5.2 The Diceyan approach

Until the end of the 1970s the Canadian courts adhered to the strict Diceyan model described in section 2. They tended to regard administrative agencies as inferior judicial tribunals, and, consequently, subjected their

[27] Scalia (1989) p. 516.

acts to intense scrutiny. This across-the-board application of the correctness-test by the courts created suspicion and distrust.[28] Since they felt that it did not do enough justice to the agencies' expertise and unduly interfered with their mandate, this approach pleased neither the agencies themselves nor the Canadian Parliament.

As a consequence, Parliament began to insert into the legislation that established new administrative agencies so-called privative clauses, under which the decisions of the agency could not be reviewed in any court of law.[29] The courts effectively by-passed these clauses, which were meant to make the decisions unreviewable, by giving them a very restrictive meaning. The courts felt that privative clauses of this kind prevented the courts only from examining lawful decisions, but they did not protect decisions that are illegal. If the authority has gone outside its jurisdiction, there is no 'decision' within the meaning of the Act. In this view illegal acts committed by the agency were perfectly reviewable by the courts since they were not considered decisions within the meaning of the provision.

This stand-off came to an end when the Supreme Court decided to give in. It acknowledged that the agencies were staffed with specialists in the field, while the judges were mere generalists who lacked the necessary expertise.[30] It also conceded that too much judicial interference would undermine the autonomy and credibility of the agencies. The Court, therefore, proved willing to self-limit the scope of its review of administrative acts. Instead of automatically subjecting those acts to a correctness-test, the Court would come up with the standard which best suited the circumstances of the case. This new attitude was called the 'pragmatic and functional approach'.

The goal of the pragmatic and functional approach is to determine which body should have the final say: the court or the tribunal.[31] If the tribunal is in the best position to deal with the issue, it should be accorded deference. If the court is best placed, no such deference is warranted. This approach has allowed administrative agencies more autonomy, while permitting the courts to maintain a supervisory role.

## 5.3 The factors to be weighed by the court

As part of this approach the Court has identified four factors, which it will weigh in each case to determine the appropriate standard of review.

---

[28] McLachlin (1998-1999) pp. 175-177.

[29] Typically a privative clause will declare decisions to be final and conclusive, as a result of which they cannot be challenged, appealed against, reviewed, quashed or called in question in any court.

[30] See the concurring opinion of Justice Wilson in *National Corn Growers Assn.* v. *Canada (Canadian Import Tribunal)*, [1990] 2 S.C.R. 1324.

[31] McLachlin (1998-1999) p. 181.

*(i) Privative clauses*

If there is a privative clause, the court should in principle show deference to the tribunal's decision. Although a privative clause will not keep a court from reviewing potentially illegal decisions under the Act, the presence of such a clause will be regarded by the court as a clear indication that deference is warranted. A more searching standard of review should be applied if the statute contains a clause that permits appeals.

*(ii) Expertise*

The second factor taken into account is the measure of expertise of the agency. The greater the agency's expertise, the greater the degree of deference that it will be accorded.

Thus, in *Pezim* v. *British Columbia (Superintendent of Brokers)* the British Columbia Securities Commission had found that the respondents, who were company directors, had contravened the Securities Act by failing to disclose material changes in their affairs.[32] Consequently, the Commission had suspended respondents from trading in shares for one year. The Supreme Court had to determine the appropriate standard for reviewing the Commission's decision. Writing for a unanimous Court, Justice Iacobucci made clear that deference was warranted, because this was the opinion of a specialised agency on issues which fell squarely within its area of expertise.

A similar line was taken by the Court in *Canada (Director of Investigation and Research)* v. *Southam Inc*, a case which shows some resemblance to *Tetra Laval*.[33] Southam owned two daily newspapers, serving the Vancouver region. The newspapers were not very successful, presumably because several so-called community newspapers were distributed in the area free of charge. In order to neutralise the competition, Southam started to acquire those community newspapers. The Director of Investigation and Research felt that this move substantially lessened competition in the market for retail print advertising in the Vancouver area. He therefore initiated proceedings in the Competition Tribunal. The Tribunal felt that there was not much of a problem, because Southam's dailies and its newly acquired community newspapers served different markets.

Both Southam and the Director appealed to the Federal Court of Appeal. The main question this court had to solve was whether the Tribunal had been right in determining that the paid-for and the free newspapers served different markets. The Federal Court felt that the Tribunal had ignored evidence supporting the view that both types of newspapers were in the same market. The Federal Court substituted its own findings for those of the Tribunal and it came to the conclusion that the evidence was more than sufficient to show that both types of newspapers were in the same market.

Southam challenged this ruling before the Supreme Court. The main question the Court had to address was whether the Federal Court of Appeal

---

32 [1994] 2 S.C.R. 557.

33 [1997] 1 S.C.R. 748.

had been justified in substituting its own findings for those of the Tribunal. In other words, had the Court of Appeal shown enough curial deference? Justice Iacobucci pointed out that there was a preponderance of persons learned in economics and commerce on the Tribunal. This reflected the view of Parliament that expertise was more desirable than knowledge of the law. Considering this expertise, the courts had to accord a measure of deference to its findings. The Federal Court should not, therefore, have ventured into a re-examination of the Tribunal's conclusions.

*(iii) The purpose of the Acts as a whole, and the provision in particular*

The third prong of the test focuses on the question which role the agency is supposed to play. When the statute intends for the agency to adopt a court-like role by defining the rights of the parties, it should be treated as an inferior judicial tribunal whose actions will be subject to close curial supervision. When, on the other hand, it is supposed to take on a policy role, deference will be the rule.

In *Pezim* Justice Iacobucci pointed out that the British Columbia Securities Commission had the broad responsibility to regulate the securities' market and to protect the general public from being defrauded by securities' traders and investment bankers.[34] To this end the Commission had an impressive arsenal at its disposal, including the authority to develop policy. Since the role of the Commission was not comparable to that of courts of law, the Court felt that deference was due.

*(iv) Law or fact*

Finally, the court will establish whether the issue raised before it is a question of law – what do the words in the provision actually mean? –, a question of fact – what did actually happen? -, or a mixed question of law and fact – do the facts satisfy the words in the provision? Ordinarily, questions of law deserve a more probing review by the courts. Through their training and experience judges are particularly good at interpreting legal texts and resolving statutory issues. Consequently, they will not hesitate to subject the interpretation given by agencies to a searching review. Questions of fact are the domain of the agencies. They serve in the frontline and are therefore able to judge the importance of evidence first hand. Over the years they build up a considerable experience in finding facts in a certain area, which cannot be matched by the courts. Therefore, questions of fact deserve a more deferential approach. Mixed questions of law and fact will be halfway between those two.[35]

---

34 [1994] 2 S.C.R. 557.

35 A very good description of the review of mixed questions of law and fact is provided by Judge Thomas Ambro in his concurring opinion in *Interfaith Community Org.* v. *Honeywell Intl., Inc.* 399 F.3d 248, 269-70 (3d Cir. 2005).

### 5.4 The standards applied by the Court

Initially the Canadian courts applied only one standard of review, *i.e.* correctness. In 1979, however, in a case called *C.U.P.E., Local 963* v. *New Brunswick Liquor Corp.*, the Supreme Court added a second, more lenient standard, *i.e.* patent unreasonableness.[36] When it applies this standard the court will seek to determine whether the position taken by the agency was so patently unreasonable that it cannot be rationally supported by the relevant legislation. This very deferential standard is akin to *Wednesbury* unreasonableness, which undoubtedly served as a model. The standard of correctness is situated at the more exacting end of the spectrum, patent unreasonableness at the more deferential end.[37]

When applying the pragmatic and functional approach the reviewing court determines how the decision scores on each of the four factors described above. It adds up the results and then the appropriate standard emerges automatically. The Court's judgment in a 1998 case called *Pushpanathan v. Canada (Minister of Employment & Immigration)* can serve as an example.[38]

Pushpanathan was a Sri Lankan national residing in Canada. After having been convicted for a criminal offence, the authorities ordered his deportation. He thereupon claimed refugee status under the United Nations Convention Relating to the Status of Refugees. This claim was referred to the Immigration and Refugee Board, which decided that it was unfounded. He then sought and obtained judicial review of this decision. The main question before the Supreme Court was which standard of review should be applied to this kind of decisions taken by the Immigration and Refugee Board. According to Justice Bastarache, for the majority the correctness-test should be applied, since there was no privative clause; the Board enjoyed only limited expertise regarding the object of the proceedings; the Board performed a function which was not too far removed from that of a court; and at issue was a question of law, not one of fact.

## 6 Conclusion

As the *Tetra Laval* judgment has once again made clear, the intensity of review exercised by courts can cause controversy. The main reason for that is that courts, when reviewing administrative action, operate between the poles of judicial oversight and agency autonomy, which both flow from

---

36 [1979] 2 S.C.R. 227.

37 In *Southam* the Court developed a new standard, situated between these two extremes, called reasonableness *simpliciter*. The difference between patent unreasonableness and reasonableness *simpliciter* has always been very subtle and hard to describe. Not surprisingly, therefore, the Supreme Court recently decided in *Dunsmuir* v. *New Brunswick*, 2008 SCC 9, to merge the two into one standard, *i.e.* reasonableness.

38 [1998] 1 S.C.R. 982.

the separation of powers. These poles correspond with two types of review, *i.e.* comprehensive and limited review. When a court applies comprehensive review it will ascertain whether the decision taken by the agency is correct, *i.e.* whether under the circumstances it would have taken the same decision. When a court applies limited review it will determine whether the decision was so patently unreasonable that no rational authority could have taken it.

Since it is the responsibility of the judges to say what the law is, issues of law will usually be subjected to the correctness-test. However, in *Chevron* the U.S. Supreme Court has adopted a more deferential approach. The *Chevron* 'two-step' requires courts ordinarily to yield to the agencies' interpretations of the statutes they administer, unless their construction was unreasonable. Issues of fact will usually require a deferential test to respect the agency's expertise. Since the agencies serve in the frontline they are able to judge the importance of evidence first hand. In addition, over the years they build up a considerable experience in finding facts, which cannot be matched by the courts. Similarly, exercises of discretion will be subjected to minimal scrutiny, because the law leaves the final say to the agency. However, in certain jurisdictions, like Germany, these two elements will be reviewed comprehensively if they touch upon rights.

To maximise the acceptance of its decisions in this field and to preserve its legitimacy, the CFI should start clarifying and explaining publicly and convincingly why it has opted for a particular test. The pragmatic and functional approach developed by the Canadian Supreme Court is very well suited for this purpose. The model acts as a kind of score-card, which allows administrative authorities to predict which test will be applied, even while they are still preparing their decisions. By adopting the Canadian model the CFI would serve legal certainty, the interests of the administrative authorities and its own position.

## Bibliography

AMAN (2001)
A.C. Aman Jr. and W.T. Mayton, *Administrative Law* (West Publishing Company, Saint Paul 2001)

ARAI- TAKAHASI (2000)
Y. Arai-Takahashi, 'Discretion in German Law: Doctrinal Discourse Revisited' [2000/6] *European Public Law* pp. 69-80

ARTHURS (1979)
H. W. Arthurs, *Rethinking Administrative Law: A Slightly Dicey Business*, 17 Osgoode Hall L.J. 1 (1979)

BURNETT HARVEY (1960-1961)
W. Burnett Harvey, 'The Rule of Law in Historical Perspective' [1960-1961/vol. 59] *Michigan Law Review* pp. 487-500

CRAIG (2006)
P. Craig, *EU Administrative Law* (Oxford University Press, Oxford 2006)

DICEY (1927)
A.V. Dicey, *Introduction to the Study of the Law of the Constitution* (London 1927)

EHLERMANN (2004)
C. Ehlermann and N. Lockhart, 'Standards of Review in WTO Law' [2004/7] *Journal of International Economic Law* pp. 491- 521

MCLACHLIN (1998-1999)
B. McLachlin, 'The Roles of Administrative Tribunals and Courts in Maintaining the Rule of Law' [1998-1999/12] *Canadian Journal Administrative Law & Practice* pp. 171- a.f.

NIEHUES (1997)
N. Niehues, 'Die bindungswirkung und Umsetzung Verfassungsgerichtlicher Entscheidungen' [1997] *Neue Juristische Wochenschrift* p. 557

SCALIA (1989)
A. Scalia, 'Judicial Deference to Administrative Interpretations of Law' [1989] *Duke Law Journal* p. 511

SCHWARTZE (2004)
J. Schwartze, 'Judicial Review of European Administrative Procedure' [2004/vol. 68] *Law and Contemporary Problems* pp. 85-106

CHAPTER 4

# Observations on Economic Proof in Economic Cases

A. Ottow

## 1 Introduction

During the past decade the Member States of the European Union, including The Netherlands, have liberalised significant sectors of their economies. This *liberalisation process* was initiated with the belief that more competition will bring welfare and consumer choice. Consequently, statutory monopolies have been partly or completely removed with the object to introduce competition in many sectors. This process required regulation to correct the existing *market failure* (lack of competition) and to ensure that the transition of the market structure is well constructed.

Liberalisation has been accompanied by considerable rules of different kinds, such as technical aspects concerning the access to networks and the protection of the public interest through universal service provisions. The liberalisation process has been introduced per specific market, resulting in *sector-specific regulation*, taking into account the specific characteristics of the market concerned (so-called regulatory frameworks).

To support this liberalisation process and to enforce these rules *independent administrative authorities* – also called regulatory bodies or regulators – were established. These authorities are given the task to ensure competition in the markets concerned and to intervene by *ex ante* regulation where necessary. Obligations are imposed on undertakings with significant market power or a dominant position to correct market failure.

In addition, general competition rules do exist to correct *ex post* anti-competitive behaviour, such as cartels or abuse of a dominant position. Cartel authorities have been empowered to enforce these competition rules, not only on a European level but also at a national level in all Member States.

The last few years a tendency can be identified for the application of competition law and sector-specific regulation. There is pressure on the authorities to have sufficient consideration for economic reality and the impact on the market.[1] They are urged to ensure that a *more economic approach* is followed. A strict legalistic application of the rules is no longer considered to be sufficient, but the authority has to give sound economic reasons for its intervention. The adverse or positive effects on the market place need to be proven. This is even more the case when the intervention includes sanctions (fines) imposed on undertakings concerned by the independent administrative authority.[2] In competition and regulatory cases there is increasing pressure on the authorities to have sufficient consideration for economic reality and the impact on the market. Per se rules are less accepted and the authority is more and more required to take the *economic context* into account and to analyse what the *effect* on competition is of the behaviour concerned.[3] For example, it is argued that the competition authority has to prove that there is an adverse effect on the market in case it wants to

1 Parret (2008).

2 Parret (2008).

3 Ottow et al (2008) pp. 170-187.

establish a prohibited restriction on competition and that an automatic *per se* application of the prohibition is no longer acceptable. A shift can be observed from a legalistic (formal) approach to a more economic effect based approach. In most competition and regulation cases this approach requires a balancing act,[4] where both pro-competitive and anti-competitive effects have to be weighed out. Per se prohibitions are less common and a more dynamic approach is required where the authority has to demonstrate this balancing act and prove the positive results of its intervention.

This approach has consequences for the legal position of the authorities when taking decisions. They will have to give more attention to the economic proof of their reasoning and substantiate their case with sufficient economic evidence, demonstrating that the assumed effects on the market concerned do or will take place. This leads to the so-called *"proof paradox"*[5]: intervention by competition or market authorities is considered to be necessary, but a (too) strict approach towards rules on proof can result in insufficient enforcement of the competition or market rules. This can lead to ineffective market control.

This leads to the question which *rules on economic proof* in relation to the intervention by independent administrative bodies on the basis of general competition law and economic regulation are needed. How can the right balance be found between the need for sufficient economic proof and the need for effective supervision on the market? Which rules on proof should be developed to reconcile the need for a more economic approach with the need for effective market regulation?

A complication in this respect is formed by the different approaches that can be used from the economic thinking towards competition policy.[6] Different theories do exist (the Harvard view, the Chicago school) which can be used to interpret vague legal concepts. Different welfare standards are introduced, which have consequences for the use of competition law. Which economic welfare criteria are used, has consequences for the proof to be delivered by the authority. How do the economic welfare criteria fit into the legal framework of the general competition rules and regulatory regimes?[7] In addition, economics have influence on the sort of evidence that can be used by the authorities and the parties concerned. The development of new techniques enables both regulatory authorities and market parties to use econometric evidence to prove their case. Central questions on competition law and regulation do relate to empirical issues, which require empirical evidence to prove the claimed effects.[8]

---

4 Van den Bergh et al (2001) p. 70.

5 See also Parret (2008) p. 10.

6 See Van den Bergh et al (2001) pp. 62-71.

7 Van den Bergh et al (2001) pp. 67-68.

8 Röller (2005), Baker et al (1999) pp. 386-435.

## 2 Competition law cases

The last few years, the Commission's application of competition rules regarding its failure to follow a more realistic economic view when interpreting these rules was criticised. This has led to a more economic approach towards the application and interpretation of European competition rules. This development has been followed in the Member States with the application of European and national competition laws. As a consequence of this new approach the standard of proof for the Commission and the national authorities has become more difficult as the authorities have to establish the economic effects of their decisions.

In the first phase this criticism focused on the application of Article 81 (1) EC Treaty (prohibition of cartels), in particular when determining whether or not an agreement restricts competition. A more economic approach was argued, resulting in allowing agreements which did not in fact restrict competition through anti-competitive effects. [9] This criticism led to the modernisation of European competition law, accepting that there should be a shift from an approach based on merely form to one more focused on effects. In evaluating its approach, the Commission accepted that a more economic and less rigid approach to vertical, horizontal and technology transfer agreements under article 81 EC Treaty was required. [10] The Commission gradually accepted a more lenient approach towards these agreements and moved away from a more interventionist policy.[11]

The burden of proof is, according to the case law of the Court of Justice, on the authority alleging an infringement of Article 81 (1) EC Treaty (see also Article para. 5 of Reg 1/2003). The Court of Justice has held that for the Commission to establish a breach "sufficiently precise and coherent proof" must be produced.[12] The economic-based approach stresses the need for more economic analysis and therefore the need for more use of economic evidence. It requires the weighing of the restrictive effects of the agreement against the economic benefits and efficiencies created by the agreement. This automatically leads to a higher standard and burden of economic proof for the cartel authorities.

In the very recent *T-Mobile case*[13] the Dutch Trade and Industry Appeals Tribunal (*College van Beroep voor het Bedrijfsleven: CBB*), the CBB, made preliminary references to the European Court of Justice on the direct applicability of Article 81 EC Treaty in relation to the standard and burden of proof regarding concerted practices. This interim judgment illustrates the increased attention for evidence issues. This tendency is clearly also present in the Dutch competi-

9 Jones et al (2008) pp. 181, 209, and 213-214.

10 Jones et al (2008), p. 214.

11 Idem.

12 Joined Cases 29/83 and 30/83 *Compagnie Royale Asturienne des Mines SA and Rheinzink GmbH* v. *Commission of the European Communities* [1984] ECR 1679.

13 CBB, 31 December 2007, AWB 06/657, 660, 661 and 662, *T-Mobile*, LJN: BC1396. See case C-8/08 T-Mobile, n.y.r.

tion practice. The Dutch competition courts have shifted away from the *object approach* (*per se* approach) to the more *effect-based approach* in its case law. Illustrative in this respect is the judgment in the *Secon case,*[14] where the court established that the NMa is required to investigate the concrete effects of the agreement concerned, also in situations where the object of the agreement is to restrict competition. This judgment has been followed in many other judgments and seems to be considered as the standard for the application of Article 6 of the Dutch Competition Act (the national equivalent of Article 81 EC).

After this phase the Commission initiated in the second phase also new reflections on the application of Article 82 EC Treaty. The same tendency towards a more flexible approach can be identified for the abuse of dominance cases. The Commission announced in 2003 that it would undertake a review of policy under Article 82 EC Treaty, bringing the application more in line with a more economic approach. This view on Article 82 EC Treaty was laid down in its Discussion Paper of 2005 and later (in a modified manner) in the recent Guidance of 2008.[15] Also in its decisions a less mechanical application of Article 86 EC Treaty is used, based on sufficient proof to establish the abuse concerned (such as predation).[16] In the case law of the European Courts, however, this effect-based approach has not yet been implemented,[17] as the courts still follow a more form-based way of reasoning.

This is contrary to the approach by the Dutch competition courts, where the courts recently seem to follow a more economic approach. In the recent case *CVR Holding BV*[18] the Court of First Instance of Rotterdam required from the Netherlands Competition Authority (*Nederlandse Mededingingsautoriteit: NMa*) that it investigates the demand side of the relevant market and to investigate whether it is difficult for competitors to make competitive offers. Instead of accepting that in principle a discount as such *can* lead to protection of the market, the court requires from the NMa to provide *actual proof* that such results do occur (the actual effects for competitors). A theoretical and mathematical proof as delivered by the NMa was not considered to be sufficient by the court.

The same counts for European and Dutch merger cases. In the *Tetra Laval* case[19] the Court of Justice stated that proof of anti-competitive conglomerate effects of a merger of the kind notified calls for a precise examination, supported by convincing evidence, of the circumstances which allegedly produce those effects. This judgment has been seen as a landmark case, where the Court

14 CBB, 7 December 2005, AWB 04/237 and 04/249, *Secon*, LJN: AU8309.

15 Discussion Paper on the application of article 82 of the Treaty to exclusionary abuses, December 2005 and Guidance on Enforcement Priorities in Applying Article 82 EC to Abusive Exclusionary Conduct by Dominant Undertakings, 3 December 2008.

16 O'Donoghue et al (2006) p. 20.

17 Case T-203/01 *Manufacture française des pneumatiques Michelin* v. *Commission of the European Communities* [2003] ECR II-4071 and case C-95/04P *British Airways* [2007] ECR I-2331.

18 CBB, 4 juli 2007, MEDED 05/3911-STRN, *CVR Holding BV*, LJN: BA9164.

19 Case C-12/03P *Commission of the European Communities* v. *Tetra Laval BV* [2005] ECR I-987.

of Justice clearly focuses more on the *effects* to be proven by the Commission and the evidence to be delivered to substantiate those effects. The same position has been taken by the *Dutch Trade and Industry Appeals Tribunal*, the *CBB*, in the merger case *Nuon/Reliant*,[20] where the court of appeal annulled the decision of the Dutch cartel authority, the NMa. The court found that the NMa used a too abstract methodology to substantiate its findings on the market and should provide more factual evidence to specify the (future) circumstances of the market concerned and the possible effects of the merger on the position of the undertakings involved.

## 3 Market regulation cases

A similar tendency can be seen in cases on market regulation, where regulators have the authority to intervene in specific markets such as telecoms, energy or transport. In these cases economic proof plays an increasingly important role. Sectors, such as telecoms and energy (electricity and gas) are regulated and supervised by special independent administrative authorities with wide powers to intervene on the relevant markets. In many of these regulated sectors the domestic regimes are strongly influenced by European rules and in those areas the main source of regulatory law is European law. Therefore, European law has a major influence on the application of the regulatory frameworks by the national independent administrative authorities who have to enforce them. Of these authorities it is expected that they effectively apply the regulation in order to achieve a level playing field in the sector concerned.

However, how to measure regulatory effects is a complicated matter. These regulatory bodies must, for example, make reliable estimates of the efficiency potential of their intervention, calculate the efficient level of costs and measure the consumer welfare gains. Illustrative in this respect is the Dutch mobile case[21] where the CBB required from OPTA, the Dutch telecoms regulator, to provide sufficient evidence ("careful study and sound argumentation") that the intervention on mobile termination rates does result in benefits for end-users and positive social effects of the imposed regulation. The court considered that OPTA did not assess these effects sufficiently, considering at the same time that the obligations imposed had far-reaching consequences and needed a more in-depth study, in order to prevent an infringement of the principle of legal certainty.

A complicating factor forms the *prospective* analysis regulators have to fulfill in analysing the market structure and the positions of the market players concerned.[22] The regulators have to make a forward looking analysis, taking into

[20] CBB, 28 november 2006, AWB 05/440, *Nuon/Reliant*, LJN: AZ3274.

[21] CBB, 29 August 2006, AWB 05/903 en 05/921-05/931, *Dutch mobile case*, LJN: AY7997. See Ottow et al (2008) and Schuurmans (2008) pp. 5-34.

[22] Ottow (2005) pp. 221-229.

account the dynamics of the market for the regulation period (normally three years). The question arises whether this prospective character of the investigation must have legal consequences for the standard of proof. In these cases *ex ante* regulation is imposed, contrary to *ex post* intervention, where the independent administrative authority will draw conclusions on past behaviour of the undertakings.

At the same time, regulators are confronted with the handicap that they do not dispose of the same information as the undertakings they regulate: the so-called asymmetry of information.[23] At the same time they are confronted with the requirements of rules of evidence to prove their results. The question arises whether this information asymmetry has to be considered when establishing reasonable rules on economic proof.

## 4 Discretion of independent authorities and judicial review

These developments raise the question whether the focus on economic proof and the heavier standard of proof still enables the independent authority to produce results that lead to more efficient and dynamic markets. It has been argued that the independent authority should have a wide margin of discretion to decide on (complex) economic matters.[24] The essential function of evidence is to establish convincingly the merits of an argument or of a decision in general. The question, however, is what the *requisite standard of proof* should be in order to provide the authority on the one hand sufficient flexibility to evaluate and establish the required competitive conditions on the relevant market (*principle of efficiency*), but on the other hand to give sufficient legal basis to the intervention by the authority (*principle of legality*). Should the standard of proof be "convincing", "not incomprehensible" or "beyond any reasonable doubt"? These different criteria reflect different views on the position of independent authorities and the *(intensity of) judicial review* of their decisions.

Whilst the Court of Justice recognises in the *Tetra Laval case* that the Commission has a margin of discretion with regard to economic matters, this does not mean that the Community Courts must refrain from reviewing the Commission's interpretation of information of an economic nature. Not only must the Community Courts, *inter alia*, establish whether the evidence relied on is factually accurate, reliable and consistent but also whether that evidence contains all the information which must be taken into account in order to assess a complex situation and whether this evidence is capable of substantiating the conclusions drawn from it. Such a review is – according to the Court of Justice – all the more necessary in the case of a prospective analysis.

Over the past years, both the European Court of Justice and the Court of First Instance have shown little reluctance to review quite intensively complex

---

23 Baldwin (1999) p. 239.

24 Ottow (2006).

legal and economic assessments in merger cases.[25] In this respect, the *Tetra Laval* judgment of the ECJ can be seen as illustrative, as in this case the ECJ sanctioned a remarkably intensive review and the subsequent annulment of a Commission merger decision by the CFI.

## 5 Principle of national autonomy

The implementation, application and enforcement of Community law takes place within the framework of national law.[26] It is enforced in judicial procedures before national courts, it is applied by national administrative authorities, and infringements are prosecuted by these authorities.[27] Member States have the authority to establish the national procedures. This is often referred to as the *principle of procedural autonomy*.[28] This principle implies that unless Community law provides otherwise, national procedural rules apply. However, on the basis of Article 10 EC the Court of Justice has established two conditions which national (procedural) rules must satisfy[29]:

i) the rules that govern a dispute with a community dimension may not be less favourable than those governing similar domestic actions (*the principle of equivalence*);
ii) the rules must not render virtually impossible or excessively difficult the exercise of rights conferred by the Community legal order (*the principle of effectiveness*).

Furthermore, the Court of Justice developed on this basis the principle of effective judicial protection, which implies that individuals should be able to enforce all rights conferred on them by Community law before the national courts. This principle may also include the rules on proof, such as the burden of proof. It also applies to an obligation on the part of the national authorities to give reasons for their decisions. In this respect, the principles of effectiveness and effective judicial protection might influence the national rules on proof and evidence.

The principle of procedural autonomy does not require the national courts to apply the standard of review used by the European Courts in reviewing decisions of national competition and regulatory authorities. On the other hand, article 10 of the EC-Treaty does require that national courts enforce the right to effective legal protection of EU citizens. It may be argued that the last mentioned right entails an obligation for national courts to refrain from a mere

[25] For an overview of the case law, see e.g. Vesterdorf (2005) pp. 3-33. He is of the opinion that the Court of Justice has done this in all cases and that there has not been a real change in its case law over the recent years.

[26] Jans (2007), pp. 35-60.

[27] Jans (2007), p. 40.

[28] Jans (2007) pp. 35-60, Ottow (2006) pp. 66-75 and Ottow (2008) pp. 265-279.

[29] Taken from: Jans (2007), p. 42.

marginal review of national decisions that execute European law. In the *T-Mobile case* the CBB raised the interesting question whether the principle of autonomy also applies in case of the direct application of European competition law by a national cartel authority. If so, then the national rules on evidence/economic proof would apply and not the European rules, as developed by the European Commission and the European courts. If not, the case law of the Court of Justice in European competition law cases becomes even more relevant and should be followed directly.

## 6 Concluding observations

The standard of judicial review cannot be studied in isolation apart from the issues relating to evidence and the rules on the standard and burden of proof. The intensity of the review has immediate consequences for the evidence to be used to substantiate allegations. A more economic approach in competition law and regulatory cases requires at the same time more economic based evidence and leads to a more critical approach by the European and national judges when analysing decisions of these authorities. Decisions merely based on form or this economic analysis will not be upheld in court, as the courts will review these decisions critically and demand more actual proof to justify the intervention by the Commission or the national authorities. The focus on economic evidence in economic cases has caused a more intense judicial review.

## Bibliography

BAKER ET AL (1999)
J.B. Baker & D.L. Rubinfield, 'Empirical methods used in antitrust litigation: review and critique' [1999/1] *American Law and Economics Review* pp. 386-435

BALDWIN ET AL (1999)
R. Baldwin & M. Cave, *Understanding regulation. Theory, Strategy and Practice* (Oxford University Press, Oxford 1999)

JANS (2007)
J.H. Jans et al, *Europeanisation of Public Law* (Europa Law Publishing, Groningen 2007)

JONES ET AL (2008)
A. Jones & B. Sufrin, *EC Competition Law* (Oxford University Press, Oxford 2008)

O'DONOGHUE ET AL (2006)
R. O'Donoghue & A. Jorge Padilla, *The Law and Economics of Article 82 EC* (Oxford University Press, Oxford 2006)

OTTOW (2005)
A.T. Ottow, 'De bewijspositie van OPTA en de rechterlijke toetsing van besluiten inzake aanmerkelijke marktmacht' [2005/6] *Mediaforum* pp. 221-229

OTTOW (2006)
A.T. Ottow, *Telecommunicatietoezicht. De invloed van het Europese en Nederlandse bestuursprocesrecht* (SDU, Den Haag 2006)

OTTOW (2008)
A.T. Ottow, 'Het gevecht tegen de windmolens. De invloed van het Europese recht op het nationale procesrecht' in N. Van Eijk & B. Hugenholtz (red.), *Dommering-bundel. Opstellen aangeboden aan prof. mr. E.J. Dommering* (Otto Cramwinkel, Amsterdam 2008)

OTTOW ET AL (2008)
A.T. Ottow & E. Doing-Bierens, 'Enige contouren van economisch bewijsrecht' [2008/4] *JBPlus* pp. 170-187

PARRET (2008)
L. Parret, 'Sense and Nonsense of Rules on Proof in Cartel Cases: How to Reconcile a More Economic-Based Approach to Competition Law with More Attention for Rules on Proof' [2008/1] *European Competition Journal* pp. 169-1999

RÖLLER (2005)
L.H. Röller, 'Using economic analysis to strengthen competition policy enforcement', in P. Bergeijk & E. Van Kloosterhuis (eds), *Modelling European mergers: theory, competition policy and case studies* (Edward Elgar, London 2005)

SCHUURMANS (2008)

Y.E. Schuurmans, 'Review of facts in administrative law procedures: the European law perspective' [2008/1] *REALaw* pp. 5-34

VAN DEN BERGH ET AL (2001)

R.J. van den Bergh & P.D. Camesasca, *'European Competition Law and Economics. A comparative perspective'* (Intersentia, Antwerp 2001)

VESTERDORF (2005)

B. Vesterdorf, 'Standard of proof in merger cases: reflections in the light of recent case law of the community courts' [2005/1] *European Competition Journal* pp. 3-33

CHAPTER 5

# Judicial Review after *Tetra Laval*

## Some Observations From a European Administrative Law Point of View

M. Schimmel and R. Widdershoven

## 1 Introduction

The rulings of the CFI and the ECJ in the *Tetra Laval* saga – which ultimately resulted in the annulment of the contested merger decision – spawned major controversy among legal scholars and practitioners alike,[1] most of which concerned the perceived increase of the intensity with which the Community judicature exerts its judicial control over the Commission's findings of fact.[2] For although the ECJ emphasised that the fact-finding process as such is to be performed essentially by the administrative institutions themselves and reiterated the well-established doctrine that the judicature should refrain from substituting its own point of view for that of the institution concerned,[3] the Court in *Tetra Laval* nevertheless demonstrated – arguably more extensively than it had before – its willingness to engage in a thorough and intensive scrutiny of the substantive legality of those findings of fact.

One of the most eye-catching features of the *Tetra Laval* rulings in this respect is formed by the fact that in that case it was made explicitly clear that the intensity of judicial control will vary according to the stage of the administrative fact-finding process under review. In this regard, the Community Courts differentiate between the review of the establishment of the facts on the one hand, and the review of the subsequent appraisal of those established facts on the other.[4] In their application of this two-staged review, the CFI and the ECJ will fully scrutinise the correctness of the established facts, but will by contrast only marginally check whether the ensuing appraisal stage meets the appropriate standard of soundness, in that the Courts will search this stage of the administrative fact-finding process exclusively for errors of assessment that are considered 'manifest'.[5] Even though the issue of whether the more explicit use of this two-staged approach during the *Tetra Laval* proceedings is actually also revelatory of a shift in the intensity of the Community Courts' control over the administrative institutions' findings of fact still remains subject to much uncertainty, the CFI's and the ECJ's rulings in that case are nonetheless very likely to have a profound influence on the way in which the process of judicial review is to be understood by both scholars and potential litigants in the future.

From a general administrative law point of view, *Tetra Laval* – and the standard of review deployed therein – gives essentially rise to four main questions:

- To what extent can the '*Tetra Laval* standard' be applied to other areas of Community law?
- In what manner do the Community Courts apply their two-staged review in practice?

1 Case T-5/02 *Tetra Laval* v. *Commission* [2002] ECR II-4381 and Case C-12/03P *Commission* v. *Tetra Laval* [2005] ECR I-987.

2 See in this regard Schuurmans (2008). See also Craig (2006) pp. 429-481.

3 See especially the Opinion of AG Tizzano in the Case C-12/03P *Commission* v. *Tetra Laval* [2005] ECR I-987 at 89.

4 Opinion of AG Tizzano in the Case C-12/03P *Commission* v. *Tetra Laval* [2005] ECR I-987 at 86.

5 Opinion of AG Tizzano in the Case C-12/03P *Commission* v. *Tetra Laval* [2005] ECR I-987 at 86.

- How does the Courts' standard of judicial review relate to questions of procedural finality?
- What are the consequences of *Tetra Laval* for the way in which national courts review administrative decisions on a national level?

These main questions will form the primary subject matter of the research presented in this article.

## 2 Applicability of the '*Tetra Laval* standard' in other areas of Community law

As the quotation marks in the above heading already indicate, the standard of judicial review that was set by the CFI, explicated – and somewhat attenuated – by the Advocate General, and then endorsed by the ECJ in the final chapter of the *Tetra Laval* saga, cannot be seen as entirely conceived only in those particular proceedings. As we shall observe below, many characteristics of that standard are applied just as well in some anterior cases pertaining to other policy areas of Community law. However this may be, the fact that the implications of the standard as applied by the Courts in *Tetra Laval* reaches far beyond the specific circumstances of the case can already be inferred from the ECJ's statement that 'such a review is *all the more* necessary in the case of a prospective analysis required when examining a planned merger with conglomerate effect'.[6]

In this paragraph the applicability of the standard in the areas of public health, environment and counterterrorism will be examined.

### 2.1 Public health policy

Similar as regards competition law, Community policy towards public health is characterised first and foremost by the scientific nature of the facts the competent administrative body will have to handle in the course of its decisional practice. On top of that, however, the decision-making process in the area of public health will very often involve a variety of policy considerations, especially regarding the – mainly political – question as to what amount of risk to the health of the public at large is still deemed acceptable, and how strict the precautionary principle is to be applied in this respect.[7]

These same fundamental aspects of public health policy can be found in the case of *Pfizer* v. *Council*,[8] which concerned an action for annulment brought by

---

6 Case C-12/03P *Commission* v. *Tetra Laval* [2005] ECR I-987, at 39. See also Bay and Calzado (2005) pp. 440, 451 and Lavrijssen and De Visser (2006) p.131.

7 It should be noted that, although these questions are political in nature, they have been 'translated' into the legal sphere.

8 Case T-13/99 *Pfizer Animal Health* v. *Council of the EU* [2002] ECR II-3303.

Pfizer against a Council Regulation which withdrew the authorisation for the use of a particular antibiotic (*virginiamycin*) as a growth promoter in animal feeding stuffs, for fear that such use might lessen the effectiveness of this antibiotic in treating human infectious diseases.[9] The Council had based its decision on a report by the Scientific Committee for Animal Nutrition (SCAN), an expert body specifically set up to advise the EC administrative institutions in scientific and technical issues relating to consumer health and food safety. During the ensuing proceedings, the CFI essentially had to rule on the question as to whether the Community institutions had erred in finding that the utilisation of *virginiamycin* in animal nutrition posed an unacceptable risk to public health.

Thereto the CFI started by making a distinction – much like the one made during the *Tetra Laval* proceedings – between the judicial review of the correctness of the Community institutions' establishment of the facts and the review of the appreciation of the established facts by that institution, as the Court indicated that:

> '[first], it will examine the argument that, in essence, the relevant findings of fact made by the Community institutions in the present case were incorrect. [Secondly], it will consider whether, on the basis of the findings of fact thus made, the Community institutions exceeded the bounds of their discretion when they held that the use of *virginiamycin* as a growth promoter constituted a risk to human health'.[10]

Hence the CFI made it clear that the contested Regulation – which had been considered to be of individual and direct concern to the applicant, making the action of Pfizer admissible – could be quashed for two main reasons, both of which are related to the administrative fact-finding process: either the Community institutions have incorrectly established the relevant facts, resulting in a (simple) error of fact, or the Community institutions' subsequent appraisal of those facts is vitiated by an error of assessment.[11] As already becomes apparent from the above quotation, however, the competent administrative institutions dispose of a certain amount of leeway during the latter stage of the fact-finding process. Just as in the areas of competition law, a simple error of assessment will form an insufficient ground to overturn the contested administrative act under such circumstances. To annul the Regulation on this count, the error will have to be *manifest*.[12]

As to the question whether the administrative fact-finding process was vitiated by an error of fact, the CFI found that the Community institutions had made no such error by relying only on certain aspects of the scientific report

9 Council Regulation (EC) 2821/98.

10 Case T-13/99 *Pfizer Animal Health* v. *Council of the EU* [2002] ECR II-3303, at 128.

11 See also Craig (2006) p. 448.

12 Case T-13/99 *Pfizer Animal Health* v. *Council of the EU* [2002] ECR II-3303, at 169.

drawn up by the SCAN, without adopting the conclusions formulated in that report, however. The Court argued essentially that the aspects of the report on which the Community institutions had relied provided a sufficient basis for the subsequent administrative appraisal.[13] The Court did consider itself to be in a position to examine the merits of other scientific evidence that might have led to a different conclusion, including parts of the same SCAN report or different interpretations thereof.[14]

With regard to the question whether or not the Community institutions made a manifest error of assessment when they concluded on the basis of the facts thus established that the use of *virginiamycin* as an additive in animal nutrition posed a risk to human health, the CFI subsequently considered that when the scientific evidence is not yet conclusive, 'the competent public authority must weigh up its obligations and decide either to wait until the results of more detailed scientific research become available or to act on the basis of the scientific information available'.[15] Under such circumstances the institutions concerned dispose of what has been called 'political discretion'.[16] Therefore, taking into account the dire consequences should the perceived risk materialise, the Community institutions were entitled to rely on the precautionary principle and did not commit a manifest error when they took preventative protective measures on what was yet an incomplete scientific basis.[17]

### 2.2 Environmental policy

The characteristics specifically pertaining to the policy area of environmental law closely resemble those relating to the EC public health policy as identified in the previous paragraph. For in this area the competent administrative authorities will also, in the course of their decision-making process, have to cope essentially with two fundamental questions, the combined answer to which will determine to a large extent the outcome of the process and the substance of the decision at hand. The first of these questions is of a technical or scientific nature and concerns the issue of assessing the level of risk to the environment emanating from particular behaviour. The second one – which is mainly political in character – subsequently relates to the fact that the Community institution concerned will have to decide what level of risk to the environment can still be regarded as acceptable.

In its 2007 *Germany* v. *Commission* ruling,[18] which concerned a dispute about the compatibility of Germany's national system of greenhouse gas emission allowances (NAP) with the criteria set forth by Directive 2003/87, the

13 Case T-13/99 *Pfizer Animal Health* v. *Council of the EU* [2002] ECR II-3303 at 199 and 204.

14 Case T-13/99 *Pfizer Animal Health* v. *Council of the EU* [2002] ECR II-3303, at 393.

15 Case T-13/99 *Pfizer Animal Health* v. *Council of the EU* [2002] ECR II-3303, at 387.

16 AG Léger Opinion Case C-40/03P, *Rica Foods* v. *Commission* [2005] ECR I-6811, at 45.

17 Case T-13/99 *Pfizer Animal Health* v. *Council of the EU* [2002] ECR II-3303, at 387 and 389.

18 Case T-374/04 *Germany* v. *Commission* [2007] ECR II-4431.

CFI first observed that the Commission disposes in this policy area of a broad margin of appreciation 'in so far as the review entails complex economic and ecological assessments'.[19] Referring, *inter alia*, to *Pfizer*, the Court stated that it follows from this assertion that:

> '[i]n its review of legality in this regard, [...] the Court of First Instance cannot take the place of the Commission where the latter must carry out complex economic and ecological assessments in this context. In this respect, the Court is obliged to confine itself to verifying that the measure in question is not vitiated by a manifest error or a misuse of powers, that the competent authority did not clearly exceed the bounds of its discretion and that the procedural guarantees, which are of particularly fundamental importance in this context, have been fully observed'.[20]

Again, the Court reiterated the view that had already been stipulated in the course of the *Tetra Laval* proceedings, i.e. that the Community judicature may not replace the administrative institution's appraisal of the facts by its own. On the other hand, the CFI made it perfectly clear that it will fully review whether 'the Commission observed the limits of the relevant rules of law'.[21]

After a particularly elaborate consideration of the manner in which the Commission had interpreted and applied the relevant legal provisions, the CFI concluded that the contested decision was vitiated by an error of law and therefore could not be upheld.[22] Nonetheless, the Court continued by examining the applicant's third plea, in which it was argued that the Commission had manifestly erred in its finding that the *ex post* adjustments provided for in the German NAP would unduly favour new entrants on the market, and that the Commission had breached its duty to state reasons as enshrined in Article 253 of the EC Treaty. Even though it did not consider whether the Commission's assessment was vitiated by a manifest error, the CFI stipulated that:

> '[c]ompliance with the obligation under Article 253 EC to state reasons [...] is of particularly fundamental importance because here exercise of the Commission's power of review under Article 9(3) of the directive entails complex economic and ecological assessments and review by the Community judicature of the legality and merits of those assessments is restricted'.[23]

---

19 Case T-374/04 *Germany* v. *Commission* [2007] ECR II-4431, at 80.

20 Case T-374/04 *Germany* v. *Commission* [2007] ECR II-4431, at 81.

21 Case T-374/04 *Germany* v. *Commission* [2007] ECR II-4431, at 81. Although the Court does not make any explicit mention of the manner in which it will review the establishment of the facts by the Community institution as it had in both *Tetra Laval* and *Pfizer*, it should be noted that the correctness of the Commission's establishment of the facts was not challenged by the applicant in the present case.

22 Case T-374/04 *Germany* v. *Commission* [2007] ECR II-4431, at 150 and 164.

23 Case T-374/04 *Germany* v. *Commission* [2007] ECR II-4431, at 168.

Consequently, the Court held that the Commission had not sufficiently motivated its decision to declare the NAP partially incompatible with Community law. This is interesting especially because it demonstrates the close link between the substantive review of the appraisal of the facts and the procedural requirement that the decision – and more in particular the appraisal stage of the fact-finding – should be duly motivated in order to avoid annulment. For even if that substantive review is limited, the Courts will severely reprimand shortcomings in the statement of reasons, as under such circumstances they are not even in a position to control the legality of the appraisal stage.

### 2.3 Counterterrorism policy

Over the past decade, the EU has witnessed a multitude of actions for annulment directed against the so-called 'terrorism lists', which contain the names of individuals and organisations allegedly involved in terrorism-related activities as a result of which their financial assets are to be frozen. The cases of *Organisation des Modjahedines du Peuple d'Iran* (*OMPI*) and *Sison* v. *Council* were the first two cases where the CFI considered itself empowered to engage in a truly comprehensive review of the contested decisions.[24] In contrast to the decisions in *Kadi* and *Yusuf*[25] the aforementioned decisions were ultimately based on a UN Security Council Resolution that leaves it up to the Member States to determine which individuals and which entities should be subjected to the counterterrorism measures.[26]

In both *OMPI* and *Sison* v. *Council*, the CFI stated that, with respect to the judicial review of the respective decisions to freeze funds pursuant to the relevant Council Regulation,[27] the Community judicature must ascertain whether in a specific case the legal conditions thereto have been fulfilled. According to the Court, this implies that:

> '[j]udicial review of the lawfulness of the decision in question extends to the assessment of the facts and circumstances relied on as justifying that decision, and to the evidence and information on which that assessment is based [...]. The Court must also be satisfied that the rights of the defence have been observed and that the requirement of a statement of reasons has been complied with and also, where applicable, that the overriding considerations relied on exceptionally by the Council, in order to escape those obligations, are justified'.[28]

---

[24] Case T-228/02 *Organisation des Modjahedines du Peuple d'Iran* v. *Council of the EU* [2006] ECR II-4665 and Case T-47/03 *Sison* v. *Council of the EU* [not yet published].

[25] Case T-315/01 *Kadi* v. *Council of the EU* [2005] ECR II-3639 and Case T-306/01 *Yusuf* v. *Council of the EU* [2005] ECR II-3533.

[26] UNSC Resolution 1373, UN Doc. S/RES/1373 (2001).

[27] Council Regulation 2580/2001 EC.

[28] Case T-228/02 *Organisation des Modjahedines du Peuple d'Iran* v. *Council of the EU* [2006] ECR II-4665, at 154 and Case T-47/03 *Sison* v. *Council of the EU* [not yet published], at para. 201.

Moreover, the CFI further added that, since the Council had restricted the rights of the defence in the cases at hand, the Court must be able to review the lawfulness and merits of the measures to freeze funds 'without it being possible to raise objections that the evidence and information used by the Council is secret or confidential'.[29]

Thus, even though the Court recognises that the Council of the EU enjoys broad discretion in these matters,[30] it does not mean that it has to restrict itself to checking the contested decision for procedural improprieties. The last part of the above quotation seems to imply that, on the contrary, a thorough review of the administrative findings of fact is considered all the more necessary when some of the procedural safeguards have been limited for objectively justified reasons.[31] Such limitations with regard to procedural prerequisites may in their turn not go so far so as to prevent the Courts from being able to judicially scrutinise the grounds on which the contested decision is based, however.

Just as in the *Tetra Laval* proceedings, the CFI made it explicitly clear that the absolute limit to the scope of the judicial review of the fact-finding process is formed by the fact that the Community judicature may not 'substitute its *assessment* of the evidence, facts and circumstances' justifying the adoption of a particular administrative measure for that of the EC institution.[32] Therefore, the Court's judicial control of such measures:

> '[m]ust be restricted to checking that the rules governing procedure and the statement of reasons have been complied with, that the facts are materially accurate, and that there has been no manifest error of assessment of the facts or misuse of power. That limited review applies, especially, to the assessment of the considerations of appropriateness on which such decisions are based'.[33]

It can be inferred from the above that in terrorism cases the Community Courts will not only intensively scrutinise whether the procedural prerequisites have been satisfied, but also whether the facts on which the Council decision rests correspond with the material truth. It is only with regard to the ensuing appraisal of the facts that, again, the Court will confine itself to ensuring that the Council has not made a manifest error of assessment during this phase of the fact-finding process. In *OMPI* and *Sison* v. *Council*, however, the CFI did not actually rule on the soundness of the administrative findings of fact, as – due

---

29 Case T-228/02 *Organisation des Modjahedines du Peuple d'Iran* v. *Council of the EU* [2006] ECR II-4665, at 155 and Case T-47/03 *Sison* v. *Council of the EU* [not yet published], at para. 202.

30 Case T-228/02 *Organisation des Modjahedines du Peuple d'Iran* v. *Council of the EU* [2006] ECR II-4665, at 159 and Case T-47/03 *Sison* v. *Council of the EU* [not yet published], at para. 206.

31 The CFI refers here to Case C-341/04 *Eurofoods* [2006] ECR I-3813, at 66.

32 Case T-228/02 *Organisation des Modjahedines du Peuple d'Iran* v. *Council of the EU* [2006] ECR II-4665, at 159 and Case T-47/03 *Sison* v. *Council of the EU* [not yet published], at para. 206.

33 Case T-228/02 *Organisation des Modjahedines du Peuple d'Iran* v. *Council of the EU* [2006] ECR II-4665, at 159 and Case T-47/03 *Sison* v. *Council of the EU* [not yet published], at para. 206.

to the lack of disclosure of some crucial evidence from the side of the Council – the Court considered itself unable to review the elements leading up to the decision to place the applicants on the terrorism list.[34] Therefore, in both actions the CFI annulled the contested decision on the ground that the Council had infringed its obligation pursuant to Article 253 EC to provide an adequate statement of reasons[35] and because of the fact that, according to the Court, during the administrative procedure the rights of the defence had been infringed on several counts.[36] Like the case of *Germany* v. *Commission* discussed above, this again demonstrates that the Community Courts will not shy away from quashing a decision that they consider vitiated by sufficiently serious procedural improprieties.

### 2.4 Conclusion

It appears that considerable similarities exist between the different areas of law as to the manner in which the Community Courts will scrutinise the administrative fact-finding process, and that the concepts as applied in *Tetra Laval* are not valid within the area of competition law alone. For in all of the policy areas considered above, the Courts make a clear distinction between the judicial review of the establishment of the facts on the one hand and the review of the subsequent administrative appraisal of the established facts on the other. And in all of these areas, the Community judicature will exert full control over the former, whilst it will limit its substantial review of the latter stage of the fact-finding process. Thus, even if the area of competition law could be conceived as the source of many of the developments concerning the Courts' methodology as regards the intensity of judicial review,[37] it can be observed that for quite a while these developments have been exported to other policy areas of Community law.

An important element that was not apparent from the *Tetra Laval* cases but which played a significant role in the cases of *Pfizer* and *Germany* v. *Commission* considered above is the notion of '*political* discretion', which curtails the Courts' abilities to review the institution's appraisal of the facts even more extensively than the margin of appreciation emanating from the *technical* (or economic) complexity of a particular case.

Thus, on the one hand it is clear that the mechanism behind the manner in which the Courts' intensity of review is curtailed at this stage is essentially

34 Case T-228/02 *Organisation des Modjahedines du Peuple d'Iran* v. *Council of the EU* [2006] ECR II-4665, at 166 and 173 and Case T-47/03 *Sison* v. *Council of the EU* [not yet published], at para. 225.

35 Case T-228/02 *Organisation des Modjahedines du Peuple d'Iran* v. *Council of the EU* [2006] ECR II-4665, at 164 and Case T-47/03 *Sison* v. *Council of the EU* [not yet published], at para. 216-218.

36 Case T-228/02 *Organisation des Modjahedines du Peuple d'Iran* v. *Council of the EU* [2006] ECR II-4665, at 160-162 and Case T-47/03 *Sison* v. *Council of the EU* [not yet published], at para. 207-214.

37 Owing largely to the fact that it is the area that has entailed by far the most litigation in this respect. See Chalmers (2006) p. 413.

the same irrespective of the type of leeway that is involved. On the other hand, however, it should be kept in mind that the intensity of the Community Courts' control over the appraisal stage of the fact-finding process in a particular policy area may vary according to whether the leeway granted to the administrative institutions consists only of a margin of appreciation or whether, on the contrary, it involves more far-reaching discretionary powers.

We shall return to this important distinction in paragraph 3.3 below.

## 3 Two stages of review

As was observed in the previous section, the clear distinction between the intensity of review of the establishment of the facts and that of the appraisal stage of the administrative findings of fact is a recurrent feature applicable across the range of Community law's different policy areas. Therefore, the present paragraph will be dedicated to a more detailed analysis of the precise workings of this two-staged review process.

### 3.1 Appraisal v. establishment

The distinction between the establishment of the facts on the one hand and the appraisal of the facts on the other is not an easy one to make in practice. For evidently, both concepts are inextricably linked in that they stand in a necessary, chronological relation to each other, as it goes without saying that an appraisal can be effectively performed only after the facts – its subject matter – have been established. Conversely, established facts will more often than not have to undergo at least some kind of assessment or weighing before the decision-maker can determine to what legal result these facts must conduce. In practice, it will often happen that the administrative institution concerned will only find out at the appraisal stage that some important or even crucial facts have not been (correctly) established, obliging it to return to the first stage of its fact-finding process, so that both stages will often be intertwined and cannot be classified in strict consecutive timeframes. Moreover, the Courts themselves will often not explicitly disentangle both notions and will rather demarcate the boundaries of the two stages of the administrative fact-finding process on functional grounds, i.e. they will decide their degree of intrusiveness of review with regard to certain elements of this process on a case-to-case basis.[38] Nevertheless, and despite the inherent difficulties in clearly separating both concepts, it seems feasible to draw an analytical delineation which is furthermore largely corroborated by the Community judicature's decisional practice.

In its most paradigmatic form, 'establishment of the facts' refers to the objective ascertainment of the existence of certain pure facts, such as that event X happened at a particular place Y at a certain time Z. It is also clear that direct

[38] Craig (2006) p. 430. See also Nicholson (2005) pp. 145-146.

inferences from those primary facts, i.e. inferences that flow automatically and logically from those facts, also belong to the stage of establishment,[39] which is thus characterised by the objectivity of the factual findings made at this stage of the decision-making process. As the correctness of such facts can be objectively verified by the Community judicature, it follows that there is no room for any margin of appreciation whatsoever.[40] Indeed, there is nothing yet to 'appreciate' at this stage, as the facts speak for themselves.[41] 'Appraisal' on the other hand implies the performance of some sort of subjective value judgment. Such a value judgment can range from a far-reaching weighing or balancing act based on a discretionary power on the side of the administrative institution, giving it considerable leeway, to the more subtle case wherein the institution has a certain margin of appreciation due, for example, to the complexity of the facts or the technicality of the assessment that is to be performed. The amount of value judgment in the decision-maker's fact-finding can thus be conceived as a sliding scale on which everything except the most self-evident primary facts will involve a value judgment of some magnitude, with the situation wherein the institution has to make important policy determinations for which the Community primary legislator has conferred considerable discretionary powers at the far end of the scale.

Notwithstanding the close intertwinement of the two stages of the review process, it appears that an analytical delineation can be made of where the first stage ends and where the second stage begins. In a general way, it could be stated that the distinction between both stages resides in the fact that with regard to the appraisal phase of the fact-finding process two *reasonable* persons can disagree with each other as to the correct outcome, whilst in respect of the first stage, in which the facts are established, they cannot.[42] For evidently – since a fact is either correct or incorrect – if two persons, of which at least one holds a reasonable point of view, disagree, the other's diverging opinion can automatically be qualified as being 'unreasonable'. Thus, a simple error at the establishment stage suffices for the Courts to overturn a contested administrative decision. The subjective nature of the intellectual effort that has to be performed at the appraisal stage means, however, that there exists a multitude of reasonable outcomes for that effort, and that the decision runs the risk of being quashed only if it exceeds the limits hence prescribed by this notion of 'reasonableness'. In other words, an error at the appraisal stage will have to be *manifest* before that decision can be annulled.

39 Legal (2006) p. 113.

40 Vesterdorf (2005) p. 15.

41 Nicholson (2006) p. 145.

42 Vesterdorf (2005) p. 17.

### 3.2 Review of the establishment stage

As follows from the above, the Community Courts will conduct a full review of the fact-finding process's establishment stage, in the course of which they are to search this stage for any errors of fact. This is only half of the story, however. For before the correctness of the established facts can effectively be fully reviewed by the Courts, it must be determined which facts should have been established by the administrative institutions in the first place. As it goes without saying that the CFI or the ECJ cannot possibly examine all facts and circumstances that might influence the outcome of the decision-making process on their true relevancy, they will have to utilise certain parameters to determine which facts should, and which facts should not, have been incorporated into the administration's findings of fact.

To this end, the Community Courts essentially dispose of three instruments to facilitate their task in this respect. The first of these concerns the fact that the Courts put the onus upon the administrative institution in question to undertake 'a thorough and painstaking investigation'.[43] The fact that this statement – even if it is general enough to leave the administration considerable space to manoeuvre – is far from being an empty threat, was aptly demonstrated during the *Tetra Laval* proceedings. For in that case, one of the primary considerations that led the CFI to the conclusion that the contested decision should be overturned, consisted of the fact that the Commission had left out of its fact-finding any elaboration on the question as to whether the illegal nature of certain anti-competitive practices would have induced *Tetra Laval* to refrain from such conduct post-merger.[44] As such an elaboration would have been plainly relevant as far as the CFI was concerned, the Commission had not lived up to its obligation to conduct a thorough investigation as to the elements that should have been integrated into its fact-finding process.

Secondly, it seems that the Courts can apply the well-established concept that by adopting policy guidelines the administrative institutions limit the exercise of their own discretion also to the question as to the facts which should form part of the subsequent appraisal.[45] In the recent merger case of *Sun Chemicals*, for example, the CFI stipulated that the Community judicature must:

> 'consider whether any possible omissions on the part of the Commission [of elements which are mentioned in the Horizontal Merger Guidelines] are capable of calling into question its finding that the present concentration does not raise serious doubts as to its compatibility with the common market'.[46]

---

43 Opinion of AG in the Case C-12/03P *Commission* v. *Tetra Laval* [2005] ECR I-987 at 88. See also Case C-12/03P *Commission* v. *Tetra Laval* [2005] ECR I-987 at 39.

44 Case T-5/02 *Tetra Laval* v. *Commission* [2002] ECR II-4381, at 159. See also Vesterdorf (2005) p. 14.

45 See with regard to this general concept, e.g., Case T-374/04 *Germany* v. *Commission* [2007] ECR II-4431, at 111 and Case T-13/99 *Pfizer Animal Health* v. *Council of the EU* [2002] ECR II-3303, at 119.

46 Case T-282/06 *Sun Chemicals* [2007] ECR II-2149, at 61.

Therefore, it appears that through guidelines the Community institutions might have effectively auto-restricted any possibly existing discretion in deciding on which facts to base their decisions if those facts cannot be established exhaustively.

Third, the procedural safeguards in the form of the rights of defence provide a valuable tool for all parties alike to ensure that no relevant facts are left out of the decision-making process. Especially the right to be heard is intimately linked to the administrative fact-finding's establishment stage. For when the contested decision's addressee is given the opportunity to express its view on the matter, it will be easy for the institution concerned to identify possible omissions on its part of factors that might indeed be material to the outcome of the decision-making process. If this procedural right has, on the other hand, not been properly observed – as was the case in *Sison* and *OMPI* considered above, for instance, – the administrative institution cannot, strictly speaking, rule out the possibility that it left important facts or circumstances unestablished (or the possibility that the facts were established incorrectly) and thus outside the scope of its subsequent appraisal. This assertion also follows from the CFI's statement in the *Reynolds* case that the right to be heard has been breached 'where it cannot be reasonably precluded that that irregularity could have had a particular impact on the content of that act'.[47] According to the Court, the breach of this procedural safeguard will always 'have a particular impact' on the content of the decision in question 'unless it is established that the person adopting the act has no discretion and was required to act as he did'.[48] Moreover, in order to safeguard the procedural propriety of its administrative decisions in respect of the right to be heard, the EC institution should include only those elements and facts on which the addressee has had the opportunity to comment in its final decision.[49] In fact, this was one of the principal reasons why the CFI overturned the Commission's merger decision in *Schneider* v. *Commission*.[50]

The procedural guarantee of the right to be heard thus provides the Community Courts with a particularly suitable instrument to control the substantive legality of the establishment stage of the fact-finding process, without having to assess which facts were omitted but should have been integrated into the administration's decision-making.

### 3.3 Review of the appraisal stage

At the second stage of the process of judicial review, the intensity of the Community Courts' scrutiny will be limited by the inherent leeway the administrative institutions dispose of as to their appraisal of the established facts. This limitation consists of the fact that the Courts will search the admin-

47 Case T-273/00 *Reynolds* [2002] ECR II-163, at 112.

48 Case T-273/00 *Reynolds* [2002] ECR II-163, at 113. See also Schwarze (2004) p. 98.

49 Bebr (1981) p.89.

50 Case T-310/01 *Schneider Electric* [2002] ECR II-4072. See also Clough (2004) p. 742.

istration's appraisal only for errors that are considered manifest. Although the question as to what the term 'manifest error of assessment' actually amounts to has never been made explicit either by the ECJ or by the CFI to a truly satisfying extent, it can generally be assumed that it denotes the situation wherein an error is evident and grave enough so as to preclude any 'potential concurrence' between the established facts on the one hand, and the conclusions drawn from these facts on the other.[51] We may recall that the appraisal stage distinguishes itself from the establishment stage because of the fact that two reasonable persons may disagree as to the correct outcome of the appraisal, and that the discretion granted to the administrative institutions can be conceived as a range of possible 'reasonable' modes of action at the disposal of those institutions under particular circumstances. Thus, it follows that the institution at hand will have committed a manifest error when it chooses to follow a mode of action that falls outside the given set of reasonable modes.[52] In that case, the institution will be found to have effectively overstepped the boundaries of its leeway.

### 3.3.1 Discretion and margin of appreciation

It follows from the above that the intensity of judicial review at the appraisal stage is directly connected to the administrative institution's amount of discretion in a particular instance. As we have already observed, however, this amount of discretion in its turn depends essentially on the source from which it emanates, i.e. the technical complexity of the case – resulting in technical discretion – or the fact that the institution has to balance different policy considerations against each other – creating political discretion.[53] In essence, 'technical discretion' is not the correct denomination of this concept. Discretion, also political discretion, refers to the situation wherein the administrative institution is empowered by the legislator to define the criteria by which a decision is reached, on its own,[54] whereas what is dubbed 'discretion of a technical nature' by Advocate General Léger has considerably less far-reaching implications.[55] Indeed, a better term for this concept is 'margin of appreciation', as a particular Community institution when performing a complex technical assessment will only dispose of some leeway within the framework of set legal criteria that may play a role in the outcome of the decision-making process.[56]

51 Van der Esch (1968) pp. 54, 73.

52 See also Ritleng (1999) p. 656.

53 AG Léger Opinion Case C-40/03P, *Rica Foods* v. *Commission* [2005] ECR I-6811, at 45-47. See also Lenaerts (2006) p. 308.

54 Bailey (2004) p. 1338.

55 AG Léger Opinion Case C-40/03P, *Rica Foods* v. *Commission* [2005] ECR I-6811, at 46.

56 It should be noted that the terms 'discretion' and 'margin of appreciation' are often used interchangeably by the Community Courts themselves. Technically, however, both terms refer to related but definitely distinct concepts.

To illustrate the sometimes subtle difference between the two concepts, one can look at the Commission's decisional practice under Article 81 (3) of the EC Treaty. Usually, the Commission will have to perform complex economic assessments in order to determine whether the criteria enumerated in that provision are fulfilled, in the course of which it disposes of a certain margin of appreciation. Sometimes, however, the Commission will go beyond the enumerated criteria and take other factors into account in deciding whether a particular Article 81 EC agreement should be exempted.[57] If the CFI then condones such administrative behaviour and upholds the exemption, one can say that the Commission has thus been allowed a degree of ('political') discretion in the true meaning of the word. In this sense, discretion essentially results from the non-justiciability of a certain element of the decision-making process because of its political character whereas allowing for a margin of appreciation is for the greatest part about technical feasibility.[58]

It can thus be observed that the Community Courts' powers of review will be more delimited in the situation where the administrative institution possesses political discretion than when the institution only disposes of a margin of appreciation.[59] This logically emanates from the fact that – as observed above – when the institution has been granted political discretion, it disposes of far greater leeway as it will essentially be able to set the criteria to be fulfilled before a certain outcome of that stage of the decision-making process is reached. In contrast, in the case of the existence of a margin of appreciation, the institution will be constrained by certain set criteria and will only have some space to manoeuvre *within* the framework created by these mandatory criteria Hence, although the manifest error standard applies just as well in both cases, the difference resides in the fact that in the latter instance the Community institution may be held more readily to have committed a manifest error, as under such circumstances the institution concerned can dispose of fewer 'reasonable' modes of action and will thus more easily overstep the bounds of its leeway.

### 3.3.2 Statement of reasons

Regardless of the type of leeway involved – technical or political – the Courts' powers of review will thus be severely limited at the appraisal stage. Therefore, it may come as no surprise that the procedural requirement incumbent upon the administrative institutions to provide an adequate statement of reasons plays an important role in the Courts' control of that stage of the fact-finding process. It was observed that the right to be heard has implications in particular with respect to the *establishment stage* of that process. The requirement that an administrative decision should be adequately motivated could be regarded as being the procedural counterpart of the substantive review

57 Bailey (2004) p. 1338.

58 See also Bailey (2004) pp. 1337-1339.

59 AG Léger Opinion Case C-40/03P, *Rica Foods* v. *Commission* [2005] ECR I-6811, at 49.

of the *appraisal stage*, as it goes without saying that a reasonable assessment will be more easily motivated than a 'manifestly erred' unreasonable one. The link between the substantive review of the administrative appraisal and the procedural scrutiny of the motivation of the contested decision is further apparent from the recurrent statement that the Courts will check whether the appraisal of the facts satisfies requirements of logic and coherency.[60] As to these requirements, it can be observed that they integrate the procedural guarantee of a proper motivation into the substantive part of the review of the fact-finding's appraisal stage.

That a breach of this procedural guarantee can and often will have far-reaching consequences is made abundantly clear when one looks at the legal proceedings in the *OMPI* and *Sison* cases considered above. For in those two terrorism cases – despite the fact that the CFI did not rule on the question as to whether the Council had committed a manifest error of assessment – the Court still overturned the contested decisions to add the names of the people concerned to the terrorism list on the ground that the Council had failed in both instances to provide adequate reasons for the outcome of the respective decision-making processes, so that the CFI was:

> '[n]ot in a position to carry out adequately its review of the lawfulness of the decision originally challenged or, in consequence, that of the contested decision, in light of the other pleas in law, grounds of challenge and substantive arguments invoked in support of the application for annulment'.[61]

Therefore, in this way, the Court did not even have to consider the question as to whether the Council had committed a manifest error of assessment; it simply annulled the contested decision because of the infringement of the essential obligation to state adequate reasons for the adopted decision. Furthermore, it clearly demonstrates the Community Courts' approach in these matters: if they cannot understand the reasons in the decision or if the decision does not contain any reasons at all, they will not be able to exercise a proper judicial scrutiny of the decision's legality.

Hence, the important implications attached to a failure to provide an adequate statement of reasons constitutes a powerful tool in the hands of the Community Courts with which they may counterbalance to a certain extent the leeway granted to the administration at the appraisal stage[62] In a sense, it could thus be stated that not only must the administrative institutions' appraisal be reasonable in order to escape annulment, but their appraisal must also *appear to be reasonable* in terms of the adequate motivation of the decision for the benefit of the parties concerned. Notwithstanding the importance of ensuring a

---

60 See, for instance, Opinion of AG in the Case C-12/03P *Commission* v. *Tetra Laval* [2005] ECR I-987, at 88.

61 CFI Case T-47/03 *Sison* v. *Council of the EU*, [not yet published], at 225.

62 Schwarze (2004) pp. 95-96.

procedurally sound administration, the frequent use of this procedural instrument to control the substantive legality of the fact-finding process might raise some important concerns as well, especially with regard to questions of procedural finality. This issue shall be examined in the subsequent paragraph of this contribution.

## 4 Judicial review and procedural finality

When a decision has been quashed by the Courts because of a procedural impropriety resulting from a breach of the rights of the defence at the establishment stage or a lack of adequately stated reasons at the appraisal stage of the fact-finding process, that fact alone will not bring the administrative dispute to an end. Just like the administrative tribunals in most Member States, the Community Courts confine themselves to the annulment of the contested decision, and leave it up to the administrative institution concerned to take a new decision in which it will have to integrate the findings of the judgment. Although this new decision may very well be in favour of the applicant, it is not uncommon for an administrative institution to repair the improprieties identified by the Court by hearing the party involved, by conducting an additional investigation or by providing further reasons for the decision, before taking a decision with the same substance and conclusion as the original one. This new decision can subsequently be challenged before the Courts, after which it may again be overturned and referred back to the administration, *et cetera*. In the Netherlands this is called the 'ping-pong effect of an action for annulment'.[63]

Most jurisdictions that recognise the possibility to bring actions for annulment are familiar with this phenomenon and, increasingly, it is perceived as a serious problem. In this manner an administrative dispute may drag on for years on end, which in its turn may come into conflict with the 'reasonable time' requirement contained in Article 6 of the European Convention of Human Rights. In addition, it will be particularly frustrating for the citizen concerned to be confronted with substantially the same administrative decision after an initial 'victory' in the courtroom, a victory which will in retrospect seem to have been Pyrrhic in character. Finally, this phenomenon is often likely to obstruct the diligence of the administrative policy in question. In the Netherlands, for instance, this last complication occurs especially in the policy area of environmental law, more in particular when decisions regarding major infrastructural projects are quashed by the Dutch administrative courts for procedural reasons. It may take the administrative authority involved considerable time to reformulate its original decision in order to comply with all formal requirements so that the administrative court, again after a lengthy procedure, can uphold the decision this time. In the meantime, the infrastructural project is idle, a

---

[63] Polak (2000).

consequence which is considered less and less acceptable from a political point of view.

Because of the aforementioned drawbacks, it is widely argued in the Netherlands that the legislature should strive to introduce a greater amount of procedural finality into Dutch administrative law. These arguments are furthermore important in the context of economic law when judges will more often quash decisions for procedural unsoundness in that area of law. A variety of techniques are applied in the Member States' jurisdictions to enhance the procedural finality of administrative disputes, which shall be briefly dealt with below.

The first of these techniques concerns the possibility to repair a procedurally flawed decision in the litigation phase recognised in multiple Member States. In Germany, for instance, the administration may complement or alter the statement of reasons underlying the contested decision during the procedure before the administrative court (*Nachschieben von Grunden*).[64] If this modified statement of reasons is subsequently considered to be sufficiently adequate, the decision may escape annulment. Moreover, the German administrative institutions can take an amended decision at the litigation stage which may subsequently be integrated into the procedure before the court. If this amended decision is considered legitimate, the dispute can definitely be settled by the judge. There exists in the Netherlands a more or less similar rule with regard to the integration of amended decisions into a pending procedure, and, just like in Germany, the administration may complement or alter a decision at the litigation stage of the dispute. Unlike the German system, however, a Dutch administrative decision cannot, in this manner, escape annulment. Nevertheless, the court at issue may rule that the legal effects of the annulled decision are to be upheld,[65] as a consequence of which the administrative institution concerned will not have to reconsider the case a second time. In France, the administration's possibilities to fix a lack of motivation at the trial stage are restricted.[66] The French administrative tribunals are, however, authorised either *ex officio* or on the request of the defendant to mend the procedural flaws of a decision by modifying the legal base of a decision (*la substitution de base légale*) or by altering the grounds of a decision (*la substitution des motifs*), in order to prevent so-called *'annulations doctrinales'*.[67] With the judgment of the *Conseil d'Etat* in *Mme Hallal*, this competence has been extended so as to enable the administrative tribunal to repair *substantive* shortcomings in the contested decision as well.[68]

---

64 In furtherance to Article 114, second phrase, *Verwaltungsgerichtsordnung*.

65 On the ground of Article 8:72, third paragraph, *Awb*. This technique – the annulment of a decision while leaving its legal effects intact – has the advantage for the claimant that his litigation costs will be reimbursed and that he may bring an action for damages, which is of course not the case when his appeal has simply been rejected.

66 Chapus (1997) p. 932.

67 Chapus (2002) pp. 915-918.

68 CE 6 February 2004, p. 48 *(Mme Hallal)*.

Secondly, some Member State jurisdictions grant the administrative courts the possibility to definitely settle the administrative dispute themselves. Thus, in such instances, the courts will not only annul the contested decision but will also take the final decision in the case. The Competition Appeal Tribunal in the United Kingdom disposes of this competence, which it occasionally applies.[69] In the Netherlands all administrative courts are, generally, authorised to take the new decision on its own account, but only in those cases where the administrative institutions at hand do not dispose of any remaining discretion after the judgment. This limitation can be traced back to the fundamental concept of the separation of powers. This concept dictates that it is up to the administration and not the judicature to decide on the manner in which it will utilise its executive leeway. As a result of this restriction, the Dutch administrative courts will replace the original decision only if it does not emanate from a discretionary power of the administrative institution involved.[70] Thus, the competence granted to the courts will be of no use in the areas of competition policy, public health, environmental law and counterterrorism policy discussed in paragraph 2, as these areas are all characterised by the significant amount of leeway the administration disposes of in choosing the optimal mode of action (discretion and/or margin of appreciation). Moreover, both the Community Courts and the administrative courts in the majority of the Member States, most notably France and Germany, are not competent to issue a replacing decision after the original one has been annulled.[71] Such a competence would seem to come into conflict with the doctrine of the separation of powers.

It follows from the foregoing that, although there exists a need for a final settling of disputes by the administrative tribunals, most Member States' jurisdictions do not provide this option when the administration still disposes of a considerable amount of leeway. To break away from this stalemate, the Dutch legislator intends to introduce the 'administrative loop', an instrument to prevent the action for annulment's ping-pong effect from occurring.[72] In short, this instrument will provide the Dutch administrative courts, when confronted with a decision that is procedurally flawed, with the possibility to render an interlocutory judgment, in which they may indicate these formal deficiencies. Whilst the case is still pending before the court, the administrative institution

69 See for example *1007/2/3/02 Freeserve.com PLC* v. *Director General of Telecommunications*, Competition Appeal Tribunal [2003] CAT 15, mentioned in the article 'Judicial Review of the Decisions of the Competition Authorities and the Economic Regulators in the UK' of Cosmo Graham in this book.

70 See for the application of this instrument in practice, B.J. Schueler, J.K. Drewes et al (2007) pp. 54-60.

71 The German administrative courts are, however, obliged to make the case 'spruchsreif', which means that they will have to review the substance of the case to such an extent that they can rule on the well-foundedness of the applicant's substantive claim. Therefore, in most cases it will be obvious which decision the administration subsequently has to take.

72 Wetsvoorstel bestuurlijke lus, *Kamerstukken* II, 2007-2008, 31 352. A somewhat similar instrument existed in Germany as of 1996, and could be found in Article 87, first paragraph, sub 7, Verwaltungsgerichtsordnung. This instrument has been withdrawn in 2002, as no use was ever made of it.

concerned is subsequently enabled either to repair these procedural flaws or to draw other conclusions from the interlocutory judgment. Depending on the nature of the flaws identified by the court, the administration can try to save the original decision by hearing particular persons, by conducting additional research or by improving the statement of reasons, but it can also take a new decision which takes the considerations of the interlocutory judgment into account. Subsequently, the court will reopen the case and may review whether the administrative institution has repaired the identified flaw in a satisfactory manner, or whether the new decision meets the standard of legality, after which the judge may definitely settle the dispute. However, if the repaired or new decision still does not meet the required standards, the court may either reinitiate the administrative loop or annul the decision and refer the case back to the administration.

The administrative loop offers the courts the possibility to definitely settle administrative disputes without having to curtail the administrative institution's discretion by replacing the institution's point of view for that of its own. For in such instances the administrative tribunal bases its judgment on the administration's modified point of view. The main advantage of this instrument is that the decision can be changed whilst the case remains before the court, and that the court can instantly determine whether the modifications can prevent the contested decision from being annulled. It seems that such a procedure will save the parties involved a considerable amount of time. However, whether this is truly so remains to be seen.

## 5 The European standard of review and national courts

As has been observed in paragraph 2, the '*Tetra Laval* standard' is slowly but surely developing into a general standard of judicial review of administrative decisions on a Community level. A subsequent question is whether this standard should be applied by the Member States' courts as well when they review national decisions that implement EC law.[73] Although such a question concerns first of all the *binding* influence exerted by Community law in this regard, it must be emphasised that the national tribunals may also let themselves be *voluntarily* inspired by the European '*Tetra Laval* standard' when ascertaining the legality of administrative decisions. Because of the fact that the application of this standard increases the transparency of the judicial review of the fact-finding process, its integration into the administrative procedure on a national level would seem a welcome step. Moreover, the voluntary application of the '*Tetra Laval* standard' by the national courts would contribute to the development of an *Ius Commune* in Europe.

Judging from the Community Courts' case law, it seems that as long as the secondary Community legislation concerned does not contain any specific provi-

73 See with regard to this question as to the situation in the Netherlands, Schuurmans (2008) pp. 5-34.

sions in that respect, the binding European influence on the national courts' review of decisions is rather limited. This follows inter alia from the *Upjohn II* case, and possibly even more so from the ECJ's recent *Arcor* ruling.[74] The *Upjohn II* case dealt with the judicial review of national decisions revoking marketing authorisations for proprietary medicinal products, and was, more in particular, concerned with the question whether national courts are empowered according to Community law to substitute their own assessment of the facts and, especially, the scientific evidence relied upon in support of the decision, for the assessment made by the national administrative authorities. The *Arcor* case was concerned with the scope of judicial review with regard to decisions of national regulatory authorities (NRAs) as to the authorisation of rates of notified operators for unbundled access to their local loop.

In both cases, the ECJ gave primacy to the procedural autonomy of the Member States.

According to the Court, in the absence of relevant Community rules it is solely for the Member States to determine the detailed rules for judicial review in accordance with the principles of equivalence and effectiveness.[75] With regard to the principle of effectiveness, the ECJ refers in *Upjohn II* to the manner in which the Court itself will review decisions that require the Community institutions to perform complex assessments in the course of which they enjoy a wide margin of appreciation. According to the ECJ, this margin of appreciation is:[76]

> 'subject to a limited judicial review in the course of which the Community judicature may not substitute its assessment of the facts for the assessment made by the authority concerned. Thus, in such cases, the Community judicature must restrict itself to examining the accuracy of the findings of facts and law made by the authority concerned and to verifying, in particular, that the action taken by that authority is not vitiated by a manifest error or a misuse of power and that it did not clearly exceed the bounds of its discretion'.

The Court continues by asserting that now that its own judicial review of decisions with regard to the authorisation of medicines is limited, a more extensive review cannot be demanded from the national administrative tribunals. It thus follows from this ruling that the national courts do not need to exert a more intrusive control over national administrative decisions than the Community Courts in similar cases.

In the *Arcor* case the Court does not make any reference to the manner in which it will review administrative decisions itself and leaves the scope of the national tribunals' judicial review entirely up to national law. The ECJ explicitly considers that:

---

74 Case C-120/97 *Upjohn II* [1999] ECR I-223, respectively Case C-55/06 *Arcor* [2008] ECR I-2931.

75 Case C-120/97 *Upjohn II* [1999] ECR I-223, at 32 respectively Case C-55/06 *Arcor* [2008] ECR I-2931, at 166.

76 Case C-120/97 *Upjohn II* [1999] ECR I-223 at 34.

> 'Community law does not lay down any rule requiring the Member States to put in place a specific means of review with respect of decisions of the NRAs (...).[77]

Although the ECJ makes it clear that the national courts must ensure that the European telecommunication rules, applicable to the authorisation of rates of notified operators for unbundled access to their local loop, are in fact complied with, those national courts are essentially subjected to national law as to the manner in which they will review the particular decisions concerned.

Hence, it appears to emanate from both cases that, in the absence of Community rules relating to this issue, the scope and intensity of judicial review are in principle a matter of national law. Therefore, under such circumstances, the Member States' courts are not obliged to apply the *'Tetra Laval* standard' to national administrative decisions.

Conversely, it also follows from the foregoing that the national courts are obliged to utilise the *'Tetra Laval* standard' when this is prescribed by secondary Community law. Neither the European medicine rules applicable in *Upjohn II* nor the telecommunication rules relevant to the *Arcor* case stipulated the scope of judicial review that should be applied by the national courts. In the area of telecommunications, however, the Framework Directive has come into force,[78] Article 4 of which prescribes a variety of requirements which have to be fulfilled by the national judicial system in the area of telecommunications. Among other things, Article 4 stipulates that the Member States are to ensure that 'the merits of the case are duly taken into account' in the course of a judicial review procedure. The provision has been incorporated into the Directive after it became apparent that there existed a significant divergence between the judicial proceedings with regard to this area of law in the different Member States, which hampered an effective national control of the telecommunication market. Against this background, it seems unlikely that the ECJ will continue to consider the judicial review in the context of this Framework Directive purely as a matter of national law. It seems probable, on the contrary, that the Community Courts will provide guidance as to the manner in which the national courts will have 'to take the merits of the case duly into account'. Although this could, of course, be done in a variety of ways, it cannot in the least be excluded that the Courts will inspire themselves in this respect on their own *'Tetra Laval* standard'. If this would be the case, the *Tetra Laval* standard would hence become binding upon national courts in the area of telecommunications.

A similar development might also occur in the area of competition law, in particular with regard to the application of the articles 81 en 82 EC. It should be remembered that after the modernisation process of 2003 the national competition authorities are subjected to the Regulation 1/2003 on the application of

---

77 Case C-55/06 *Arcor* [2008] ECR I-2931 at 169.

78 Directive 2002/21/EC, on a common regulatory framework for electronic communication networks and services, OJ 2002, L 188, p. 33.

Articles 81 and 82 EC.[79] Although this Regulation does not contain any provisions on the scope of review to be applied by the national courts, it does not – in our opinion – necessarily have to mean that the ECJ will grant primacy to the principle of national procedural autonomy in this area. Such an interpretation would not only hinder the uniform application of European Competition policy, but would also fit badly into the logic of Regulation 1/2003. In this regard it can be recalled that, since the Regulation does not provide for a strict separation of competences between the Commission on the one hand and the NCA's on the other, it will be more or less accidental whether an infringement of the competition rules will be persecuted by the Commission or by one of the NCA's. When one takes this into consideration, it only seems reasonable that the legal protection of an undertaking will be the same regardless of the fact whether the contested decision has been formulated by the Commission or by an NCA. For the situation wherein two undertakings would be confronted with two different scopes of judicial review – dependant on the enforcement institution – would appear to come into conflict with the principle of equality. Therefore, it seems likely that in competition cases the ECJ will prescribe the same intensity of review as applied by itself in similar cases,[80] which would lead to the result that the *'Tetra Laval* standard' would be binding upon national courts when adjudicating in the area of European competition law.

## 6 Concluding remarks

In paragraph 2 of this article, it was established that the Community Courts do not only utilise the *'Tetra Laval* standard' in Competition cases, but also in the areas of public health policy, environmental law and counterterrorism policy. In all of these policy areas the Community courts, when reviewing an administrative decision, make a clear distinction between the judicial review of the establishment of facts by the administrative authority on the one hand and the review of the subsequent administrative appraisal of the established facts on the other.

With regard first of all to the establishment of the facts, the Community Courts in principle exert full control of this stage of the administrative fact-finding process. The question the Courts will have to answer in this respect is whether the administrative authority concerned undertook 'a thorough and painstaking investigation'. Often, the Courts will not establish exactly which

79 Regulation (EG) no. 1/2003, OJ 2003, L1, p. 1.

80 Whether the Court will actually do so will appear from its answer to the preliminary questions formulated by the *College van Beroep voor het bedrijfsleven* in its interlocutory judgment of 31 December 2007, in the *T-Mobile* case (CBb, decision of 31 December 2007, AWB 06/657, 06/660, 06/661, 06/662 9500, *Mobiele Operators*, LJN: BC 1396). The case concerns the question as to whether the rules on the standard of proof following from the Court's case law are binding upon national tribunals in cases concerning the application of Article 81 EC.

facts should have been taken into account during this process, but will rather review whether the administration did not infringe the procedural safeguard of the rights of defence, more in particular the right to be heard (paragraph 3.2). If this is not the case, it cannot be ruled out that the administrative institution left some important facts unestablished and therefore outside the scope of its subsequent appraisal. Under these circumstances the Community Courts will have to annul the contested decision.

With regard to the appraisal of the established facts, the review by the Community Courts is limited in the sense that the Courts will only quash the decision if the administration has committed a 'manifest error' at this stage of its findings of fact. The extent of this auto-limitation will depend, *inter alia*, on whether the administrative institution in question disposed of a broad 'political' discretion or whether, on the other hand, it only disposed of a 'margin of appreciation' in the course of the complex technical assessment it has to perform. Whereas, in the first situation, the administrative institution has a far-reaching leeway which compels the Courts to greatly restrain their reviewing powers, the authority in question will dispose of fewer 'reasonable' modes of action in the second case and will thus more easily overstep the bounds of its leeway (paragraph 3.3.1). It is furthermore remarkable that also with regard to the Courts' control over the appraisal stage the judicial review has focused primarily on the procedural aspects of the contested decision. Indeed, it is quite rare for the Community Courts to explicitly state in its judgments that an administrative institution has manifestly erred with respect to the substance of a case. In most instances, the ECJ or the CFI will rather scrutinise whether the institution concerned has provided an adequate, coherent and logical statement of reasons (paragraph 3.2.2). The failure to do so may conduce the Courts to overturn a decision on procedural grounds without the need to adjudicate on the question whether the institution committed a substantive manifest error of assessment.

The established *'proceduralisation'* of the Community Courts' application of the *'Tetra Laval* standard' means that decisions are not so much annulled because of a substantive defect, but rather because the administrative institution concerned has failed to take sufficiently into consideration the rights of defence (at the establishment stage) and/or did not provide an adequate motivation (at the appraisal stage). This might raise concerns as to the procedural finality of the legal or administrative proceedings. With this in mind, a variety of measures introduced in some Member States to enhance the definite settling of disputes have been discussed in paragraph 4 of this contribution, which might form a source of inspiration for other Member States in this regard.

Finally, in paragraph 5 it has been examined to what extent the *'Tetra Laval* standard' will (have to) be applied by national administrative courts. Although in our opinion several reasons can be identified for a court to apply this standard voluntarily, Community law does not prescribe such an application in a binding way in respect of *all* decisions that implement Community law. The scope of judicial review is in principle a matter of national law, which enjoys a certain degree of procedural autonomy. Different are the cases, however, wherein a provision of secondary Community law prescribes the application of a common European standard of review. Considering the relevant rules to which the policy areas of telecommunications and competition are subjected, it cannot be precluded that the Community Courts will regard the application of the '*Tetra Laval* standard' in these areas as being binding upon national courts in the future.

## Bibliography


BAILEY (2004)
D. Bailey 'Scope of Judicial Review under Article 81 EC' [2004/6] *Common Market Law Review*, pp. 1327-1360

BAY, CALZADO (2005)
M. Bay and J. Calzado 'Tetra Laval II: the Coming of Age of the Judicial Review of Merger Decisions' [2005/4] *World Competition*, pp. 433-454

BEBR (1981)
G. Bebr, *Development of judicial control of the European Communities* (BRILL, The Hague 1981)

CHALMERS (2006)
D. Chalmers, European Union Law: text, cases and materials (Cambridge University Press, Cambridge 2006)

CHAPUS (1997)
R. Chapus, *Droit administratif général* (Montchrestien, Paris 1997)

CHAPUS (2002)
R. Chapus, *Droits de contentieux administratif* (Montchrestien, Paris 2002)

CLOUGH (2004)
M. Clough, 'The Role of Judicial Review in Merger Control' [2004] *Northwestern Journal of International Law and Business*, pp. 729-754

CRAIG (2006)
P. Craig, *EU Administrative Law* (Oxford University Press, Oxford 2006)

VAN DER ESCH (1968)
B. Van der Esch, 'Pouvoirs discrétionnaires de l'Exécutif européen et contrôle juridictionnel', in: *Europese Monografieën Nr. 12* (Kluwer, Deventer 1968)

LAVRIJSSEN AND DE VISSER (2006)
S. Lavrijssen and M. Visser, 'Independent administrative authorities and the standard of judicial review' [2006/2] *Utrecht Law Review*, pp. 111-135

LEGAL (2006)
H. Legal, 'Standards of Proof and Standards of Judicial Review in EU Competition Law' [2006] *Annual proceedings of the Fordham Corporate Law Institute 2005*, pp. 107-116

LENAERTS (2006)
K. Lenaerts, D. Arts, and I. Maselis, *Procedural Law of the European Union* (Sweet & Maxwell, London 2006)

NICHOLSON (2005)
M. Nicholson, *et al.*, 'The Scope of Review of Merger Decisions under Community Law' [2005/1] *European Competition Journal*, pp. 123-152

POLAK (2000)
J.E.M. Polak, *Effectieve bestuursrechtspraak*, Inaugural Lecture, University of Leiden (Kluwer, Deventer 2000)
RITLENG (1999)
D. Ritleng, 'Le juge communautaire de la légalité et le pouvoir discrétionnaire des institutions communautaires' [1999] *L'Actualité juridique – Droit administrative*, pp. 645-667
SCHUELER (2007)
B.J. Schueler, J.K. Drewes et al, *Definitieve geschillenbeslechting door de bestuursrechter* (Boom Juridische Uitgevers, The Hague 2007) (with a summary in English)
SCHUURMANS (2008)
Y. Schuurmans, 'Review of Facts in Administrative Law Procedures – A European
Community Law Perspective' [2008/1] *Review of European Administrative Law*, pp. 5-34
SCHWARZE (2004)
J. Schwarze, 'Judicial Review of European Administrative Procedure' [2004/1] *Law and Contemporary Problems*, pp. 85-106
VESTERDORF (2005)
B. Vesterdorf, 'Standard of Proof in Merger Cases – Reflections in the Light of Recent Case Law of the Community Courts' [2005/1] *European Competition Journal*, pp. 3-33

CHAPTER 6

# Administrative Discretion and Judicial Review in Germany

## New Tendencies in the Field of Economic Regulation

J. Terhechte

## 1 Introduction*

For a very long time the concept of administrative discretion and its (potential) judicial review by courts was one of the most prominent examples to demonstrate the different approaches in the European legal tradition, especially in the field of administrative law.[1] Because of the multitude of legal traditions and concepts in Europe, the intensity of scrutiny exercised by administrative courts can differ significantly while reviewing discretionary decisions launched by public bodies. The *French administrative law*, for example, always operated with a relatively wide margin of discretion granted to the executive branch which is not subject to judicial review by the French administrative courts (the various *Tribunaux Administratifs* and the *Conseil d'Etat*).[2] The idea of the French approach is to trust in the abilities of the administration, relying as well on the good results this approach has delivered in the past.[3]

In the *United Kingdom*, as another example, the judicial review of decisions launched by the executive branch must be seen in the light of the principle of sovereignty of parliament.[4] Due to the central role of the British parliament in the legal system of the United Kingdom, a considerable period of time had to pass before it was possible to establish an overall concept of administrative law with a concept of judicial review in regard to discretionary decisions by public bodies. In addition, the control of the executive branch in the United Kingdom is based not only on the idea of judicial review by courts or specialised tribunals but also emphasises the far-reaching role of political control and other forms of accountability.[5] Thus, the question of judicial review of administrative discretion and the relevant standards of proof are not as important as in other European countries.[6]

On the supranational level of the European Communities, the standards of judicial review,[7] especially in the field of competition rules, have been the centre of impassioned debates since the *Tetra Laval* judgment of the European Court of Justice in 2005.[8] Until this judgment, the Court had a tendency to grant (sometimes) a relatively wide margin of discretion to the Commission in

* I am grateful to Professor *Cosmo Graham*, University of Leicester School of Law for his very useful comments.

1 See for example Schwarze (2005) p. 246 et seq.

2 See De Laubadère (1974) p. 531 et seq.; Schwarze (2005) p. 248 et seq.; Hoffmann-Riem (2006) § 10 para 7; Lerche (1993) p. 1 et seq.

3 Hoffmann-Riem (2006), *Ibid.*

4 The relevance of this principle is outlined by Tomkins (Oxford 2003) p.102 et seq.

5 See Cane (Oxford 2004) p. 185 et seq. with a detailed analysis.

6 Cane (2004), ibid; Paul Craig (1986) p. 79 et seq.; see also Herdegen (1992) p. 42 et seq.

7 For general considerations concerning the standard of judicial review under EC law, see Craig (2006) p. 429 et seq.; Schwarze (2005) p. 280 et seq.; Von Danwitz (2008) p. 299 et seq.

8 Case C-12/03P [2005] ECR p. I-987; this judgment is analysed by Howarth (2005) p. 369; Jalabert-Doury (2005) p. 499; Pieters (2005) p.128; Ruiz Calzado (2005) p.433; Wirtz (2005) p.145.

view of complex economic assessments it was undertaking, especially under the Community's competition rules.[9] With *Tetra Laval* the landscape of European law changed considerably: for the first time, the Court provided a detailed programme of judicial review with reference to the Commission's margin of discretion in competition cases.[10] Today, one has to ask to what extent the Commission has a margin of discretion under Art. 81 or 82 EC Treaty or in the field of the community's merger control at all.[11] In the *Impala* judgment of 2006 the Court of First Instance affirmed this new approach in a spectacular manner: At the end of its finding the CFI outlined:

> 'It follows from all of the foregoing considerations that the first and second pleas in law are well founded in that the Decision is vitiated by, first, inadequate reasoning and, second, a manifest error of assessment in so far as the elements forming the basis of the Decision do not constitute all the relevant data that must be taken into consideration and are not sufficient to support the conclusions drawn from them'.[12]

Therefore, it seems that the European law is in a process of large-scale changes regarding its standards of judicial review. Coming from the old French tradition, in which extensive judicial review played a limited part, the Union is looking for a new, more detailed, concept of judicial review.

In contrast to these developments, the situation in Germany is totally different: For a long time the German legal system worked, for historical reasons, with an extremely detailed model of judicial review.[13] A look at the current situation in the field of economic regulation and competition law in Germany reveals that the system is apparently trying to change. Especially in the field of economic regulation (e.g. in the field of telecoms regulation), some courts established a wide discretion for the regulatory agency (the *Federal Network Agency*). After some confusing judgements of lower administrative courts, the Federal Administrative Court of Germany delivered a landmark decision in 2007 which, in all probability, will have an extensive influence on the whole issue. At the moment we are witnessing a new tendency evolving in German law towards a more marginal standard of judicial review combined with a new doctrine of

9 Case 56 and 58/64 *Consten/Grundig* [1966] ECR 321 (396). The *Consten* Case of the Court deals with questions of the exemption conditions under Art. 81 III EC Treaty. Here the Court stated that the Commission has a wide margin of discretion in view of the question whether the exemption conditions are met or not. It is important to mention that the Court never accepted a margin of discretion regarding to Art. 81 I or Art. 82 EC Treaty, see for example Case 42/84 *Remia* [1985] ECR 2567 para 34; Case 142 and 156/84, *BAT and Reynolds* [1987] ECR 4487 para 62; Terhechte (2004) p. 42 et seq.; Anselm Adam (1993).

10 See for an analysis of the Court's approach Lippert (2008) p. 492 et seq.; Schwarze (2005) p.280 et seq.

11 Regulation No. 139/2004, OJ 2004 No. L 24/1.

12 Case T-464/04 *Impala* [2006] ECR II- 2289, para 542. See for more information concerning this case Frenz (2007) p.138-144.

13 See Maurer (2008), § 7.

discretion which could be named 'regulatory discretion' (*'Regulierungsermessen'*).[14]

The following remarks seek to illuminate this new approach in Germany and the impact of the European level on German legal doctrine in different steps: A first step will examine the constitutional background of judicial review in Germany. After this, it is useful to have a look at the special organisation of the enforcement of economic regulation and the competition rules in Germany. In some fields of German economic law, the structures differ significantly from the general approach of administrative law. This could potentially have an impact on the standards of judicial review. In a next step this paper demonstrates that there are in principle different concepts of judicial review in the field of economic regulation in the various sectors, like telecoms, on the one side, and the general approach of the German competition law on the other side. The remarks will conclude with a look to future developments and the influence of European law.

## 2 The general background of judicial review in Germany

### 2.1 The central role of the judiciary in the German legal order

From a general point of view, it is important to see that there exists a direct connection between the standards of judicial review and the principle of separation of powers.[15] Especially the role of the judiciary becomes more important in the case where judges are entitled to review nearly every (or even every) decision by public authorities. Therefore, the very central role of the Federal Supreme Court (*Bundesverfassungsgericht*) and the other Federal and State Courts in Germany create a unique legal situation.[16]

The overall architecture of the German legal system and the central role of the judiciary are causally related to the very bad experiences of the past, where the executive branch was evidently too powerful (especially the head of the *German Reich*, the *Reichspräsident*).[17] To avoid such an 'executive centralism' in Germany, the Basic Law (*Grundgesetz* – GG[18]) delegated extensive powers to the courts. The main outcome of this delegation is a very intensive concept of judicial review with only very few exceptions.[19]

---

14 See for general information Pache (2001); Bullinger (1984) p. 1001; Schmidt-Aßmann, (1997) p. 281 et seq.

15 Starck (1995) p. 133

16 See Di Fabio (2004) § 27 para 25 et seq.

17 Gusy (1997) p. 102 and 403 et seq.; Huber (1981) p. 322 et seq.

18 An official English translation of the GG is available under <http://www.bundestag.de/htdocs_e/parliament/function/legal/germanbasiclaw.pdf>.

19 It is not a new concept in history to establish powerful courts to control the executive and the legislative branch. From time to time constitutional courts authorise themselves to do so. A good example is the

## 2.2 The constitutional background

As a guiding principle of judicial review in Germany the Basic Law provides that 'should any person's right be violated by public authority, he may have recourse to the court' (Article 19 [IV] GG; so called *'Garantie auf rechtliches Gehör'*). This passage contains a fundamental guarantee of judicial review to *any* person who is potentially violated in his rights by *any* act of a German public authority.[20] This usually applies without any exception not only on the constitutional level but also in the field of economic regulation and competition law.[21]

In fulfilling its task under Article 19 [IV] GG, the judicial branch is only bound by law and justice (Article 20 [III], Art. 97 GG).[22] In addition, Article 97 GG provides that judges shall be independent and subject only to the law. Finally, Article 1 [III] GG states that the basic rights (*'Grundrechte'*: Article 1 to 19 GG) shall bind the legislature, the executive, and the judiciary as direct applicable law. Taking these constitutional provisions together, one can say that the standard of judicial review in Germany is not very flexible. In general, the constitution permits space for executive acts free from judicial review only under exceptional circumstances.[23] Certainly, two examples can be found where the constitution itself excludes any form of judicial review (see Article 10 [2][24] and Article 44 [4][25] GG).

---

famous case of the U.S. Supreme Court *Marbury* v. *Madison*, 5 U.S. (1 Cranch) 137, 2 L.Ed 60 (103); see for that case *Nowak* (2004) p. 3 et seq. The phenomenon could be named as self-authorisation, see Höreth (2008) with an analysis of self-authorisation of the U.S. Supreme Court and the European Court of Justice.

20 See Huber (1999) Art. 19 Abs. 4 para 348 et seq.; Schmidt-Aßmann (1983) p. 1 et seq.

21 See Heyde (1995) § 33 para 46: *'Entsprechend der materiell-rechtlichen lückenlosen Individualrechtsgarantie des Art. 2 Abs. 1 GG gewährt Art. 19 Abs. 4 GG einen verfahrensrechtlich möglichst lückenlosen gerichtlichen Schutz gegen die Verletzung der Rechtssphäre des einzelnen durch Eingriffe der öffentlichen Gewalt.'*

22 An official English translation of the GG is available under <http://www.bundestag.de/htdocs_e/parliament/function/legal/germanbasiclaw.pdf>.

23 See *Schmidt-Aßmann*, in: Theodor Maunz/Günter Dürig/Roman Herzog (eds), *Grundgesetz* – Commentary, München (Loose-leaf), Art. 19 Abs. 4 GG para 71; *Jarass* (2006) Art. 19 para 43.

24 Art. 10 I GG provides that the privacy of correspondence, posts and telecommunications shall be inviolable. Art. 10 II provides that restrictions may be ordered only pursuant to a law. If the restriction serves to protect the free democratic basic order or the existence or security of the Federation or of a Land, the law may provide that the person affected shall not be informed of the restriction and that recourse to the courts shall be replaced by a review of the case by agencies and auxiliary agencies appointed by the legislature. Whether Art. 10 II is constitutional is under discussion; see for more information Jarass (2006), Art. 10 para 20 et seq.

25 Art. 44 GG provides that the German Parliament *(Bundestag)* shall have the right, and on the motion of one quarter of its Members the duty, to establish an investigative committee, which shall take the requisite evidence at public hearings. According to Art. 44 IV the decisions of investigative committees

The crucial question is, however, which burden of proof does Art. 19 [IV] GG imply? Does the Article 19 [IV] GG provide only the possibility for appeal in general or is a special standard of proof also a dimension of this provision? The Federal Constitutional Court found very early that Art. 19 [IV] GG does not only provide for access to the courts but also demands an intensive review standard. The provision forces the courts to check decisions by public authorities from the legal perspective as well as from their virtual background.[26] Having a conclusive view on the constitutional background in Germany, it can be said that there is no space for decisions without or with restrictive judicial review by courts. Under normal circumstances, courts are always entitled to review all dimensions of a decision by public authorities.

## 3 The distinction between discretion and the interpretation of open textured legal phrases under German administrative law

### 3.1 *Ermessen* and *Beurteilungsspielsraum* as discretionary elements

It has to be noted that the German administrative law draws a clear distinction between two dimensions of discretion. Most administrative law provisions grant 'action-possibilities' to the authority in charge. This phenomenon is called '*Ermessen*' under German law.[27] This means that a public authority has a *choice* which measure to take in a special situation.[28] The German courts developed a special concept of judicial review in the field of *Ermessen*. The core idea of this concept is the restriction of judicial review to specific facets of *Ermessen*.[29] § 114 of the German Administrative Courts Procedure Code (*Verwaltungsgerichtsordnung* – VwGO) defines the burden of proof in cases in which the administration decided within its *Ermessen*.[30] According to this provision, administrative courts have to prove, first, whether administrative bodies acted beyond the margin of discretion granted by a special provision or, secondly, whether the discretionary power was used in a manner separate from its function at all. Yet, this burden of proof initiated a very detailed and sophisticated concept of judicial review in that field.

---

shall not be subject to judicial review. The courts shall be free to evaluate and rule upon the facts that were the subject of the investigation. See also Di Fabio (1988); Hilf (1987) p. 537.

26 Entscheidungen des Bundesverfassungsgerichts 78, p. 214 (226); 101, p. 106 (123);. p.118, 352 (357).

27 See Maurer (2008) § 7 para 7 et seq.

28 Cane emphasises that having a choice is the essential basis for all varieties of discretion, Cane (2004) p. 185.

29 Maurer (2008) § 7 para 4 et seq .

30 For more information Schwarz (2006) § 114 VwGO para 1 et seq. This provision has to be seen in the light of § 40 of the German Administrative Procedure Act *(Verwaltungsverfahrensgesetz – VwVfG)*.

It is important to distinguish between *Ermessen* on the one side and '*Unbestimmter Rechtsbegriff*' on the other side.[31] '*Unbestimmter Rechtsbegriff*' describes the phenomenon that many legal phrases are unclear and have to be interpreted.[32] In the case that a provision contains '*unbestimmte Rechtsbegriffe*' the law grants no clear direction for the interpretation. As a result of this, German courts accepted a so-called '*Beurteilungsspielraum*' for the administration.[33] *Beurteilungsspielraum* names therefore a special margin of discretion while interpreting open-textured norms. Regarding to the fact that there is a margin, numerous scholars proclaimed a restrictive concept of judicial review.[34] The German courts, however, never accepted such a restrictive approach. Only under special circumstances, which have to be evaluated in a next step (see under 3.2), a margin of discretion is granted in which a court is not entitled to intervene. In general, *all facets* of interpretation of unclear provisions are subject to judicial review. [35]

The German approach with its distinction between different levels of discretion seems to be unique in Europe. Neither European law[36] nor the law of most of the member states draws this distinction[37]. The distinctions between *Ermessen, unbestimmter Rechtsbegriff* and *Beurteilungsspielraum* makes the German approach hard to handle. Thus, tendencies are emerging to change this approach, especially in the field of economic regulation.[38] The aim is to establish just one concept of discretion and judicial review without any differentiations as part of a new idea of the role of judicial review in administrative law. The new approach does not just bring the concept of judicial review by courts into the main focus of administrative legal doctrine, but rather the 'action-possibilities' of the administration as a whole (so-called '*Neue Verwaltungsrechtswissenschaft*').[39] If the ideas of this new approach succeed in influencing the legal doctrine in the future, and this seems indeed to be a possibility, the centre of interest of administrative scholarship would shift from the focus on judicial to the administrative procedure and the decision-making process of the executive branch.[40] However, it is important to mention that there have always been special circumstances under which German courts denied a judicial review of administrative decisions. The *Neue Verwaltungsrechtswissenschaft* aims to broaden this approach. Whether courts will accept this new tendency in general

31 This legal doctrine goes back to Bachof (1955) p. 97.

32 In fact, this approach has to be seen from a practical perspective because all legal provisions are 'unclear' to some extent, see Hart (1997), p. 124 et seq.

33 Schwarz (2006) § 114 VwGO para 89.

34 Schenke (2005) § 114 VwGO para 23 et seq.

35 See Maurer (2008), § 7 para 35 et seq.

36 See Schwarze (2005), p. 280 et seq.

37 *Ibid*, p. 246 et seq. with a detailed analysis of some European Country's administrative legal orders.

38 See Maurer (2008) § 7 para 41.

39 For more information about *Neue Verwaltungsrechtswissenschaft* see Voßkuhle (2006) § 7.

40 See Hoffmann-Riem (2004) p. 9 et seq.

is open at the moment, but especially newer judgements of the Federal Administrative Court seem to confirm this approach.

### 3.2 Traditional fields of executive discretion without judicial review

As the courts have to act in the field of '*Ermessen*' accordingly to § 114 VwGO, the concept in the field of '*Unbestimmte Rechtsbegriffe* and *Beurteilungsspielraum*' remains unclear. Of course, some examples can be found where the Federal Constitutional Court accepted an exception from full blown judicial review, e.g. in the case of decisions regarding *examinations and tests*[41] (today the courts operate a very restrictive approach to these cases[42]), or in the case of decisions by a *body of experts* that is formed on a balanced basis[43] (examples for this exception are decisions by the *Federal Department for Media Harmful to Young Persons*[44]). But this, as was mentioned before, does not reflect the common approach. Usually, German administrative courts are obliged to prove all dimensions of the administrative interpretation of unclear legal phrases.[45] This can be seen as the current state of art in the field of judicial control of administrative action.

In the context of these remarks, however, a new tendency can be identified in the field of economic regulation. Since the 1990s the deregulation of some special markets like electricity, telecoms and traffic has been one of the major challenges for administrative law in Europe, and subsequently in Germany as well.[46] In the context of deregulation some of the traditional doctrines of administrative law had to be reassembled and the structure of public administration has changed considerably.[47] The current discussion in Germany reflects this expansion of new ideas. The law of deregulation represents a new field of administrative law with new doctrines and problems.[48] The question is whether these new ideas and doctrines are capable of affecting even the traditional concept of discretion under German law.

---

41 See Entscheidungen des Bundesverfassungsgerichts 84, 34; Entscheidungen des Bundesverwaltungsgerichts 104, 203.

42 See Maurer (2008) § 7 para 43.

43 Entscheidungen des Bundesverwaltungsgerichts 12, 20; 62, 330 (337 et seq.); 91, 211.

44 See Entscheidungen des Bundesverfassungsgerichts 83, 198; 91, 211; Schenke (2005) § 114 para 26.

45 Maurer (2008) § 7 para 35 et seq.

46 See Stober (2007) p. 176 et seq.

47 See Ruffert (2004) p. 165 (184 et seq).

48 A comprehensive overview is delivered by Badura (2008) p. 226 et seq.; see also Rolf Stober (2007), p. 176 et. seq.

## 4 Some remarks on the enforcement process in Germany

Before the different concepts of judicial review concerning economic regulation in Germany can be analysed, it is worthwhile to have a look at the relevant actors in this field. It is an interesting and maybe important detail of the German legal order that different courts have jurisdiction in the field of economic regulation and competition law. This could potentially have a great impact on their judgments in case they have different assessments.

In the field of economic regulation, e.g. telecoms, media, railway regulation and postal services the relevant laws define the jurisdiction of the German administrative courts. Nevertheless, the German law includes some important exceptions to this approach. Especially decisions by the competition authorities and decisions by the Federal Network Agency in the field of energy market regulation under the *Energiewirtschaftsgesetz (EnWG)* are subject to review by *civil courts*, which are governed by other procedural principles than administrative courts.[49]

For example, the German civil procedure is guided by the old principle *'da mihi factum, dabo tibi jus'* meaning that courts are, in general, not entitled to decide cases from their own point of view, but from the legal and real arguments delivered by the parties.[50] In terms of judicial review standards, the principle leads to the consequence that only arguments delivered by the parties can be part of the court's review. The situation under German administrative procedural law is very different. Administrative courts review and decide on an *ex officio* basis. Therefore it is their duty to discover the real background and the arguments of the parties as well as the legal background from every possible perspective.

The question is, however, whether German law really accepts different standards of judicial review due to a splitting of courts and procedures resulting from a different historical background. To cut a long story short: in principle it does not, of course. But the approach is different: While in the case of energy market regulation and competition law a high standard of judicial review is explicitly demanded by the relevant provisions of the law, other fields of economic regulation do not contain such provisions. Because of this, the courts tend to react in a different manner: In the fields where we can find provisions dealing with standards of judicial review, the practical application is subject to judicial self-restraint by the courts while in all other fields some courts try to establish a wide margin of discretion in favour of the Federal Network Agency. Therefore, one can identify the same effects caused by different approaches.

---

49 See for general information Saenger (2007), Einleitung para 64.

50 *Ibid.*

## 5 The case of judicial review of sectoral regulator's decisions

### 5.1 Current standards

At first blush, some regulation laws in Germany include a very intensive standard of judicial review, such as the German law concerning the energy markets (*Energiewirtschaftsgesetz – EnWG).*[51] § 83 [V] EnWG provides that the courts are entitled to review *all* dimensions of a decision launched by the Federal Network Agency, especially the exercise of its discretion and the statutory limits to this discretion. This provision is unique in the field of economic regulation apart from the competition law. The fact that this field is subject to the jurisdiction of the civil courts may serve as an explanation. The German legislator wanted to ensure the same standards of judicial review in this area as they would be applicable under the jurisdiction of the administrative courts. Apart from the written law, the practical application in the field of energy market regulation demonstrates that one can find a variety of decisions including discretionary elements. This is a typical case of judicial self-restraint caused by the fact that courts accept the expertise of regulating agencies under normal circumstances.

The *German telecom law* (TKG),[52] displaying a counter-example, does not include such a provision. Thus, there is an ongoing debate concerning the standards of judicial review. In an important judgment, the higher administrative court ('*Oberverwaltungsgericht*') of Northrhine-Westfalia in Münster rejected all arguments in conjunction with a low standard of judicial review and found that all dimensions of the regulation of connection fees in this sector could be subject to judicial review.[53] Moreover, German courts have ruled in the past that the reasonableness of connection fees could be subject to private claims too.[54] In that case, the standard of judicial review is guided by § 315 (I) of the German Civil Code (*Bürgerliches Gesetzbuch* – BGB), which provides that where a performance is to be specified by one of the parties to the contract, then in the case of doubt it is to be assumed that the specification is to be made at the reasonably exercised discretion of the party making it. This could be applied in the case of increasing connection fees, for example. This is very important for the context of this paper because this is a form of *private law control of discretion* conferred on public bodies.

On the other hand, the courts in other cases refused to undertake a very detailed analysis of decisions by the Federal Network Agency. This reflects the current standard: for example, the administrative court in Cologne decided in

51 See *Bundesgesetzblatt* (Officical Gazette) I 2005, 1970.

52 See *Bundesgesetzblatt* (Officical Gazette) I 2004, 1190.

53 *Oberverwaltungsgericht Münster,* Case 13 A 1521/03, *Computer und Recht* (CR) 2006, 101.

54 *Bundesgerichtshof für Zivilsachen,* Case KZR 36/04 *(Netzentgelte I), Neue Juristische Wochenschrift (NJW)* 2006, 154, see for critical remarks to this judgment Reinhard Bork, Über die Billigkeitsprüfung nach § 315 BGB bei Preisabsprachen für die Stromnetznutzung, Juristenzeitung (JZ), 2006, p. 682 et seq.

2007 that the specialised knowledge of the Federal Network Agency may permit the court to grant it a wide discretion.[55] A few months later, the same court went even further while finding that the judicial review of a decision by the Federal Network Agency was restricted in general. Only the procedural framework, the proper handling of all circumstances of a case, and the constitutional background could be subject to judicial review.[56] Thus, it follows that the situation in Germany is somewhat confusing. Some courts tend to a very extensive standard of judicial review while other courts demonstrate a tendency to restrict their own ability to review decisions.

### 5.2 The Federal Administrative Court and regulatory discretion

In 2007 the Federal Administrative Court of Germany (*Bundesverwaltungsgericht*) affirmed in a landmark decision a more restrictive approach regarding its burden of proof concerning discretionary decisions launched by the Federal Network Agency.[57] In this case the plaintiff called for more regulatory activities in the telecom sector, meaning that the dominant market player, *Deutsche Telekom*, should be subject to several regulatory duties, e.g. to expand the capacity of the network, to allow more co-operation within the network and to grant more transparency. The Federal Network Agency as defendant claimed that its discretion under the German telecom laws, especially under § 21 TKG, could not be challenged by an application by third parties. The open texture of § 21 TKG and the whole structure of the provision would make it impossible for courts to review all aspects of a decision based on § 21 TKG.

The Federal Administrative Court affirmed this interpretation of § 21 TKG. It conceded that a decision concerning special regulatory duties is always complex by nature. The Federal Network Agency has to weigh the interests of the public and of private actors. In general, the court emphasised, the agency has no discretion whether a regulatory action is needed or not, because the applicable law defines the relevant circumstances, especially when the agency identified a market which should be regulated in the sense of § 10 and § 11 TKG.[58]

But the crucial question is whether the law also defines the concrete action of the agency after having determined a market that has to be regulated. § 13 of the TKG enumerates a multitude of possible (and, of course, different) actions of

---

55 *Verwaltungsgericht Köln*, Case 1 L 1997/06, *Multimedia und Recht* (MMR) 2007, 680.

56 *Verwaltungsgericht Köln*, Case 21 K 4193/06 (available under *juris* database).

57 *Bundesverwaltungsgericht* (Federal Administrative Court of Germany), Case 6 C 42.06 of (28. November 2007), *Deutsches Verwaltungsblatt (DVBl.)* 2008, 659; the judgment is available under http://www.bundesverwaltungsgericht.de/media/archive/6001.pdf, the judgment is reviewed by Thorsten Attendorn, Das Bundesverwaltungsgericht, die Bundesnetzagentur und die Sinnenprüfung – planerische Gestaltungsfreiräume bei der Zugangsanordnung nach § 21 TKG? , *Deutsches Verwaltungsblatt (DVBl.)* 2008, p. 1408 et seq.

58 *Bundesverwaltungsgericht* (above n 57), para 28.

the agency and gives no advice which concrete action has to be taken. Because of this, the court found that the agency has a wide margin of discretion over which concrete measures have to be taken.

In the next paragraph of its judgment the court delivered a very new approach towards the doctrine of discretion in German administrative law. It decided that because of the very special structure of the relevant provisions, it was impossible to distinguish between elements of discretion and the interpretation of unclear and open-textured phrases. Because of the vague ideas of the provision and the very complex dimensions of the concrete decision of the agency, it is not possible for courts to review all aspects of such decisions.[59] According to the judgment, courts can only review, first, whether all relevant interests of the parties involved were properly investigated and, secondly, whether all relevant facts of the case were explored, thirdly, whether all relevant matters were considered in the case, and, finally, that no arguments were taken into consideration, which had or have no connection to the case.[60]

At the moment the intention of the Federal Administrative Court is difficult to discern.[61] Does the judgment establish a new standard or just a sole finding in a very special case? The answer to this question cannot be given in view of this judgment only; the whole debate has to be taken into account.

### 5.3 'Regulatory Discretion' as an overall concept?

Because of these (different) standards and judgments, heated academic debates revolve around the concept of judicial review in the different sectors of economic regulation in Germany (e.g. in the field of energy, telecoms, postal services or railway regulation). Some scholars proclaim a restrictive concept of judicial review in the whole area. The idea is to establish the new doctrine of 'Regulatory Discretion' (*Regulierungsermessen*). Decisions or part of decisions based on complex economic assessments should not be subject to judicial review or the judicial review should be at least restricted. The Federal Administrative Court affirmed this approach in regard to § 21 TKG in its judg-

59 *Bundesverwaltunsggericht* (above n 57), para 29: ,*Diese Normstruktur schließt es aus, die durch zahlreiche unbestimmte Rechtsbegriffe gesteuerte Abwägung von einer sich etwa daran erst anschließenden Ermessensbetätigung zu trennen und erstere der vollen gerichtlichen Kontrolle zu unterwerfen. Vielmehr ist die Abwägung ein untrennbarer Bestandteil des Regulierungsermessens selbst, das der Bundesnetzagentur bei zweckentsprechender Auslegung des Gesetzes insoweit eingeräumt ist. Der Senat übersieht dabei nicht, dass die Konkretisierung unbestimmter Rechtsbegriffe grundsätzlich Sache der Gerichte ist, die die Rechtsanwendung der Verwaltungsbehörden uneingeschränkt zu überprüfen haben. Doch kann ein gesetzlich vorgegebenes Entscheidungsprogramm wegen hoher Komplexität oder besonderer Dynamik der geregelten Materie so vage und seine Konkretisierung im Nachvollzug der Verwaltungsentscheidung so schwierig sein, dass die gerichtliche Kontrolle an die Funktionsgrenzen der Rechtsprechung stößt* (...).

60 Federal Administrative Court of Germany (above n 57), para 31.

61 Thorsten Attendorn (above n 57), p. 1408 et seq.

ment, and in some following judgments.[62] At this point one can say that the idea of 'regulatory discretion' took on its triumphal course.

This is part of an overall concept, however, which has been discussed in Germany for a few years now. The main aim is to assemble all sectoral regulations in German economic law into just one law.[63] Keeping in mind the dynamics and unpredictability of the real background in regulated industries, the complex accumulation of aims of the different regulations in this field, the open texture of most of the provisions in the field of economic regulation, and the ambiguity of regulation effects, the proponents of this approach claim that only a (mere) marginal judicial review could secure the effective enforcement of such a legislation.[64] The concept of a mere marginal standard of judicial review is also an outcome of the academic debate about *'Neue Verwaltungsrechtswissenschaft'* and will influence the whole concept of administrative law in Germany for the next decade.[65]

## 6 The case of judicial review of decisions by the National Competition Authority

Is this approach restricted to special economic regulations or is it part of a whole concept in German law? To give an answer to this question, more parts of German law have to be evaluated. Because of the strong connection of deregulation issues and the general provisions of competition law, an analysis of the German Act against Restraints of Competition (*'Gesetz gegen Wettbewerbsbeschränkungen'* – GWB)[66] could be very useful.

### 6.1 Legal background

The GWB contains a special provision which deals with the burden of proof of the German courts while reviewing decisions of the national competition authority (the *Bundeskartellamt – BKartA*). § 70 [V] (1) GWB provides that the court has to qualify a decision [this means a decision by the BKA] as *inadmissible or unfounded if the cartel authority has improperly exercised its discretionary powers, in particular if it has exceeded the statutory limits of its discretionary powers or if it has exercised its discretion in a manner violating the purpose*

[62] See *Bundesverwaltungsgericht* Case 6 C. 38.07 (available under juris database); *Bundesverwaltungsgericht* Case 6 C 15.07 WuW/E DE-R 2340-2347.

[63] Masing (2006) p. 152 et seq.; Röhl (2002) p. 191 et seq.

[64] Johannes Masing, ibid.; Martin Burg (2006) p. 2439.

[65] See for more information Voßkuhle (1999) p. 445 et seq.; Hoffmann-Riem (2001)184; see also Wahl (2006) p. 87 et seq.

[66] An English version of the Act is available under <http://www.bundeskartellamt.de/wEnglisch/download/pdf/GWB/0712_GWB_mitInhaltsverzeichnis_E.pdf>.

*and intent of the GWB*.[67] It is interesting to see, however, that § 70 [V] (2) GWB contains one exemption from this standard of judicial review by the German courts. § 70 [V] (2) GWB provides that the appraisal by the cartel authority of the general economic situation and trends shall not be subject to review by the courts. This provision of the GWB leads to confusion. The function of the whole provision can be interpreted in different ways: Does § 70 [V] (2) GWB mean a restriction of the court's power? Or is it the other way round – does the provision demand for a full-fledged judicial review without any space for discretion of the competition authorities? Further more the role of the 'general economic situation exception' remains unclear.

After early judgements with another focus,[68] the courts interpret § 70 [V] GWB today as the duty to prove all legal and real dimensions of a case. This can only be understood by keeping the whole enforcement process in Germany in mind. As was outlined before, competition matters are subject to the jurisdiction of civil courts. Their standard of judicial review differs from the standard of administrative courts. § 70 (V) GWB attempts to transfer the standards of the administrative procedure into the proceedings of the civil courts. Thus, the broader sense of § 70 [V] GWB is to bring all activities of the BKA under judicial review. This can strengthen the *role of the law* through the *rule of law*. Not least of all, the background of this aim is to be seen in the vague language of competition rules. As *Stephen Calkins* once noted, antitrust is an Alice in Wonderland world where words do not always mean what they say.[69] A quick look at the provisions of the German GWB, but also at Article 81 and 82 EC-Treaty, underlines this sentence. For example: What is the meaning of the term 'competition'? What is a 'distortion' of competition? Or what exactly is an abuse? Competition authorities dispose of a wide range of interpretation possibilities for these words. § 70 [V] GWB attempts to bring two worlds together: the wide interpretation possibilities on the one side, and the rule of law on the other (maybe *Tetra Laval* is nothing but this is on the Community's level). As a result of this, the standard of judicial review in German competition law is very high. Some voices claim it is even higher than in the field of German administrative law in general (compare above § 114 VwGO).[70]

§ 70 [V] GWB includes a sort of general economic exception. According to the second part of the provision, it is not applicable in case of an appraisal by the cartel authority of the general economic situation and trends. This is a special implementation of the 'political question doctrine' in German law which also influences US antitrust laws and other competition regimes around the world. Consequently, German courts are not entitled to review assessments in that

67 Schneider (2008) §12 para 206.

68 Entscheidungen des Bundesgerichtshofs für Zivilsachen 49, 367 (369, 372), *Neue Juristische Wochenschrift (NJW)* 1968, 1037 (1039).

69 Calkins (2000) 495 (520).

70 Mees (2006) § 71 para. 30.

field. The scope of application of the 'political question doctrine' is extremely restricted, however.

Only in case of an appeal against an exemption decision by the Minister of Economics in the sense of § 42 GWB (so called ministerial authorisation – '*Ministererlaubnis*') under German merger control enforcement, can judicial review be restricted as a result of § 70 (V) GWB. § 42 GWB states that the Federal Minister of Economics and Labour shall, upon application, authorise a concentration prohibited by the BKA if in a specific case the restraint of competition is outweighed by advantages to the economy as a whole following from the concentration, or if the concentration is justified by an overriding public interest.[71]

### 6.2 Practice of the courts

The 'modern' interpretation of § 70 [V] GWB regards the standard of judicial review in the field of competition law as very high and, as an outcome of this, the margin of discretion of the authorities remains potentially low. In fact, however, the situation is different: The last case in which a court dismissed a decision by the German competition authority because of the economic assessment of the decision was in 1994. In the *Hochtief/Philipp Holzmann* case the Higher Court of Berlin (*Kammergericht*) rejected the approach of the BKA regarding its approach in a dominance case.[72] Since this judgment, no decision of the BKA has been overturned. Therefore, it appears that the standard of judicial review in Germany required by the constitution is nothing but a theoretical boundary lacking practical relevance.

## 7 Towards a mere marginal standard of judicial review and the separation of powers

It follows that Germany is shifting towards a more marginal standard in the field of economic regulation and in the field of competition law, but the approach to this shift seems to be diverse: while in the field of economic regulation (like in the telecoms sector) a restrictive standard is introduced by the courts as a consequence of the special arrangement of the provisions of the telecom law, the situation in the field of competition law is somewhat different. The GWB demands a very detailed analysis of decisions launched by the federal competition authority. In fact, we have come across only a few decisions where courts overturned the approach of the *BKartA*. This is not only because of the very high standards of *BKartA* decisions, but also owing to the fact that,

[71] Orth (2008) §12 para 489 et seq.

[72] See *Kammergericht* WuW/E DE-R 94, 98 – Hochtief/Philipp Holzmann, see also Schmidt (1977) p. 551 et seq; Schmid (1992) § 70 para 35 et seq.

for example, the courts are well aware of the difficulties in handling complex economic assessments.

Coming from a tradition of intensive judicial review, this process will need more time to have a broad effect. But it is important, however, that these developments are not only a question of the practice of the courts but also give rise to thinking about the concept of the separation of powers in the German legal system. The more space for administrative action without detailed judicial review is available, the more influence is delegated to the executive branch.

What can this mean for the European level? Maybe the new developments, especially the *Tetra Laval* case, give occasion to think about the general role of the judiciary and the executive branch in the EC and their relationship to each other. It is commonly known that this relationship cannot be described in terms of national legal orders. In fact, the EC has its own model of separation of powers, which is called the *principle of institutional balance*.[73] Therefore, the EC has different standards of judicial review than its Member States. But – and this is maybe the main benefit of *Tetra Laval* for the community's legal order – while expanding the role of the judiciary through an intensive standard of judicial review, the institutional architecture of the Community is automatically changed. In particular, the Commission's role is subject to more pressure. This is not only an outcome of the *Tetra Laval* case but also of some judgments of the Court of First Instance in the field of merger control law.[74]

From this perspective the question of administrative discretion deals not only with special facets of judicial review in economic regulation, but also with fundamental questions of the European constitutional order. Is *Tetra Laval* only the beginning of an overall concept of the Court of Justice to interpret the community provisions in the light of the rule of law? Will the Community adopt a more intensive standard of judicial review? The German example could mark the boundaries of such an approach. Because of the special characteristics of legislation in the field of economic regulation and competition it is, of course, not possible to review every interpretation of the vague and open textured rules as well as it is not possible to review all dimensions of the economic assessments in these special fields. Germany is looking for new concepts and so is the European Community!

73 See Case 9/56, *Meroni*, [1958] ECR 1; Case 138/79, *Roquette Frères*, [1980] ECR 3333; see also Lenaerts (1991) p. 11 et seq.; Terhechte (2004) p. 384 et seq.

74 See CFI Case T-342/99 *Airtours* v. *Commission* [2002] ECR II-258; Case T-301/01 *Schneider Electric* v. *Commission* [2006] ECR II-4071; Case T-5/02 *Tetra Laval* v. *Commission* [2006] ECR II-4381.

## Bibliography

ANSELM ADAM (1993)
Winfried Anselm Adam, *Die Kontrolldichte-Konzeption des EuGH und deutscher Gerichte* (Nomos, Baden-Baden 1993)

BACHOF (1955)
Otto Bachof, 'Beurteilungsspielraum, Ermessen und unbestimmter Rechtsbegriff' [1955] *Juristenzeitung* (JZ), p. 97

BADURA (2008)
Peter Badura, *Wirtschaftsverfassung und Wirtschaftsverwaltung*, 3. ed. (Mohr Siebeck, Tübingen 2008)

BULLINGER (1984)
Martin Bullinger, 'Das Ermessen der öffentlichen Verwaltung – Entwicklung, Funktionen, Gerichtskontrolle' [1984] *Juristenzeitung* (JZ), p. 1001

BURGI (2006)
Martin Burgi, 'Übergreifende Regelung des Rechts der Regulierungsverwaltung – Realisierung einer Kodifikationsidee?' [2006] Neue Juristische Wochenschrift (NJW), p 2439

CALKINS (2000)
Stephen Calkins, 'California Dental Association: Not a Quick Look but not the Full Monty', 67 [2000] *Antitrust Law Journal* 495 (520)

CANE (2004)
Peter Cane, *Administrative Law*, 4. ed. (Oxford University Press, Oxford 2004)

CRAIG (1986)
Paul Craig, 'Discretionary Power in Modern Administration', in: Martin Bullinger (ed.), *Verwaltungsermessen im modernen Staat* (Nomos, Baden-Baden 1986)

CRAIG (2006)
Paul Craig, *EU Administrative Law* (Oxford University Press, Oxford 2006)

VON DANWITZ (2008)
Thomas von Danwitz, *Europäisches Verwaltungsrecht* (Springer, Berlin/Heidelberg 2008)

DI FABIO (1988)
Udo Di Fabio, *Rechtsschutz im parlamentarischen Untersuchungsverfahren* (Duncker & Humblot, Berlin 1988).

DI FABIO (2004)
Udi Di Fabio, 'Gewaltenteilung', in: Josef Isensee/Paul Kirchhof (eds), *Handbuch des Staatsrechts*, Vol. II (Verfassungsstaat), 3rd ed. (Müller, Heidelberg 2004)

HEYDE (1995)
Wolfgang Heyde, 'Rechtsprechung', in: Ernst Benda/Werner Maihofer/Hans-Jochen Vogel (eds), *Handbuch des Verfassungsrechts,* 2th ed (De Gruyter, Berlin/New York 1995)

HILF (1987)
Meinhard Hilf, 'Untersuchungsausschüsse vor den Gerichten', *Neue Zeitschrift für Verwaltungsrecht* [1987] (NVwZ) p. 537

HUBER (1981)
Ernst Rudolf Huber, *Deutsche Verfassungsgeschichte seit 1789*, Kohlhammer, Stuttgart 1981, Vol. VI (Die Weimarer Reichsverfassung)

FRENZ (2007)
Walter Frenz, 'Die Kontrolle von Fusionsgenehmigungen als Spiegelbild von Untersagungen – Die Fortführung der Entscheidungen Kali & Salz, Tetra Laval, BaByliss und Airtours im Urteil Impala/Kommission' [2007] Wirtschaft und Wettbewerb (WuW), p.138-144

GUSY (1997)
Christoph Gusy, *Die Weimarer Reichsverfassung* (Mohr Siebeck, Tübingen 1997)

HART (1997)
Herbert L. A. Hart, *The Concept of Law*, 2nd ed. (Oxford University Press, Oxford 1997)

HERDEGEN (1992)
Matthias Herdegen, 'Landesbericht Großbritannien', in: Jochen Abr. Frowein (ed.), *Die Kontrolldichte bei der gerichtlichen Überprüfung von Handlungen der Verwaltung* (Springer, Berlin/Heidelberg 1992)

HOFFMAN-RIEM (2004)
*Wolfgang Hoffmann-Riem*, 'Methoden einer anwendungsorientierten Verwaltungsrechtswissenschaft', in: Eberhard Schmidt-Aßmann/Wolfgang Hoffmann-Riem (eds), *Methoden der Verwaltungsrechtswissenschaft* (Nomos, Baden-Baden 2004)

HOFFMAN-RIEM (2006)
Wolfgang Hoffmann-Riem, 'Eigenständigkeit der Verwaltung', in: Wolfgang Hoffmann-Riem & Eberbard Schmidt-Aßmann & Andreas Vosskuhle (eds), *Grundlagen des Verwaltungsrechts*, Vol. 1 (Beck, München 2006)

HOFFMAN-RIEM (2001)
Wolfgang Hoffmann-Riem, ,Schlüsselbegriffe' der Verwaltungsrechtsreform, Veraltungsarchiv 2001, 184

HORETH (2008)
Marcus Höreth, *Die Selbstautorisierung des Agenten* (Baden-Baden 2008).

HOWART (2005)
David Howarth, 'Tetra Laval/Sidel: Microeconomics or Microlaw?' [2005] *European Competition Law Review*, p. 369

HUBER (1999)
Peter Michael Huber, in: von Mangoldt/Klein/Starck (eds), Bonner Grundgesetz – Commentary, Vol. 1 (Art. 1-19), 4th ed. (Franz Vahlen, München 1999)

JALABERT-DOURY (2005)
Nathalie Jalabert-Doury, 'Tetra Laval/Sidel: la Cour approuve le niveau de preuve élevé exigé par le TPI' [2005] *Revue de droit des affaires internationales*, p. 499

JARASS (2006)
Hans Dieter Jarass, in: Hans Dieter Jarass/Bodo Bieroth, Grundgesetz – Commentary, 8th ed., (München 2006)

DE LAUBADERE (1974)
A. de Laubadère, 'Le contrôle juridictionnel du pouvoir discrétionnaire dans la jurisprudence récente du Conseil d'Etat français', in: *Mélanges offerts à Marcel Waline*, Vol. 2 (Montchrestien, Paris 1974)

LENAERTS (1991)
Koen Lenaerts, 'Some Reflections on the Separation of Powers in the European Community' [1991] *CMLRev.* 28

LERCHE (1993)
Clemens Lerche, 'Landesbericht Frankreich', in: Jochen Abr. Frowein (ed.), *Die Kontrolldichte bei der gerichtlichen Überprüfung von Handlungen der Verwaltung* (Springer, Berlin 1993)

LIPPERT (2008)
André Lippert, 'Abwägungsentscheidungen im Europäischen Wettbewerbsrecht' [2008] *Deutsches Verwaltungsblatt* (DVBl.), p. 492 et seq.

MASING (2006)
Johannes Masing, 'Soll das Recht der Regulierungsverwaltung übergreifend geregelt werden?' *Gutachten D zum 66. Deutschen Juristentag* (Mohr Siebeck, München 2006)

MAURER (2008)
Hartmut Maurer, *Allgemeines Verwaltungsrecht*, 17 th ed. (Beck, München 2008)

MEES (2006)
Hans-Kurt Mees, in: Ulrich Loewenheim/Karl M. Meessen/Alexander Riesenkampff (eds), *Kartellrecht*, Vol. II (GWB) (Beck, München 2006)

NOWAK (2004)
John E. Nowak/Ronald D. Rotunda, *Constitutional Law*, 7 th ed. (Thomson West, St. Paul 2004)

ORTH (2008)
Mark-E. Orth, in: Jörg Philipp Terhechte (ed.), *Internationales Kartell- und Fusionskontrollverfahrensrecht/International Cartel and Merger Enforcement Law* (English Summaries) (Gieseking Verlag, Bielefeld 2008)

PACHE (2001)
Eckhard Pache, *Tatbestandliche Abwägung und Beurteilungsspielraum: zur Einheitlichkeit administrativer Entscheidungsspielräume und zu deren Konsequenzen im verwaltungsgerichtlichen Verfahren* (Mohr Siebeck, Tübingen 2001)

PIETERS (2005)
K.F.H. Pieters, 'Groen licht voor Tetra/Sidel' [2005] *Nederlands tijdschrift voor Europees recht*, p.128

ROHL (2002)
Hans Christian Röhl, *Die Regulierung der Zusammmenschaltung* (Frankfurt a. M. 2002)

RUFFERT (2004)
Matthias Ruffert, 'Die Methodik der Rechtswisssenschaft in anderen Ländern der Europäischen Union', in: Eberhard Schmidt-Aßmann/Wolfgang Hoffmann-Riem (eds), *Methoden der Verwaltungsrechtswissenschaft* (Nomos, Baden-Baden 2004)

RUIZ CALZADO (2005)
Javier Ruiz Calzado, 'Tetra Laval II: the Coming of Age of the Judicial Review of Merger Decisions' [2005] *World Competition*, p. 433

SAENGER (2007)
Ingo Saenger, in: Ingo Saenger (ed.), *Zivilprozessordnung (ZPO) – Commentary*, 2 ed, (Nomos, Baden-Baden 2007)

SCHENKE (2005)
Wolf-Rüdiger Schenke, *Verwaltungsgerichtsordnung – Commentary*, 14th ed. (Beck, München 2005)

SCHMIDT-AßMANN
Eberhard Schmidt-Aßmann, in: Theodor Maunz/Günter Dürig/ Roman Herzog (eds), *Grundgesetz – Commentary* ( München)

SCHMIDT-AßMANN (1983)
Eberhard Schmidt-Aßmann, 'Art. 19 IV als Teil des Rechtsstaatsprinzips' [1983] *Neue Zeitschrift für Verwaltungsrecht* (NVwZ), p. 1 et seq.

SCHMIDT-AßMANN (1997)
Eberhard Schmidt-Aßmann, 'Die Kontrolldichte der Verwaltungsgerichte: Verfassungsrechtliche Vorgaben und Perspektiven' [1997] *Deutsches Verwaltungsblatt* (DVBl.), p. 281 et seq.

SCHMIDT (1977)
Karsten Schmidt, *Kartellverfahrensrecht* (Heymann, Köln 1977)

SCHMIDT (1992)
Karsten. Schmidt, in: Ulrich Immenga/Ernst-Joachim Mestmäcker, (eds), GWB – Commentary, 2. ed. (1992)

SCHNEIDER (2008)
Hans-Helmut Schneider, in: Jörg Philipp Terhechte (ed.), *Internationales Kartell- und Fusionskontrollverfahrensrecht/International Cartel and Merger Enforcement Law* (English Summaries) (Bielefeld 2008)

SCHWARZE (2005)
Jürgen Schwarze, *Europäisches Verwaltungsrecht*, 2. ed. (Baden-Baden 2005)

SCHWARZ (2006)
Kyrill-Alexander Schwarz, in: Michael Fehling/Berthold Kastner/ Volker Warendorf (eds), *Verwaltungsrecht (VwVfG/VwGO) – Commentary* (Baden-Baden 2006)

STARCK (1995)
Christian Starck, *Der demokratische Verfassungsstaat. Gestalt, Grundlagen, Gefährdungen* (Tübingen 1995)

STOBER (2007)
Rolf Stober, *Besonderes Wirtschaftsverwaltungsrecht*, 14 th. ed., (Stuttgart 2007)

TERHECHTE (2004)
Jörg Philipp Terhechte, *Die ungeschriebenen Tatbestandsmerkmale des europäischen Wettbewerbsrechts*, (Nomos, Baden-Baden 2004)

TOMKINS (2003)
Adam Tomkins, *Public Law* (Oxford 2003)

VOßKUHLE (1999)
Andreas Voßkuhle, 'Die Reform des Verwaltungsrechts als Projekt der Wissenschaft' [1999] *Die Verwaltung* 32, p. 445 et seq.

VOßKUHLE (2006)
Andreas Voßkuhle, 'Neue Verwaltungsrechtswisenschaft', in: Wolfgang Hoffmann-Riem/Eberhard Schmidt-Aßmann/Andreas Voßkuhle (eds), *Grundlagen des Verwaltungsrechts*, Vol. 1 (München 2006)

WAHL (2006)
Rainer Wahl, *Herausforderungen und Antworten: Das öffentliche Recht der letzten fünf Jahrzehnte* (Berlin 2006)

WIRTZ ET AL (2005)
Markus M. Wirtz/Silke Möller, 'Fusionskontrolle: Das Tetra Laval-Urteil des EuGH' [2005] *Europäisches Wirtschafts- und Steuerrecht* (EWS), p.145

CHAPTER 7

# Judicial Review in French Competition Law and Economic Regulation

## A Post *Commission* v. *Tetra Laval* Assessment

N. Petit and L. Rabeux

## 1 Introduction[1]

The present article seeks to assess the degree of judicial scrutiny performed by French courts when reviewing decisions of National Competition Authorities ('NCAs') and National Regulatory Authorities ('NRAs') in the aftermath of the seminal ruling handed down by the European Court of Justice (the 'ECJ') in *Commission* v. *Tetra Laval*.[2]

In this judgment, the ECJ considered that the European Community ('EC') courts should refrain from engaging in a *de novo* assessment of the decisions adopted by the European Commission (the 'Commission'), when enforcing EC competition rules and, arguably, in other fields such as sector-specific regulation.[3] Yet, the Commission's complex economic assessments should not be left unchecked. The EC Courts must verify whether the Commission's analysis is convincing, accurate, reliable, consistent and exhaustive.

In light of the general duty of Member States to fully ensure the *effet utile* of EC legislation, the question arises whether the *Tetra Laval* standard of judicial review promoted by the ECJ has been endorsed by national courts when reviewing decisions of NCAs and NRAs.[4] With this, one must keep in mind that the equally ranking principle of *procedural autonomy* implies that national legal orders should remain free to decide the degree of judicial scrutiny applicable to decisions from national regulators.[5]

The present contribution examines whether the French courts have drawn inspiration from the ECJ's moderate standard of judicial review in *Commission* v. *Tetra Laval*, or if, on the contrary, a stricter standard prevails under French law. To that end, it is divided into four paragraphs, which follow a chronological approach. The first paragraph provides an overview of the characteristics of the French judicial review system in the pre-*Tetra Laval* world. As in the French judicial system many courts have jurisdiction over regulators' decisions, it seeks to clarify who judges the regulators, the judicial remedies available to regulated entities and the degree of judicial scrutiny traditionally exercised over regulators' decisions in the pre-*Tetra Laval* period. The second paragraph offers a brief analysis of *Commission* v. *Tetra Laval* where the Court introduced a new standard of judicial review different from that found in previous case law. It argues that the ECJ's judgment marks a striking piece of judicial deference towards regulators' decisions. The third paragraph determines whether the *Tetra Laval* judgment has impacted on the degree of judicial scrutiny applied in practice by

---

1 The authors thank Alexis Brunelle, Elise Provost and Anne-Lise Sibony for their helpful comments.

2 See Case C-12/03 P *Commission* v. *Tetra Laval BV* [2005] ECR I-987.

3 The concept of sector-specific regulation should be understood in this article as the various pieces of secondary legislation adopted by EC institutions to promote the opening up to competition of former monopolistic network industries such as telecommunication, energy *etc.*

4 See Article 10 of the EC Treaty.

5 See notably Case 33-76 *Rewe-Zentralfinanz eG et Rewe-Zentral AG* v. *Landwirtschaftskammer für das Saarland* [1976] ECR 1989.

French courts when reviewing regulators' decisions in the areas of competition law (including merger control and antitrust) and sector-specific regulation. We find that French courts have not followed the *Tetra Laval* ruling in the area of competition law, and, to the contrary, that they scrutinize intensively both the procedural aspects and the merits of the NCAs' decisions. By contrast, French courts display a much higher degree of deference with respect to NRAs' decisions in the field of sector-specific regulation. The fourth paragraph offers a brief conclusion.

## 2 An overview of the French judicial system in the pre-*Tetra Laval* world

### 2.1 The French courts' system: NCAs and NRAs under the scrutiny of two judges

The French legal order is organised around two separate bodies of law, namely 'civil' (private) law and 'administrative' (public) law, each of which is subject to the jurisdiction of a specific type of court. The civil courts, at the head of which sits the 'Supreme Court of Appeals' (*'Cour de cassation')*, are responsible for deciding on issues of private law. On the other hand, the administrative courts, at the head of which sits the 'Council of State' (*'Conseil d'Etat'*), have jurisdiction over issues falling within the scope of public law.

As a matter of principle, decisions of the French administrative authorities fall within the exclusive jurisdiction of the administrative courts.[6] Deeply rooted in the political history of France, the rationale for sheltering the French administrative authorities from the scrutiny of the civil courts deserves a short explanation.[7] In the years following the 1789 French revolution, civil courts – which also enjoyed legislative powers at the time – became widely distrusted in political circles. Shortly thereafter, revolutionary leaders, and later on Napoleon, came to the view that an absolute separation of powers between civil courts and the administration was necessary. Civil courts were accordingly barred from adopting legislative or regulatory acts and from scrutinizing decisions

6 The civil courts remain nevertheless competent to decide on a certain number of disputes involving administrative decisions, notably those in the area of legal/marital status and those involving fundamental rights such as the right to private property.

7 During the *'Ancien Régime'* (the political system in vigour before the French Revolution in 1789), the local Parliaments (which at the time acted both as superior courts and as legislative bodies) were suspected by the French revolutionaries of having abused their authority to counter administrative and economic reforms in order to protect the interest of their class. For this reason, French revolutionaries were wary that these courts would systematically oppose the important revolutionary reforms needed to build a new political and economic system. This 'revolutionary' distrust led to the creation of two separate orders in order to ensure that civil judges would be precluded from having any undue influence over the French administration. See Chapus (1997) at paras. 950 and following.

of legislative and administrative bodies.[8] A new administrative courts system was instituted, composed of magistrates recruited amongst experienced civil servants, and entrusted with jurisdiction over appeals against decisions issued by administrative authorities.[9]

Whilst, approximately two centuries later, decisions of NCAs and NRAs should logically have been subject to the scrutiny of administrative courts,[10] a convoluted judicial architecture was instead established in the field of competition law and economic regulation. Endorsing the view that those disciplines belonged at least as much to administrative law from an institutional standpoint than to private law from a conceptual standpoint, the French legislator gradually and significantly entrusted the civil courts through specific derogatory legislative provisions with jurisdiction over NCAs and NRAs decisions. For instance, when establishing the Competition Council in 1987, the French legislator deemed it apt that, in the interest of a 'good administration of justice', disputes arising from the Competition Council's decisions be brought within the exclusive jurisdiction of the civil courts system[11] and, in particular, within the sole jurisdiction of the Paris Court of Appeals.[12] A key explanatory factor for the French legislator's decision was the view that competition law would be better

8 See Bonnard (1934) at para. 79.

9 As a result of this absolute separation, the French administration was left solely accountable before its own judge, coming from its own ranks, and who acted as a 'judge-administrator'. At the time it was felt that this judge-administrator would be best placed to understand the problems, the needs and the realities underlying the actions of the administration. See Chapus (1997) at para. 982. This reasoning is well encapsulated in the the saying that 'To judge the administration is still administering' ('*Juger l'administration, c'est encore administrer*'). See Sandevoir (1964).

10 See Article R311-1 of the French Code of Administrative Justice. NCAs and NRAs fall within the broader category of independent Administrative Authorities ('IAAs'). IAAs are administrative bodies with both impartiality and technical expertise that are responsible for the regulation of various sectors such as competition law, telecommunications, audiovisual services, energy, privacy issues, *etc.*

11 It was felt that, in the case of the Competition Council, a strict application of the principle of separation between civil courts and administrative courts would lead to risks of divergence or even contradictory interpretations of competition law. Indeed, the French dualistic judicial system has already led a number of times to contradictory case law. See Chapus (1997) at para. 979.

12 The Paris Court of Appeals is an ordinary appellate court that belongs to the civil courts system (there are 35 Court of Appeals in France). Like any other appellate court, it is in principle only competent to hear disputes which fall within its territorial jurisdiction. Since the Paris Court of Appeals had the reputation of having the greatest number of specialized judges in the area of competition law and economic regulation, it has usually been chosen by the French legislator as the competent judge with regard to administrative decisions falling within these areas of law. With regard to competition law, the Paris Court of Appeal has no longer exclusive jurisdiction over antitrust matters at first instance. Since 2006 a limited number of courts of first instance are competent to hear disputes concerning Article L.420-1 to L.420-5 of the French commercial code and Articles 81 EC and 82 EC (see new Article L.420-7 of the French commercial code). The Paris Court of Appeal has been given exclusive jurisdiction to hear appeals against decisions rendered by the Competition Council and by these courts of first instance in

applied by the already experienced civil courts. Indeed, civil courts routinely heard disputes in the area of commercial, civil and criminal law which often involved issues of competition law by virtue of the direct effect of Article 81 and 82 EC.

A similar, albeit less radical, derogation was later introduced in the telecommunications and energy sectors, where *certain decisions* of the French Telecommunications and Post Regulator ('ARCEP') and the Commission for Energy Regulation ('CRE') were made subject to the jurisdiction of the civil courts. Under the impetus of EC secondary legislation, the French legislator endowed NRAs with dispute settlement duties, for example with respect to issues arising in the context of interconnection pricing negotiations, *etc.* Whilst, formally, a NRA's settlement decision is an administrative act which should fall within the jurisdiction of the administrative courts, it is in substance comparable to a judgment rendered by a civil court in the context of a typical commercial law, and, more specifically, competition law dispute.[13] Hence, the legislator entrusted the civil courts, and in particular the Paris Court of Appeal, with the power to review NRAs' dispute settlements decisions. The Council of State remains competent to review the legality of all the other decisions taken by NRAs.

In sum, under French law, two types of courts are competent to review decisions of the NCA and NRAs, namely the administrative courts and the civil courts. The administrative court is in theory the natural venue for actions against their decisions. For instance, NRAs' decisions declaring that a market player enjoys 'significant market power' ('SMP') or ordering remedies, are normally challengeable before the Council of State. Yet, as explained previously, the administrative courts' legal monopoly has been significantly curtailed over the years and, in practice, the Paris Court of Appeal is now the primary venue for challenging decisions of the Competition Council,[14] as well as dispute settlement decisions of NRAs.

In spite of a certain degree of complexity, this dual judicial system does not, as such, generate significant problems in respect of the effectiveness and the

antitrust matters. A specific chamber of the Court (1st Chamber Section H) is entrusted with the review of all competition and regulation cases.

13 See Bonnard (1934) at para. 79.

14 Whilst until recently decisions over merger transactions were taken by the French Minister of Economy and were therefore challengeable before the Council of State, in August 2008, a new legislation has transferred these decisions to the Competition Council as a result of which the Paris Court of Appeal has now jurisdiction over its decisions in the field of merger control. This law (The Law on the Modernisation of the Economy) substantially amends the procedural rules in French merger control. The Minister of Economy ceases to have jurisdiction over merger control and its powers are transferred to a new authority (the 'Competition Authority') which (subject to a number of limited exceptions) becomes the sole authority competent to take decisions in the area of merger control. The new Competition Authority also replaces the Competition Council and centralizes the power of investigation and the power to impose sanctions and fines which were previously exercised by the General Directorate for Competition Policy, Consumer Affairs and Fraud Control and the Competition Council respectively.

quality of judicial review.[15] Both the civil and the administrative courts appear equally qualified to review decisions adopted in the field of competition law and economic regulation. The Paris Court of Appeal, on the one hand, boasts professional judges with significant expertise in technical commercial disputes between private parties. The Council of State, on the other hand, is composed of high-profile civil servants (a good part of them was trained in the prestigious *Ecole Nationale d'Administration*), who are accustomed to deal with sensitive public policy issues, such as those encountered by NRAs in their daily market regulation activities.

Furthermore, the duality of judicial fora in the field of competition law and economic regulation offers additional well-known advantages such as, for instance, cross-fertilisation dynamics, experimentation and benchmarking.

### 2.2 General principles governing the intensity of judicial review pre-*Tetra Laval* – in-depth assessment vs. 'sliding-scale' approach

The purpose of the present section is to describe the principles that have traditionally governed the intensity of judicial review of the decisions of NCAs and NRAs in the pre-*Tetra Laval* world. In that respect, a salient feature of the French dualist courts system consists of the asymmetrical principles applicable to the intensity of judicial review in the field of competition law and economic regulation. Whilst it has been generally undisputed that the Paris Court of Appeal *had* to scrutinize 'in depth' all aspects of NCAs and NRAs decisions (1), the ability of the Council of State to perform similar assessments has been less obvious, and was instead subject to a 'sliding-scale' approach (2).

#### 2.2.1 The duty of the Paris Court of Appeal to scrutinise thoroughly decisions submitted to its review

In the context of its judicial review activities, the Court of Appeal of Paris has been traditionally placed under the duty to painstakingly scrutinize the Competition Council's decisions. This, in turn, is primarily explained by the so-called *effet dévolutif* ascribed to the constitutionally-protected right of appeal. The *effet dévolutif* means that the Court of Appeal has both (i) the obligation to examine fully the grounds of the Competition Council's decision in fact and in law; and, if it subsequently declares the appealed decision void, (ii) the duty to replace (or *reform*) it with its own decision in order to terminate the dispute.[16]

---

[15] We refer to the effectiveness of judicial review from an applicant's standpoint.

[16] Article 561 of the new French Code of Civil Procedure. See also, Supreme Court of Appeal, Commercial Chamber 31 January 2006, *Colas Midi Méditerranée/Bonna sabla and others* where the Supreme Court of Appeals confirmed that, in antirust matters, although there are specific procedural rules applicable to

The relatively uncontroversial nature of the Court of Appeals' extensive judicial prerogatives has often been attributed to the French Constitution itself, which explicitly entrusts civil law courts with the duty to protect fundamental freedoms (and, in particular, the right to be heard by an independent judge). In addition, the rulings of the Court of Appeal may be subject to a further appeal (*pourvoi en cassation*)[17] on points of law to the Supreme Court of Appeals, which obviates concerns of arbitrary judgments and inconsistent interpretation and application of the law.[18]

### 2.2.2 The Council of State's fluctuating standard of judicial review

By contrast, the Council of State has not been entirely free to apply a similarly high standard of judicial review when scrutinizing administrative decisions. Rather, the Council of State's standard of judicial review varied according to the circumstances of each case, pursuant to a well-established 'sliding scale' which is intrinsically linked to the degree of discretion statutorily enjoyed by the administrative authority under review.[19]

The first and most limited standard of review, the so-called 'marginal review' (*contrôle restreint*) has traditionally been applied where – by virtue of statutory provisions – the administrative authority enjoys discretionary power (*pouvoir discrétionnaire*), i.e. when it is free to choose between different measures to regulate a certain factual situation.[20] In this case, the Council of State simply assesses whether the decision is vitiated by a 'manifest error of appraisal', defined as 'a blatant error, which a reasonable man would not have made'.[21] For instance, when a civil servant acts unlawfully, the administration may either initiate a disciplinary procedure or consider that such action is not necessary, for example, because the civil servant has an outstanding record. In this case,

annulment proceedings or reversal proceedings brought against decisions of the Competition Council, the principle of the *effet dévolutif* of the appeal remained fully applicable.

17 This appeal is not suspensive. Provisional measures may, however, be requested and obtained.

18 The Supreme Court will nevertheless review whether the law has been correctly applied to the facts of the case, and, thus, what kind of facts must necessarily be mentioned in the judgment under appeal to do so. Thus, in case the Supreme Courts concludes that the judgment has not mentioned certain facts or that the facts are inadequate or inaccurate, the Court will annul the ruling as these defects have hindered its review of the law. See the 'mobile telephony' case, where the Supreme Court of Appeal criticized the Paris Court of Appeal for failing to review all the criteria constitutive of an anti-competitive information exchange (see Supreme Court of Appeal, Commercial Chamber, 29 June 2007, *Mobile Telephony*).

19 See Chapus (1997) at para. 1253.

20 See Rivero (2006) at p.559.

21 See conclusions of the *Commissaire du gouvernment* G. Braibant in case Council of State, 15 February 1961, *Lagrange* : *'une erreur évidente, invoquée par les parties et reconnue par le juge, et qui ne fait aucun doute pour un esprit éclairé'*.

the Council of State's review must not go beyond a mere marginal review of the decision. To take an example in the field of competition law, this standard should logically be applied in the area of merger control in cases where, for example, the Minister of Economy would examine[22] a merger leading to a tight oligopoly and where it could choose between (i) prohibiting the transaction; (ii) clearing the transaction unconditionally; or (iii) clearing it subject to conditions.[23]

The second standard of review, the so-called 'standard review' (*contrôle normal*) has been applied where the administrative authority has a 'duty to act in a certain way' (*compétence liée*), *i.e.* where the administrative authority must, by virtue of the law, take a specific decision with regard to a given factual setting. In this case, the Council of State has normally applied a thorough standard of judicial review. Administrative courts have to apply a *contrôle normal,* for instance in retirement cases where the administration has a duty to ensure that the civil servant has the right to retire, thereby giving him a right to pension. In the field of economic regulation, the same standard of review has been applied by administrative courts where they examined whether, for instance, the regulatory authority has complied with the fundamental principle of the right to be heard, including the right to have access to the key documents on which the administration has based its decision[24] or the right to submit observations.[25]

Both standards of review share common features and, when applying these standards, the Council of State has been under an obligation to review whether the NCA/NRA has:

i) Made an error of law – the legal basis for the decision, or the criteria applied, are erroneous. For example, in the field of economic regulation, this could happen where a NCA has found a non-dominant firm guilty of an infringement of Article 82 EC, or its national equivalent;

ii) Made an error on the facts – the factual basis for the decision is non-existent, or erroneous. For example, in the field of economic regulation, this would be the case where a NCA has found a low pricing strategy abusive on the basis of an alleged increase in the market share of the dominant firm, whilst in fact, its market share has decreased;

iii) Misused its powers – the underlying purpose of the decision is alien to the protection/promotion of competition. For example, in the field of economic regulation, this could happen where a NCA sanctions an efficient foreign firm in the sole purpose of protecting domestic companies from increased rivalry;

iv) Incorrectly characterised the facts in law – a NCA or NRA characterizes facts in law when it translates the factual setting which is subject to its review (for instance, a price cutting commercial practice) in a legal concept (to take the

---

22 See footnote 13.

23 See ex-Article L. 430-5 *Code de Commerce.*

24 See for instance Council of State, 22 May 1985, *Société Cabot Corporation* or Council of State, 31 May 2000, *Société Wienergerger Baustoffindustrie AG.*

25 Council of State, 9 April 1999, *Société Interbrew.*

same example, an *abusive* predatory strategy). The facts are incorrectly characterized in law when the factual setting at the origin of the decision does not fulfil the conditions for being translated into a legal concept. For example, in the field of economic regulation, this would be the case where a NCA finds that a tight oligopolistic market is akin to a collective dominant position, whilst the market does not exhibit sufficient price transparency to give rise to joint dominance.

Under well-established case law, it is only in respect of the fourth parameter namely the 'legal characterization of the facts', which is by far the most subjective[26], that the standard of judicial review of the Council of State can fluctuate, depending on whether the administration has the 'duty to act in a certain way' or, on the contrary, if it has a 'discretionary power'. If, on the one hand, the administrative authority has the duty to act in a certain way, the Council of State exercises a 'standard' review and examines the decision thoroughly. It tracks down any error in the application of the law to the facts and may even, pursuant to a 'third' degree of control, namely the 'proportionality assessment', examine (i) whether the measure is suitable to achieve its intended purpose and (ii) whether its expected benefits do not exceed its costs. If, on the other hand, the administrative authority enjoys a discretionary power, the Council of State – considering that the administration should nonetheless be subject to a certain, albeit limited, degree of judicial accountability – exercises a marginal review.

In this context, it becomes critical to determine the degree of discretionary power that competition authorities and sector-specific regulators enjoy at the time of the adoption of the decision. This issue becomes particularly intricate when the judge must review complex economic assessments performed by regulators. To take just one example, given previously, of a merger leading to a tight oligopoly, we saw that the Minister of Economy could choose between (i) a prohibition decision; (ii) an unconditional clearance decision; or (iii) a clearance decision subject to conditions. This naturally led to the conclusion that the Minister enjoyed a 'discretionary power' in merger control. However, on closer examination, the Minister was clearly bound by various well-defined case law criteria for the purposes of deciding whether the merger gave rise to a joint dominant position. Since the fulfilment of these conditions was a necessary requirement for a finding of joint dominance, the Minister could also be deemed, in reality, to be under a 'duty to act in a certain way'.

This latter view of duality generally prevailed in the case law of the Council of State in the pre-*Tetra Laval* era. The Council of State usually considered that most complex economic assessments in the field of competition law constituted factual, objective, issues, over which – disputably – the deciding authority enjoyed in fact little discretionary power.[27] Accordingly, NCAs decisions were

[26] See Rivero (2006) at p.557, para. 641.

[27] See Legal (2005) p.107.

subject to a *contrôle normal* in those fields. This applied, for instance, with regard to the delineation of the relevant product and geographic market.[28]

### 2.3 Consequences and outcome of the French courts' judicial review

In the field of competition law and economic regulation, the Court of Appeal of Paris and the Council of State's task is not to review – and resolve – disputes between parties. Rather, they scrutinize the legality of an administrative decision taken by a public authority. In this respect, actions against regulators' decisions bear close resemblance to annulment actions brought before the Community courts on the basis of Article 230 EC.[29] If, whilst reviewing a NCA/NRA decision, the courts find a ground for annulment, they should normally quash the decision.[30] As explained previously, to ensure expediency in judicial matters, the Court of Appeal of Paris additionally has the power to reform the decision, in part or in full. Much like a second-level regulator, it can issue a new decision (formally, a judgment) exempt from any illegality. For instance, if in a cartel case the Court has found exculpatory evidence sufficient to reduce the amount of the fines imposed on one of the cartel members, it can issue a judgment providing for a different, lower fine.[31]

The ability to reform decisions has been extended to the Council of State, but only in the exceptional circumstance where the regulators impose sanctions on operators.[32] For instance, where an operator with Significant Market Power has not complied with the remedies ordered by the regulator and, as a result, has been sanctioned, for example, by means of suspension of his authorisation to provide services for a period of X months,[33] it can challenge that decision before the Council of State, which may decide to reduce or increase the sanction.

---

28 See Council of State, *Analyse de la jurisprudence, 1991-1999, Droit économique 1999*, available at http://www.conseil-etat.fr/ce/jurispa/index_ju_aj9910.shtml.

29 See Geradin (2005) p. 393, *available at*: http://papers.ssrn.com/sol3/papers.cfm?abstract_id=877967. It is common knowledge that French administrative law has initially influenced the structure of the Community courts and the permissible grounds of annulment under Article 230 EC. Thus, Article 230 EC allows a party to attack a Community act on four grounds: lack of competence, infringement of an essential procedural requirement, infringement of the Treaty or of any rule of law relating to its application, misuse of powers. These terms are borrowed from French administrative law. However, these concepts have later been used and interpreted by the Community courts far differently from the French administrative courts.

30 The regulator may subsequently take a new decision, exempt from the illegality.

31 See Case T-111/05 *UCB S.A.* v. *Commission* [not yet reported].

32 The law instituting the regulator must provide for that possibility. Otherwise, it would be unconstitutional, as explained by the Constitutional Council in its Decision 88-8 DE of 17 January 1989.

33 With the possibility of fines up to 5% of the annual turnover in case of a second offence.

# 3 ECJ case law on judicial review and its relevance for the French courts

## 3.1 Standard of judicial review applied by EC courts

In its most recent judgments to date, the ECJ has – often implicitly – lambasted the Court of First Instance' ('CFI') intrusive scrutiny of the Commission's decisions and, in particular, of the Commission's economic assessments.[34] In what appears, at times, inscrutable court-speak, the ECJ defined in *Commission* v. *Tetra Laval* a more traditional,[35] arguably moderate,[36] standard of judicial review compared to the stringent appraisal performed by the CFI in the *Airtours, Schneider,* and *Tetra Laval* merger cases.[37] Whilst the ECJ recognized that the EC Courts can review 'the Commission's interpretation of information of an economic nature',[38] it endorsed a system of 'selected' review, whereby the EC Courts' scrutiny only targets a limited set of features of the Commission's decisions.

> 'T]he Community Courts [must], *inter alia*, establish whether the evidence relied on is factually accurate, reliable and consistent but also whether that evidence contains all the information which must be taken into account in order to assess

---

[34] In its appeal in *Tetra Laval*, the Commission criticised the CFI for having exceeded the judicial review standard laid down in former case law by examining the Commission's economic analysis too closely. See Case C-12/03 *Commission* v. *Tetra Laval BV* [2005] ECR I-987 at paras. 25 et seq. See, for a description of this stringent standard, Petit (2007) at Chapter III. See also Sibony (2008) at paras. 1221, 1237, 1246 and 1285. A number of scholars considered that the standard of judicial review performed by the CFI was overly intrusive. See, amongst others, Bailey (2003) p.845; Siragusa (2004).

[35] This standard seems more in line with its earlier case law (see for instance Case 42/84 *Remia BV and others* v. *Commission* [1985] E.C.R. 2545 or Case C-68/94 *Kali und Salz* [1998] E.C.R. I-1375).

[36] But the ECJ refused to uphold the minimalist standard of review proposed by the Commission and AG Tizzano. See Opinion of AG Tizzano at para. 89: 'The rules on the division of powers between the Commission and the Community judicature, which are fundamental to the Community institutional system, do not however allow the judicature to go further, and particularly – as I have just said – to enter into the merits of the Commission's complex economic assessments or to substitute its own point of view for that of the institution'.

[37] Case T-342/99 *Airtours plc* v. *Commission* [2002] ECR II-2585; Case T-310/01 *Schneider Electric* v. *Commission* [2002] ECR-II 4071; Case T-5/02 *Tetra Laval* v. *Commission* [2002] ECR II-4381.

[38] See Case C-12/03 *Commission* v. *Tetra Laval BV* [2005] ECR I-987 at para. 39: 'Whilst the Court recognises that the Commission has a margin of discretion with regard to economic matters, that does not mean that the Community Courts must refrain from reviewing the Commission's interpretation of information of an economic nature'. The Court also insisted on the importance of such review in the context of merger control: 'Such a review is all the more necessary in the case of a prospective analysis required when examining a planned merger with conglomerate effect'.

a complex situation and whether it is capable of substantiating the conclusions drawn from it [...]'.[39]

To focus only on a few salient points, three conclusions can be drawn from this judgment. First, the EC Courts' judicial review should be confined to whether the substantive economic analysis, the facts and evidence convincingly characterize, as a matter of law, the infringement sanctioned by the regulator. Second, the EC Courts should seek to ascertain whether the economic evidence which supports a legal characterization of infringement is accurate, reliable, consistent and exhaustive. Third, annulment proceedings do not constitute a second chance for disappointed parties to change the Commission's substantive findings. In fields involving substantial economic analysis, the EC Courts must not perform a *de novo* investigation, and therefore cannot substitute the Commission's analysis – and in particular the theories of competitive harm – with their own assessment. For instance, in the case of a merger that has been prohibited on the basis of a unilateral effects theory of harm, the CFI cannot substitute a finding of coordinated effects.

Most of these principles were subsequently endorsed by the CFI in its notorious *Microsoft* judgment of 2007. Drawing the lessons from *Tetra Laval*, the Court held that:

'although as a general rule the Community Courts undertake a comprehensive review of the question as to whether or not the conditions for the application of the competition rules are met, *their review of complex economic appraisals made by the Commission is necessarily limited* to checking whether the relevant rules on procedure and on stating reasons have been complied with, whether the facts have been accurately stated and whether there has been any manifest error of assessment or a misuse of powers;

Likewise, in so far as the Commission's decision is the result of complex technical appraisals, those appraisals are in principle subject to only limited review by the Court, which means that the Community Courts cannot substitute their own assessment of matters of fact for the Commission's.

However, while the Community Courts recognise that the Commission has a margin of appreciation in economic or technical matters, that does not mean that they must decline to review the Commission's interpretation of economic or technical data. The Community Courts must not only establish whether the evidence put forward is *factually accurate, reliable and consistent* but must also determine whether that evidence contains *all the relevant data* that must be taken into consideration in appraising a complex situation and whether it is capable of substantiating the conclusions drawn from it (*emphasis added*)'.[40]

---

39 See Case C-12/03 *Commission* v. *Tetra Laval BV* [2005] ECR I-987 at para. 39.

40 See Case T-201/04 *Microsoft Corp.* v. *Commission* [2007] ECR II-3601 at paras. 87-89. See, similarly, Case T-340/03 *France Télécom SA* v. *Commission* [2007] ECR II-107 at para. 129: 'As a preliminary point, it should be recalled that, as the choice of method of calculation as to the rate of recovery of costs entails

Finally, in *Bertelsmann AG and Sony Corporation America* v. *Impala*,[41] where the Court had to rule on the CFI's judgment invalidating the Commission's *Sony/ BMG* merger clearance decision, the Community judicature found it necessary to – yet again – rehearse the above principles. In the judgment, which is already widely interpreted as a striking piece of judicial deference,[42] the ECJ sought to preserve the Commission's discretion when carrying out complex economic assessments.[43] However, this self-imposed limited power of appraisal entails the risk that the Commission's broad powers in the field of competition law[44] are not sufficiently counterchecked. The risk of abuse is even recognized by the Chief economist of the Directorate General for Competition himself.[45]

### 3.2 Relevance of the EC standard of judicial review in the French courts system

The standard of judicial review promoted in *Commission* v. *Tetra Laval* does not compare one on one with any of the standards of judicial review prevailing until then under French law as described under section I.[46] A former French judge at the CFI has nonetheless attempted to reconcile both standards,

a complex economic assessment on the part of the Commission, the Commission must be afforded a broad discretion [...]. The Court's review must therefore be limited to verifying whether the relevant rules on procedure and on the statement of reasons have been complied with, whether the facts have been accurately stated and whether there has been any manifest error of appraisal or a misuse of powers'. Finally, in the *Alrosa* case, the CFI further suggested that, whilst under Article 81 and 82 EC judicial review of complex economic assessments should necessarily be limited, in the field of merger control, the intensiveness of judicial review could even be lower. See T-170/06 *Alrosa* v. *Commission* [2007] ECR II-2601 at para. 108: 'the level of review carried out by the Court of the analyses carried out by the Commission on the basis of the competition rules of the Treaty must take into account the margin of discretion which underlies each decision under consideration and is justified by the complexity of the economic rules to be applied. Having regard to the effect of decisions taken under Articles 81 EC and 82 EC on the fundamental economic freedoms guaranteed by the Treaty, cases involving a limited review must be restricted to those in which the contested decision is based on a complex economic assessment, save in fields, such as concentrations, where the existence of a discretionary power is essential to the exercise of the powers of the regulatory institution [and where it could be lower, implies the Court in quoting *Tetra Laval*]'.

41 See Case C-413/06 P *Bertelsmann AG and Sony Corporation America* v. *Impala* [not yet published].

42 See Brandenburger (2008); Hirsbrunner (2008).

43 See Hisbrunner (2008) at p.19.

44 See Geradin (2005).

45 See Neven (2008).

46 In the *Remia*, *Matra Hachette* and *Kali und Salz* cases, the ECJ had promoted a standard of judicial review that bore close resemblance with the standard applied by the Council of State when reviewing decisions taken in the context of "discretionary powers". The Court confined its review to: "verifying whether the relevant procedural rules have been complied with, whether the statement of the reasons for the decision is adequate, whether the facts have been accurately stated and whether there has been

in a somewhat stylized reasoning. If we follow H. Legal's interpretation of *Tetra Laval*, complex economic assessments are subject to a control that, without amounting to a *contrôle normal* ('standard review'), nonetheless goes beyond the *contrôle restreint* ('marginal review') and by the same token of the 'manifest error of appraisal'.[47] Put simply, the standard hinges on reviewing 'the consistency, relevance of the reasoning and sufficiency of the documentation on the sides of facts'.[48]

In spite of this, however, it remains unclear whether the ECJ ruling in *Commission* v. *Tetra Laval* holds the potential to influence the standard of judicial review applied by the French courts and, in particular, the Council of State, whose reluctance to developments in EC case law is notorious.[49] Indeed, no single piece of EC legislation expressly requires national courts to abide by specific standards of judicial review when examining competition authorities and regulators' decisions. Moreover, it is doubtful that the general principles of EC law, such as the duty of loyal cooperation or the principle of *effet utile*, entail an obligation on national courts to follow the standards of judicial review applied by the Community courts. On the contrary, in its recent *Arcor* judgment, the ECJ – albeit implicitly – held that the principle of national procedural autonomy took precedence over other EC law rules and principles in so far as judicial review is concerned:

> 'Community law does not lay down any rule requiring the Member States to put in place a specific means of review with respect to decisions of the NRAs [...] It follows from all of the above considerations that the answer to Question 3(d) must be that it is a matter solely for the Member States, within the context of their *procedural autonomy*, to determine, in accordance with the principles of equivalence and effectiveness of judicial protection, the competent court, the nature of the dispute and, consequently, the detailed rules of judicial review with respect to decisions of the NRAs (*emphasis added*)'.[50]

In addition, certain endogenous features of the French courts system appear manifestly incongruous with the principles enshrined in *Commission* v. *Tetra Laval*. Of particular importance is the fact that the intrusive standard of judicial review applied by the Paris Court of Appeal is consubstantial to the constitutionally protected right of appeal. Any lowering of the Paris Court of Appeal's standard of judicial review could thus entail a violation of the French Constitution.

---

any manifest error of appraisal or a misuse of powers". See Case 42/84 *Remia BV and others* v. *Commission* [1985] ECR 2545 at para. 34.

47 See Legal (2005) at pp.114-115.

48 See Legal (2005) at pp.114-115.

49 Until 1989, the Council of State for instance refused to abide by the case law principle of primacy of EC law (see Council of State, 1 March 1968, *Syndicat Général des Fabricants de Semoules de France* [1970] CMLR 395). Concretely, the Council refused to set aside French legal provisions that infringed EC law.

50 See Case C-55/06 *Arcor AG & Co. KG* v. *Bundesrepublik Deutschland* [not yet reported] at paras. 169-170.

## 4 What is the standard of judicial review in France post-*Tetra Laval*?

The present section seeks to determine empirically whether, since the adoption of the *Commission* v. *Tetra Laval* judgment, the French Courts have applied in their jurisdictional practice the standard of judicial review established by the ECJ and, by the same token, whether they have departed from the principles outlined under Section I. To that end, we have reviewed a number of recent decisions of the Council of State and the Court of Appeal of Paris, rendered since February 2005.

Our overall finding is that of a clear divide between competition law and sector-specific regulation. In the field of national competition law, French courts have maintained a standard of judicial review that is clearly more stringent than the principles enshrined in *Commission* v. *Tetra Laval* (sub-paragraph A below). By contrast, decisions of NRAs in the field of sector-specific regulation are subject to a marginal, cursory, review by the French courts, which seems slightly lower than the standard promoted in the ECJ judgment (sub-paragraph B below).[51]

### 4.1 Intensive standard of judicial review in national competition cases

The cases reviewed below provide undisputable evidence that in the aftermath of *Commission* v. *Tetra Laval*, NCA decisions rendered in the entire spectrum of national competition law remain subject to a *contrôle normal* ('standard review'), remote from the ECJ judgment. To start with the area of merger control, a field in which the Council of State holds jurisdiction, the Minister's decisions have been persistently subject to a high degree of judicial scrutiny.[52] In the *De Longhi* case, the Council of State rejected an annulment action brought by De Longhi,[53] a manufacturer of small household electrical equipment, against a decision of the minister re-authorising a concentration between two compet-

---

[51] It ought to be noted that it is uneasy to interpret the extent of judicial review performed by the Courts on the basis of a reading of a judgment. French courts usually deliver very short rulings, and their reasoning is subject to the customary rule, *'Imperatoria brevitas'*. See, on this, Pacteau (2001) at p. 358.

[52] In the past, the Council of State has examined: the legal qualification of the factual situation (for instance whether the transaction is a "concentration" (Council of State, Sect., 31 May 2000, *Société Cora and Société Casino-Guichard-Perrachon*, Lebon p. 194); the minister's concrete appraisal of the economic setting (relevant market, anticompetitive effects, efficiencies generated by the operation (Council of State, Sect., 9 April 1999, *Société The Coca-Cola Company*, Lebon p. 119; Council of State, Sect., 6 October 2000, *Société Pernod-Ricard, Lebon*, p. 397); the proportionality of the remedies imposed (Council of State, Sect., 9 April 1999, *Société The Coca-Cola Company*, Lebon p. 119); the minister's application of the criteria of the *failing firm* defense (Council of State, Sect., 6 February 2004, *Société Royal Philips Electronic et autres*, Lebon p. 28).

[53] See Council of State, Sect. 13 February 2006, *De Longhi*.

ing French manufacturers, Seb and Moulinex.[54] In doing so, the Council of State carefully reviewed the Minister's competitive assessments and agreed that the merger would not significantly lessen competition in the market. A perhaps more telling illustration is the *Fiducial* case, where the Council of State had to rule on annulment proceedings against the Minister's clearance of the merger between CEGID and CCMX.[55] Fiducial, a competitor of the merged entity, claimed in its application that the decision was vitiated by a number of economic contradictions. Chief in these allegations was the fact that the Minister had cleared the concentration although it had acknowledged that the merged entity would hold a market position three times larger than its closest competitor and that no entry had taken place on the market. The Council of State subjected the Minister's decision to a *contrôle normal* and ultimately decided to quash it. It is noteworthy, however, that the apparent reasoning of the Council of State's ruling bears an intriguing optical resemblance to the *Commission* v. *Tetra Laval* judgment. In particular, the Council of State observed that the Minister's analysis lacked 'consistency' and, as a result, it was 'unconvinced' that the transaction would not stifle competition.[56]

In the area of antitrust law, i.e. the national equivalents to Article 81 and 82 EC, the Paris Court of Appeals has sustained its traditional standard of judicial review, engaging into a meticulous examination of the Competition Council's decisions. In the *Sandoz* case – which involved the Competition Council's decision finding Sandoz guilty of abuse of dominance for bundled rebates in the pharmaceutical sector – [57] the Court scrutinised every single step of the Competition Council's analysis.[58] The Paris Court of Appeal in particular departed from the Competition Council's geographic market definition. Upon examination of the relevant facts, the Court substituted its own economic assessment of the relevant market as national in scope, and found that the Competition Coun-

54 The Council of State had indeed annulled the first clearance decision on the basis that the minister's decision had not fulfilled all the criteria of the 'failing firm' defence (Council of State, Sect., 6 February 2004, *Société Royal Philips Electronic and others*, Lebon p. 28). However, the decision of the Council did not lead to the de-merger of Seb/Moulinex. This case is also interesting in that the Council of State was given the opportunity to review the concrete effects of a concentration on competition on the basis of historical data and not on the basis of prospective data, as is usually the case in merger control.

55 See Council of State, Sect., 20 July 2005, *Société Fiducial Informatique and others.*

56 Faced with a difficulty of appraisal, the Council of State required the Competition Council to issue an advisory opinion on the concentration. Later on, in another decision, the Council of State rejected the complaint after an in-depth analysis of the economic and competitive state of the market (Council of State, Sect., 13 January 2006, *Société Fiducial Informatique and others*).

57 See Competition Council, 24 July 2003, decision no 03-D-35, *Holopanoragramme.*

58 From relevant market to dominance and abuse. In other words, on the basis of the facts of the case, whether the latter has correctly defined the relevant market or the anticompetitive effects of a practice, whether it has adduced enough evidence of an infringement *etc.*

cil's determination of a relevant local market was incorrect.[59] The *Pharma-Lab* case[60] is another example – albeit less explicit – of the Paris Court of Appeal's intensive review of the Competition Council's legal and economic determinations.[61]

This being said, the most interesting – and perhaps most conclusive – evidence we have found that the ECJ ruling in *Commission* v. *Tetra Laval* has not altered the French courts' standard of judicial review originates from a judgment of the Supreme Court of Appeals (which, in the same way as the ECJ, occasionally formulates the applicable principles governing lower courts judicial duties). In *Bouygues Télécom*,[62] the Supreme Court of Appeals quashed a judgment of the Paris Court of Appeals upholding a Competition Council's decision that had sanctioned an information exchange agreement between firms active on an oligopolistic market.[63] Of importance is the fact that the Supreme Court of Appeals admonished the excessively lax standard of judicial review applied by the Court of Appeal.[64] It came to the view that the Court of Appeals duty of

---

59 See Paris Court of Appeal, 30 March 2004, *SAS Novartis Pharma* v. *Competition Council*. The Competition Council had concluded that the relevant geographic market was local in scope, being limited to the demand of each of the customers (hospitals) concerned by the rebates. The Court of Appeal, after reviewing the facts of the case concluded that the geographic markets were not local but, on the contrary, were national in scope.

60 See Paris Court of Appeal, 20 December 2005, *Pharma-Lab*.

61 The Paris Court of Appeal dismissed annulment proceedings brought against a decision of the Competition Council which had found no objections in respect of the following practices of pharmaceutical laboratories (i) to implement a quota system with regard to drugs supplied to wholesale distributors which had distribution activities within and outside France and (ii) to refuse to supply drugs at the price fixed by the State to those distributors which exclusively re-exported the drugs outside of France. The Court found that, on the basis of the evidence of the case, the Council was right to conclude that there was no agreement contrary to Article 81 EC (the quotas resulted from a unilateral act); and that the pharmaceutical laboratories' refusal to supply was not an abuse under Article 82 EC and was justified by their right to defend their 'commercial interests'. In doing so, the Court of Appeal carefully examined the Competition Council's economic and legal reasoning.

62 See Supreme Court of Appeal, Commercial Chamber, 29 June 2007, *Mobile Telephony*.

63 See, on this, Petit (2008) p.5.

64 The Supreme Court of Appeal apparently reached a similar conclusion in the *France Télécom and SFR* case. See Supreme Court of Appeal, Commercial Chamber, 10 May 2006, *X France and Minister of Economy* v. *France Télécom and SFR*. In *France Télecom and SFR*, the Supreme Court of Appeals reversed a decision of the Paris Court of Appeals which annulled a decision of the Competition Council on the basis that there was insufficient evidence of an abuse. The case concerned two vertically integrated operators in the fixed and mobile telephony markets who had implemented 'price squeeze' practices by offering retail 'landline to mobile' services to firms at prices that did not cover their costs of supply. This prevented non-vertically integrated rivals from offering competitive services to these customers by 'direct' interconnection (i.e. by directly routing the call from the landline network to the mobile network). The Court of Appeal annulled the Competition Council's decision on the basis that the Council had not adduced sufficient evidence that rival operators had no other choice but to opt for the

judicial review entailed a concrete determination as to whether the impugned conduct could likely allow anticompetitive coordination. It furthermore noted that the Court's duty – arguably much like a second-level regulator – should carefully review the characteristics of the market, the nature, the level of aggregation of the data exchanged as well as the periodicity of such exchange.

### 4.2 Marginal standard of review in the field of sector-specific regulation

In contrast to the situation in the field of competition law, both the Council of State and the Paris Court of Appeals have subjected NRA decisions to a much laxer standard of judicial review. Most, if not all, the judgments rendered in the field of sector-specific regulation display a striking degree of judicial deference to the regulators' economic assessments, and accordingly do not go beyond a marginal review which hinges on verifying whether the NRA made a 'manifest error of appraisal'. This finding holds true for the entire range of issues dealt with by NRAs: dispute settlement issues,[65] market definition, designation of SMP operators, remedies,[66] market authorisations and licences,[67] and public service obligations.[68]

A judgment handed down by the Council of State in December 2007 has nonetheless created the optical illusion that the applicable standard of judicial review had been elevated. In *Région Rhône Alpes*, the Council of State held that ARCEP's (the French electronic communications NRA) decision to dismiss the *Région Rhône Alpes's* application to use radio spectrum resources was not vitiated by any 'error of appraisal', implying that it scrutinised the adequacy of ARCEP's economic assessment.

Yet, we believe that the surreptitious semantic shift from 'manifest error of appraisal' to 'error of appraisal' does not conceal any elevation of the standard of judicial review in the field of sector-specific regulation. A careful reading of the judgment indeed reveals that the Council of State simply did not review ARCEP's economic assessment. Rather, the Council stressed that the data submitted by the *Région Rhône Alpes* in support of its application was so cryptic, that the NRA was simply left with no choice but to dismiss it. In other words,

---

direct interconnection solution. See Paris Court of Appeal, 12 April 2005, *France Télécom and SFR* v. *Competition Council*. The Supreme Court of Appeal rejected the Court of Appeal's analysis in that it had not examined whether the Competition Council had sufficiently demonstrated that the "price squeeze" practices had an anticompetitive object or effect on market.

65 See Paris Court of Appeal, 28 May 2002, *France Télécom* v. *Free Télécom* ; Paris Court of Appeal, 30 January 2007, *SFR* v. *Afone*.

66 See Council of State, 29 December 2006, *Societe UPC France*; Council of State, 25 February 2005, *France Télécom* v. *Telecom Regulation Authority*.

67 See Council of State, 29 December 1999, *Société Viatel Operations* v. *Telecom Regulation Authority*.

68 See Council of State, 10 July 2006, *Cégétel and other* v. *Telecom Regulation Authority*; Council of State, 25 April 2007, *Bouygues Télécom and others* v. *Telecom Regulation Authority*.

no 'error of appraisal', let alone no 'manifest error of appraisal', could have been made by ARCEP in the present case.

## 5 Conclusions

To conclude, we would like to formulate two remarks. First, the rationale for different standards of judicial review in French competition law and sector-specific regulation remains obscure. In particular, most of the tentative explanations for this appear at first glance unconvincing: *ex post* nature of competition law vs. *ex ante* nature of regulation,[69] *sector-specific* nature of regulation vs. *general* nature of competition law,[70] etc.

Second, at the core of the debate on the intensiveness of judicial review in economic regulation is a trade-off between, on the one hand, the risk of arbitrary/biased regulatory decisions in fields involving debatable economic assessments and, on the other hand, the risk of regulatory inefficiency, if courts can – and do – systematically second-guess NRAs and NCAs decisions thereby delaying the entry into force of regulatory measures and weakening the legal value attached to them in the first place.[71]

In the context of the French legal order, one may argue that both concerns are adequately addressed through a set of particular institutional features. To be clear, French regulatory authorities are composed of many individuals that are drawn from the highest civil and administrative courts.[72] As a result, regulators' decisions are already subject to a certain degree of internal judicial scrutiny, which arguably would eradicate the risk of regulatory abuses.[73] The upshot of this is that the standard of judicial review in France should primarily be tailored with a view to mitigating the risk of regulatory inefficiency. Accordingly, a

---

69 In sector-specific regulation, NRAs also intervene *ex post*, in the context of their dispute settlement duties. In competition law, NCAs intervene *ex ante* in the field of merger control, but also Article 82 EC, when they sanction abuses on the basis of their likely effects.

70 One could argue that sector specific regulation requires so much technical, expert knowledge, that the discretion of the NRA shall be guaranteed, whilst competition law involves less intricate technical assessments. It goes without saying that NCAs also deal with complex technical matters, for instance in fields involving high-technology markets. Furthermore, most of the concepts applied by NRAs originate in general competition law (significant market power, market definition, *etc.*).

71 This is, for instance, a serious problem in the US where the rulings of the federal agencies often give rise to lengthy litigation. In addition, it could be considered that courts of law are ill-equipped for evaluating technical and economic regulatory acts. See Geradin (2004) p. 137.

72 For example, the settlement dispute resolution body of the Energy Regulator ('CRE') is composed of two judges at the Council of State and two judges at the Supreme Court of Appeals. This indicates that decisions are already taken by judges, and therefore may limit the extent of subsequent judicial review. The Competition Council, which is composed of 17 members included 5 former administrative or civil law judges in 2008.

73 See Marimbert (2003) pp. 26-37 who speaks of regulators as 'quasi-judges'.

moderate standard of judicial review – such as the standard promoted by the ECJ in *Tetra Laval* v. *Commission* – should prevail in order, amongst other things, not to create too many incentives for litigation against regulators' decisions.

Whilst it is not the purpose of this contribution to take a position on this issue, we believe that what primarily matters in fields involving complex economic assessments, is the possibility to submit decisions taken by NRAs and NCAs – and in particular, their economic components – to a second, impartial and novel, examination. This also guarantees that the parties will have their legal situation properly and fairly reviewed, in line with the principle of right to appeal laid down by the European Court of Human Rights.[74] This outcome could certainly be attained through the institution of review panels within regulators. Yet, no such institutional setting is ever capable of providing as many guarantees against abuses/mistakes as the possibility to challenge a decision before an independent, distinct court. Internal peer review mechanisms are indeed fraught with numerous shortcomings, such as, for instance, biases affecting the review panels' decisions,[75] lack of transparency, etc.

Moreover, to ensure the efficacy of this institutional setting, we believe that an intensive standard of judicial review – such as the one applied by the French courts in the field of competition law – is warranted as a necessary '*checks and balances*' mechanism against the broad powers enjoyed by NRAs and NCAs. There are several reasons for this. First, by virtue of their independent nature, the French NCA and NRAs are (legitimately) insulated from any form of political control and subject to no other scrutiny than judicial review. Second – and maybe more importantly – once adopted, NCA and NRAs decisions over complex economic issues (*e.g.*, delineation of the relevant market(s), findings of dominance/SMP, applicable cost-benchmarks) exert a significant precedential influence in subsequent proceedings before other *foras* (such as, for instance, courts and authorities from the same or other Member States). In the course of their daily activities, national ordinary courts often refer to rulings previously adopted by NRAs and NCAs.[76] We thus believe that it is legitimate – and desirable – to allow for an in-depth review of NRAs and NCAs' decisions which, often, will produce long-lasting and widespread 'sunshine' effects over other organs.[77]

74 See Geradin (2005).

75 Be it a 'favourable' bias arising from the coalitional spirit of the reviewers, or an 'unfavourable' bias arising in the case of internal agency competition between the reviewing and reviewed organs.

76 To take only one example, in the context of its efforts to promote the private enforcement of EC competition rules, the Commission has proposed that decisions taken by a NCA finding an infringement of the EC competition rules be accepted as an 'irrefutable proof of the infringement' in subsequent civil litigation. In addition, such decisions should be deemed to constitute evidence of 'fault', for the purposes of claiming damages. See White Paper on Damages actions for breach of the EC antitrust rules, COM(2008) 165, 2 April 2008.

77 See, for a discussion of the concept of 'sunshine' enforcement and effects, Petit (2009). The effects of such decisions also are also likely to influence firms other than the regulated entities, when designing their legal strategies.

Finally, the usual concerns associated with intensive standards of judicial review are not necessarily present in the case of the French courts. In France, courts indeed appear well-qualified to review complex economic assessments as they are increasingly composed of economists.[78] In addition, issues such as regulatory lags or disruptive litigation are of little concern since annulment proceedings before the French courts have in principle no suspensive effect.[79]

---

78 F. Jenny, a notorious competition economist, was previously a judge at the Paris Court of Appeals, and now sits with the Supreme Court of Appeals.

79 In French public law, decisions taken by the French administration are presumed legal as a result of which administrative decisions are immediately applicable. This principle has been recognized as a "fundamental principle of public law" by the Council of State in *Huglo* (Council of State, 2 July 1982, *Huglo and others*). For this reason, judicial review can only take place *a posteriori* and appeals before the administrative judge have no suspensory effects (see Chapus (1997) at para. 1021). However, it is possible to initiate summary proceedings before the administrative judge to request a stay of execution if certain restrictive criteria are met (see Article L511-1 of the French code of Administrative Justice). For instance, the Council of State in *Fiducial* (Council of State, 19 May 2005, *Société Fudicial Informatique*) suspended the decision of the minister authorizing the merger on the basis that the decision did not provide sufficient justifications as to why the merger would not foreclose new entry on the market. Similarly, appeals to the Paris Court of Appeal with regard to decisions taken by the Competition Council have no suspensory effect (see Article L464-7 of the French Code of Commerce). However, it is also possible to be granted a stay of execution of the Competition Council's decision (see Article L464-8 al.3 of the French Code of Commerce). For instance, a stay of execution was granted in a case where the *rapport* (a document representing an important procedural stage in the procedure before the Competition Council) had not been notified to the concerned parties (see Court of Appeal of Paris, 23 January 2007, *Eiffage Construction*).

## Bibliography


BAILEY (2003)

D. Bailey, 'Standard of Proof in EC Merger Proceedings: A Common Law Perspective' [2003] *Common Market Law Review* pp. 845-888

BONNARD (1934)

R. Bonnard, *Le contrôle juridictionnel de l'administration* (Dalloz 1934)

BRANDENBURGER (2008)

R. Brandenburger, T. Janssens and J. Aitken, 'Bertelsmann and Sony Judgment: Welcome Clarity for EC Merger Review of the EU's Highest Court' [2008/2] *GCP – Online Magazine for Global Competition Policy*

CHAPUS (1997)

R. Chapus, *Droit administratif général 11ème édition* (Montchrestien, Paris 1997)

GERADIN (2005)

Geradin and N. Petit, 'Judicial Remedies Under EC Competition Law: Complex Issues Arising from the Modernization Process', in: B. Hawk (ed.), *Fordham Corporate Law Institute* (Fordham 2005) p. 393, *available at*: http://papers.ssrn.com/sol3/papers.cfm?abstract_id=877967

GERADIN (2004)

D. Geradin and N. Petit, 'The Development of Agencies at EU and National Levels: Conceptual Analysis and Proposals for Reform', (2004) 23 Yearbook of European Law, p. 137

HIRSENBRUNNER (2008)

S. Hirsenbrunner and C. v. Köckritz, 'Rebalancing EC Merger Control: The ECJ Judgment in Case C-413/06P, Bertelsmann AG and Sony Corporation America vs. Impala, not yet reported', [2008/2] *GCP – Online Magazine for Global Competition Policy*

LEGAL (2005)

H. Legal, 'Standards of Proof and Standards of Judicial Review in EU Competition Law', in: B. Hawk (ed.), *Fordham Corporate Law Institute* (Fordham 2005) p.107

MARIMBERT (2003)

J. Marimbert, 'Régulateurs et juges', *Forum de la régulation*, n° 17 du 23 janvier 2003, pp. 26-37

NEVEN (2008)

D. Neven, '*The role of economics in European Competition Enforcement and Policy*', FIW Symposium Innsbruck, 7 February 2008, available at http://ec.europa.eu/dgs/competition/economist/speeches.html

PACTEAU (2001)

B. Pacteau *Traité de contentieux administratif* (Puf, Paris 2001)

PETIT (2007)

N. Petit *Oligopoles, collusion tacite et droit communautaire de la concurrence* (Emile Bruylant, Brussels 2007)

PETIT (2008)
N. Petit, 'L'actualité du droit des ententes en 2007' [2008/133] *Les petites affiches* p. 5

PETIT (2009)
N. Petit and M. Rato, 'From Hard to Soft Enforcement of EC Competition Law – A Bestiary of "Sunshine" Enforcement Instruments', forthcoming in C. Gheur and N. Petit (eds), *Alternative Enforcement Techniques – A New Paradigm of EC Competition Law* (Emile Bruylant, Brussels 2009)

RIVERO (2006)
J. Rivero and J. Waline *Droit administrative* (Dalloz, Paris 2006)

SANDEVOIR (1964)
P. Sandevoir, 'Etudes sur le recours de pleine juridiction', LGDJ, 1964

SIBONY (2008)
A-L. Sibony, Le juge et le raisonnement économique en droit de la concurrence, LGDJ, 2008, at paras.1221, 1237, 1246 and 1285

SIRAGUSA (2004)
M. Siragusa, 'Judicial Review of Competition Decisions under EC Law', *Speech delivered at the Competition Commission Lectures*, 21 September 2004

CHAPTER 8

# *Tetra Laval* à la Hongroise

K. Cseres and J. Langer

## 1 Introduction

This paper assesses the degree of judicial scrutiny performed by administrative courts in Hungary when reviewing decisions by the Hungarian Competition Authority (*Gazdasági Versenyhivatal*, the Office of Economic Competition, hereinafter: the 'GVH') in the light of the landmark ruling handed down by the European Court of Justice (the 'ECJ') in *Commission vs. Tetra Laval*.[1]

In this judgment, the ECJ defined an arguably moderate standard of judicial review of competition decisions taken by the European Commission.[2] The ECJ considered that Community courts must not perform a new investigation and substitute the Commission's analysis with their own assessment. Nonetheless, the Commission's assessment must not be left unchecked.[3] The courts must fully verify whether the evidence put forward is accurate, reliable, consistent, exhaustive and capable of substantiating the conclusions drawn from it.[4] Yet, the appraisal of complex economic issues should be reviewed in a marginal way. Under this limited test, courts should check whether the procedural requirements are satisfied, the reasons for the decision taken are properly stated, the facts are accurately stated and whether there has been no manifest error of assessment or a misuse of powers.

The present paper examines whether the Hungarian courts have drawn inspiration from the above Community standard of judicial review. To that end, the paper is divided into four parts. The first part provides an outline of the Hungarian Competition Act and sets the scene for the present contribution. The second part offers a brief overview of the general principles of judicial review of the Hungarian administrative authorities' decisions. The third part examines against the backdrop of landmark cases whether the *Tetra Laval* ruling has influenced the degree of judicial scrutiny applied by Hungarian courts when reviewing the GVH's decisions. The fourth part offers a brief conclusion and weaves together the various threads that can be found throughout the paper.

## 2 Background

### 2.1 Act on the Prohibition of Unfair and Restrictive Market Practices

The first Hungarian Competition Act based on market principles was introduced in 1990. This act was replaced in 1996 by the Act on the

---

1 See Case C-12/03P *Commission* v. *Tetra Laval BV* [2005] ECR I-987.

2 Cf. Case 42/84 *Remia BV and others* v. *Commission* [1985] ECR 2545 and Case C-68/94 *Kali und Salz* [1998] ECR I-1375.

3 See further contribution by Meij.

4 See also Case T-201/04 *Microsoft* v. *Commission* [2007] ECR II-3601, paras. 87-89.

Prohibition of Unfair and Restrictive Market Practices (hereinafter: the 'HCA').[5] Besides competition law in the classical sense, the HCA deals with unfair competition and consumer information issues. The HCA's unique feature is that it not only includes the prohibitions of restrictive agreements and abuse of dominant position as well as rules regarding control of concentrations but also prohibitions of unfair competition and unfair manipulation of consumer choice. The enforcement of the HCA is entrusted to the GVH. The GVH is an independent administrative authority that reports to the Hungarian Parliament. The President of the GVH annually submits a report to the Parliament on the GVH's activities. The GVH is also entrusted with a number of enforcement duties under the Act on Trade, the Act on Business Advertising Activity and the Act on Price Setting. On the basis of Section 44 HCA, the supervisory duties of the GVH are governed by the Public Administrative Procedures Act of 2004. However, proceedings in relation to the provisions on unfair competition belong on the ground of Section 86 HCA to the competence of the administrative courts and are therefore governed by the Act on Civil Procedures of 1952.

### 2.2 Recent amendments

The HCA and its following amendments are by and large in line with EU competition law. Amendments to the HCA in 2000 resulted in further harmonisation. On 26 May 2003 the Hungarian Parliament passed further amendments, bringing the act fully in line with EU competition law. These new provisions entered into force when Hungary joined the EU on 1 May 2004. The most recent amendments of the HCA took effect on 1 November 2005. These changes relate to the coming into force of the new Public Administrative Procedures Act (hereinafter: the 'PAPA') as well as bringing the HCA in alignment with the developments at Community level where the European Commission's monopoly under article 81(3) EC has been abolished.

## 3 Judicial review in general

### 3.1 Introduction

The decisions of the GVH are subject to review by the Budapest Municipal Court. The Budapest Court of Appeal is competent to review the rulings by the Budapest Municipal Court. In exceptional cases, decisions are subject to appeal to the Hungarian Supreme Court.

### 3.2 Legal standard for the GVH

Most competition decisions discussed in this paper were adopted on the basis of Act IV of 1957 on Administrative Procedures. Today,

[5] The HCA is available in English: http://www.gvh.hu/gvh/alpha?do=2&st=2&pg=96&m19_act=4.

however, the GVH enforces the provisions of the HCA on the basis of the PAPA. The PAPA applies to the GVH's investigations only insofar as the procedural rules of the HCA do not differ from those of the PAPA. For the present discussion the following provisions are relevant. Section 50 (1) of the PAPA requires the administrative body to determine the relevant facts of the case during its investigation. If the information available is insufficient, it may initiate a procedure *ex officio* or upon request to obtain evidence. Section 72(1) sub e of the PAPA requires that the administrative authority's decision contains in its operative part, *inter alia*, the relevant facts and evidence used for the decision, the evidence presented by the plaintiff and found inadmissible, an explanation for the authority's opinion, the reasons for any seizure carried out, the statutes upon which the authority has adopted its decision. Section 26(1) of the Act on Administrative Procedures of 1957 contains exactly the same provision as Section 50(1) of the PAPA. Section 43(1) sub c of the Act on Administrative Procedures states that the administrative authority's decision has to contain in its operative part, *inter alia*, the relevant facts and evidence, the evidence presented by the client and found inadmissible, and the reason for this finding and the name of the special authority involved.

A quick comparison shows that previously no requirement existed of 'resolutions adopted under the principle of weighing and deliberation, the criteria and facts employed, the explanation for the special authority's opinion, the reasons for any seizure carried out in the proceeding.' This requirement targets the considerations underlying and supporting the appraisal of the administrative agency, and the Explanatory Memorandum of the PAPA notes that the aim was to achieve balanced administrative decisions.[6] This legislative development touches upon exactly the same part of the judicial review as discussed by the Community Courts in the *Tetra Laval* ruling: appraisal of the established facts.

### 3.3 Judicial review by lower courts

Relevant for the appeal proceedings is Chapter XX of Act III of 1952 on the Code of Civil Procedures. According to Section 327(1) of this Act, a decision can be appealed by any party to the proceedings or by anybody whose rights and obligations are directly affected by the decision. Such a person can be the complainant or other participants in the proceedings, like competitors. The general statutory standard of review can be found in Section 339/B Code of Civil Procedure:

> 'An administrative decision reached as a result of deliberation is regarded as lawful when the administrative authority adequately disclosed the facts, complied with the procedural rules, the considerations of the deliberation can be ascer-

6 The Explanatory Memorandum of the PAPA notes that this requirement was introduced on the basis of the experience gained over the years. 2004. *évi* CXL. *törvény indokolása a közigazgatási hatósági eljárás és szolgáltatás általános szabályairól.*

tained (are clear) and the reasoning of the decision demonstrates the reasonableness of the deliberation of the evidence.'

This standard consists of four elements: accurate establishment of the facts, compliance with relevant procedural rules, the assessment of the facts is clear and the characterisation of the evidence in law is reasonable. When this standard is compared with the *Tetra Laval* standard as laid down in paragraph 39 of the judgment and further elaborated on by the Court of First Instance in *Microsoft,*[7] *Alrosa*[8] and *Impala,*[9] the Hungarian legislator seems to follow the Community standard.

On the basis of Section 339(1) of the Code of Civil Procedures, the competent court is entitled to annul the administrative decision appealed. The court can also order the initiation of a new investigation (with compulsory instructions as to how the GVH should conduct this investigation) or, on the basis of Section 339(2) sub q, the court can alter the decision appealed when the law allows it. Article 83(4) of the HCA stipulates that the court may overrule the decision made by the GVH. On the basis of this provision, courts are allowed to actually change and replace the authority's decision by their own decision on the basis of their own assessment of a file. But courts can only review the administrative decision within the limits set by the application for review, i.e. the decision shall not go beyond the relief sought by the applicant. As a result, if the court establishes that there is no infringement, it cannot abrogate the relevant decision based on another infringement of law. If the challenged decision complies with the law or merely a minor infringement of the procedural rules is established, a court will confirm the administrative decision under review.[10]

There are special rules for judicial review by the Supreme Court. In practice, administrative courts have relied on the above standard. In this regard, the Supreme Court noted as follows:

'A lawsuit for judicial review can be based on the violation of procedural or substantive legal rules, but it is not possible for the Supreme Court as the court of review to examine the conclusions based on reasonable assessment or to re-establish the facts instead of the demonstrated facts by newly assessing the available evidence.'[11]

The extent of review is crucial to the present discussion. Article 83(4) HCA provides a certain competence for the courts that can have far-reaching consequences in judicial review. In all the above-mentioned judgments, the European Courts do not extend their competence of judicial review further than reviewing

7 Case T-201/04 *Microsoft Corp.* v. *Commission* [2007] ECR II-3601, paras. 87-89.

8 Case T-170/06 *Alrosa* v. *Commission* [2007] ECR II-2601, para. 108.

9 Case C-413/06 P *Bertelsmann AG and Sony Corporation America* v. *Impala* [2008] ECR I-0000.

10 M. Kárpáti, 'Hungarian administrative jurisdiction'.

11 Legf. Bír. Kf.X.27.608/1998/5, Vj-144/1995 (Supreme Court).

whether the evidence relied on is factually accurate, reliable and consistent and contains all the information which must be taken into account in order to assess a complex situation and whether it is capable of substantiating the conclusions drawn from it,'[12] According to the CFI, the review of the complex economic appraisals made by the Commission is necessarily limited.'[13] In contrast, the Hungarian courts are entitled to substitute the GVH's decision with their own assessment and thus the courts are allowed to engage in judicial review of a similar intensity such as was criticised by AG Tizziano in the *Tetra Laval II* judgment.[14] This will be illustrated below in the Budapest Municipal Court's judgment concerning the acquisition of *Népszabadság Rt.* by *B.V. Tabora.*[15] In sum, the Hungarian legislation provides wide competence for the Hungarian courts to review decisions of administrative authorities. Beyond reviewing whether the facts have been accurately established, the procedural rules have been complied with and the considerations of the deliberation are clear, the courts are allowed to change the decision of the administrative agency and replace it by their own decision. However, they cannot re-establish the facts of the case. Yet, this competence seems to go further than what the ECJ has set out in the *Tetra Laval* ruling.[16]

## 4 Judicial review of competition cases

### 4.1 Statistics

Approximately half of the GVH-decisions establishing an infringement are appealed by the parties concerned, which has been a representative tendency since 1997. In more recent years there is a slight decrease of appeals. The reason for this is that the number of consumer fraud cases has significantly increased (as from 75% in 2006 to 94% in 2007).[17] More than two thirds of the 412 appeals of the decisions brought under the present HCA have become final. In 20 cases the underlying decisions by the GVH were altered in part or in its entirety. In these cases, the Budapest Municipal Court and the Supreme Court (or the Court of Appeal) changed the decision of the GVH in respect of its legal basis. In another 17 cases the fine imposed was reduced.[18] As to the subject of the decisions, the following can be said. Decisions brought in consumer fraud cases were mainly accepted and not appealed due to the

12 Case C-12/03 *Commission* v. *Tetra Laval BV* [2005] ECR I-987, para. 39.

13 Case T-201/04 *Microsoft Corp.* v. *Commission*, [2007] ECR II-3601, para. 87.

14 Opinion of AG Tizziano, delivered on 25 May 2004, Case C-12/03 P *Commission* v. *Tetra Laval*, paras 86 and 89.

15 Legf. Bír. 7.K.33364/2003/10 (Budapest Municipal Court).

16 Case C-12/03 *Commission* v. *Tetra Laval BV* [2005] ECRI-987, para. 39.

17 Annual report on competition policy developments in Hungary, 2007, DAF/COMOP(2008)9/27, p.3.

18 Annual report on competition policy developments in Hungary, 2007, DAF/COMOP(2008)9/27, p.3.

moderate levels of fines imposed. However, the GVH added that the more severe sentencing policy recently adopted is expected to bring changes in this field. Contrary to the situation concerning the fraud cases, virtually all prohibition decisions in cases of cartel agreements and abuse of dominance were appealed, even if fines were low or insignificant. In the case of cartels, decisions based on leniency applications were not appealed.[19] In merger cases, the decisions are rarely appealed.[20]

These statistics raise the following questions. Is the GVH doing its job so well that virtually all its decisions are upheld in appeal? Or are administrative courts not sufficiently critical when reviewing the decisions taken by the GVH? What does this mean for the accountability of the GVH? Below we seek to answer these questions. At this point, we note that the GVH seems to consider that accountability is not an issue. In its annual reports, the GVH has repeatedly stated:

> *'...there is harmony in law enforcement between the GVH and the courts.'*[21]

Beyond the issue of accountability, the cases discussed below examine whether and to what extent in competition cases Hungarian courts have endorsed the Community standard of judicial review as set out in the *Tetra Laval* ruling.

## 4.2 Landmark cases

### 4.2.1 General remarks

Perhaps the most extensive and detailed review of a decision by the GVH is to be found in a case concerning the acquisition of *Népszabadság Rt.* by *B.V. Tabora* in the Hungarian newspaper market. This case exhibits several interesting similarities with the issues discussed in the *Tetra Laval* ruling. The Hungarian court handed down its judgment in 2004 and with its restraint review it actually seems to have been a forerunner of the ECJ's landmark ruling. In order to be able to evaluate the relevance of this case, it seems indispensable to contrast the ruling with a number of other cases handled by the Hungarian courts.

### 4.2.2 Restrictive agreements

As mentioned before, most of the decisions by the GVH on restrictive agreements are being appealed by the parties concerned. The decisions that have been successfully appealed concern issues like the reliance upon

19 Annual report on competition policy developments in Hungary, 2005, DAF/COMOP(2006)7/27, p.5.

20 *Országgyűlési beszámoló* 2002 (Annual Report, GVH) 2003, p.42.

21 GVH's annual reports are available in English: http://www.gvh.hu/gvh/alpha?do=2&st=2&pg=99&m5_doc=2321&m174_act=7.

insufficient deliberation of the available evidence,[22] inadequate characterisation of the facts in law,[23] the absence of proper reasoning for the imposition of fines and insufficient evidence.

Case Vj-137/1999/18 is illustrative in the way that the GVH's motivation for setting fines has been scrutinised by the courts. In this case, the GVH established that the Chamber of Hungarian Physicians violated the HCA by fixing minimum medical fees in its Ethical Code. The Budapest Municipal Court upheld this decision, but the Court of Appeal disagreed with the reasoning given by the GVH for the imposition of fines. According to the Court of Appeal, the GVH's reasoning was controversial and incomplete as it had failed to consider the mitigating circumstance that consumers were harmed. The Appeals Court changed the GVH's decision and accordingly reduced the fine.[24] In cases of restrictive agreements, courts have only intervened when the GVH made a manifest error, either because the reasoning stated was not coherent or clear or because the GVH has misread the obvious meaning of a memorandum. The courts seem to have been reluctant to intensively review decision taken by the GVH.

### 4.2.3 Abuse of dominance

In comparison with the way the courts review GVH-decisions on restrictive agreements the courts engage in a more detailed analysis when they review cases concerning abuse of a dominant position. In these cases, the courts have more extensively discussed substantive issues of the GVH-decisions and occasionally referred to European case law. Therefore, these cases provide more insight into the considerations the courts take into account when they engage in judicial review of GVH-decisions.

Many appeal cases where the decisions were overturned concerned unfair contract terms and excessive pricing. In these cases, the GVH struggled to identify, on the one hand, what constitutes unfair contract terms[25] and, on the other

22 2.Kf.27.347/2006/5. *Fővárosi Ítélőtábla* (Budapest Court of Appeal).

23 In case Vj-169/2001/37 the GVH had conditionally exempted an agreement concerning a fidelity card based on a rebate system that has been created by MOL, the Hungarian Oil and gas Company, OTP, the National Savings Bank and the Hungarian Telecommunications Ltd. According to the Court, the GVH failed to show in its reasoning how the arrangement under investigation restricted or could restrict competition. The Court held that the GVH has not demonstrated all the elements of the allegedly anti-competitive agreement and it has not managed to unambiguously qualify the behaviour under investigation as illegal. More specifically, the GVH did not take into consideration the potential reactions that the competitors could take. In the end, the Court held that the GVH violated Section 43(1) sub c of the Act on Administrative Procedures. 2.K.32971/2002/11. *Fővárosi Bíróság* (Budapest Municipal Court).

24 Kf.II.40.072/2000/5. *Legfelsőbb Bíróság* (Supreme Court).

25 The GVH has dealt with this issue in details in its decision against UPC Hungary Kft's policy concerning the structuring of programme packages. Vj-126/2000. The GVH interpreted the term 'unjustified advantage' under Article 21(a) of the HCA as an objective category, but in the absence of a separate defi-

hand, finding an accurate method for the establishment of excessive prices.[26] There are no clear guidelines on what amounts to an 'unjustified advantage'. This term has neither been defined under the HCA nor in the GVH's practice. The same legal uncertainty applies to the establishment of excessive pricing in the GVH's practice. In the appeal cases, these legal uncertainties provided potential room for the courts to intensely review the GVH's decisions. Therefore, these cases represent good examples to examine the intensity of the Hungarian courts' judicial review.

In a case concerning the unilateral alteration of standard contract terms in cable television services[27] the GVH found a violation of Article 21a HCA. The GVH examined whether the change in the programme packages took place by taking the consumer interests into account and concluded that the service provider's standard contract terms contained no adequate guarantees for subscribers. While the court at first instance affirmed the GVH's decision, the Budapest Court of Appeal found that the GVH did not satisfy the requirements of disclosing the relevant facts of the case and adequate motivation as laid down in Section 26(1) and 43(1) sub c of the Administrative Procedures Act of 1957. The decision was incomplete and therefore it was unsuited to establish the harm of consumer interests and abuse of a dominant position. On the basis of Section 253(2) of the Code of Civil Procedures, it annulled the GVH's decision and ordered new proceedings, instructing the GVH to assess whether the price calculation of the undertaking was in conformity with competition law rules and whether the undertaking concerned held a dominant position on the relevant market. According to the Court of Appeal, the GVH had not answered these questions. It therefore had to re-examine the price formation and had to identify how it had taken account of consumer interests by establishing the dominant position in the light of substitutability and the relevant market.[28] Similarly, in a case concerning unilateral modification of a cable television company's standard contract terms by increasing service fees and changing programme packages,[29] the Budapest Court of Appeal dismissed the GVH's decision and ordered new proceedings. It explained that the GVH's disclosure of the relevant facts, the examination of the existence of dominance as well as the characterisation of

nition of this term under the HCA, it made reference to Article 209/B of the HCC. GVH, *A kábeltelevíziós szolgáltatók műsorjelelosztó szolgáltatásával kapcsolatos versenyfelügyeleti eljárások tapasztalatai alapján megfogalmazott szabályozási javaslatokról*, 2003, pp. 59-61. For a more detailed discussion on unfair contract terms as violation of competition rules see K.J. Cseres, What has competition done for consumers?

26 This HCA provision is equivalent to Article 82(a) EC prohibiting the imposition of unfair contractual terms or prices.

27 Vj-88/2003/35.

28 2.Kf.27.542/2006/6. *Fővárosi Ítélőtábla* (Budapest Court of Appeal).

29 In Vj-11/2002/23 the GVH has established that *T-Kábel Magyarország Kft.* violated Article 21a HCA by reserving the possibility of unilateral contract modification in its standard contract terms by increasing service fees and changing its programme packages.

the facts in law were incomplete. The Budapest Court of Appeal added that in its new procedure the GVH had to examine separately and together the decisive factors that are indispensable to establish violation of Articles 21 and 22 HCA. Moreover, it had to examine special sector specific regulation, the relevant provisions of Act XI of 2001 on telecommunications, in order to examine the substitutability of the service provided by a cable television company in the relevant market as well as the relevant provisions of the HCC on standard contract terms. The Budapest Court of Appeal added that the clearly established concepts help to adequately disclose and interpret the facts as laid down in Article 22 HCA.[30]

This case also illustrates clearly how the appeal courts review the lower courts' judgment. The case has first been annulled by the Budapest Municipal Court as court of first instance. Consequently, this decision was appealed to the Budapest Court of Appeal, finding the judgment of the lower court unsuited for review as it violated procedural rules by failing to motivate its judgment. The Budapest Court of Appeal referred the case back to the court of first instance and ordered new proceedings. The new proceedings of the Budapest Municipal Court were again appealed.[31]

As mentioned above, the Hungarian courts have the competence to change the decision of the GVH. In a case concerning the offer of Budapest Electricity Works Inc. to modify its public utilities service contract the GVH established the abuse of this company's dominant position as refusing this offer resulted in harmful consequences for consumers.[32] Budapest Electricity Works Inc. introduced a new system of partial billing but consumers had to react to the new offer at their own costs. Acceptance or refusal were both at the consumers' own costs. The GVH was of the opinion that this arrangement violated both Article 21a HCA, as well as the general prohibition of abuse of a dominant position under Article 22 HCA. The Supreme Court ruled on the question whether the contract modification to the partial billing system violated the general (Article 21 HCA) or specific prohibition of abuse of dominance (Article 21a HCA). It held that the GVH did not balance the advantages against the disadvantages of the partial billing system and thus no violation of Article 21a HCA took place. Still, the Supreme Court found that the general prohibition of abuse of dominance

---

30 2.Kf.27.257/2006/5. *Fővárosi Ítélőtábla* (Budapest Court of Appeal).

31 This 'ping-pong' effect between the higher court and the lower court is even clearer in the next case. In Vj-14/2003 the GVH has established that VidaNEt Zrt. violated Article 21 a, HCA by imposing excessive prices for cable television services. The court of first instance dismissed the GVH decision and ordered new proceedings. The court found the GVH decision unfounded with regard to the relevant market and dominant position as substitutability was incompletely proved. In appeal, the Court of Appeal found that the court of first instance correctly established the relevant facts but that it made incorrect conclusions and thus partly approved the GVH decision. The Court of Appeal then explained and it analysed the definition of the relevant market and the issue of substitutability of services and concluded that it was the GVH and not the court of first instance that established the substitutability of the cable television services at issue correctly.2.Kf.27.483/2007/7. *Fővárosi Ítélőtábla* (Budapest Court of Appeal).

32 Vj-106/2000/16.

as laid down in Article 21 HCA was infringed and thus imposed a fine. On the basis of Article 83(4) HCA the Supreme Court changed the decision of the GVH – it omitted the infringement of Article 21 a and d, but established the infringement of Article21 HCA and reduced the fine.[33]

This case shows that the courts review whether the considerations of the GVH's appraisal had been accurate, but they are reserved to review the appraisal of the GVH.

With regard to excessive prices the GVH has struggled to find an accurate method for the establishment of this infringement.[34] The GVH has drafted a so-called benchmark method, based on the comparison with competitive prevailing prices and economic values.[35] However, in the cable television sector the GVH applied another test based on the assessment of how fees change in time.[36] Tóth demonstrates that in a number of recent cases the GVH (Vj-25/2006; Vj-27/2005; Vj-156/2005) did not pursue the case relying on the lack of public interest. The GVH indicated that its lack of resources was not balanced with the gravity of the infringement.[37] The fact that the GVH refrained from proceedings in these cases questions whether the GVH has complied with the legislative requirements of decision-making as laid down in the Act of Administrative procedures mentioned in section 2 of this contribution. Such insufficiencies provide room for the courts' judicial review as formulated in Section 339/B Code of Civil Procedures. The courts again showed restraint in their review.

The following case is an illustration of the above mentioned enforcement problem. In this case the reviewing court stated that the GVH needs to apply several economic methods in order to draw balanced conclusions on excessive pricing. The case concerned proceedings against MOL, the largest oil and gas supplier in Hungary and the setting of resale and wholesale prices of fuels in the period 1997 to 2000. The GVH terminated its proceedings as it could not establish the existence and the abuse of a dominant position. When the GVH

---

33 Kf.II.39.894/2001/6. *Legfelsőbb Bíróság* (Supreme Court).

34 Excessive pricing generally occurs when a dominant undertaking raises its prices that are not justified by the change in the undertaking's economic circumstances. Moreover, when it significantly exceeds the economic value of the services, i.e. the sum of the economically reasonable costs and the fair profit attributable to the particular sector, prices are held to be excessive. Vj-27/2005, GVH, Annual Report (2006) p.36, A GVH *versenytanácsának elvi állásfoglalásai*, 21.4; 21.7 (Guidelines of the GVH in applying the HCA).

35 The method compares the price in question with the prices of the relevant product at stake in another (competitive) geographic relevant market or in the same product market but in another time period with different competition factors or the prices of products or services that are similar in characteristics and technical features with the relevant product and service and in all cases including all justified costs. Tóth (2008) p.3.

36 The GVH argued that it was not the extraordinary profit that signals excessive prices but whether the firm raises prices, including the higher profit margins, above the levels justified by the change in its economic circumstances. The GVH itself, however, acknowledged that this method is too simplistic.

37 Tóth (2008) pp. 6-7.

examined the question whether the prices charged by MOL were excessive it did not rely on a costs-based analysis. In the practice of the GVH excessive pricing is established when prices significantly exceed the economic value of the services, i.e. the sum of the economically reasonable costs and the fair profit attributable to the particular sector.[38] However, the GVH has acknowledged that both national and international practice have restrained from applying this costs-based method because of the difficulties in enforcement. The GVH established several times that there is no particular prevailing cost allocation method, any deviation from which would entail an infringement of competition law.[39] The decision of the GVH was appealed by the Hungarian Auto Club and the court of first instance dismissed the GVH-decision and ordered new proceedings. The Budapest Municipal Court argued that the GVH had not adequately disclosed the relevant facts and it has not engaged in an extensive cost-based price analysis, which was indispensable. In second instance the Supreme Court overturned the GVH's decision. In its pleadings before the Supreme Court the GVH referred to *United Brands*[40] and argued that national and international jurisprudence has not applied the cost-based analysis because of its difficulties. Therefore, the GVH stated that there was no need for the analysis of all costs involved; it sufficed to compare the prevailing prices with competitive prices in order to exclude the presence of highly excessive prices. The Supreme Court disagreed and held that when there are several reasonable methods to determine whether prices are excessive, these methods should be applied and the results of the several methods should be evaluated in their entirety in order to make the overall decision whether violation of competition law has taken place.[41] This case is very illustrative to demonstrate the dividing line between how a court can review whether the administrative authority has based its appraisal on clear and balanced considerations but restrain from reviewing the appraisal itself.

As an interim conclusion, the following can be said. Even though the Hungarian courts have far-reaching legislative competence to review decisions of the GVH including the alteration of these decisions, they have in practice restrained from intensely reviewing the content of the GVH's (economic) assessment of the disclosed facts. The above discussed cases illustrate that the Hungarian courts are critically reviewing GVH decisions where the facts have been inadequately disclosed or where the characterisation of the disclosed facts

---

38 Vj-27/2005, GVH, Annual Report GVH (2006) p.36.

39 It should be noted that excessive pricing is a cautiously and exceptionally enforced part of competition law and its enforcement is not without controversies. A solid benchmark of unfair or excessive prices is missing. Uncertainties of enforcement are even greater in the network industries, where *ex ante* tariff regulation is often necessary to create efficiency-driven prices and *ex post* regulation is thus not appropriate in this case. For a more detailed overview see M. van der Woude, Unfair and excessive prices in the energy sector, 2007 *EU Competition Law and Policy Workshop/Proceedings*, European University Institute, Robert Schuman Centre for Advanced Studies.

40 Case C- 27/76 *United Brands* v. *Commission* [1978] ECR 207.

41 Kf. II. 39. 048/2002/13. *Legfelsőbb Bíróság* (Supreme Court).

in law were incorrect. The last case in this section truly demonstrates that the courts are also prepared to overturn GVH-decisions when the considerations of the economic assessment are illogical, unclear or incomplete, but they do not exceed their legislative competence and engage in a full-flush analysis of the GVH's appraisal. The Supreme Court has clearly affirmed the above formulated finding in a case where it has reviewed the GVH's decision on the amount of fine for misleading consumers. In this case the Supreme Court has restated the borderlines of a restrained judicial review by saying:

> 'the court is entitled to examine whether the administrative authority has taken account of all possible considerations of its assessment and whether it has explained the acceptance or refusal of these considerations. In this case, it cannot be established that the administrative authority has violated a legal provision and thus the amount of the fine cannot be changed, the court is not entitled to reconsider the administrative authority's assessment.'[42]

### 4.2.4 Acquisition of *Népszabadság*: pre-'*Tetra Laval* standard'

Most, if not all, judgments rendered in the field of the cartel prohibition and abuse of dominance display a striking degree of judicial deference to the GVH's (economic) assessments and accordingly do not go beyond a marginal review which hinges on verifying whether the GVH made a manifest error of appraisal. Yet, in the field of merger control the Budapest Municipal Court seems to be willing to depart from this. Illustrative is the acquisition of *Népszabadság Rt.* by *B.V. Tabora,* a member of the Swiss Ringier Group, which is active in the newspaper market in many European countries. This case is not only interesting because it concerns the application of the portfolio theory of competitive harm but also because the Hungarian court's approach is arguably in line with the principles of judicial review laid down in the *Tetra Laval* ruling, even though it was handed down on 23 September 2004.

The facts of the case are as follows. The Swiss newspaper group Ringier intended to acquire a direct competitor in the Hungarian market for political dailies. The acquisition was vetoed by the GVH, because it was concerned about the direct horizontal effects as well as the portfolio effects of the acquisition in the market for national dailies (i.e. sport dailies, tabloids, political dailies) and in the market for advertising. For the purpose of this paper, we focus on the GVH's appraisal of portfolio effects. In Hungary, three groups belonged to the Ringier Group, active in the markets for daily tabloids, weekly tabloids, daily sports papers and political daily newspapers. According to the GVH, the Ringier Group was dominant on the Hungarian market for sports dailies and on the Hungarian market for tabloids. After the acquisition of *Népszabadság,* a daily political paper, it would also become dominant on the Hungarian market for political dailies. The GVH considered that as a consequence of the acquisi-

42 Kf. V. 39. 361/2001/4. *Legfelsőbb Bíróság* (Supreme Court).

tion the Ringier Group would have created a large portfolio of national dailies. Such a strong portfolio would reinforce its position on the market for advertising as advertising campaigns are generally a mix of all kinds of media, including the various forms of printed media. This would in turn reinforce the Ringier Group's position on the market for national dailies. Relevant for this conclusion was the fact that the market for advertising was characterised by high entry barriers, according to the GVH.

In appeal, the Budapest Municipal Court annulled the GVH's decision. The judgment is very interesting for answering the research question of this paper: an intensive review of the economic evidence supporting the GVH's decision, but a more restrained review of the theory of competitive harm itself.

The GVH listed a number of human resources factors, financial and material barriers to enter the market for national dailies, and emphasised that competitors needed high volumes to successfully enter this market. The GVH further believed that the market segment for political dailies was not expected to grow. The GVH also noted that readers would be unlikely to switch between political newspapers given readers' stable political orientation, thus creating an entry barrier. In support of its analysis, the GVH emphasised that since 1990 no successful entry has been made to the market for national dailies. Moreover, it found no adequate structural, behavioural or informational remedies that could balance the detrimental effects of the concentration and thus result in approval. Even though the divestment of *Magyar Hírlap* would have remedied the horizontal effect in the national dailies market, it could not remedy the portfolio effect in the other readers' and advertisements' markets.

The Budapest Municipal Court exercised full review as to the accuracy of these facts and their adequacy to substantiate GVH's conclusions that the market is characterised by high entry barriers. First, assessing all the documentation available, the Court found the GVH's conclusion that since 1990 no entry was successful, inaccurate. Competitors had entered, so held the court, the market, although one of the new entrants was not active anymore as it had now merged with another competitor. This circumstance was not taken into account by the GVH and therefore the GVH came to an incorrect and illogical conclusion. The Court also held that the lack of cross-reading due to the political orientation of readers did not qualify as an entry barrier. Against this background and the presence of (potential) competitors with large capital and with volumes even larger than the acquired undertaking, the Court concluded that it was not reasonable to argue that the market for national dailies was characterised by entry barriers.

With regard to the portfolio effect, the considerations of the Budapest Municipal Court are also worth mentioning, because here the Court showed more restraint in the review of the GVH's findings. In line with the *Tetra Laval* ruling, the Court reiterated that:

> 'within the framework of judicial review there is no room for reconsideration in case the authority has reasonably deliberated on the basis of adequately disclosed facts.'

Therefore, the Court accepted *as fact* that the portfolio effect on the market for dailies strengthened a dominant position and thus has detrimental effects on competition. Surprisingly, the Court, nonetheless, reviewed whether the economic analysis, the facts and evidence convincingly characterised the claimed detrimental effects. The Court first stressed that these effects are realised in a long process of several steps, deriving from the market for advertising, where plaintiffs are not dominant. It questioned whether in the long run the concentration indeed restricts competition and raises entry barriers. According to the Court, the segmentation of the market for dailies on the basis of political orientation reduces the detrimental consequences of the portfolio effects. The Court held that such effects can be counterbalanced by undertakings with large financial, material and personal assets in the market for advertising. In the words of the court:

> 'The Court emphasises that it does not question the appraisal of the authority, but has examined the disclosed facts and circumstances that were taken into account in the [GVH's] assessment. Furthermore, it has disclosed the blatantly unreasonable conclusions and dismissed the incorrect facts (i.e. lack of supply side substitution) and substituted them for facts based on the available data.'

Therefore, the GVH's decision was quashed. The Budapest Municipal Court has also made some remarks on the competence of the Hungarian courts to change the decisions of the GVH. The Court found that even though it could substitute the GVH's decision by imposing remedies for the merger under investigation, it refrained from doing so for procedural reasons. The Court noted that on the basis of the Code of Civil Procedures it cannot impose obligations on an undertaking not party to the case. In the present case, this would mean ordering the divestiture of a part of the undertaking which is not party to the proceedings. The Court concluded that the HCA is therefore not in conformity with the Code of Civil Procedures.

To conclude, the *Népszabadság* case shows that under merger control the legal and economic determination of the facts is subject to a high degree of judicial scrutiny. This case also shows, on the one hand, that there is a floating and perhaps grey zone in both the European and national case law where the borderline of judicial review of the (economic) appraisal of national authorities is situated. Yet, it seems to be the core issue in the whole discussion of judicial review. On the other hand, the case affirms the conclusion of the previous section, namely that the Hungarian courts exert limited review of the GVH's assessment of competitive harm as long as its reasoning is clear and is based on correctly disclosed facts and evidence.

## 5 Conclusions

The aim of this contribution was to examine whether and to what extent the Hungarian courts endorsed the standard of judicial review as established by the European Court of Justice in *Tetra Laval*. At first sight the answer to this question is that the Hungarian courts seem to draw little or no inspiration at all from the Community Courts' case law and thus the impact of the *Tetra Laval* ruling is actually none. However, a deeper analysis on how the Hungarian courts review decisions of the Hungarian competition authority leads to a more balanced conclusion. In essence, irrespective of the developments in European jurisprudence the Hungarian courts have developed a finely tuned and restrained judicial review of the GVH decisions.

While the Hungarian legislation provides wide competence for the Hungarian courts to review decisions of administrative authorities, the case law of the courts as discussed above shows that the courts are cautious in the extent of how they review the assessment of the GVH and well aware of the borderlines of their powers. Even though the courts are allowed to change the decision of the administrative agency and replace it by their own decision, they do not engage in re-establishing the facts of the case or intervene with the appraisal of the GVH. The above-reviewed cases and especially the *MOL* case on excessive pricing and the *Népszabadság* acquisition case clearly demonstrate that the Hungarian courts restrict their review to controlling the reasonableness and the consistency of the assessment of the GVH. What is more, the Hungarian courts seem to have been able to find a reserved position in the floating zone between restrained and intense judicial review when it comes to the review of the (economic) appraisal of national authorities. The identification of the exact borderline between marginal and intense judicial review of the administrative authorities' decisions could perhaps be further discussed by using a cross-country comparison.

Still, the question remains why the Hungarian courts do not refer to and rely on European law more often. Currently there is a high degree of convergence between national and thus Hungarian substantive competition rules and the European competition law provisions. Accordingly, it could reasonably be expected that the enforcement of these closely aligned national rules follow the guidelines provided by the European Courts. But this is not the case. An extensive answer to what the underlying reasons for this discrepancy might be is beyond the scope of this contribution. Still, one possible explanation could be that, unlike the national competition authorities who actively participate in the European Competition Network, national courts are still more embedded in their national legal system and focus more on national legal rules and jurisprudence.

## Bibliography

CSERES (2008)

K.J. Cseres, 'What has competition done for consumers in liberalised markets?' [2008/4] *Competition Law Review* pp. 5-48

KÁRPÁTI

M. Kárpáti, 'Hungarian administrative jurisdiction', http://www.juradmin.eu/fr/members/pdf/Hungary.pdf

LAVRIJSSEN (2006)

S. Lavrijssen and M. de Visser, 'Independent administrative authorities and the standard of judicial review' [2006/2] *Utrecht Law Review* pp. 111-135

NAGY CSONGOR (2008)

I. Nagy Csongor, *Kartelljogi kézikönyv* (HVG-ORAC Budapest, 2008)

TÓTH (2008)

A. Tóth, 'A Gazdasági Versenyhivatal túlzó ár megállapításával kapcsolatos gyakorlata' [2008/3] *Gazdaság és jog* pp. 3-8

ZAVODNYIK (2004)

J. Zavodnyik, 'A Gazdasági Versenyhivatalhoz benyújtott bejelentések megítélésének egyes kérdései a bírói gyakorlatban' [2004/9] *Gazdaság és jog* pp. 16-20

CHAPTER 9

# Judicial Review of Regulatory Decisions in Italy

## Changing the Formula and Keeping the Substance?

R. Caranta and B. Marchetti

## 1 Introduction[1]

One of the crucial issues of the modern administrative law systems concerns the nature and scope of judicial review of agency action.[2] Administrative authorities are created to carry out public functions and their administrative powers, established by statutes, have to be exercised in accordance with the law. Sometimes the powers accorded to the agency for implementing the law are discretionary in nature and consequently the administrative authority has to make policy choices, evaluating the different interests at stake. In other areas, in order to adopt its final decision, the administrative authority has simply to apply the law to a set of facts, without any possibility to make policy choices. This happens, for example, when the authority has to verify whether simple legal requirements are fulfilled before granting a license or a benefit. Finally, sometimes the agency has to apply an ambiguous statutory term to a set of facts. In doing so it has to interpret the statute, as a condition to enact its final decision (this is the area of so-called mixed questions of law and fact, involving *technical appraisals of complex facts*).

Judicial review has the fundamental goal to guarantee that administrative decisions are legally enacted. The scope of this control can be more or less intrusive, however, depending on the degree of power accorded to administrative authorities. In most western legal systems, courts show a certain degree of deference towards administrative authorities when reviewing discretionary decisions. Quite often, this orientation towards policy choices is referred to either by saying that review is limited to legality and does not cover the merits or expediency of the decision taken, or by establishing a distinction – as is the case in England – between review and appeal. This phenomenon depends on the assumed preferred allocation of decision-making powers between courts and agencies that may suggest that the politically accountable and expert administrative agencies are to be the preferred subjects to make policy choices.[3]

By contrast, when the administrative decision is simply the result of the application of law to fact, no discretionary power for the agency is recognised, and the court may perform a *de novo* review, substituting its own statutory interpretation for that of the administrative authority. As a result, the judge may quash the challenged decision based on an erred interpretation of law and will refer the decision back to the administrative agency.

---

1 Paragraphs 1, 2 and the conclusions were written by B. Marchetti; paragraphs 3 to 5 were written by R. Caranta.

2 The terms 'administrative authorities' and 'agencies' will be used here interchangeably, since the solutions to most of the issues discussed in this paper do not depend on an administrative authority also being an agency in the sense of independent from political oversight (see generally Caranta (2004) p. 93).

3 For an American view, see Pierce (1999) p.357: 'it is part of the standard litany of judicial review of agency action that a reviewing court cannot substitute its judgment for that of an agency, but must instead assume a much more limited role'. Recently see also Travi (2008).

Major problems occur, however, when the administrative decision depends on the application of ambiguous statutory terms to facts, because then it is not clear whether or not it is the agency that is the preferred subject to solve that statutory ambiguity and whether or not the courts can review these mixed legal and factual issues on the basis of a *de novo* (or substitutive) review.

This problem of who is best suited to resolve statutory ambiguity in mixed cases presents itself clearly in the judicial review of antitrust decisions: the antitrust agency has to apply certain undetermined statutory terms – such as abusive conduct, dominant position, unfair or deceptive trade practices – to a set of facts. Its decision is the outcome of a complex statutory interpretation effort. What is the scope of judicial review in these cases? Can courts substitute their own interpretation for that of the relevant administrative agency? Or do courts have to exercise some deference towards the statutory construction of the agency? The answer to these questions depends on the approach chosen with regard to the allocation of policymaking powers between courts and agencies, as well as on the consideration of who is the best equipped subject for these complex technical assessments.

The *Chevron* case,[4] which is the famous American leading case in the matter, answered the question of deference by giving preference to the agency construction to a judicial interpretation of statutes: 'policy arguments are more properly addressed to legislators or administrators, not judges. (...) The agencies considered the matter in a detailed and reasoned fashion and the decision involves reconciling conflicting policies'. As the U.S. Supreme Court reasoned: 'Judges are not experts in the field and are not part of either political branch of government. Courts must, in some cases, reconcile political interests but not on the basis of the judge's personal policy preferences. In contrast, an agency to which Congress has delegated policymaking responsibilities may, within the limit of that delegation, properly rely upon the incumbent administration's views of wise policy to inform its judgement.' Thus, if the agency's construction of the statute involves the 'wisdom' of the agency's policy, the court has a duty to respect legitimate policy choices, because the responsibility for these assessments is not a judicial one. The court only has the power to check whether the agency's statutory construction is permissible. It cannot verify whether the agency's construction is the right one, but only that it is one of several possible constructions of the statutory terms.

This approach, related to the specific constitutional context of the USA, is not irrelevant for the European legal tradition. Even though in the European legal tradition the power to interpret the law seems to be firmly in the judge's hands, the European Court of Justice seems to share the same approach as the Supreme

4 *Chevron U.S.A. v. Natural Resources Defense Council, Inc.*, 467 U.S. 837 (1984).

Court in reviewing mixed questions of law and fact.[5] In the *Upjohn* case,[6] for example, an English court asked the European Court of Justice whether community law requires national courts, when reviewing an administrative decision, to substitute their own technical assessments for those of the public authorities. The Court of Justice answered that a judicial review system in which the court exercises a certain degree of deference towards the complex technical statutory construction of the administrative agencies, without substituting its own assessment to the agency one, was compatible with Community law.

For a long time, the same deferential standard of review was applied by the Community courts in their review of Commission decisions in competition law.[7] In fact, the economic assessments of the Commission were met with a considerable degree of judicial deference. Specifically, 'provided the Commission decision contains adequate reasoning, is supported by probative evidence and is free from any obvious errors, the margin of appreciation enjoyed by the Commission means that the Court of First Instance will generally refrain from second guessing its conclusion'.[8] Similarly to the approach of the Supreme Court in *Chevron*, the European Court of Justice thus avoided addressing the Commission's assessment of complex economic matters; the more complex the assessment, the more likely it was that more than one plausible interpretation could be identified.

Nevertheless, in 2005, the Court of Justice is considered to have changed its direction. As has been noted, the *Tetra Laval* case seems to have showed a more incisive judicial review of the Commission's decision in the competition law area.[9] The starting point of the judgment of the Court was the consideration of the discretion accorded to the Commission by Regulation n. 4064/89 on the control of concentrations, especially with respect to assessments of an economic nature.[10] However, moving from this legal perspective and recognising the

5 In US experience, and specifically in *Chevron*, the EPA (Environmental Protection Agency) interpreted a statutory term (the term 'stationary source') and the Court recognised some deference to this statutory interpretation; on the contrary, in the European context it is the application of an ambiguous statutory term to a set of facts that is usually 'reserved' to the administrative agency.

6 Court of Justice, 21 January 1999, in causa C-120/97, annotated by R. Caranta, Tutela giurisdizionale effettiva delle situazioni soggettive di origine comunitaria ed incisività del sindacato del giudice nazionale (Kontrolldichte), *Riv. it. dir. pubbl. comun.*, 1999, 503.

7 See Bailey (2004) p.1328. In European case law see Case 42/84 *Remia and others* v. *European Commission* [1985] ECR 2545; Joined Cases C-142/84 and 156/84 *British American Tobacco, Company Ltd and RJ Reynolds Industries Inc.* v. *European Commission* [1987] ECR 4487.

8 Bailey (2004) pp. 1332-1333.

9 Case C-12/03P *Tetra Laval* [2005] ECR I-987.

10 Case C-12/03P *Tetra Laval* [2005] ECR I-987; p. 19. In the first instance judgment, the community judge held that the Commission committed manifest errors of assessment in its findings and therefore annulled the Commission's decision. The first instance tribunal decision was appealed by the European Commission. One of the grounds of appeal refers to the scope of power of judicial review: in particular, there was the complaint that the judge whilst «claiming to apply the test of manifest error of assessment, in fact applied a different test requiring the production of 'convincing evidence'.

correlated limitation on judicial review, the Court held that this 'does not mean that the Community Courts must refrain from reviewing the Commission's interpretation of information of economic nature'. The European judges have thus not only to 'establish whether the evidence relied on is factually accurate, reliable and consistent but also whether the evidence contains all the information which must be taken into account in order to assess a complex situation and whether it is capable of substantiating the conclusions drawn from it'.[11]

Looking at the *Tetra Laval* judgment, it has been said that the Court of Justice, in so doing, moved towards a more intrusive and substantial review of the economic assessments made by the Commission. Moreover, this judgment is said to raise the problem of the allocation of the decision-making authority in the European Community as regards competition regulation.[12] With the Italian perspective in mind (see section 3 below), we would like to add that some reflections are certainly needed on the adequate tools for the investigation of evidence that the Community courts need to perform this kind of a more intense review. We can imagine, for example, that the Court will be asking frequently for experts' reports (see article 70 of the Procedural rules of Court of First Instance), because it seems clear that no court can substitute its own decision for that of the agency if it cannot have appropriate expert support.

## 2 The Italian experience: the 'technical discretion' and the idea of a marginal judicial review

Decisions taken by Italian administrative authorities may be subjected to legality review. Legality review is distinguished from merits review. Normally, courts must confine themselves to legality review. Merits are a no go area for courts. Decisions may be challenged for their merits before an authority which is hierarchically superior to the one having taken the decision.

Since the close of the 19th century, the grounds for legality review have been incompetence, breach of legal rules and *eccesso di potere*. The former two relate to cases where the administrative authorities are not vested with discretionary powers. What is at stake is the interpretation of legal rules and/or the application of these rules to simple facts.

Very close to the French notion of *détournement de pouvoir, eccesso di potere* was originally referred to by Italian courts in order to strike down decisions that on their face value were taken to pursue goals falling outside the scope of the enabling legislation. Starting with the beginning of the 20th century, *eccesso di*

In the Commission's view, in doing so, the judge infringed article 230 of the Treaty that prescribes the judicial restraint in reviewing discretionary decisions of the Commission with regard to complex factual and economic matters. On the Court's decision Pieters (2005) p. 155; Völcker (2005). On this point, see also Geradin (2006).

11 Case C-12/03P *Tetra Laval* [2005] ECR I-987, par. 39.

12 Völcker (2005).

*potere* has developed to cover different situations that the courts considered to be symptoms of misuse of power, such as insufficient or inconsistent reasoning and the different treatment of similar situations. Recently, *eccesso di potere* has become associated (if not confused) with an illogical or manifestly unreasonable decision. These developments hardly contribute to make it easier to distinguish between legality questions that are reviewable by courts, and questions of merits, which generally are not. To this date, Italian courts have yet to structure their review on rigid (but predictable) lines as in the case of proportionality review performed by German courts.

*Eccesso di potere* allowed courts a (marginal) review of discretionary decisions. Right before WWII two competing theories of discretion were advanced in Italy. According to Mortati's broad view, discretion was the room for choice left by the law to the decision-maker by using open-ended and/or ambiguous legal and/or factual words and phrases (discretion in the broad sense).[13] In Giannini's stricter reading, discretion was the power to choose between conflicting interests (proper discretion).[14]

While Giannini's view soon became prevalent in scholarly circles, courts continued following Mortati's much more generic approach. The practical difference did not concern discretion properly. Policy choices introduced by vague and imprecise legal terms such as public order or general interest were considered to be discretionary choices under both theories. The practical difference concerned the application of open-ended and/or ambiguous legal and especially factual words and phrases, such as those referring to complex facts.[15] In the Italian legal system, it has traditionally been recognised that the existence of a certain degree of statutory ambiguity may imply an authority's 'technical discretion'.[16]

For a long time the inclusion of cases involving problematic statutory constructions in the 'discretion area' has had the effect to equalise discretionary decisions involving policy choices with decisions involving technical evaluations, even though the two ambits of deference have to be considered to be quite distinct.[17]

Mortati's view allowed courts to go on talking of *discretionalità tecnica* submitting the administrative authority's technical findings and assessments to marginal review under *eccesso di potere*. In other words, simple facts only were subjected to a full review. The reticence of courts to look more thoroughly into complex factual assessments could also be explained with reference to proce-

13 A seminal work was Mortati (1939) p. 76 ff.; Mortati's works have been analysed by G. Azzariti (1989) p. 347 ff.

14 The defining work was Giannini (1939); Giannini's theory has been analysed by Scoca (2000) p. 1045 ff.

15 See further Caranta (2008) p. 191 f.

16 For an historical frame of the traditional Italian reconstruction of the administrative technical evaluation activity see De Pretis (1995); Idem, Cassese (2006) p. 6176.

17 Specifically on this point R. Caranta (1999), Il sindacato giurisdizionale sugli atti dell'Autorità garante del mercato e della concorrenza, cit., 250-251; Protto (2001) p. 866.

dural issues. Administrative courts could not (until recently) have recourse to expert advice. Therefore, if the administrative authorities claimed, just to give two instances, that a building deserved to be listed or that a person was or was not fir for service in the army, courts had no tool to disprove it.

In the past 10 years or so, courts have started to apply more precisely the distinction between 'technical appraisals' and other kind of administrative evaluation activities, especially in the judicial review of decisions of independent agencies.[18] This means that, on the one hand, if an undetermined statutory term requires the application of technical and professional expertise by the agency, the need for proper 'technical appraisals or assessments' arise. On the other hand, the undetermined statutory term can simply empower the administrative authorities to make policy choice decisions, without implying the application of specialist expertise. This is the case, for example, when the statute talks about 'good conduct' or 'public security reasons' or 'dangerous conduct': the agency statutory construction does not require the application of specialist technical expertise, and courts will normally defer to the choice made by the decision-maker.

Considering the sphere of 'technical appraisals' in more detail, it then becomes possible to discern differing standards of judicial review. Particularly, if the statutory language provides for technical factual analysis and the administrative agency has specific institutional expertise in the matter, a weak judicial review (based on grounds of legality) could be justified. By contrast, if the administrative authority does not have specific expertise and the statute provides for complex assessments of technical nature, a *de novo* (strong) review will generally be accorded. Therefore, the court could be entitled to substitute its own construction to that of the administration.

The case law is still in flux and scholarly opinions are nothing but divergent. The terminology itself is not really consistent and the variance is further proof of the uncertainty in the law on the proper boundaries of judicial review.

The reconsideration of the boundaries of the 'technical discretion area' involving the possibility, failing a specific expertise of the administrative agency, of a *de novo* review by the judge on administrative technical assessments, could have been very difficult without strengthening the courts power to seek evidence.

In the past, one of the reasons for a limited judicial review of technical discretionary decisions seems to have been the impossibility for the court to have access to the disputed facts. In the Italians system it has never been clear if the idea of a reserved area of administrative discretion in technical assessments was the consequence of a determined allocation of decision-making power (between courts and administrative agencies, as mentioned in paragraph 1, above) or simply the effect of a limitation of the judicial investigative powers as to the facts of the dispute.[19]

---

[18] See Consiglio di Stato, IV, n. 601/1999; Consiglio di Stato IV, n. 5287/2001.

[19] Travi (2008).

Before 2000, courts could only gain access to evidence either through the file records of the court case, or through inspections by and clarifications from the administrative authority, usually the same as the one having taken the decision,[20] without there being any possibility to ask for an expert's technical report. These limitations made a substantial review on complex technical facts extremely difficult, so that the judge was *de facto* only able to marginally review administrative decisions.

In 2000, the Italian Parliament enacted a statute to introduce a general reform of judicial review procedures.[21] One of the important statutory amendments granted the administrative court the possibility to ask an expert's advice. This has been a strong innovation in the field of judicial review of technical appraisals of administrative authorities, because the courts gained an incremented degree of expertise in reviewing the administrative decision founded on technical assessments.

## 3 The Antitrust Authority and the Administrative Courts

The *Autorità garante per la concorrenza e il mercato* (hereafter: the Antitrust Authority) was set up as an independent authority whose members are named by the chairs of the two Houses of Parliament.[22] It must be pointed out that the Italian antitrust law is not based on an adversarial model according to which the opposite views of the Antitrust Authority and the concerned firms are confronted before and adjudicated upon by courts. Quite the contrary, like the European Commission, in the administrative phase of the proceedings the Antitrust Authority acts both as prosecutor and court. Affected parties may then seek judicial review of the decision taken by the Antitrust Authority, challenging the decision before administrative courts.[23] Seen from another point of view, once the Antitrust Authority has taken its decision, it is up to the affected parties to show that it is vitiated in some aspects, and therefore illegal.

The Italian system of judicial review of administrative actions, including those of the Antitrust Authority, is somewhat complex. According to the relevant

---

20 The Italian rules on evidence in administrative cases were discussed by Advocate General Darmon in Case C-236/92, *Comitato di Coordinamento per la Difesa della Cava*, ECR [1994] I-483.

21 L. 21 luglio 2000, n. 205.

22 By L. 10 October 1990, n. 287; the Competition Law Act.

23 This point is stressed by Cons. St., Sez. VI, 8 febbraio 2008, n. 594, *Shell Italia*, n.y.r., point 3, *'I provvedimenti dell'Autorità sono impugnabili davanti al giudice amministrativo, il quale, a differenza del giudice penale o di quanto avviene in sistemi antitrust adottati da altri Stati, non deve assumere una decisione, verificando le tesi dell'accusa e della difesa, ma deve verificare la correttezza della decisione assunta dall'Autorità'* (In contrast with what is the case with criminal courts and with antitrust cases in other jurisdictions, administrative courts are not to adjucate between the conflicting submissions of the Antitrust Authority and the concerned parties; they are to check whether the decision taken by the *Autorità* was the right one).

provision of the administrative justice act of 1865,[24] which is still the rule of general application even if challenged by a growing number of exceptions, civil courts are competent when civil and political rights are at stake. Administrative courts, on the contrary, are competent with reference to *interessi legittimi*. The distinction between (subjective) rights (*diritti soggettivi*) and *interessi legittimi* is somewhat like the English dichotomy distinguishing private and public law rights. To make a matter simple which has been a subject of hot dispute for well over a century, a few broad rules may be given. First, the person asking for a decision from an authority has no right, just an *interesse legittimo*. For instance, those asking for a licence to open a shop, for a building permission, a school grant or any other benefit, or submitting a bid to a public procurement procedure, are all said to be entitled to an *interesse legittimo*. Since most economic activities in Italy are (or at least till fairly recently were) made conditional upon the granting of a licence or permission, *interessi legittimi* are widespread. Second, when discretionary powers are vested in an administrative authority, only *interessi legittimi* are said to be present. This is even so when a subjective right (*diritto soggettivo*) would have been present if the case were analysed under civil law. For instance, the landowner is said to have no more than an *interesse legittimo* when confronted with an administrative decision in an expropriation procedure; this is the case quite independently from the question whether the decision is legal or not.[25] Under civil law, however, the landowner would have a subjective right (*diritto soggetivo*).

In some areas, the administrative courts have exclusive jurisdiction (*giurisdizione esclusiva*), meaning that they are competent to adjudicate both on subjective rights (*diritti soggettivi*) ánd *interessi legittimi*, and in those areas civil courts have no jurisdiction. Even when arrangements are more complex than this, civil courts may still be competent in some cases.

One of such areas of law concerns jurisdiction over antitrust cases. Under the Competition law act, the Administrative court of Lazio (the *Tribunale amministrativo regionale per il Lazio*) at first instance and the Council of State (the *Consiglio di Stato*) on appeal, have exclusive jurisdiction to hear cases brought against the decisions taken by the Antitrust Authority.[26] The legislative preference for the jurisdiction of administrative courts in cases challenging decisions taken by the Antitrust Authority is justified by the idea that they are the most competent to address and review the administrative action and decisions. However, the same provision gives civil courts jurisdiction over antitrust litigation between private parties.

Moreover, administrative courts have jurisdiction on the merits (*giurisdizione di merito*) concerning the fines inflicted by the Antitrust Authority, meaning that the courts may not just quash the fine but can substitute their own findings

---

24 That is: art. 2 of l. 20 March 1865, n. 2248, All. E

25 This last judge-made rule has been subject to strong academic criticism but still stands: Cannada Bartoli (1958) p. 670; Cannada Bartoli (1972) p. 13; Angeletti (1980).

26 Art. 33 of L. 10 ottobre 1990, n. 287.

on the amount of the fine for that of the Authority.[27] This is a special power that is seldom conferred upon *administrative* courts but entirely consistent with the power enjoyed by *civil* courts over other fining decisions taken by administrative authorities. As we have seen in section 2, Italian courts are generally expected to review the legality of administrative decisions but to steer clear from the merits (*merito*), meaning they cannot substitute their view for that endorsed by the administrative decision-maker. A wide and generic concept of discretion tends to extend the realm of what is said to be the merits of the case.

Finally, the *Corte di cassazione* is charged to police the court system, including administrative courts, to make sure no court oversteps the bounds of its jurisdictional power. In antitrust cases, this means that it is up to the *Corte di cassazione* to check that the administrative courts, when performing their review on aspects other than the amount of the fines imposed, do not go into the merits of the administrative decision taken.[28]

## 4 General remarks on the case law on the margins of review on antitrust decisions

It is worth noting that several antitrust cases reached the Council of State (*Consiglio di Stato*) more or less at the same time that the debate on the review of technically complex decisions was kicking off.[29] Indeed, antitrust cases have often been instrumental in shaping the more general evolution of the rules of judicial review and have in turn been influenced by the changes in the legislative framework portended by the new Judicial Review act of 2000.[30] However, as always, the theorisation of the problems involved in judicial review should be distinguished from the actual review performed. Prudence suggests not taking for granted that the deeds of the courts follow their words. In this sec-

---

27 See Art. 31 of the Competition Law Act.

28 Other jurisdictional errors are not covered; e.g., a decision by the *Consiglio di Stato* cannot be challenged in front of the *Corte di cassazione* by simply maintaining that the reasons given for the decision are wanting: Cass., Sez. un., 28 February 2007, n. 4630, *Foro It.*, 2007, I, 1428; Cass., Sez. un, 29 April 2005, n. 8882, *Giur. It.*, 2005, 2186; *Foro amm. CDS*, 2005, 2468, note by M. Antonioli, Legge antitrust, giurisdizione esclusiva e sanzioni amministrative al vaglio delle sezioni unite.

29 The first decision by the *Consiglio di Stato* in this matter, albeit not focusing on the limits of judicial review, was Cons. di Stato, Sez. VI, 30 dicembre 1996, n. 1792, *Giur. It.* 1997, III, 1, 604, note R. Caranta, Il Consiglio di Stato, la concorrenza ed i principi del diritto comunitario di cui alla legge antitrust; Foro It. 1997, III, 215; notes R. Pardolesi and D. Liantonio, Accordi, addio! Antitrust e giustizia amministrativa; *Resp. civ. prev.* 1997, 755, note P. Magnani, Il cartello assicurativo in una decisione del Consiglio di Stato; *Gazzetta Giur.* Giuffré / *Italia Oggi* 1997, n. 7, 3, notes G. Libertini, *Pratiche concordate e accordi nella disciplina della concorrenza*, and C.G. Corvese, *'Accordi' tra imprese di assicurazione e applicabilità dell'art. 2 comma 2 della legge antitrust italiana: l'interpretazione del Consiglio di Stato.*

30 Law 205/2000.

tion several of the cases, relevant to the purpose of discussing judicial review in antitrust cases, will be held up for closer scrutiny.

## 4.1 The insurance cartel: no intense review

A first relevant case concerned an insurance cartel which had been sanctioned by the Antitrust Authority. In its judgment the *Consiglio di Stato* developed a complex doctrine of judicial review. It distinguished between 'simple facts' and *'valutazioni tecniche opinabili'*. The latter facts, involving technical appraisals of complex facts, are quite similar to complex legal and factual assessments, the emphasis of the Court being on the idea that the outcome of these assessments can never be beyond all doubt or above discussion. This distinction is linked to a difference in the intensity of the scrutiny by the courts. According to the judgment, where simple facts are concerned, the court may, after having recourse to expert witnesses if necessary, check whether the appraisal of the Antitrust Authority was the right one. If not, the court will strike down the decision. By contrast, however, concerning *'valutazioni tecniche opinabili'*, review of the court is limited, peripheral, soft or weak (or: *'debole'*); courts are not allowed to substitute their views for those of the decision-maker and must confine themselves to strike down unreasonable, illogical or inconsistent decisions. In passing the *Consiglio di Stato* also remarks that most decisions based on economic reasoning are open to doubt. In such cases, judicial review is shaped according to the traditional way the review is fashioned on the ground of *'eccesso di potere'* (*ultra vires*, or *détournement de pouvoir*). Therefore the Council of State allowed itself a 'harder' look (a more intense review) only in relation to the amount of the fines imposed on the firms involved.[31] The *Consiglio di Stato* upheld its stance by referring to the case law by the Community courts, which was said to run along the same lines.[32]

On this theoretical basis of discerning between simple facts and 'technically complex facts' and by linking this distinction to a more or less intense scrutiny, the *Consiglio di Stato* ruled out the need to have recourse to expert advice to rebut the submission of the insurance firms, and found that most of the decision by the Antitrust authority was well grounded in the findings made during the proceedings. However, the Council of State did quash parts of the decision concerning some of the supposed participants in the agreement restricting

---

[31] Cons. St., Sez. VI, 23 aprile 2002, n. 2199, RCAuto, in *Giornale di diritto amministrativo* 2003, 358, note A. Lalli, *Il sindacato giurisdizionale sui provvedimenti dell'Autorità garante della concorrenza e del mercato*; see also Cons. St., Sez. VI, 1° ottobre 2002, n. 5156, *Enel/Infostrada*, in *Urbanistica e appalti*, 2003, 448, notes F. Agnina and M. Di Cagno, *Discrezionalità tecnica e sindacato giurisdizionale: scelta la strada della coerenza, another decision concerning a merger*; in this case, however, the Antitrust Authority had red-lighted the merger, claiming it led to create a dominant position on the market for fixed-line telecommunications.

[32] See also Cons. St., Sez. VI, 1° ottobre 2002, n. 5156, cit., end of point 8.

competition, because the investigation had not been thorough enough as to their actual involvement.[33]

The judgment was challenged by some insurance firms, complaining that the *Consiglio di Stato* had not gone far enough in probing the Antitrust Authority's decision, and specifically in not having recourse to expert advice. However, the judgment was mostly upheld by the *Corte di cassazione*.[34] The highest court of Italy held that the administrative court had been right in allowing itself to review simple facts and considering the merits of the fines imposed by the Antitrust Authority, lowering their amount. As to the question, central here, of which kind of review is appropriate for '*valutazioni tecniche opinabili*', the *Corte di cassazione* was happy to say that the choice for a specific standard of review falls outside of the area of errors of jurisdiction which are challengeable in front of the highest court. Therefore it left undisturbed the choice by the *Consiglio di Stato*.[35]

The reading of the Community case law by the *Consiglio di Stato*, while commended by some, also met with criticism that pointed out that the judgment had picked up some general remarks found in ECJ case law rather than to follow the Community law in action.

### 4.2 The *CONSIP* case: a more intense review

The highest administrative court changed its doctrinal reasoning somewhat in later cases. One of these later cases concerned an agreement restricting competition between a number of service providers which had colluded in the presentation of the bids to a public procurement for meal vouchers to be handed to public servants. The procurement was passed by CONSIP s.p.a., the central procuring agency, and the firms had co-ordinated their bids for different lots. They were fined by the Antitrust Authority and brought judicial review proceedings against that decision. One of the questions that rose in court was whether the Antitrust Authority was right in its delimitation of the relevant market. On appeal the *Consiglio di Stato* felt it necessary to expand on the bounds of judicial review.[36] First of all, the *Consiglio di Stato* stopped short of talking of 'technical discration' (*discrezionalità tecnica*); the Antitrust authority was said to operate in an environment of what the French would call *compétence liée*, even if complex assessments are involved. In this framework, courts may

33 See point 6.3.

34 Cass., Sez. un, 29 aprile 2005, n. 8882, *Giur. It.*, 2005, 2186; *Foro amm. CDS*, 2005, 2468, note by M. Antonioli, *Legge antitrust, giurisdizione esclusiva e sanzioni amministrative al vaglio delle sezioni unite*.

35 See points 5.1. and 7 of the decision; the focal point of this judgment has somehow eluded some commentators, who pretend that the *Corte di cassazione* endorsed the decision taken by the *Consiglio di Stato* as to the boundaries to its powers: e.g. M. Antonioli, *Legge antitrust, giurisdizione esclusiva e sanzioni amministrative al vaglio delle sezioni unite*, cit., 2485.

36 Cons. St., Sez. VI, 2 marzo 2004, n. 926, *Buoni pasto*, *Urbanistica e appalti*, 2004, 817, note by S. Mirate, *Autorità antitrust e controllo giurisdizionale sulle valutazioni tecniche*.

check and re-evaluate the economic analysis performed by the Antitrust Authority, to see whether the ambiguous statutory concepts (*concetti giuridici indeterminati*) have been correctly interpreted and applied in the case under review.[37] The *Consiglio di Stato* then avowed that to speak of *controllo debole* (weak or soft review) was somewhat misleading, and should be avoided. Anyway, according to the judgment, a clarification is needed, the real point being that, after having fully reviewed the facts on which the decision is based and the assessments (*valutazioni*) made by the decision-maker, the courts must take a step back. They should not substitute their decision for the one taken by the Antitrust Authority if they find the assessments were correct, reasonable, proportionate and reliable (*'corrette, ragionevoli, proporzionate ed attendibili'*).[38]

A certain detachment from theoretical discussions as to the proper boundaries of judicial review is apparent from the continuation of the reasoning by the *Consiglio di Stato*, which maintains that what is important are not the words but the way in which the review is actually performed.[39] Again, the case law of the Community courts is used as the necessary yardstick for judicial review of antitrust decisions at national level. According to the Council of State this is even more relevant after the entry into force of Regulation 2003/1/EC on the implementation of the rules on competition laid down in Articles 81 and 82 of the Treaty. The *Consiglio di Stato* then recalls that European courts are ready to verify whether the rules on procedure and on the statement of reasons have been complied with, whether the facts have been accurately stated and whether there has been any manifest error of appraisal or misuse of powers.[40] The highest administrative court of Italy is ready to concede that Community courts have at times given a very probing look at the Commission's antitrust decisions, but it maintains that the judicial review as performed by Italian courts is no less stringent.[41]

Finally, concerning the possible recourse to expert advice, the *Consiglio di Stato* remarks that conflicting expert evidence provided by the parties is usually enough to highlight the weak points in the assessment made by antitrust authorities. In any case, even Community courts, while being in principle favourable to having recourse to expert advice, in practice very seldom make use of this prerogative.[42]

In the end, the *Consiglio di Stato*, without feeling the need to have recourse to expert advice, upheld most of the findings by the Antitrust Authority, but

---

37 See point 3.3.

38 Again point 3.3.

39 Again point 3.3.

40 Again point 3.3.; the ECJ decisions quoted are Case 42/84, *Remia*, point 34; joined cases 142/84 and 156/84, *BAT and Reynolds*, point 62; Case C-7/95, *John Deere*, point 34; joined cases C-204/00 and C-219/00, *Aalborg*, point 279 and Case T-231/99, *Joynson*.

41 Again point 3.3; Cons. St., Sez. VI, 1° ottobre 2002, n. 5156, *Enel/Infostrada*, is quoted here.

42 Case C-89/85, *Woodpulp*, is quoted here (point 3.3).

lowered the fines imposed on the firms responsible for the breaches of competition law.[43]

The change in the approach is remarkable. Indeed, the *Consiglio di Stato* allowed itself what it had always denied, the possibility to give a hard look at (to intensely review) the specific application of an ambiguous statutory concept (*concetto giuridico indeterminate*). This means that the self-restraint practised by the court does no longer refer to the review of the decision, but only to the possibility to take a decision in the place of the Antitrust Authority.[44]

### 4.3 The *Codacons* case: consolidation of change

This new approach of a more intense review was followed by a case concerning misleading advertising, another matter falling under the jurisdiction of the Antitrust Authority. CODACONS – a well-known consumer protection group – challenged a decision by the Antitrust Authority to the effect that a commercial ad in a newspaper advertising a fast speeding car was not misleading for the consumers. This time, in its judgment the *Consiglio di Stato* overruled the Antitrust Authority and stated that it was wrong to hold that the advertisement was not misleading for consumers.[45] In this case the highest administrative court did not content itself with checking whether the reasons given by the authority were reasonable enough. It rather performed a *de novo* review, substituting its view to those expounded by the Antitrust Authority.

Therefore, from the above mentioned case law it would seem that there has been a change in the deference paid by the Italian administrative courts to decisions of the Antitrust Authority. Instead of a relaxed approach, a more intensive review, even if matters of technically complex appraisals and ambiguous statutory terms are involved, areas which historically have been part of only legality review (see paragraph 2), is now undertaken by the *Consiglio di Stato*. However, as the following paragraph will show, the court is not entirely consistent in its approach.

## 5 The law as it stands: the ambiguity of the jet fuel cases

Doubts as to the consistency displayed by administrative courts in dealing with the review of decisions taken by the Antitrust Authority are justified. Reading the case law, the impression is that 'old language' pops up here and there and maybe the new language does not make a difference in the practice of the courts anyway. In light of the central question of the contributions in this book it must also be mentioned that, even though the *Consiglio di Stato*

43 Case C-89/85, *Woodpulp*, is quoted here (point 6). Mirate (2004).

44 See Mirate (2004) p. 822.

45 Cons. St., Sez. VI, 7 aprile 2005, n. 280, in *Foro amm. CDS*, 2005, 886, note by M. Antonioli, *L'Autorità garante della concorrenza e del mercato e i terzi: appunti in tema di legittimazione a ricorrere.*

often refers to case law of the European Court of Justice, it is a remarkable fact that the *Tetra Laval* litigation and the stir it has caused in the doctrinal debate, has not yet been mentioned even once in Italian case law.[46]

A more definitive answer as to the question of the depth of judicial review of the decisions taken by the Antitrust Authority would imply an extensive analysis of all the judgements handed down in this area. Judgements should be indexed to check both the 'doctrinal' statements issued and the actual review performed. With reference to the latter, an admittedly more complex assessment, a number of issues should be considered. Among them are: 1) whether the decision challenged is either an authorisation given or refused, or taken as following an investigation into anticompetitive behaviour; 2) whether the decision challenged also imposed a fine and therefore falls under a review of the merits (*giurisdizione di merito*); 3) what each of the issues risen in court were about or, in other words, which enabling legal clauses (the words and phrases in the legislation) were discussed. In this context, more specifically, it is necessary to analyse: 3a) what the legal clauses are which are held to vest the Antitrust Authority with the power to take a decision involving technically complex assessments (*decisione tecnica opinabile*) and what clauses contain statutory ambiguous concepts (*concetto giuridico indeterminate*) and whether the two categories are interchangeable; and 3b) whether the categories of decisions involving technically complex assessments (*decisione tecnica opinabile*) and statutory ambiguous concepts (*concetto giuridico indeterminate*) are consistently applied, also taking into account the different category of 'simple facts'. Furthermore, such a study should include: 4) what kind of review was performed, taking into account a number of variants such as: 4a) whether the burden of proof as to the legality of the decision about each relevant issue was placed on the defending authority or upon the applicant; 4b) against what grounds the reasoning by the Antitrust Authority was checked (including overall consistency; rebuttal of adverse arguments risen during the proceedings; procedural fairness; economic considerations referred to, etc.); 4c) whether reasonableness and/or proportionality principles were applied; and lastly, 4d) whether recourse to an expert opinion had actually been provided and, if so, to what extent, if any, the judgment relied on the expert's opinion.

This task is quite complex and time consuming. A meaningful – even if not entirely satisfactory – shortcut is to consider the handful of decisions taken by the Italian highest administrative court in the recent jet fuel litigation.

The jet fuel litigation cases issued from the situation existing in relation to the provision of airplane fuel in Italian airports. Fuel was provided by several oil

---

46 A repeated search for "Tetra Laval" on the website www.giustizia-amministrativa.it, the official website of administrative courts reporting all the decisions they have taken, brought no query (even if it must be admitted that the effectiveness of the search engine of this site has ample margins for improvement and its reliability is not absolute).

companies[47] through a number of companies they jointly held.[48] Furthermore, concerning the Rome airports, fuel was provided through essential facilities (including storage tanks and pipelines) owned by a company which was jointly owned by some of the same oil companies.[49] Following the complaint of a competitor, Tamoil, which claimed to have been denied access to the market, the Antitrust Authority started a thorough investigation, confiscating a number of documents and consequently finding out that the jointly held companies had allowed the oil companies to exchange information and factually co-ordinate their business and pricing policies while at the same time excluding potential new entrants from the market. At the conclusion of its investigation, the Authority took a decision ordering 1) the oil companies involved to disband the jointly owned companies (a structural measure), 2) all the oil companies involved to stop sharing information (a behavioural measure) and 3) to pay hefty fines.

Unsurprisingly, all the companies involved sought judicial review. They challenged the decision separately, which is hardly surprising since most of the companies maintained that they had had either a minor role or no role at all in the overall scheme. However, most of the arguments put forward by the companies were very similar (although since fines were imposed on the oil companies only, they were not discussed in the cases brought by the other companies). The issues involved in the litigation included the following: *a*) the proper delimitation of the relevant market; *b*) the proof of the agreement restricting competition, *c*) the effects of the agreement on the market; *d*) the appropriateness of the measures ordered by the Antitrust Authority, including the severeness of the sanctions levied. Reasoning along German lines, we could say that the first issues (*a* through *c*) refer to *Tatbestand* and the latter (*d*) to *Rechtsfolge*. It can also be said that the issues *a*) the relevant market, and *c*) the effects of the agreement on the market, clearly involve either ambiguous statutorial concepts (*concetti giuridici indeterminate)* and/or technical appraisals (*valutazioni tecniche opinabili),* for which the question of deference arises, whereas the issues *b*) proof of the agreement, and *d*) appropriateness of the ordered measures, mainly focus on more traditional legal issues to be solved according to familiar legal concepts such as legitimate expectation, proportionality and, culpability.

The first instance court struck down the decision to order the disbandment of the jointly held companies, because it was held to be disproportionate to the end of stopping the restriction of competition, and upheld the rest of the measures taken by the Antitrust Authority.[50] Subsequently, the companies involved, including the complainant Tamoil, and the Antitrust Authority all lodged appeals and cross-appeals to the *Consiglio di Stato.*

47 Eni s.p.a., Esso Italiana s.p.a., Kuwait Petroleum Italia s.p.a., Shell Italia s.p.a., Shell Italia Aviazione s.r.l., Tamoil Italia s.p.a. and Total Italia s.p.a.

48 Hub s.r.l., Par s.r.l., RAM s.r.l., Rai s.r.l. e Disma s.p.a.

49 Seram s.p.a.

50 T.A.R. Lazio, Roma, Sez. , 27 febbraio 2007,

What makes this litigation particularly interesting is that the appeals were heard by panels (consisting of five *Consiglieri,* including the President) having a slightly different composition, and that the drafting of the judgements was entrusted to different *Consiglieri* (judges with the *Consiglio di Stato*). The *Consiglieri* were all present at the same hearing, so a certain consistency between the judgements is assured. Indeed, all the appeals and cross-appeals were rejected. But the vocabulary and the reasoning in the different judgements show remarkable variances; this is so even though some of the *Consiglieri* seem to have borrowed relevant sections of the reasoning of the judgements from each other. A further look at the different judgements is instructive for the issue of legal review of antitrust decisions, because it is (amongst others) in this area where the judgements show remarkable differences.

For example, the reasoning in the judgements penned by Consigliere De Michele start with the characterisation of the Antitrust Authority as an independent administrative authority with high technical expertise. Judicial review of its decisions is possible but, due to the presence of wide margins of technical discretion (*discrezionalità tecnica*), it is confined to legality review along the traditional lines of *eccesso di potere* (*ultra vires* or *détournement de pouvoir*), insufficient and inconsistent reasoning foremost amongst the grounds for review. Any incursion into the merits of the decision – including the way the special technical knowledge of the Antitrust Authority is translated in specific measures – is to be excluded. The courts may review the correct application of special technical knowledge to a given set of facts only in so far as they are capable of objective assessment. Only the interpretation given by the Antitrust Authority to legal clauses referring to ambiguous legal concepts (*concetti giuridici indeterminati*) may be fully reviewed by the courts.[51]

The traditional approach could hardly be more piously followed. Moreover, it must be remarked that concerning the legal clauses containing technical or ill-defined/ambiguous terms referred to in the judgment – such as for instance 'relevant market' or 'dominant power' – the interpretation of the rule is not easily distinguishable from its application. The approach adopted in this judgment therefore barely masks a very limited or restrained review. Accordingly, the reasoning of the judgment is terse, also when compared to the other judgements in the jet fuel litigation, handed down on the same day and concerning the same litigation. Indeed, in this judgment the *Consiglio di Stato* mainly remarks that the overall reasons given by the Antitrust Authority are globally persuasive, at the same time refusing to be tricked too much into a detailed assessment of the specific findings referred to and of arguments concerning the challenged measures of the Authority, which are held to fall within the boundaries of unreviewable discretion.

---

[51] Cons. St., Sez. VI, 8 febbraio 2008, n. 421, *SERAM*, at the beginning of the *'Diritto'* section; the same section is repeated word for word in Cons. St., Sez. VI, 8 febbraio 2008, n. 423, *HUB*, penned again by Cons. De Michele.

The appeal lodged by the Authority itself is similarly disposed of, by holding that dismantling the jointly owned companies was indeed not the only option available to avoid future restraint of competition, less invasive measures being possible and indeed having been taken.

For his part, *Consigliere* Buonvino is not inclined to theorisation. Indeed, in the judgment by his hand, he does not refer often to the usual terminology concerning discretion, technical assessments and so on. The reasoning in this judgment centres on the possible evidence of the agreements restricting competition and the burden of proof. He remarks that it is usually impossible to find the smoking gun pointing at the conclusion of an agreement restricting competition. In this vein, he finds that all that is needed in judicial review proceedings is to see whether or not the Antitrust Authority was capable of offering a logical and coherent reconstruction of the relevant facts, as demonstrated by the evidence collected. This, he finds, was the case since the oil companies failed to offer convincing elements to the contrary (such as a possible alternative reading of the evidence by the Authority, capable of explaining what happened as a perfectly legal commercial practice rather than an unlawful restriction of competition).[52]

In contrast, a much deeper theorisation is to be found in the judgment penned by *Consigliere* Bellomo. Referring to the precedent in the *Consip* case (see paragraph 5 above), he maintains that the measures taken by the Antitrust Authority are the object of a very probing analysis (*'penetrante scrutinio'*). This means that the courts may reconsider the technical choices and impose their reading of *'concetti giuridici indeterminati'*; there is no reason to distinguish between soft review (*'sindacato debole'*) and intensive review (*'sindacato forte'*).[53] The only limit to the courts' power is the impossibility to substitute their decision for the one taken by the competent administrative authorities. What then becomes relevant is the measure in which the enabling legal clause refers to non-legal technical rules. The more the application of these rules is uncertain and/or leads to uncertain and debatable results, the less the court may go in second-guessing the application of the rules by the Antitrust Authority. In this case, the decision taken by the authority may be left standing since it is based on a perfectly possible reading of uncertain non-legal rules.[54]

On this basis, the judgment does not contend itself with assessing the global rationality of the antitrust measures. It assesses the consistency of every step in the reasoning, only stopping short of allowing an adversarial confrontation of the opposite thesis by the authority and the companies involved. Lastly, the proportionality issue affecting the structural measure is in turn analysed in depth, along a three steps analysis of proportionality. In the end the measure is found wanting under the adequacy (a rather strict proportionality) step.

52 Cons. St., Sez. VI, 8 febbraio 2008, n. 422, *PAR*, point 7.

53 Cons. St., Sez. VI, 8 febbraio 2008, n. 424, *TAMOIL*, point 5.

54 Cons. St., Sez. VI, 8 febbraio 2008, n. 424, *TAMOIL* point 6.

On similar lines one can read two judgements written by *Consigliere* Chieppa,[55] a judge with the *Consiglio di Stato* who also writes extra-judicially, has considered aspects of judicial review of antitrust measures.[56] Referring to the *Consip* case (see paragraph 5 above), he maintains that the highest administrative court has been inclined to abandon the previous hands-off approach. In sharp contrast with the position expounded by *Consigliere* De Michele, *Consigliere* Chieppa maintains that the court may have recourse to the same technical knowledge – including economic analysis – as the Antitrust Authority. As a consequence, he claims that review is now intense, complete and effective (*'forte, pieno ed effettivo'*), the only limit, again, being the impossibility to take the decision in the place of the competent administrative authority.[57]

Accordingly, when considering whether the relevant market was properly delimited by the Antitrust Authority, *Consigliere* Chieppa analyses the structure of the market, points at the elements which must be considered and concludes that the Antitrust Authority was right in its assessment.[58] As to the proof of the agreement restricting competition, the starting point is again the difficulty in finding direct evidence (a smoking gun), such as a document laying down the contents of the agreement. The evidence is necessarily circumstantial, depending on facts from which a given picture – the agreement – may be inferred. Administrative courts, however, must make sure that each specific fact has been properly ascertained and taken into account. Accordingly, the judgment then goes into all the specific and relevant facts, including the huge exchange of information between the different companies involved (taking place mainly through the jointly owned companies), to the co-ordination of the selling policies, to attempt to exclude new entrants, to the high prices paid by Italian airlines when compared to other companies operating in Europe. Moreover, *Consigliere* Chieppa insists that the reconstruction of the overall picture from the different facts must be based on the principles of corroboration and cumulative redundancy;[59] in other words, the picture painted by the Antitrust Authority must be the only possible logical explanation of the facts ascertained or – at least – by far the more compelling one.[60] As to the fines imposed, *Consigliere* Chieppa upholds the decision taken, noting that they were fixed according to the Communication on fines of the Commission.[61] Moreover, there was even written evidence (in the form of e-mail exchanges) as to the knowledge by the perpetrators of the illegality of the behaviour of the different firms involved and

55 Cons. St., Sez. VI, 8 febbraio 2008, n. 594, *Shell Italia* and n. 597, *R.A.I.* and *R.A.M.*

56 Chieppa (2005) p. 103.

57 Cons. St., Sez. VI, 8 febbraio 2008, n. 594, *Shell Italia*, point 3.

58 Cons. St., Sez. VI, 8 febbraio 2008, n. 594, *Shell Italia*, point 5 *in fine*.

59 Cons. St., Sez. VI, 8 febbraio 2008, n. 594, *Shell Italia* and n. 597, *R.A.I.* and *R.A.M.*, points 4.

60 Cons. St., Sez. VI, 8 febbraio 2008, n. 594, *Shell Italia* and n. 597, *R.A.I.* and *R.A.M.*, points 4.

61 Communication of the EC Commission 98/C9/03.

the commitments the oil company was ready to offer were not very incisive when compared to the gravity of the breach of competition law at issue.[62]

Lastly, the judgment written by *Consigliere* Volpe with reference to two appeals brought by another oil company and another jointly held company, is quite similar – often word for word – to the judgment of *Consigliere* Chieppa.[63]

The reader cannot be but bewildered by such a multifarious take on what, in the end, was the same case. On the one hand, one could say that different philosophies did not beget different outcomes. But they very well could have in other cases. Indeed, as many of the *Consiglieri* remarked, in the jet fuel litigation there was hardly any doubt as to the main facts of the case, there was almost no issue of appraisals of a technical nature (*valutazioni tecniche opinabili*), and no need for expert advice, but of course this might not always be so. To add to the confusion, the *Corte di cassazione* recently seems to have come back to the idea of soft review ('*controllo debole*') as it was referred to in the older case law of the *Consiglio di Stato*.[64] Therefore, the picture is one of confusion as to what exactly is the standard of judicial review applied by the administrative courts in reviewing decisions by the Antitrust Authority.

## 6 Concluding remarks on antitrust decisions and the scope of judicial review in light of European developments

As we remarked above, antitrust decisions are frequently the result of the application of ambiguous statutory terms to a set of facts. The Antitrust Authority has to choose a determined statutory construction to be able to adopt the consistent decisions. Frequently it has to decide, in practical circumstances, whether there is an 'abusive conduct', a 'dominant position', an 'unfair or deceptive trade practice', or an 'incompatible concentration'. These are technically complex issues. We saw that the question arises as to whether it is possible to grant a *de novo* review in these cases or if it is more expedient to only allow a review in which the court does not substitute its own appraisal to the agency's one.[65] For the above-mentioned reasons (see paragraph 1), judicial review should not be substitutive if the administrative authority has an institutional and specialist expertise in the matter, because then the administrative agency can be considered to be the best-equipped subject in carrying out these technical appraisals, while the role of the court should properly be that of the guardian. However, in the absence of this subjective condition of the adminis-

62 Cons. St., Sez. VI, 8 febbraio 2008, n. 597, *R.A.I.* and *R.A.M.*, point 12.1.

63 Cons. St., Sez. VI, 8 febbraio 2008, n. 595, Esso Italiana, and n. 595, Disma.

64 Cass., Sez. un., 17 marzo 2008, n. 7063, *Menarini*, [not yet reported].

65 On the specific profile of the judicial review of independent administrative agencies see Lazzara (2001); Chieppa (2004) p. 1019; De Pretis (2004) p. 997; Merusi (2003) p. 175; Cintioli (2005); Mirate (2004) p. 817; Ramajoli (2006) p. 80.

trative agency, it could be more convenient to allocate to the judicial branch the interpretative function of statutory (ambiguous) terms.

Looking at the Italian legal system, the Antitrust Authority seems to be specifically created for the purpose of having recourse to a specialised administrative authority to implement competition law. It was one of the first administrative (independent) agencies institutionalised in the Italian system to assure specialist and technical expertise in the competition regulation. Moreover, in addition to the 'expertise element', the Antitrust Authority is also characterised by a particular constitutional position in the institutional framework. It is independent with respect to the executive power and its members are nominated in a particular way in order to assure impartial and neutral decisions.

Its independence constitutes another crucial element that traditionally could be used as an argument against a 'substitutive review' of its decisions by courts (even though its independence can lead to other tricky accountability problems). Consequently, the mentioned subjective (expert) status of the Antitrust Agency and the technical nature of its decisions may be considered by courts to be elements in favour of a non-substitutive judicial review.

But which is, more precisely, the scope of a legality review? Does it merely mean a formal review or is its 'weakness' compatible with a substantive control of the authority's decision-making? Which standards have to be guaranteed in the review of these technical administrative decisions, considering the need to protect both the private parties affected by agency action and the administrative agency autonomy? Taking the *Tetra Laval* case as an example, the starting point of both the judgment of the Court of First Instance and the Court of Justice is the existence of discretion for the European Commission with respect to assessments of an economic nature. Nevertheless, the Court of First Instance and the Court of Justice did not contend themselves with checking whether the Commission decision not to allow the merger (between *Tetra Laval* and *Sidel*) was based on 'cogent and consistent' evidence,[66] but asked the Commission to produce convincing evidence, so limiting the Commission's discretion in cases involving complex factual and economic matters.[67]

In particular, the Community judges looked into the Commission's technical analysis to verify whether the evidence provided contained all the information which must be taken into account in order to assess a complex situation, and whether it was capable of substantiating the conclusions drawn from it. The Community court found the Commission to have failed to show with convincing evidence its prospective analysis on the anticompetitive effects of

[66] This was the standard of proof established by the community courts in some judgements before *Tetra Laval*.

[67] Specifically, considering the prospective character of the economic analysis, the Court held that 'the quality of the evidence produced by the Commission in order to establish that it is necessary to adopt a decision declaring the concentration incompatible with the common market is particularly important, since that evidence must support the Commission's conclusion that if such a decision were not adopted, the economic development envisaged by it would be plausible' (Court of Justice Judgment, par. 44).

the merger and carried out its analysis through a 'hard look' at the evidentiary record performed by the European Commission. Even though this revised standard of proof seems to create a kind of presumption in favour of the legality of mergers,[68] the Court did not have the intention to substitute its own technical analysis for that of the Commission. Instead, the Court of Justice (and the Court of First Instance) looked closely at the Commission's evidentiary record to verify if there was a convincing scientific basis for the appraisals of the challenged merger decision.[69]

Looking at the *Tetra Laval* judgment with an Italian eye, we can claim that the review operated by the court is very close to a reasonableness scrutiny. The courts do not substitute their decisions for that of the administrative authority, but control whether the facts are truthful, whether the decision-making process, moving from assessed premises to its conclusions, is logical and reasonable, and whether a link exists between the factual findings and the consequent decision. If the factual and technical basis of the decision is not consistent, and if there is no convincing evidence to support the Commission's factual analysis, the Court has to quash the decision because it is irrational, illogical and not well-founded. These are the typical grounds of the reasonableness of judicial review.

It is not surprising that very similar standards of review were developed by the Italian *Consiglio di Stato* in its judgements *Buoni Pasto* and *Codacons*,[70] in which the meaning of 'weak review' was specified in relation to the judicial review of independent agencies decisions. In the cases considered in this contribution, the Italian judges recognised that the limitation of judicial review due to the technical expertise of the administrative agency (its 'weakness character') does not lead to a limitation in the judicial assessment of facts, in the review of the decision-making process or in reviewing the final assessments of the Authority. It only means that the judge cannot substitute its own assessments for those of the administrative agency. In other words, the recognition of a reserved area of complex technical appraisal due to the specific expertise of a public authority does not seem to imply a merely formal or marginal review of the administrative decisions founded on these assessments. On the contrary, judicial control seems to be full – even though it is not substitutive – that is to say that the court has a duty to assess the facts, to check the application

68 In this sense see the Commission's symmetry argument in the judgment. Völcker (2005) cit., 4.

69 Specifically, the Court held that 'the evidence produced by the Commission was unfounded by stating that, of the three independent reports cited by the Commission, only the PCI report contained information on the use of PET for milk packaging'. In the judgment under appeal (par. 213), 'the Court of first instance merely stated that the Commission's analysis was incomplete, which made it impossible to confirm its forecasts, given the differences between those forecasts and the forecasts made in the other reports'.

70 Cons. St., Sez. VI, 2 marzo 2004, n. 926, *Buoni pasto*, in *Foro. it.*, 2005, III, 6, con nota di S. Bastianon, *Dai buoni pasto ai 'concetti giuridici indeterminati'. Ovvero: come cambia il sindacato giurisdizionale sugli atti dell'Autorità antitrust*; ; in *Giorn. dir. amm.*, 2004, con nota di De Pretis (2005), n. 280.

of correct standards and to verify the reasonableness of the decision-making process, in order to be sure that the administrative decision is well-founded.

Particularly, with regard to the last of the decisions annotated above, the PAR judgment, the *Consiglio di Stato* decided to waive the distinction between 'weak' and 'strong' review, seeking standards of substantial judicial review compatible with the community legal framework and its fundamental principle of an effective judicial protection.[71] However, as was remarked above, the more recent case law seems to show all the uncertainties of a developmental phase, both as to its theoretical and doctrinal underpinnings as to the practical performance of judicial review tasks (see paragraph 5). So far, in this phase, the more recent European cases, even if they are a possible source of inspiration for some of the trends discernible in the case law, are not openly discussed in the judgements handed down by the administrative courts. However, at the end of the stage of development judicial review in Italy may be converging with the standard of judicial review in European cases.

[71] As mentioned in footnote 51.

## Bibliography

ANGELETTI (1980)
A. Angeletti, *Aspetti problematici della discriminazione delle giurisdizioni e Stato amministrativo* (Giuffré, Milano 1980)

AZZARITI (1989)
G. Azzariti, 'Discrezionalità, merito e regole non giuridiche nel pensiero di Constantino Mortati' [1989] *Pol. dir.*, p. 347 ff.

BAILEY (2004)
D. Bailey, 'Scope of Judicial Review under Article 81 EC' [2004/5] *Common Market Law Review* pp. 1327-1360

BARTOLI (1958)
E. Cannada Bartoli, *'Affievolimento', in Enciclopedia del Diritto vol. I* (Milano 1958)

BARTOLI (1972)
E. Cannada Bartoli, 'Voce Interesse (diritto amministrativo)', *in Enciclopedia del Diritto vol. XXII* (Milano 1972)

CARANTA (2008)
R. Caranta, 'On Discretion' in S. Prechal and B. van Roermund (eds.), *The Coherence of EU Law. The Search for Unity in Divergent Concepts* (Oxford University Press, Oxford 2008)

CARANTA (2004)
R. Caranta, 'Independent Administrative Authorities in Italian Law' in R. Caranta, M. Andenas and D. Fairgrieve (eds), *Independent Administrative Authorities* (British Institute of International and Comparative law, London 2004)

CASSESE (2006)
S. Cassese, Valutazioni tecniche della pubblica amministrazione, S. Cassese (ed), *Dizionario di diritto pubblico* (Giuffré, Milano 2006)

CHIEPPA (2004)
R. Chieppa, *Il controllo giurisdizionale sugli atti delle autorità antitrust* (*Dir. Proc. Amm.*, n. 4/2004, 1019)

CHIEPPA (2005)
R. Chieppa, 'Jurisdictional control over the decisions of the Antitrust Authorities', in: Enrico Adriano Raffaelli (ed.), *Antitrust between EC Law and National Law*, VI Conference LIDC, (Bruyliant and Giuffré, Bruxelles – Milano 2005)

CINTIOLI (2005)
F. Cintioli, *Giudice amministrativo, tecnica e mercato. Poteri tecnici e 'giurisdizionalizzazione'* (Giuffré, Milano 2005)

DE PRETIS (1995)
D. de Pretis, *Valutazione amministrativa e discrezionalità tecnica*, Pubblicazioni del Dipartimento di scienze giuridiche dell'Università di Trento, (Cedam, Padova 1995)

DE PRETIS (2004)
D. de Pretis, 'Antitrust, valutazioni tecniche e controllo giurisdizionale' [2004], *Diritto e formazion* pp. 997-1005
DE PRETIS (2005)
D. de Pretis, 'Antitrust, valutazioni tecniche e controllo giurisdizionale' [2005/280] *Giur. it.*
GERADIN (2006)
D. Geradin, N. Petit, 'Diritto della concorrenza e ricorsi per l'annullamento nell'era della post-modernizzazione', in E. Ferrari, M. Ramajoli,M. Sica (editors) *Il ruolo del giudice di fronte alle decisioni amministrative per il funzionamento del mercato* (Giappichelli, Torino 2006)
GIANNINI (1939)
M.S. Giannini, *Il potere discrezionale della pubblica amministrazione* (Giuffré, Milano 1939)
LAZZARA (2001)
P. Lazzara, *Autorità indipendenti e discrezionalità* (Cedam, Padova 2001)
MERUSI (2003)
F. Merusi, *Giustizia amministrativa e autorità indipendenti*, Annuario 2002 Associazione italiana professori diritto amministrativo (Milano 2003)
MIRATE (2004)
S. Mirate, Autorità antitrust e controllo giurisdizionale sulle valutazioni tecniche, [2004/7] *Urbanistica e Appalti* p. 817
MORTATI (1939)
C. Mortati, 'Potere discrezionale', *Nuovo Digesto Ital.*, vol. X (Torino 1939), p. 76
PIERCE (1999)
R.J. Pierce, S.A. Shapiro, P.R. Verkuil, *Administrative Law and Process* (Foundation Press, New York 1999)
PIETERS (2005)
K. Pieters, 'Commission versus Tetra Laval: Another Defeat of the European Commission' (Rs C-12/03); *European Law Reporter* 2005 p. 153
PROTTO (2001)
M. Protto, 'La discrezionalità tecnica sotto la lente del G.A.' [2001/8] *Revista Urbanistica e Appalti* p. 866
RAMAJOLI (2006)
M. Ramajoli, 'Potere di regolazione e sindacato giurisdizionale', *Diritto processuale amministrativo,* [2006/1] p. 80
SCOCA (2000)
F.G. Scoca, 'La discrezionalità nel pensiero di Giannini e nella dottrina successiva' in *Riv. trim. dir. pubbl.,* 2000, p. 1045e ss ff.

TRAVI (2008)

A. Travi, 'Valutazioni dell'amministrazione e valutazioni del giudice' in G. Falcon (edt.), *Il procedimento amministrativo nel diritto e nei diritti europei* (Cedam, Trento 2008)

VÖLCKER (2005)

S.B. Völcker, P. Charro, 'Tetra Laval – A Landmark Judgement on EC Merger Control' [2005/4] *Competition Law Insight* pp. 3-5

CHAPTER 10

# More Intensive Judicial Review in Competition Law and Economic Regulation in the Netherlands

## Vice or Virtue?

S. Lavrijssen

## 1 Setting the scene

The last decade has been characterised by a rise of independent administrative authorities in the EU Member States. With the entry into force of the liberalisation directives and Regulation 1/2003, the Member States founded national regulatory authorities (NRAs) and national, independent competition authorities (NCAs) charged, respectively, with the task of promoting competition in liberalised sectors and safeguarding competition by the enforcement of Articles 81 and 82 EC.[1]

To a certain extent, independent national authorities operate independently from the political arena to ensure fair, impartial and consistent decision-making.[2] The powers of the NRAs and the NCAs are exercised on the basis of complex legal and economic assessments, requiring a high degree of expertise of the specialists employed by the authorities. The decisions of the national authorities may have enormous financial consequences for the incumbents, for their competitors as well as for the consumers. In the light of the foregoing, the political accountability of the authorities has been the subject of constitutional debate in several Member States. Authors in several Member States have argued that the position of the authorities violates the principle of the separation of powers as well as the principle of Parliamentary sovereignty, as they would be able to exercise discretionary powers, which would imply discretion in assessment or discretion in policy, at a distance from politics.[3]

The national courts play a crucial role in the debate on the accountability of the independent national authorities in ensuring the right to effective legal protection of the market parties and holding the agencies legally accountable for their acts. However, the tasks of the national courts are becoming increasingly complex. In the first place, economic regulation and competition law are more and more characterised by the introduction of complex econometric models to forecast potential and uncertain market developments and problems of market power. This raises the question how the courts can verify whether the economic models are economically sound and whether the results can serve as a basis for regulating the market parties when assessing the legal acts of the authorities. Should the courts defer as much as possible to the choices the authorities have made, and merely review marginally whether they have reasonably exercised

1 See e.g. Article 3 of Directive 2002/21/EC of the European Parliament and of the Council of 7 March 2002 on a Common Regulatory Framework for Electronic Communications Networks and Services (Framework Directive), OJ 2003 L 108/33, Article 23 of Directive 2003/54/EC of the European Parliament and of the Council of 26 June 2003 Concerning Common Rules for the Internal Market in Electricity and Repealing Directive 96/92/EC, OJ 2003 L 176/37 and Article 25 of Directive 2003/55/EC Concerning Common Rules for the Internal Market in Gas and Repealing Directive 98/30/EC, OJ 2003 L 176/57.

2 Hancher (2003) p. 355-389.

3 See for an overview of the discussion in different Member States: Verhey (2003) p. 155-169 and Caranta (2004).

their powers, or should they review intensively whether the authorities have correctly exercised their powers in order to protect the right to effective legal protection of the market parties? To what extent is the case law of the ECJ, such as the *Tetra Laval* case, dealing with the standard of review of Commission decisions, of relevance for the way national courts scrutinise the legal acts of national authorities applying and interpreting European law?[4]

Furthermore, the application and enforcement of the European liberalisation directives or European competition law (Articles 81 and 82 EC) by the national authorities takes place in a setting of multi-level governance in which there is vertical co-ordination between the European Commission and the national authorities as well as horizontal co-operation between the national authorities themselves. For instance, the European Commission has the power, in the interest of a uniform application of European law, to intervene ex ante in national procedures by making comments,[5] vetoing decisions[6] and/or removing a national authority from a case.[7] In addition the Commission has increasingly used 'hybrid' forms of regulation to supervise and regulate the work of the national authorities, e.g. by the adoption of soft law documents, such as recommendations and guidelines, and through the establishment of independent European networks of national authorities.[8] Within these networks, the independent national authorities of the 27 Member States must co-operate with each other and with the Commission to guarantee uniform application of European law, among other things by exchanging information and by the formulation of soft law, such as best practice guidelines.

In the light of the aforementioned developments, national courts are faced with new challenges. They face an important challenge in allocating responsibility for decision-making in a setting in which the European Commission, the European networks and the national authorities co-operate in the application of European law.[9] Furthermore, the national courts are also responsible for the determination of the standard of review and the standard of proof to be applied to increasingly complex decisions taken by the national authorities specialised in competition law and/or economic regulation. In this regard they should also decide on the weight that should be given to informal and formal interventions of the European Commission and the European networks of national authorities

---

4 Case C-12/03P *Tetra Laval* [2005] ECR I-987.

5 See Article 7, par. 3 of Directive 2002/21/EC and Article 11, par. 3 and par. 4 of Council Regulation 1/2003.

6 Article 7, par. 4 and 5 of Directive 2002/21/EC. For similar powers of the Commission in other areas, see also Article 27 of Directive 2003/55 EC and Article 7 of Council Regulation 1228/2003/EC.

7 Article 11, par. 6 of Council Regulation 1/2003.

8 These networks include the European Energy Regulators Group (ERGEG), the European Regulators Group for Communications Networks and Services (ERG) and the European Competition Network (ECN).

9 Hofmann (2007) p. 267.

in determining and applying the standard of review and the standard of proof when reviewing the legal acts of the national authorities.

This contribution focuses on the question how the national administrative courts in the Netherlands deal with these challenges when reviewing the acts of the NRAs and the Dutch Competition Authority. The goal is to establish how the Dutch administrative courts find the balance between the safeguarding of the right to effective legal protection on the one hand and an effective and efficient functioning of the national authorities in a multi-level governance setting on the other hand.

It should be noted at the outset that the required level of judicial protection and the intensity of legal review will vary depending on the types of measures at stake. In so far as general binding measures are subject to political control, generally speaking courts tend to exercise only a marginal review of their legality.[10] This type of review focuses on whether the procedural rights of the interested parties have been respected, and whether conflicting interests have been balanced in a proportionate way. In the light of the increasingly intensive judicial review of individual administrative decisions by the ECJ and the CFI and the national courts, it is argued in this contribution that where such measures are adopted by the Commission or the national authorities, these are generally subject to a more intense review than general measures, including the safeguarding of substantive and procedural rights which individuals derive from European law.[11]

### 1.1 Structure

In seeking an answer to the main question, this contribution consists of six sections. Section 2 defines the main concepts used in this contribution and how these are interpreted in Dutch administrative law. The following concepts will be dealt with: discretion, judicial review and the intensity of review. The section also analyses what the view of administrative law doctrine is on the standard of review and the standard of proof to be applied by national administrative courts when reviewing national decisions. Section 3 outlines the competent administrative courts which review the decisions of the NRAs and the NCA in the Netherlands. Section 4 discusses, on the basis of some important examples of jurisprudence, how the competent Dutch courts review decisions of the Dutch NCA which applies Articles 81 and 82 EC and the national merger control regime. Section 5 examines the judicial review of decisions of the Dutch NRAs, focussing on decisions from the Independent Post and Telecommunications Authority (OPTA). Section 6 highlights some recent court cases to

10 See on this Hofmann (2007) p. 268. In this contribution, the term general measures refers to measures that have general applicability and that apply to an unidentified group of cases/persons. The term specific or individual measures refers to measures that relate to a specific situation and that have specific addressees.

11 Hofmann (2007) p. 268. See e.g. Case C-12/03P *Tetra Laval* [2005] ECR I-987.

show how the national courts deal with interventions of the European Commission when determining and applying the standard of review while reviewing national administrative decisions. The contribution ends with a number of conclusions.

## 2 Definitions and concepts

### 2.1 Judicial review and discretion

When this contribution uses the term judicial review, it refers to administrative judicial review of the legality of administrative acts on the basis of the General Administrative Law Act (GALA). This legality review may encompass a full review of the facts and the law of the case. The national courts may substitute the findings of the authority with regard to the establishment and the assessment of the facts with their own judgment. Unlike the ECJ and the CFI, the national courts may even definitively decide the case by determining that their judgment will replace the decision of the authority concerned. However, the courts only make use of this power in those cases where the administrative institutions concerned do not dispose of any discretion after the judgment.[12]

Dutch administrative law doctrine generally distinguishes two forms of discretion; discretion in policy and discretion in assessment. Discretion in policy (*beleidsvrijheid*) implies that the relevant legislation does not prescribe what kind of decision the authority should take if the legal conditions for exercising a power are fulfilled.[13] The Dutch authorities may also possess powers that imply discretion in assessment (*beoordelingsvrijheid*). In the case of discretion in assessment it is up to the judgment of the administration to determine whether the legal requirements for the exercise of powers have been met in the case at hand.[14]

### 2.2 Standard of review, standard of proof and discretion

In order to get a clearer picture of the standard of review national courts apply with regard to decisions of national authorities, doctrine makes a distinction between the establishment of the facts, the assessment of the facts in the light of the law and the interpretation of the law.[15] In Dutch administrative law it is generally assumed that the competent courts have the power to fully review the facts of the case as well as the interpretation of the

12 See contribution of Schimmel and Widdershoven in this book.

13 Van Wijk (2005) pp. 141-151.

14 Van Wijk (2005) p. 141 and Stroink (1995) p. 86.

15 See also Legal (2006) pp. 107-116.

law.[16] However, in making assessments of the facts in the light of the law, there is reason for the courts to defer to the legal and economic choices made by the national authorities. This deference is, amongst others, based on the constitutional division of tasks between administrative bodies on the one hand and the courts on the other; the former may make legal and economic choices under the supervision of political bodies or politically controlled bodies whereas the latter should review the legality of decisions. Moreover, courts may defer to administrative bodies in case decisions are taken on the basis of a specific technical and economic expertise which may be lacking at the courts.

The competent courts review decisions that are taken on the basis of policy discretion only marginally, since they can merely establish whether or not the authority concerned acted reasonably.[17] Decisions that are made on the basis of discretion in assessment are also reviewed marginally.[18]

If the national authorities have discretion in assessing the facts in the light of the law, this will not only lead to a marginal review by the courts of the assessment of the facts, but also to a marginal review of the establishment of the facts. So in practice, because of the difficulty to make a distinction between the establishment of the facts and the assessment of the facts in the light of the law, full review of the facts hardly takes place. National courts tend to defer to the national authorities in establishing the relevant facts and merely review whether the authorities have gathered the facts via careful procedures and whether the investigation concerned was complete on the basis of the duty of due care (Article 3:2 GALA).[19]

There is a link between the standard of review and the standard of proof. If the national courts apply an intensive standard of review, this will impact the standard of proof and *vice versa*. Generally, on the basis of Dutch administrative law, national authorities should take care that their decisions are based on an adequate factual basis (Article 3:2 GALA).[20] The actual standard of proof will depend on the circumstances of the case, such as the legislative text and the goals of the power concerned, the availability of information and European law requirements of legal protection, including the principles of effectiveness and equivalence.[21] Where national authorities can dispose of discretion in policy and/or in assessment, they have freedom to determine which facts are legally relevant, which weakens the standard of proof and with respect to which the

---

16 Schuurmans (2007) p. 116.

17 Verhey (2005) p. 313. See also Kortmann (2005) p. 65.

18 Van Wijk (2005), Verhey (2005) p. 313. It should be noted that in practice it is not always easy to establish whether the powers concerned leave discretion in assessment or whether the administrative authorities concerned should interpret vague legal norms. In the latter case the courts can fully review the interpretation of the law, whether in the former case they will review marginally the assessment of the facts in the light of the law.

19 Schuurmans (2007) pp. 118-120.

20 Ottow (2006) pp. 220-223.

21 Ottow (2006) pp. 227-232.

national courts must apply a more marginal standard of review than in the situation where there is no such discretion.

## 2.3 Standard of review, standard of proof and European law

Since EC law generally does not provide rules for the standard of review and the standard of proof to be applied by national courts when assessing national decisions with EC law aspects, these rules come within the realm of the national procedural autonomy. It is up to the national legislator to draft the relevant procedural rules, provided the widely echoed European principles of effectiveness and equivalence are respected.[22] In Dutch administrative law doctrine, it is generally assumed that the above-mentioned marginal standard of review (section 2.2.) on the basis of the duty of due care complies with these principles.[23] In this respect the *Upjohn* case of the ECJ is frequently cited as authoritative, where the ECJ considered that European law does not require the national courts to apply a more intensive standard of review than the ECJ applies in comparable cases, implying an appreciable margin of discretion for the European Commission in exercising its powers.[24]

It may be submitted, however, that the national courts should play a more active role in reviewing the assessment of the facts of the case in order to ensure the right of effective legal protection of the market parties.[25] In this regard it is of importance that the CFI itself has moved towards a more intensive review of complicated legal and economic assessments by the European Commission in competition cases, which was approved by the ECJ in *Tetra Laval*.[26] Although formally the CFI reviews Commission decisions on the basis of the marginal standard of 'manifest error of assessment', in practice it tends to scrutinise the assessment of the facts as well as the facts of the case intensively, although it does not substitute the Commission's opinion with its own.[27] More pervasive

22 Schuurmans (2007) p. 121. Case 33/76 *Rewe* [1976] ECR 1989.

23 Schuurmans (2005) p. 122 and Jans (2002) pp. 132-133.

24 Case C-120/97 *Upjohn* [1999] ECR I-233.

25 Jans argues that the principle of equivalence may be violated if national courts structurally avoid a substantive assessment of decisions in the light of European law and merely deal with European law problems by assessing whether the authorities have acted in a careful way, while the national courts are inclined to intensively review 'pure' national decisions. He does not seem to be conclusive as regards the duties that follow from the principle of effectiveness, although he suggests that the assessment on the basis of the duty of due care would be less favorable in terms of the effectuation of European law than a substantive assessment of the European law aspects of a case. Jans (2005).

26 Case C-12/03P *Tetra Laval* [2005] ECR I-987, par. 39: 'Not only must the Community Courts, inter alia, establish whether the evidence relied on is factually accurate, reliable and consistent but also whether the evidence contains all the information which must be taken in account in order to assess a complex situation and whether it is capable of substantiating the conclusions drawn from it.'

27 See Lavrijssen (2006) II and Bay (2005) pp. 443-440 and L. Parret (2008) pp. 169-1999. Vesterdorf (2003) p. 136-144. Vesterdorf argues that the CFI has not applied a new, more intensive standard of

control by the Community Courts also brings with it a higher standard of proof for the Commission.[28] The Commission must support its decisions with sufficient reasoning and convincing evidence, obtained after a thorough investigation, leading to the realisation of the essential function of evidence, which is to establish convincingly the merits of an argument.[29]

In the light of the foregoing clarifications and considerations, the next sections will examine how the competent administrative courts review the decisions of national authorities in the area of competition law and economic regulation in the Netherlands.

## 3 Competent courts

The decisions of the Netherlands Competition Authority – *Nederlandse Mededingingsautoriteit (NMa)* – are reviewed exclusively by the specialised Rotterdam District Court.[30] The District Court is part of the administrative court structure. Appeals are taken to the specialised Trade and Industry Appeals Tribunal – *College van Beroep voor het Bedrijfsleven (CBB)*.[31] To speed up legal proceedings the amended Telecommunications Act stipulates that the most important regulatory decisions taken by the Independent Post and Telecommunications Authority (OPTA) can only be appealed before the CBB – no further appeal being possible.[32] Also in the energy sector the CBB is generally the only appeals body to review decisions of the Dutch Energy Regulator (*Energiekamer*), which is a separate entity falling under the responsibility of the NMa.[33] As regards decisions imposing sanctions of the OPTA and the *Energiekamer*, the appeals procedure provides for two instances, i.e. the Rotterdam District Court decides in first instance and higher appeal is taken to the CBB.[34]

---

review: 'CFI has simply been more exacting latterly than it arguably was previously when applying the well established principles to which I have referred'.

28 On the relation between the standard of review and the standard of proof see also: Bailey (2004) pp. 1327-1360.

29 Case C-12/03P *Tetra Laval* [2005] ECR I-987. par. 41.

30 This in deviation from Article 8:7 Awb [General Administrative Law Act].

31 Article 93 Mw [Dutch Competition Act].

32 Article 17.1, par. 1 Tw [Dutch Telecommunications Act], referring to decisions taken pursuant to Chapter 6 [interoperability of services], Chapter 6A [obligations for SMP operators], Chapter 6B [the Articles 6 and 7 Framework Directive procedure], Chapter 12 [dispute settlement] and Chapter 15 [enforcement], with the exception of decisions pursuant to Article 15.2.a [preventing an operator from offering electronic communications services or networks] and 15.4 [fines and periodic penalty payments].

33 Article 82 of the Electricity Act 1998 and Article 61 of the Gas Act.

34 Article 17.1 par. 2 Tw. This provision applies in deviation from Article 8.7. Awb.

# 4 Competition Law; Articles 81 and 82 EC

## 4.1 General remarks

The District Court Rotterdam and the CBB commonly engage in an intensive review of NMa decisions concerning the application of Articles 81 and 82 EC and their Dutch equivalents, Articles 6 and 24 of the Competition Act 1998. The District Court applies a particularly pervasive control.[35] The District Court has at times substituted its own assessment for that of the NMa, a practice approved by the CBB on appeal.[36] In some cases the CBB also substituted its judgment for that of the NMa.[37] For instance in the *Modint* case, the CBB held, after an intensive review of the economic and legal analysis conducted by the NMa, that in the light of the legal and economic context in which the agreement at hand functioned, the NMa was wrong in establishing it had the object to restrict competition.[38]

It is of relevance that both the District Court Rotterdam and the CBB review extremely intensively the decisions to impose fines and that both Courts are willing to substitute the NMa's assessment of a fine with their own.[39] The courts have, however, been more reluctant to fully review the application of the criteria for an exception of the cartel prohibition, since this necessarily entails a balancing exercise for which broader discretion is deemed appropriate.[40] Below, this

35 For an extensive analysis of the standard of judicial review regarding the different types of decisions by the Netherlands Competition Authority, consult Lavrijssen (2004) p. 34 and Lavrijssen (2006) pp. 251-299.

36 For instance District Court Rotterdam, 26 November 2002, 00/1002 MEDED, *NEA BV* v. *DG NMa*, LJN: AF1111. On appeal the CBB endorsed the substantive findings by the District Court but lowered the fine imposed on the basis of a very intense review: CBB, 28 May 2004, AWB 03/76, *NEA* v. *DG NMa*, with annotation by GC, *AB* 2004/449. See also District Court Rotterdam, 11 March 2003, *Carglass and Glasgarage* v. *DG NMa*, MEDED 01/2674-RIP, MEDED 01/2629-RIP, LJN: AF8902, appealed to the CBB who endorsed the judgment by the District Court to the extent that it found that the NMa had failed to properly examine a discount offered by Carglass and had failed to offer adequate reasoning in support of its decision: CBB, 17 November 2004, AWB 03/614, 03/621 en 03/659, *Glasgarage Rotterdam and Carglass* v. *DG NMa*, with annotation by GC, *AB* 2005/81.

37 See for examples of an intensive review by the CBB: CBB, 28 October 2005, AWB 04/794, AWB 04/829, Modint, LJN:AU5316 with annotation by Coumans (2006) p. 47-55 and CBB 15 July 2004, AWB 03/132, NOS v. NMa, judgment on appeal against the judgment by the District Court of Rotterdam of 11 December 2002, *LJN* AQ1727.

38 See on this case Lavrijssen (2006) pp. 118-119.

39 For instance District Court Rotterdam, 26 November 2002, 00/1002 MEDED, *NEA BV* v. *DG NMa*, LJN:AF1111; CBB, 28 May 2004, AWB 03/76, *NEA* v. *DG NMa*, with annotation by GC, *AB* 2004/449; District Court Rotterdam, 18 June 2003, Case 01/621 MEDED, *X* v. *DG NMa*, LJN:AH9702; and CBB, 12 March 2004, AWB 03/916 and 03/946, with annotation by GC, *AB* 2004/170.

40 See Lavrijssen (2004) pp. 26-27.

contribution will discuss two landmark cases which are very illustrative for the way the District Court and the CBB review decisions of the NMa.

### 4.2 *Secon*

The *Secon* case has attracted – and deserved – quite some attention from academics and practitioners.[41] This case, amongst others, concerned certain clauses on minimum prices and advice prices that were included in distribution agreements relating to the supply of luxurious jeans that de facto amounted to price fixing. Consequently, the clauses at issue were qualified as having the object to restrict competition, which was confirmed by the District Court in appeals and by the CBB in higher appeals.

In harmony with the *Grundig Consten* case of the ECJ,[42] the CBB and the District Court considered that in case an agreement has the object to restrict competition, the NMa does not have to investigate the concrete effects of the agreement anymore. However, unlike the practice of the District Court and the NMa at that time, the CBB applied established case law of the ECJ, such as *Völk* v. *Vervaecke*, and considered that the cartel prohibition does not apply to agreements that do not have an appreciable effect on competition in the relevant market.[43] The CBB considered that although generally agreements that have the object to restrict competition will affect the relevant market to an appreciable extent, it is still possible that such agreements do not appreciably restrict competition in the relevant market because of the insignificant position of the parties concerned.[44] The CBB specified how the NMa should assess the appreciability of a restriction, in that the NMa should take into account the concrete situation in which the agreement generates its effects and especially the economic and legal context within which the undertakings operate, the nature of the goods and services that are the subject of the agreements, the structure of the relevant market and the actual conditions within which the market operates. As the NMa had not performed this kind of economic analysis of the appreciability of the effect of the restrictions in their concrete market context, the CBB annulled the decision of the NMa on the basis of a lack of adequate reasoning.

It may be argued that *SECON* is not a good example for illustrating the standard of review and the standard of proof applied by the CBB, as the latter merely applied established case law of the ECJ. Nevertheless the case shows the critical approach of the CBB towards decisions of the NMa. Moreover, the case shows the CBB is not afraid to clarify the case law of the ECJ by giving the NMa directions on how it should conduct an economic analysis on the appreciable effect of agreements.

---

41 CBB, 7 December 2005, AWB 04/237 en 04/249, *SECON*, LJN: AU8309, with annotation by Loozen (2006) pp. 88-92. See Ottow (2008) pp. 170-187.

42 Joined Cases 56/64 and 58/64 *Consten and Grundig* [1966] ECR 299.

43 Case 5/69 *Volk Vervaecke* [1969] ECR 295.

44 Par. 6.5.

### 4.3 *T-Mobile*

In the *T-Mobile* case the District Court quashed an NMa decision, imposing sanctions on five mobile network operators for violating the cartel prohibition by engaging in a concerted practice through the exchange of confidential information on the prices and conditions of post and pre-paid packages for mobile telephony.[45] The decision was appealed by the NMa and by the mobile network operators. Unlike the District Court, the CBB explicitly dealt with the standard of review and the standard of proof to be applied. It considered, recalling previous case law, that the NMa enjoys a certain margin of appreciation when assessing economic facts and circumstances in the light of the provisions of the Competition Act. However, this does not prevent the court from reviewing whether the NMa has made it sufficiently plausible that the conditions for the application of the Competition Act are fulfilled. The court should not only assess whether the decisions have been carefully prepared and are adequately motivated, but also whether the NMa has interpreted legal concepts in a correct way and has made it sufficiently plausible that the facts and circumstances comply with the legal conditions of the law.[46]

A closer examination of the standard of review applied by the CBB reveals that it is very similar to the one applied by the ECJ in *Tetra Laval*. This is confirmed by the fact that the CBB itself refers implicitly to the *Tetra Laval* case by citing the exact consideration in paragraph 39 of this case when clarifying the standard of legal review it applies:

> ' Not only must the court, inter alia, establish whether the evidence relied on is factually accurate, reliable and consistent but also whether that evidence contains all the information which must be taken into account in order to assess a complex situation and whether it is capable of substantiating the conclusions drawn from it.'

Taking into account the abovementioned standard of review, the CBB carefully scrutinised the NMa decision and concluded that the NMa had failed to make it plausible that the mobile network operators were engaged in a concerted practice as regards the conditions and prices of the pre-paid subscriptions. With regard to the assessment of the alleged concerted practices concerning the post-paid subscriptions, the CBB considered it necessary to submit preliminary questions to the ECJ to ask for clarifications on legal issues affecting the standard and burden of proof of the NMa. Recently the ECJ handed down its preliminary ruling in the *T-Mobile* case.[47]

---

45 District Court Rotterdam, 13 July 2006, MEDED 04/3242, *Mobiele operators*, LJN:AY4035.

46 CBB, 31 December 2007, AWB 06/657, *Mobiele operators*, LJN: BC1396, par. 9.2.

47 Case C-8/08 4 June 2009, *T-Mobile* n.y.r.

### 4.3.1 Preliminary questions and answers

The first question raised by the CBB relates to the problem of the way in which to determine whether an agreement has the object to restrict competition. In this regard, the CBB reiterates the case law of the ECJ requiring an examination of the actual economic and legal context in which the agreements at issue function to characterise a restriction of competition.[48] The CBB considers that the establishment of an object restriction has an impact on the standard of proof of the NMa, as, according to settled case law of the ECJ, in case of an object restriction the NMa does not have to conduct an economic analysis into the effects of an agreement.[49]

In the case at hand the NMa decided that concerted practices with regard to price fixing, as well as any other forms to restrict price competition, such as the exchange of data and the number of price changes, including discounts and retributions, by their nature restrict competition, making an examination into the effects of the agreement superfluous. However, the CBB considers that the behaviour at issue concerned a reduction of the benefits that are paid by the mobile network operators to the services providers. Therefore, it cannot be assumed that the concerted practice has the object to fix the prices at the retail market. Indeed, the prices at the retail market are primarily determined by the mobile network operators themselves. Moreover, in the circumstances of this case it cannot be assumed there is a direct link, functioning independently from the market conditions, between the sales activities of the service providers and the benefits they receive from the mobile network operators. The CBB seems to doubt that, taken into account the economic and legal context of the agreement, the behaviour at issue can by its nature be detrimental for the consumer interest and be qualified as an agreement that has the object to restrict competition. It suggests that further economic analysis is necessary to assess whether there is a direct link between the concerted practice and its effects on consumer prices and the position of the mobile network operators on the retail market. In the light of the foregoing the CBB asks the ECJ to clarify how to interpret the words 'have the object' from Article 81(1) EC and to specify which criteria should be taken into account by the CBB in determining whether an agreement has the object to restrict competition.[50]

The ECJ requires a less far-reaching economic analysis for the establishment of an object restriction on the basis of Article 81 EC than was suggested by the CBB.[51] It takes a rather traditional approach by considering there is no need to consider the effects of a concerted practice where its anti-competitive object is established. The ECJ point outs that in order for a concerted practice to be regarded as having an anti-competitive object, it suffices that the practice has

48 Case 56/65 *Société Technique Minière* [1966] ECR 235.

49 Joined Cases 56/64 and 58/64 *Consten and Grundig* [1966] ECR 299.

50 CBB, *Mobiele operators*, par. 9.5.3.

51 Case C-8/08, par. 23-43.

the potential to have a negative impact on competition. Furthermore, the ECJ, rules that contrary to what the referring court would appear to believe, in order to find that a concerted practice has an anti-competitive object, there does not need to be a direct link between that practice and consumer prices.

The other two preliminary questions relate to the application of the *ANIC* judgment of the ECJ.[52] In the *ANIC* case the ECJ ruled that there is a presumption of proof of the existence of a causal link between the concerted practice and the parallel behaviour in case the undertakings engaged in the concerted practice remain active on the relevant market, unless they can provide evidence to the contrary.[53] The CBB asks firstly whether the rule established in *ANIC* only relates to the application of the competition rules by the European Commission or whether it is also binding for the national competition authorities, superseding national procedural rules, when they apply European competition law. The CBB indicates that two lines of reasoning can be followed. The first line of reasoning is based on the principle of national procedural autonomy, implying that the burden of proof should be determined on the basis of national law, provided that the principles of equality and effectiveness are respected.[54] According to the second line of reasoning the presumption of proof is seen as a substantive element of the concept of concerted practice of Article 81(1) EC, meaning that the national courts and national authorities are also bound by it when applying Article 81(1) EC. The ECJ is of the opinion that the presumption of a causal link stems from Article 81(1) EC as interpreted by the Court, and consequently forms an integral part of applicable community law.[55] Secondly, the CBB asks the ECJ to clarify whether the ANIC presumption of proof is only valid when the market players have participated in a series of meetings or whether it is also applicable when they have attended only one meeting, such as in the case at hand. Here the ECJ rules that it is not so much the number of the meetings held between the participating undertakings as whether the meeting or meetings which took place afforded them the opportunity to take account of the information exchanged with their competitors in order to determine their conduct on the market in question and knowingly substitute practical co-operation between them for the risks of competition.[56]

## 4.4 Competition law: Merger control

### 4.4.1 General remarks

Due to the complex prospective analyses that must be undertaken by the NMa in merger cases, the standard of review applied can differ

[52] CBB, *Mobiele operators*, par. 9.5.5.

[53] Case C-49/92P *ANIC* [1999] ECR p. I-4125.

[54] Joined Cases C-222/05-C-225/05 *Van Weerd* [2007] ECR I-4233.

[55] Case C-8/08, par. 44-53.

[56] Case C-8/08, par. 54-62.

from the one applied in cases concerning the cartel prohibition and the prohibition of the abuse of a dominant position. The case law showed a divergence between the District Court and the CBB in this respect.[57] The District Court has reviewed NMa merger decisions intensively, even substituting the NMa's opinion with its own, whereas the CBB has applied a standard of review between marginal and intense, which subsequently was adopted by the District Court in new cases.[58] Like in the *Mobiele Operators* case dealing with the cartel prohibition, the CBB consistently applies the 'plausible' standard when reviewing merger decisions of the NMa, which is a standard that resembles the *Tetra Laval* standard applied by the ECJ when reviewing Commission decisions (see section 4.3). Although a closer look shows that both courts are inspired by the case law of the ECJ in formulating and specifying the standard of review and the standard of proof, they usually do not refer explicitly to specific ECJ case law.

The next section discusses the *Nuon/Reliant* case to illustrate how the abovementioned standard of review and standard of proof are applied by the courts in merger cases.

### 4.4.2 *Nuon/Reliant*

#### 4.4.2.1 District Court

After the *Tetra Laval* judgment of the ECJ, the District Court of Rotterdam has applied an intensive standard of review for assessing a complicated merger decision in the electricity sector; however, without mentioning the source of inspiration for the standard chosen. In *Nuon/Reliant* the District Court stated that Article 41 of the Competition Act implies that it should be shown with a high degree of certainty that the conditions for the refusal of approval or the approval subject to conditions of a proposed merger have been met.[59]

In the case at hand, the proposed merger did not lead to any problems from a structural viewpoint, given the modest market shares of the undertakings concerned. But the problem was that in the electricity sector market shares can vary greatly depending on the time of day. Typically, at times when demand for

---

57 Lavrijssen (2006) p. 119.

58 Compare: District Court of Rotterdam, 20 September 2000, MEDED 00/874-SIMO and MEDED 00/875-SIMO, *Wegener* v. *d-g NMa*, with annotation by Leeflang (2001) pp. 20-33 and CBB, 5 December 2001, AWB 00/867 and 00/8709500, *Wegener* v. *d-g NMa*, with annotation by Mok (2002) p. 422. See also: CBB, 27 September 2002, AWB/01/633, *Essent* v. *d-g NMa*, with annotation by Leeflang (2002) pp. 171-176. See also Verheij (2005).

59 District Court of Rotterdam, MEDED 04/135-WILD, *NUON* v. *NMa*, LJN: AT6440, with annotation by Albers (2005) pp. 169-173. The merger decision in this case was taken on the basis of the old substantive test, in that the NMa had to prove the creation or the strengthening of a dominant position. Recently the substantive test of the merger control regime of the Competition Act has been amended and has been brought in harmony with the substantive test of Regulation 139/2004 (significant impediment of competition, in particular as a result of the creation or strengthening of a dominant position).

electricity is high, the so-called flexible power stations are used as a last resort, because these power stations are able to quickly supply the electricity demanded. Even if an undertaking possesses a modest market share, the electricity producers can still drive up the price for electricity by refusing to use the capacity of the flexible power stations they possess. The decision by the NMa was based to a large extent on a quantitative analysis linked with economic principles related to game theory, which, according to the NMa, demonstrated that the merger would create greater possibilities for the merged entity to engage in such strategic anti-competitive behaviour due to wider access to flexible electricity capacity. However, the time, nature and extent of such behaviour and the effects of the merger on these aspects were uncertain and difficult to demonstrate. Partly based on these considerations the District Court held that the NMa had failed to justify why a traditional competition law based analysis would be insufficient to prove the effects of the proposed merger. In addition, the quantitative analysis used was based on the assumption that the undertakings concerned would actually engage in strategic behaviour. However, the NMa had failed to prove that in the past such behaviour had occurred. The NMa appealed the judgment and argued that the District Court had applied a too strict standard of review and a too high standard of proof, making the work of the NMa very difficult indeed.[60]

#### 4.4.2.2 CBB

On appeal, the CBB referred to its previous case law regarding the standard of review in merger cases, once more stressing that the NMa had to make it sufficiently plausible that the conditions for the disapproval or the conditional approval of a merger of the Competition Act have been met.[61] Although the CBB already applied this standard before the *Tetra Laval* case, it referred implicitly to the above-mentioned paragraph 39 of this case in order to specify what its standard requires from the NMa (see also section 4.3).

Furthermore, like the ECJ in *Tetra Laval*, the CBB emphasised that the standard of review applied will not be altered by the specific nature of a prospective analysis of the kind required in merger control, making it necessary to envisage various chains of cause and effect with a view to ascertaining which of the possible scenarios are the most likely.[62] This analysis must be carried out with great care since it does not entail the examination of past events – for which many items of evidence are often available, which make it possible to understand the causes – and therefore provides another certainty than retrospective analyses. According to the CBB such an analysis generally does not exclude the use of certain economic models or theories. A model which forms the basis of a prospective analysis should be based on realistic assumptions about the behav-

60 See for a critical comment Kalbfleisch (2005).

61 CBB, AWB 05/440, *NUON* v. *NMa*, LJN: ZA3274.

62 See par. 8.3.4. The comments of the CBB are very similar to those made by the ECJ in case C-12/03P, par. 42-44.

iour of the market parties on the relevant market and should be transparent and consistent both with regard to the assumptions on which they are based and with regard to their results. The prospective analysis should be based on real facts and circumstances that are made sufficiently plausible by the NMa. The NMa cannot confine itself to a general and abstract or theoretical description of the market situation as a basis for the prospective analysis.

Subsequently the CBB considered that although the District Court used the words 'with a high degree of certainty', it actually did not apply a stricter test and merely examined whether the NMa has made it sufficiently plausible whether the conditions for the conditional approval of the proposed merger were met. Subsequently the CBB thoroughly reviewed the facts of the case, although it did not substitute the NMa's assessment. The Court largely confirmed the findings of the District Court, in that it considered the NMa could not substantiate the expected market power problems of the proposed merger with adequate factual findings. The NMa limited itself to an abstract and theoretical description of the possibilities for strategic behaviour in the electricity sector, without examining the specific market positions of NUON and Reliant or whether they were actually engaged in anti-competitive behaviour. As the econometric models were also based on the same theoretical assumptions about the behaviour of NUON and Reliant, the CBB concluded that their results could not substantiate the conclusions of the NMa.

### 4.5 Observations

On the basis of the foregoing, it may be observed that, despite the fact that the NMa may enjoy a considerable degree of discretion in assessment when exercising its powers, both the District Court Rotterdam and the CBB tend to intensively scrutinise the different decisions the NMa may take. Especially the decisions applying Articles 81 and 82 EC may be reviewed intensively, sometimes leading to a substitution of the NMa's opinion by the courts. Generally, the courts apply a more restrained test in merger cases; they carefully review whether the NMa has sufficiently substantiated the existence of a competition problem, but refrain from substituting the assessment already made by the NMa.

Unlike the District Court, the CBB is more explicit on the standard of review it applies, by considering that the NMa should make it 'plausible' on the basis of sufficient evidence that the legal conditions of the competition provisions are met. A closer examination of the case law reveals that the standard of review, which was already applied by the CBB before the *Tetra Laval* case, in practice resembles the *Tetra Laval* standard. Although European competition law (Articles 81 and 82 EC) and the national merger control regime are applied and enforced on the basis of national procedural law, there are indications that both courts are inspired by the *Tetra Laval* case of the ECJ when reviewing the decisions of the NMa. Particularly, the CBB will refer, implicitly but literally, to paragraph 39 of the *Tetra Laval* case to clarify what is meant by the 'plausible standard' it applies.

The CBB applies the 'plausible standard' to review Article 81 and Article 82 decisions and merger decisions, without differentiating according to the different types of decisions. However, it seems that the plausible standard and consequently also the *Tetra Laval* standard leaves sufficient scope for the courts to attune the actual standard of review to the specifics of each case, e.g. by taking into account the specifics of a prospective analysis, which is always characterised by a certain degree of uncertainty. Of course the case law is not yet clarified at this point. Both for the sake of transparency and legal certainty for the NMa and the market parties it is advisable for the courts to continue to give the NMa guidance on the requirements that follow from the standard of proof which may differentiate dependent on the type of case at hand. At the same time these requirements should not be cast in stone, but leave sufficient flexibility to deal with the specifics of each case as well as for innovations in economic theory and modelling.[63]

Both the District Court and the CBB clearly reject a formalistic application of competition law by the NMa and require a sound economic analysis of the competition problems. The NMa should examine the actual economic and legal context within which certain undertakings operate and should not base its analysis and models on assumptions that are merely theoretical. For instance, in *Secon* the CBB firmly rejected the practice of the NMa not to investigate the appreciable effect of agreements that had the object to restrict competition. The CBB did not merely apply the standard case law of the ECJ in this case but it went a step further by clarifying the way in which the NMa should conduct its economic analysis of the appreciability of competition restrictions.

In addition, in *T-Mobile* the CBB indicated that with regard to the determination of object restrictions the NMa should investigate, taking into account the actual legal and economic context within which the practices function, whether the behaviour by its nature can actually be detrimental to the consumer interest. It should be noted that in the *T-Mobile* case the line of reasoning of the CBB very much resembles the reasoning of the CFI in the *Glaxo Smith Kline* case. In the latter case the CFI annulled a Commission Decision condemning an agreement in the pharmaceuticals sector restricting parallel trade by wholesalers, on the grounds that the Commission refrained from conducting an analysis into the actual economic and legal context of the agreement to justify its presumption that by its nature it could be detrimental for consumer welfare.[64] It was the first time that the CFI required the Commission to prove the possible harm to consumer welfare when qualifying restrictions as object restrictions, thus tightening the economic analysis the Commission has to deliver and the standard of proof it has to comply with.[65] However, at a time in which the economisation

63 See also: Parret (2008).

64 Case T-168/01*GlaxoSmithkline Services* [2006] ECR II-2969.

65 See the annotation by Van Ginneken (2007) pp. 56-60.

of the application of competition law is high on the agenda of the European Commission, it may be argued that the ECJ in its preliminary ruling in the *T-Mobile* case limits the effects of the economisation of competition law on the burden of proof for the Commission and the national competition authorities when applying Article 81 EC. When establishing an object restriction the competition authorities do not have to prove that the restrictive practice has an actual effect on competition or that there is a direct link between the restriction and consumer prices. It is sufficient that it is proven that the practice is capable of restricting competition within the common market. The Commission has appealed the judgment of the CFI in *Glaxo Smith Kline*. The judgment of the ECJ in higher appeal will probably shed more light on the requirements for the application of Article 81 EC and the resulting burden of proof for the Commission and the national competition authorities.

The following section discusses the way in which the national courts review the decisions of the Independent Post and Telecommunications Authority (OPTA).

## 5 Judicial review in the electronic communications sector

### 5.1 General remarks

The National Regulatory Authorities in the electronic communications sector enjoy considerable discretion in assessment and/or in policy in exercising their powers to *ex ante* regulate the market parties. The powers of the NRAs to some extent resemble the powers of the NCAs to assess mergers: the former have to make a prospective analysis to assess whether the market parties concerned will have Significant Market Power, i.e. a position which amounts to a dominant position in the sense of Article 82 EC, in the coming three years.

Under the old Telecommunications Act 1998, many of the OPTA's decisions had been annulled by the CBB for formal reasons – read lack of competence – due to the restrictive drafting of the Act.[66] However, the few judgments that did address the substance of the case indicate that the District Court and the CBB did not shy away from carefully scrutinising decisions of the OPTA which concerned complex legal and economic assessments. The District Court generally applied an intensive standard of review, whereas the CBB applied a standard of review between marginal and intensive, depending on the circumstances of the case.[67] Also under the amended Telecommunications Act, implementing the 2002 Electronic communications directives, the CBB critically assesses the reasoning, facts and evidence on which the OPTA's decisions are

---

[66] Ottow (2006) pp. 102-119.

[67] Ottow (2005) pp. 227-228 and Lavrijssen (2006) pp. 114-117.

based, but without substituting OPTA's opinion with its own.[68] Although generally the CBB is less explicit about the standard of review in economic regulation cases, in fact it resembles the 'plausible' standard that is applied by the CBB in competition law cases (see section 4).[69] In one provisional judgment the CBB explicitly dealt with the standard of review by considering that to some extent a prospective analysis is always speculative and that the OPTA is the appropriate body to give a judgment on the most likely market developments, based on an appropriate analysis. Furthermore, the CBB considered that it was not up to the court to substitute the OPTA's judgment with its own, where the OPTA's conclusions are based on transparent and adequate reasoning.[70]

As argued by Pietermaat and Ottow,[71] the standard of review applied by the CBB is in harmony with Article 4 of the Framework Directive,[72]stipulating that:

> 'Member states shall ensure that effective mechanisms exist at national level under which any user or undertaking providing electronic communications networks and/or services who is affected by a decision of a national regulatory authority has the right of appeal against the decision to an appeal body that is independent of the parties involved. (......) Member States shall ensure that the merits of the case are duly taken into account and there is an effective appeal mechanism. (...)'

The English language version of the Framework Directive implies that the competent appeals bodies should fully review the merits of the case, which means that they may, if necessary, substitute the NRAs' assessment. Therefore the English language version seems to imply a more intensive review than the Dutch version where it is stated 'that the facts of the case should be duly taken into account'. In any event, article 4 of the Framework Directive seems to prevent the competent courts from reviewing the decisions of the NRAs merely marginally, without, however, requiring the courts to substitute the opinion of

---

68 Pietermaat (2007) pp. 343-350. See e.g. CBB, 24 July 2007, AWB 06/322, *Casema et al* v. *OPTA*, LJN: BB0186 and CBB 11 May 2007, AWB 06/125, 06/127, 06/128 and 06/129, *Tele2 et al.* v. *OPTA*, LJN: BA4880.

69 Art. 1.3(4) of the Telecommunications Act now requires OPTA to demonstrate with reference to both qualitative and quantitative indicators that any measure which has a significant effect on the relevant market is necessary for achieving the objectives of the Telecommunications Act as well as proportionate to achieve those objectives. In the light of the rather intensive review being applied by the CBB before the entry into force of this article, it is argued that this article as such has not exerted much impact on the standard of review and the burden of proof.

70 Vzr. CBB, 10 February 2006, *KPN* v. *OPTA*, LJN: AV1487.

71 Pietermaat (2007) p. 347.

72 Directive 2002/21/EC of the European Parliament and of the Council of 7 March 2002 on a Common Regulatory Framework for Electronic Communications Networks and Services (Framework Directive), OJ 2003 L 108/33.

the NRAs with their own.[73] At times the standard of review applied by the CBB when reviewing decisions of the OPTA can be very pervasive. One good example of this is the review of the decision concerning the regulation of the mobile terminating access tariffs.

### 5.2 Mobile terminating access tariffs

In harmony with the Commission Recommendation on Relevant markets,[74] the OPTA came to the conclusion that mobile terminating access at each of the networks of the mobile network operators should be qualified as separate relevant markets.[75] Since there is currently no other alternative than the network of the mobile operator concerned for terminating telephone calls destined for its subscribers, each of the mobile network operators has a market share of 100% on his own mobile terminating access network. OPTA decided that, taking into account the market shares of the mobile operators, the absence of alternatives and the absence of buying power, each of the mobile operators had a Significant Market Power position on the market for mobile terminating access. As the OPTA was of the opinion that the mobile operators charged excessive prices for mobile terminating access, it wanted to regulate the mobile terminating access tariffs on the basis of the principle of cost orientation. The mobile operators appealed against this decision to the CBB.

The CBB intensively reviewed OPTA's reasoning, the facts of the case and the evidence provided by the parties.[76] According to the CBB, the OPTA had not thoroughly examined the specific market position of each of the mobile operators on the market for mobile terminating access on the basis of the available evidence. Moreover, it had insufficiently taken account of the information provided by the mobile operators or of the comments they had made. For instance, the OPTA had not adequately addressed the comments of several operators that they could not abuse their position since KPN, the incumbent of the fixed network, could exercise buying power e.g. by not paying the mobile terminating access tariffs. If OPTA's opinion that KPN could not exercise buyer power would prove to be right, it was still necessary to consider what would be the cause of this. According to the CBB it was not unthinkable that the strong position of the mobile network operators as well as the absence of buying power on

73 Pietermaat (2007) p. 347 and Prechal (2005) pp. 39-40.

74 OJ 2003 L 114/45. The NRAs should take this recommendation into account when defining and analysing relevant markets in the electronic communications sector. They may deviate from this recommendation if this is justified by national market conditions and approved by the European Commission on the basis of Article 7 Directive 2002/21/EC.

75 Mobile terminating access refers to the service the mobile operators deliver to each other and to the operators of the fixed telephone networks by terminating telephone calls that originate from another operator's network onto their own network in order to ensure that the subscribers of the different networks can communicate with each other.

76 CBB, 29 September 2006, AWB 05/903 en 05/921-05/931, *Mobile Terminating Access*, LJN: AY7997.

the part of KPN was caused by the fact that OPTA regulated the fixed terminating tariffs of KPN. Consequently KNP could not react to the rise of the mobile terminating access tariffs by raising its own tariffs for terminating mobile calls on the fixed network, causing an imbalance between the mobile network operators and KPN. As OPTA based its market analysis on the starting point of a situation of no regulation, it should have dealt with the question to what extent the regulation of the fixed terminating tariffs could be taken as a given and to what extent it influences the market position of the mobile operators. Furthermore, the CBB was of the opinion that OPTA's decision lacked adequate reasoning and evidence for several other aspects. For instance, it considered that the OPTA did not adequately deal with the question whether tariff regulation was really necessary to deal with the possible problems of market power. Here it referred to the fact that the tariffs already went down substantially in recent years. Irrespective of whether this decrease was caused by a threat of the NMa to take enforcement action or by other factors, the CBB suggested that the OPTA should have examined whether it was possible to tackle the perceived competition problems on the basis of general competition law. On the basis of the foregoing the CBB annulled OPTA's decision.[77]

Although the CBB did not substitute OPTA's assessment for its own, it very critically reviewed the reasoning and assessment made by the OPTA. It is interesting to note that the CBB took this critical stance despite the fact that the European Commission had already approved the decision concerned by making no comments on the basis of Article 7 of the Framework Directive. It is also interesting to note that the CBB handed down its judgment after the UK Competition Tribunal had been very critical of the reasoning and evidence put forward by the OFCOM to regulate the mobile terminating access tariffs of the UK mobile operators, in particular on the part relating to the presence of countervailing buyer power on the part of the incumbent British Telecom, resulting in an annulment of the decision.[78] It is not clear, however, whether the CBB had taken notice of the latter judgment, since it does not refer to it.

## 6 The role of the European Commission

As mentioned before, the European Commission has several powers to interfere in national administrative procedures, e.g. by making comments on draft national decisions, by raising serious doubts or by blocking draft decisions on the basis of the electronic communications directives.[79] This raises the question to what extent the Commission interventions may influence the standard of review and the standard of proof applied by the national courts. The

---

77 Following the CBB' s judgment the OPTA adopted a new decision that was again annulled by the CBB on the basis of a lack of adequate reasoning. CBB, 23 July 2008, AWB 07/674, UPC et al, LJN: BD8280.

78 CAT 29 November 2005, *Hutchinson 3G UK Limited* v. *OFCOM* [2005] CAT 39.

79 See Article 7 of Directive 2002/21/EC.

answer to this question will depend on the type of act of the Commission and its legal effects vis-à-vis the national authorities. For this purpose the following acts can be distinguished: veto decisions, no comments, comments and serious doubts.

Obviously, in harmony with the *Masterfoods* case law, the national courts will have to respect binding Commission Decisions vetoing draft decisions when reviewing decisions of the National Regulatory Authorities.[80] When the national courts have doubts on the validity of those decisions, they have to submit preliminary questions to the ECJ on the basis of Article 234 EC.

As shown in the *Mobile terminating access* case, it often happens that a National Regulatory Authority notifies a draft decision to the European Commission and the Commission implicitly approves it by stating it has no comments. This means the Commission is of the opinion that the draft decision is in harmony with European law and does not frustrate the creation of the internal market. One would think that an implicit approval by the European Commission would make it easier for the authority to argue that the decision concerned satisfies the legal conditions of the law. However, despite an approval of the European Commission, the CBB and the CAT have not refrained from strictly reviewing the decisions concerned. It is submitted that this is the right approach. If the European Commission has concluded on the basis of a more abstract analysis that a decision does not violate European law, the national court will take note of this when assessing the national decision. One could even argue that the national courts should take into account the opinion of the Commission on the basis of Article 10 EC, requiring the courts to loyally cooperate with the European Commission when applying European law, although they can deviate from it by providing adequate reasons.[81] Nevertheless, it is still up to the national courts to protect the right to effective legal protection of the market parties by verifying whether the decisions concerned are carefully prepared, well reasoned, based on convincing evidence and whether the substantive and procedural rights which the market parties derive from European law are protected.

In other cases the Commission made comments or made suggestions in order to improve the reasoning and evidence of the decision of the NRA concerned. Article 7 of the Framework Directive requires the NRAs to take those comments into account when exercising their powers. An analysis of the case law shows that the CBB does take note of these types of suggestions and comments, but still makes an assessment of a decision on the basis of all the evidence gathered in a case.[82] For instance, in one case the European Commission suggested that the OPTA should impose the regulatory remedy of separate accounts it made KPN subject to on the market for access to the local loop also on the market for wholesale low quality broadband access. The OPTA pointed

80 Case C-344/98 *Masterfoods* [2000] ECR I-11369.

81 See for this argument Lavrijssen (2006) p. 132 ff.

82 Pietermaat (2007) p. 345. See for instance: CBB, AWB 06/120 en 06/136, *TeLe2 et al*, LJN: BA4656.

out that the Commission merely made this suggestion in order to give the OPTA better possibilities to monitor the market concerned, and not because regulation of the second market was necessary as a consequence of the risk for anti-competitive leveraging between the first and second market. In that light the CBB considered that the OPTA had adequately motivated why the suggested extension was not necessary.[83] The foregoing means that when the national authority has not followed the Commission suggestions, but has adequately explained why, it is up to the market parties to put forward convincing arguments that the remarks of the Commission should be taken into account by the national authority.

When the Commission has raised serious doubts concerning a draft regulatory decision, which is the step before the adoption of a binding veto decision, it is likely that the national court will critically assess the elements of the decision to which the Commission objects, raising the standard of proof of the national authority to illustrate it has adequately dealt with the Commission's objections. The Commission has at one time raised serious doubts concerning a draft decision of the OPTA relating to the regulation of the retail tariffs for the transmission of broadcasting signals. However, since the OPTA came to an agreement with the Commission on the amendment of the decision, leading to a withdrawal of the serious doubts, the CBB considered that it could assume the OPTA has adequately addressed the objections of the Commission.[84] Therefore OPTA was not obliged to fully reconsider the case. Nevertheless, the CBB considered that this would not prevent the market parties from showing that the objections that were raised by the Commission were still so weighty that the OPTA could not have taken the decision without opening a new investigation.

## 7 Conclusion

Taking into account that the case law of the European courts and the national courts relating to the standard of review and the standard of proof is still evolving, four concluding observations can be made.

First, despite the fact that the NRAs and NCAs enjoy considerable discretion in applying economic regulation and/or competition law, the foregoing analysis shows that the national courts do not shy away from intensively scrutinising the assessment of the facts in the light of the law. At times, particularly the District Court may be tempted to substitute the national authorities' assessments, whereas the CBB usually follows a middle course between a marginal review and a full review on the merits.

Although the exact standard of review applied is attuned to the specifics of each case, the District Court and the CBB generally review the facts and evidence of the case critically and require the national authorities to provide

83 CBB, judgment of 2 May 2007, AWB 06/134, 06/135 and 06/137, *BBNED et al.* v. *OPTA*, LJN: BA4461.

84 CBB, 24 July 2007, AWB 06/322, *Casema et al.* v. *OPTA*, LJN: BB0186, par. 9.1.3.

sufficiently plausible evidence of the existence of a competition problem. A closer examination reveals that the 'plausible' standard in fact resembles the *Tetra Laval* standard applied by the ECJ to review Commission Decisions. The national authorities should substantiate their decisions with convincing evidence, based on a realistic and high quality factual basis and not on abstract and theoretical assumptions. If they make use of econometric models, it should be ensured that the models concerned are transparent, in that they are based on realistic and consistent assumptions and deliver transparent and consistent results. The analysis also shows that the national courts are not prevented from safeguarding the substantive and procedural right the market parties derive from European law by thoroughly reviewing decisions that were implicitly approved by the European Commission.

Secondly, although the national courts are not obliged to follow the standard of review and the standard of proof applied by the ECJ when reviewing Commission Decisions, there are indications that the District Court and the CBB are inspired by the case law of the ECJ, and by the *Tetra Laval* case in particular. The CBB refers implicitly to paragraph 39 of the *Tetra Laval* case to specify what its 'plausible' standard of review means and how it influences the standard of proof that has to be met by the NMa. However, neither the CBB nor the District Court of Rotterdam explicitly mention the relevant cases of the European courts or motivate why it is relevant for them, which would be advisable for the sake of transparency and legal certainty.

Furthermore, it can be observed that, like the European courts, the national courts increasingly require the national authorities to base their decisions on sound economic analysis. The District Court and the CBB reject a rigid application of competition law by the NMa and require an adequate economic analysis of the economic and legal context within which agreements function, and their appreciable effect on the relevant market. For instance, in applying European law, the CBB in *SECON* has specified how the NMa should assess the appreciable effect of (object) agreements. Moreover, both the CFI and the CBB require the competition authorities to consider, taken into account the actual legal and economic context, whether certain behaviour may actually be presumed to be detrimental to consumer welfare in order to qualify it as an object restriction. It is submitted that as the European and national courts increasingly tend to impose strict requirements on the competition authorities with regard to the economic analysis of object agreements, the standard of proof in these cases has risen. Consequently, the traditional boundary between object and effect restrictions has become blurred. However, in its *T-Mobile* judgment the ECJ seems to have put a hold on the economic requirements that have to be met for the application of Article 81 EC. The awaited judgment of the ECJ in *Glaxo Smith Kline* will probably shed more light on the requirements for the application of Article 81 EC and the resulting burden of proof for the Commission and the national competition authorities.

The fourth observation that can be made is that the CBB applies the 'plausible' standard of review to different types of decisions of the NMa, such as merger decisions and decisions relating to the cartel prohibition. Therefore, the 'plausible' standard of review and the resulting standard of proof, resembling the *Tetra Laval* standard of review, seem to be flexible enough to take into account the specifics of each case, such as the distinction between *ex post* and *ex ante* analysis. However, where this latter point is concerned, the case law is not yet clarified. This gives the courts the opportunity to formulate more guidance for the manner in which this standard should apply to different cases and the requirements which should follow for the national authorities, provided they leave sufficient room for dealing with the specifics of each case and for innovations in economic theory and modelling.

It is submitted that the development of a more intensive review of decisions of national authorities with regard to the application of competition law and/or economic regulation is a vice from the perspective of the right to effective legal protection of the market parties. Indeed, the actual standard of review applied will differ depending on the type of decision under review, in that generally specific decisions will be reviewed more intensively than the adoption of general binding rules. Nevertheless, it is advocated that even in the latter case, the national courts should not apply a very marginal standard of review. On the basis of the principle of effective legal protection and the proportionally principle they should assess whether the general rules at issue were carefully prepared, including a public consultation of the interested stakeholders and an assessment of the costs and benefits of the different regulatory alternatives, and amount to a proportionate balancing of conflicting interests.

Of course the national courts should also take into account the inherent complexities of economic analysis and take care that they do not prevent the national authorities from exercising their tasks in an effective way. Moreover, in a setting of multi level governance, decision-making is often a joint responsibility, as more European and national public entities and private parties may be involved in the decision-making process. Therefore, in each case the courts will have to balance between the right to effective legal protection with the need for efficient and effective multi-level decision-making processes. In this regard the *Tetra Laval* standard may be a good starting point. By applying this standard the courts may serve as a catalyst to ensure that decision-making procedures are proper, including the consultation of all interested parties, and that the evidence basis is of high quality, encompassing all relevant facts. This enables the national courts to review whether all conflicting interests are weighed in a proportionate way, but without substituting the opinion of the competent bodies with their own.[85]

[85] In this regard Scott and Sturm refer to the catalyst function of the courts, Scott (2007) pp. 565-594.

## Bibliography


ALBERS (2005)

H.S.J. Albers, [2005/4] *Nederlands Tijdschrift voor Energierecht* 2005 pp. 169-173

BAILEY (2004)

D. Bailey, 'Standard of Proof in EC Merger Proceedings: A Common Law Perspective' [2004/5] *Common Market Law Review* pp. 1327-1360

BAY (2005)

M.F. Bay & Calzado, 'Tetra Laval II-The Coming Age of the Judicial Review of Merger Decisions' [2005/4] *World Competition* pp. 443-440

CARANTA (2004)

R. Caranta, M. Andenas & D. Fairgrieve, *Independent Administrative Authorities* (British Institute of International and Comparative Law London 2004)

COUMANS (2006)

J.J.A. Coumans [2006/2] *Markt en Mededinging* pp. 47-55

HANCHER (2003)

L. Hancher, P. Larouche & S. Lavrijssen, 'Principles of Good Market Governance' [2003/4] *Journal of Network Industries* pp. 355-389

HOFMANN (2007)

H.C.H. Hofmann & A. Türk, 'The Development of Integrated Administration in the EU and its Consequences' [2007/2] *European Law Journal* p. 267

JANS (2002)

J.H. Jans, R. de Lange, S. Prechal & R.J.G.M. Widdershoven, *Inleiding tot het Europees Bestuursrecht* (Ars Aequi Libri Nijmegen 2002)

JANS (2005)

J.H. Jans, *Doorgeschoten? Enkele opmerkingen over de gevolgen van de Europeanisering van het bestuursrecht voor de grondslagen van de bestuursrechtspraak* (Europa Law Publishing Groningen 2005)

KALBFLEISCH (2005)

P. Kalbfleisch, President of the Board of the NMa, '*Intensiteit van rechterlijke toetsing van besluiten van marktautoriteiten*', speech on the occasion of the fiftieth anniversary of the CBB, www.nmanet.nl

KORTMANN (2005)

C.A.J.M. Kortmann, *Constitutioneel recht*, (Kluwer Deventer 2005)

LAVRIJSSEN (2004)

S. Lavrijssen, 'De rol van de Nederlandse administratieve rechter bij het toezicht op de mededinging' [2004/1] *SEW* p. 34 ff.

LAVRIJSSEN (2006)

S. Lavrijssen & M. de Visser, 'Independent Administrative Authorities and the Standard of Judicial Review' [2006/1] *Utrecht Law Review* pp. 111-135

LAVRIJSSEN (2006) II

S. Lavrijssen, *Onafhankelijke mededingingstoezichthouders, regulerende bevoegdheden en de waarborgen voor good governance* (Boom Juridische Uitgevers Den Haag 2006)

LEEFLANG (2001)

F.J. Leeflang and K.J.M. Mortelmans [2001/1] *Mediaforum* pp. 20-33

LEEFLANG (2002)

F.J. Leeflang, [2002/9] *Actualiteiten Mededingingsrecht* pp. 171-176

LEGAL (2006)

H. Legal, 'Standards of Proof and Standards of Judicial Review in EU Competition law', in: *Annual Proceedings of the Fordham Corporate Law Institute: International Antitrust and Policy* (Juris Publishing 2006) pp. 107-116

LOOZEN (2006)

E. Loozen [2006/3] *Markt & Mededinging* pp. 88-92

MOK (2002)

M.R. Mok [2002/11] *SEW* p. 422

OTTOW (2005)

A.T. Ottow, 'De bewijspositie van de NMa en de rechterlijke toetsing van besluiten inzake aanmerkelijke marktmacht' [2005/6] *Mediaforum* pp. 227-228

OTTOW (2006)

A.T. Ottow, *Telecommunicatietoezicht, De invloed van het Europese en Nederlandse bestuurs(proces)recht* (SDU Den Haag 2006)

OTTOW (2008)

A.T. Ottow & E. Doing-Bierens, 'Enige contouren van het economisch bewijsrecht', [2008] *Jbplus* pp. 170-187

PARRET (2008)

L. Parret, 'Sense and Nonsense of Rules on Proof in Cartel Cases: How to Reconcile a More Economic-Based Approach to Competition Law with More Attention for Rules on Proof' [2008/1] *European Competition Journal* pp. 169-1999

PIETERMAAT (2007)

E. Pietermaat & A. Ottow, 'De rechterlijke toetsing van OPTA's marktanalyses, Procedurele aspecten' [2007/11] *Mediaforum* pp. 343-350

PRECHAL (2005)

S. Prechal et al., *'Europeanization' of the Law: Consequences for the Dutch Judiciary*, report for the Dutch Council of the Judiciary, October 2005, pp. 39-40

SCHUURMANS (2007)

Y. Schuurmans, 'De toetsing van de feitenvaststelling in Europees perspectief', in: T. Barkhuysen, W. den Ouden & E. Steyger, *Europees recht effectueren* (Kluwer Alphen aan den Rijn 2007)

SCOTT (2007)

J. Scott & S. Sturm, 'Courts as Catalysts; Re-thinking the Judicial Role in New Governance' [2007/3] *Columbia Journal of European Law* pp. 565-594

STROINK (1995)

F. Stroink, 'Judicial Control of the Administration's Discretionary Powers (le bilan executive-juge administrative)', in: R. Bakker, A.W. Heringa & F. Stroink (eds), *Judicial Control, Comparative Essays on Judicial Review*, (Antwerp-Apeldoorn 1995)

VAN GINNEKEN (2007)

P. van Ginneken, [2007/2] *Markt en Mededinging* pp. 56-60

VAN WIJK (2005)

Van Wijk, Konijnenbelt en Van Male, *Hoofdstukken van Bestuursrecht* (Elsevier Juridisch, Den Haag 2005)

VERHEY (2003)

L. Verhey & T. Zwart, *Agencies in European and Comparative Perspective* (Intersentia Antwerpen-Oxford-New York 2003)

VERHEY (2005)

L.F.M. Verhey & N. Verheij, 'De macht van de marktmeesters, markttoezicht in constitutioneel perspectief', in: *Toezicht, Handelingen Nederlandse Juristen Vereniging* (Kluwer Deventer 2005)

VESTERDORF (2003)

B. Vesterdorf, 'Certain Reflections on Recent Judgments Reviewing Commission Merger Control Decisions', in: M. Hoskins & W. Robinson (eds), *A True European: Essays for Judge David Edward*, (Hart Oxford 2003.

CHAPTER II

# Judicial Review in Competition Law and Economic Regulation in Spain

I. Del Guayo

## 1 Introduction

This contribution attempts to analyse whether the standard of judicial review applied in Spain has been, or will be, influenced by EU Law, and, in particular, by the judgment of the ECJ in the *Tetra Laval* case, issued in 2005.[1] Section 2 of this chapter gives a short description of a number of key concepts and institutions of the Spanish legal order. In order to properly set in context the analysis of the influence of *Tetra Laval* on the Spanish legal order, and keeping in mind that the *Tetra Laval* judgment not only has to do with an economic concentration of two companies but also means a shift in the intensity of the review applied by the EU Courts, there is the need to briefly describe the provisions of the Spanish Constitution in three main areas: i) the economy (section 3.1), ii) the respective positions *vis-à-vis* of, on the one hand, the Judiciary, and, on the other hand, the Government and the public administration (section 3.2); and iii) the judicial review of governmental and administrative activities (section 3.3). The chapter then moves into a brief description of how the Spanish Judiciary reviews decisions in economic areas (section 4). The extent of the influence of *Tetra Laval* in economic concentration cases is subject to evaluation, in the light, among others, of two controversial judgments of the Spanish Supreme Court (the *Sogecable/Vía Digital*, and the *Endesa/Gas Natural* cases, in section 5). The next section is devoted to the prospective influence which the new Defence of Competition Act 2007 may have on judicial review (section 6), and finally, a concluding remark is attached (section 7).

## 2 Some key concepts and institutions

In an attempt to clarify these issues from the very outset, amidst the remarkable conceptual and terminological divergences within the EU, this section seeks to offer a basic description of a number of crucial concepts and institutions in Spanish Law, related to the issues involved in the *Tetra Laval* case.

In Spain, the Government and the public administration enjoy discretion, whenever it is so stated by an Act of Parliament, but the Constitution expressly prohibits arbitrariness. Moreover, the Constitution awards the Government the role of deploying its own policies, including economic policy, by which it chooses from a number of options. These choices can not be overturned by the Judiciary when reviewing the decisions of the Government. This constitutional role of the Government differs from discretion in that the choice of a policy is not the choice from a number of legal options. Judicial review of these choices of the Government has a wide scope, and includes not only review of the legality of decisions, but also a check whether discretion has been exercised, or not, within the limits established by the relevant Act of Parliament, and, in any

[1] Case C-12/03P *Tetra Laval* [2005] ECR I-987.

case, whether it has turned, or not, into arbitrariness. For example, the lack of sufficient explanations of the grounds on which a discretionary decision has been adopted, is considered to be arbitrary. The burden of proof within judicial review of administrative and governmental decisions follows the ordinary rules of procedure on civil matters, so that it is up to the party (either the Public Administration or the private subject), to affirm the existence of a fact and to give enough evidence of its existence. No particular limits exist in the number and intensity of proofs which can be used within this procedure. In a few words, Spanish courts are constitutionally empowered to exercise an intense review of administrative action in accordance with the relevant Act of parliament, but there is a limit that courts do not, and cannot trespass. This limit lies in the subjective opinion of the Government in areas where it enjoys discretion, an opinion which the court cannot replace with its own view. There are, however, some judgments of the Spanish courts, which are clearly neither within nor beyond said limit.[2]

With regard to economic concentrations issues, the Spanish Government adopted decisions under the 1989 Act for the Defence of Competition which could be appealed before the judicial review division of the Supreme Court, which is the highest Court within the Judiciary. This adoption took place after a prior report of the Tribunal for the Defence of Competition. This Tribunal was an independent body of the Public Administration and not a member of the judiciary, but rather organisationally located within the Ministry for Economy (hereafter: TDC). The new 2007 Act for the Defence of Competition, repealing the Act of 1989, replaces the former TDC with a National Commission for Competition (hereafter CNC). The CNC is also an independent body of the Public Administration. The difference with the former situation is that the CNC adopts final decisions, except when it decides either to prohibit a concentration to proceed or to subordinate it to the fulfilment of certain commitments proposed by the notifying parties or to subordinate it to certain conditions. In cases of prohibition or subordination of a concentration, the Government is empowered to allow the concentration to proceed or to modify or annul the conditions whenever it thinks it is appropriate, on grounds of a number of reasons not linked to the maintenance of competition in the market.[3] Decisions of the CNC relating to concentrations may be appealed to the judicial review division of the National Audience. This is a court, a member of the Judiciary, whose jurisdiction extends to the whole country and whose judgments may in turn be appealed to the judicial review division of the Supreme Court. Decisions of the Government relating to economic concentrations may directly be appealed to the judicial review division of the Supreme Court.[4]

An assessment of the influence of *Tetra Laval* on Spanish Courts can only be reached by means of a prior determination of what *Tetra Laval* has really meant

---

[2] See further sections 3.2 and 3.3.

[3] See further section 6 of this contribution.

[4] See further sections 4, 5, and 6 of this contribution.

to EU Law. If *Tetra Laval* is understood as a full deployment, or the logical consequence, of the traditional review based on the manifest error test, its influence will be restrained to reinforce a trend already in existence in Spain. If, on the contrary, *Tetra Laval* is understood to have meant a review of the appreciation of economic facts of the European Commission or, even further, an evaluation of the appropriateness of the decision of the European Commission (rather than its legality), as a matter of principle Spanish courts will not be ready to support that trend.[5]

## 3 Constitutional framework

### 3.1 The Spanish Constitution and the economy

The Spanish Constitution was approved in 1978, and is divided in ten Titles, dealing, respectively, with fundamental rights and duties, the Crown, the Spanish Parliament, the Government and the public administration, the relationship between Parliament and Government, the judiciary, economy and taxes, the territorial distribution of powers, the Constitutional Court, and amendments to the Constitution. It is the Fundamental Act, and any other norms are subordinated to it.

There are a number of constitutional provisions on the fundamental rights and freedoms which apply to economic activities, such as the right to own private property, subject to those social obligations which Parliamentary Acts may impose; accordingly, no expropriation of private goods can occur unless there is a public social interest in such expropriation, which is then subject to indemnification.[6] The Constitution also recognises freedom of enterprise within the framework of a market economy; public authorities guarantee and protect it, and foster productivity, in accordance with the exigencies of the national economy and, as the case may be, with those of planning.[7] Therefore, the Constitution limits governmental intervention in the business of private companies, as it must be based on the general interest.

On the one hand, the Constitution authorises the Public Administration to run commercial activities, which is just a possibility, not a constitutional exigency. This authorisation means that the Public Administration can create public companies in whatever fields it thinks appropriate. Under this provision neither special privileges nor monopolistic rights can be awarded to those public undertakings.[8] On the other hand, the Constitution states that 'from time to time, a Parliamentary Act may reserve to the public sector the management

5 See further, on the meaning of *Tetra Laval*, Calviño (2007) pp. 220-224.

6 Article 33.

7 Article 38.

8 Article 128 (2, first sentence).

of essential resources or services, especially those of a monopolistic nature'.[9] Roughly speaking, this provision would be the basis for the establishment of public services. 'Essential services' has a wider meaning than 'public services' and in this respect it is considered that all public services are essential, but not all essential services will be public services. After the accession of Spain to the EU in 1986, there was a switch of interest from the concept of public services to the concept of services of general economic interest.[10] Moreover, reservations of essential services may be, under certain circumstances, against EU Law. In any case, the freedom which the Public Administration enjoyed, prior to the accession of Spain to the EU, to choose how a public service (a reserved essential service) should be managed, including by monopoly, has been narrowed by EU Law, since it prohibits the maintenance of State monopolies of an economic nature or the creation of new ones.[11] The focus is now on how public or universal service obligations can impose restrictions on competition and liberalisation.

The current distribution of powers between central ('the State'), regional (the seventeen Autonomous Communities), and local (around 8,000 Municipalities) government levels implies a remarkable decentralisation that includes economic matters.

### 3.2 The Government, the Public Administration, and the Judiciary

There is a constitutional distinction between the Public Administration and the Government, which may have an influence on the extent and scope of judicial review. The Constitution states that the Public Administration serves the general interest with objectivity and acts in full subordination to the law.[12] With regard to the Government, the Constitution states that it conducts domestic and foreign policy, civil and military administration and the defence of the State; it exercises executive authority and has the power to make statutory regulations in accordance with the Constitution and the laws.[13] The leadership of domestic policy is understood to include economic policy.

Within the Spanish Legal Order, the Judiciary (judges and courts) is a power that operates independently from Parliament and Government (and Public Administration).[14] There are decisions of ordinary courts divided into sections dealing, respectively, with civil, social, criminal, commercial, military, and administrative issues. The judges and courts belonging to the administrative division are the ones called on to exercise judicial review of administrative action. Besides the ordinary courts, the Constitutional Court also has the task

9 Article 128 (2, first part of the second sentence).

10 Article 86 EC Treaty.

11 Article 31 EC Treaty.

12 Article 103.

13 Article 97.

14 Article 117.

of solving disputes between the Central Government and the Autonomous Communities. Furthermore, the Constitutional Court has exclusive rights to repeal an Act of Parliament if it considers that the Act concerned contravenes the Constitution. Moreover, the Court is entrusted with the task of the protection of certain fundamental rights of citizens by means of a special application (*recurso de amparo*).

### 3.3 Judicial review of governmental and administrative decisions

In accordance with the Spanish Constitution, every person has the right to obtain effective protection from the judges and the courts in the exercise of their rights and legitimate interests, and in no case may there be a lack of legal protection.[15] This is one of the grounds for the courts to review the whole administrative action, and for citizens to seek protection from the courts whenever any of their rights have been affected by an activity of the Public Administration.

According to the Constitution, the courts control the rule-making power of the Public Administration, and the legality of the administrative action, as well as the full compliance of said action with the aims for its justification.[16] This constitutional provision is the legal basis for a universal jurisdiction of the courts over administrative decisions, as well as over the lack of proper action by the Public Administration.

There is, however, a debate going on whether such universal jurisdiction over Public Administration can also be extended to the Government, particularly when its activity is not subject to administrative law; that is when the Government acts as a political body, and not as the Public Administration. In that regard the evolution of the Spanish legal order shows that the number of decisions which are to be described as *governmental political acts*, as opposed to *governmental administrative acts*, is being progressively narrowed, and there is consensus that this kind of acts are limited to the dissolution of Parliament (and the call for general elections), the decision to send a Draft Act to Parliament or to withdraw it, calling for a referendum, the establishment of diplomatic relations with a third country and, in general terms, those decisions which do not result in external legal effects on any person. Moreover, the Spanish Legal order has evolved in the sense that even those governmental political decisions can be reviewed by courts in two regards: first, for the protection of fundamental rights; second, for the review of those aspects of the decisions which are not discretionary, but are subject to specific rules, such as procedural ones. The notion of discretion is closely linked to the notion of *undefined legal concepts* and the doctrine of the margin of *appraisal*,[17] but in dealing with political decisions

---

[15] Article 24.

[16] Article 106 (1).

[17] See further, on discretion in Spanish Law, Alonso García (2008) pp. 130-133.

it will be useful to refer to the notion of judicially accessible concepts (*conceptos judicialmente asquibles*), particularly with respect to judicial review of economic regulatory decisions. Those judicially accessible concepts are the limits or prior requirements to which governmental decisions, leading policies, are bound. Although said decisions are immune to judicial review, those limits and/or requirements would be helpful to the review in case of *ultra vires* or a lack of compliance.[18]

In simple terms, the distinction between Public Administration and Government may lead to the identification of two streams of legal thinking among Spanish lawyers. On the one hand, there are those who emphasise the need not to leave any aspect of administrative and governmental activity outside the scope of judicial review and therefore, highlight the need to allow courts to get to the core of public decisions by strictly limiting the concept and scope of political governmental decisions. On the other hand, there are those who accentuate the need to respect a scope for the Government to exercise the discretionary powers it has been allocated by the Constitution and the legal order, so that courts do not interfere in policy decisions. This simplification attempts to put the issues involved in the *Tetra Laval* Decision in a wider context. However, it must be mentioned that it does not reflect the whole of the arguments of either the former or the latter, nor does it honour the many remarks and variations one may find in the arguments of the followers of any of those two streams.

Since *Tetra Laval* deals with the intensity of judicial review over discretionary powers, it must be underlined that the Spanish constitutional order lays down the basis for a fundamental distinction between discretion and arbitrariness. In that regard the Constitution guarantees the prohibition of arbitrary action of public authorities,[19] which obviously includes the prohibition of arbitrariness imposed upon the Government and the Public Administration. This prohibition offers the courts enough grounds to follow the same doctrine as the one included in *Tetra Laval*, insofar that the courts could rely upon it to review whether the evidence contained information of an economic nature, on which the reviewed decision relies 'is factually accurate, reliable and consistent, and also whether such evidence contains all the information which must be taken into account in order to assess a complex situation'.[20]

It has also been pointed out that 'the existence of discretionary powers does not exclude judiciary control since, in any case, public actions must conform to the principle of legality and the protection of individual rights and legitimate intersts. This means, as the Spanish Court has stated, that the scope for judicial review must be enhanced to allow for substituting the administrative act with

18 Decisión of the Supreme Court, of 4 April, 1997, in the case of the Spanish Intelligence Service (CESID).

19 Article 9 (3).

20 Case C-12/03P *Commission* v. *Tetra Laval BV* [2005] ECR I-987, no 39.

a judicial decision if the law provides all the relevant features to determine the content of that decision'.[21]

The progressive implementation of the *Estado de Derecho* in Spain (literally translated into English as *State of Law*, or *Rule of Law*, in accordance with the British tradition, or *Rechtsstaat*, following the German expression) has meant the progressive reduction of public discretion and, in parallel, the progressive statutory design of when and how discretion is to be exercised by public authorities. The current relatively more intense judicial review in Spain, in comparison with other EU countries, might be explained by historical reasons, as a pendulum-like motion after a long-lasting non-democratic political system (from 1939 to 1975) and therefore the lack of proper control of Government, but that conclusion would not be entirely accurate. An argument like that could be valid with regard to governmental acts, but not with regard to administrative acts. The 1956 Judicial Review Act, which was in force until 1998, i.e., for twenty more years after the entry into force of the 1978 Constitution, contributed to the creation of a *State of Legality*, yet far from a proper *State of Law*, by which courts were empowered to intensively review administrative action, even though crucial areas of governmental action were outside the scope of judicial review.[22]

## 4 Judicial review of administrative and governmental decisions on economic issues

As a starting point of the analysis, we may agree upon a degree of reluctance on the side of the courts not only to quash administrative decisions on economic issues, but also to review the core of the decision on grounds related to, on the one hand, the technical discretion which is involved in such decisions, a discretion which they can not substitute with their own, and on the other hand, the fact that the decisions have been adopted in the light of reports produced by specialised bodies.

This approach can be summarised by quoting a paragraph of three judgments of the Supreme Court in three appeals dealing with the authorisation of the Government, which was awarded to SEPI (a state Agency holding governmental stakes in several companies), to privatise three former public enterprises:

> 'The scope of judicial review has two limits. Firstly, because the reviewed authorisation enjoys a discretionary nature and it is a decision adopted within the economic policy of the Government, which is outside the scope of judicial review. Secondly, because the authorisation itself, as an instrument of governmental

[21] Alonso García (2008) pp. 131 and 153.

[22] I am thankful to Adam Scott, from the UK Competition Appeal Tribunal, for pointing out this issue at the Seminar which was held at the *Europa Institute* of Utrecht University School of Law, on 22 and 23 May 2008.

> control on SEPI, can not have such a wide scope, so that it may interfere with the commercial strategy of SEPI' *(authors translation)*.[23]

This was also the attitude of the Spanish Supreme Court towards the decision of the Bank of Spain, of 28 December 1993, to substitute the Board of Directors of *Banco Español de Crédito* (BANESTO) by a number of administrators the Bank of Spain appointed itself, a decision based on the risky financial situation of BANESTO.[24]

However, a number of judgments of the Spanish Supreme Court show its readiness to deal with the substance of the decision. A remarkable and very controversial judgment of the Supreme Court was the one adopted in 1989, by which the decision of the Municipality of Barcelona to set up a commercial company called *Iniciatives* was quashed by the Court. The Supreme Court found that the Municipality had violated the procedural rules to set up a commercial company, since in that regard it had not properly followed the provisions of the Local Act 1985. If the judgment of the Court had stopped there, it would not have been worth mentioning here, since the review of procedural aspects and the quashing of an administrative decision on procedural grounds has always been an option for the courts, the core of the decision to create a commercial company remaining untouched. However, the Court went further in that it found the purpose of the corporation to be too vague, so that the Municipality had not properly justified why the setting up of such a company was in the general interest of the people of Barcelona. The Court argued that the creation of public undertakings is subject to the principle of specificity or specialisation, an argument that some commentators found to be an invention of the Court. The Court, however, connected this principle with European Community Law insofar as the ambiguity of the purpose of the corporation *Iniciatives*, linked with the fact that its activities were going to be publicly funded, violated the principles of the European Internal Market and in particular the state aid rules.

This last judgment therefore shows that in certain circumstances the Spanish courts may depart from their relatively deferential attitude and go to the heart of administrative economic decisions.

## 5 Judicial review in economic concentration cases and the influence of *Tetra Laval*

### 5.1 General remarks

The extent of judicial review in competition cases must be linked with those provisions contained in the relevant Defence of Competition Act, since in Spanish law discretion is to be exercised when parliamentary Acts

[23] Decisions of 4 June 2001, 4 February 2003, and 26 January 2004.

[24] Decisions of 26 November 2001, 5 May 2004, and 14 March 2006.

so state, and in the way that it is stated. Consequently, judicial review will be confined to check whether discretion has been properly exercised by the relevant authority in accordance with what the parliamentary Acts state. In particular the courts will be empowered to check whether, taking all information into consideration, the decision is not arbitrary.

The defence of competition, including anticompetitive conducts, economic concentrations and state aids, is a key element of economic policy, since it promotes productivity and competitiveness. Spain has a new Defence of Competition Act 2007, which has substituted and repealed the former Defence of Competition Act of 1989. The new Act contains relevant changes for the issue to which this paper is devoted, since on the one hand it makes a switch of powers on economic concentrations from the Government to the new National Competition Commission (the CNC, which is set up to replace the former Tribunal for the Defence of Competition), and on the other hand it tries to tune the powers of the Government to allow an economic concentration to proceed whenever it has been banned by the CNC.

Before going into the new provisions of the Defence of Competition Act 2007 and its foreseeable effects on judicial review, I will give a brief explanation of the prior system and of the influence of *Tetra Laval* within the context of the former Act.

Under the Defence of Competition Act 1989, whenever the Service for the Defence of Competition (hereafter: SDC) of the Ministry of Economic Affairs so advised, the Ministry of Economic Affairs would refer to the TDC for a report when the Ministry thought a concentration would create an obstacle for the maintenance of effective competition in the market. Once produced, the Ministry of Economic Affairs would submit the report of the TDC to the Government and the Government would adopt any of the following decisions, within a maximum period of one month:

a) the decision to allow the concentration to proceed; or
b) the decision to subject the concentration to the fulfilment of a number of conditions capable to sufficiently contribute to the economic and social progress, so that they compensate the restrictive effects on competition; among other conditions, they may refer to the divestiture of a number of businesses or assets or to the imposition of limitations;[25] or
c) the decision holding a declaration of the concentration to be inadmissible.

The report of the TDC was not binding for the Government, but if the Government departed from the opinion of the TDC, the burden to justify why it did so fell on the Government's shoulders. The wording of the Act (*sufficiently contribute to the economic and social progress*) gave the Government a wide discretion, both in the number and quality of conditions it could impose on the concentration and in the determination of what social and economic progress meant.

---

[25] These provisions were adopted by Royal Decree-law no 2, of 2 February 2001, and Act no 9, of 4 June 2001.

The *Tetra Laval* judgment has had, as such, a limited impact on the jurisprudence of Spanish courts, if that impact can be measured by the number of times that judgment is referred to in judgments of the Spanish courts. Collaterally, I would like to note that in the day to day practice, Spanish courts do not refer as often to decisions of the ECJ as the case seems to be in other EU jurisdictions, due partially to the fact that Spain is a relatively young member of the EU. If *Tetra Laval* is, however, understood to have marked a starting point towards an intensive review of administrative discretion in competition cases, several recent key judgments of the Spanish Supreme Court show that our courts were already (prior to *Tetra Laval*), and are still, following that path.

There are, however, several examples of a relatively intensive review of governmental decisions in concentration cases, undertaken without reference to the *Tetra Laval* judgment of the Court of Justice. For example, in the judgment in the *Unión Radio* case, the Supreme Court[26] stated that the decision imposing conditions is an administrative act, whose control is located with the judges and courts of the administrative (judicial review) division. It decided to declare null and void the authorisation by the Government of two radio broadcasting companies to pass on the partial management of its activities to a third company. In doing so, the Supreme Court held that economic concentration of media companies can not only be analysed on grounds of the principles related to freedom of enterprise (Article 38 of the Spanish Constitution), but also on grounds of information pluralism (Article 20 of the Spanish Constitution). In other words, whereas in some economic sectors the functioning of the economic system does not impose the need of a plurality of competitors, in the media sector the decrease of competitors endangers political pluralism and therefore democracy.

In its judgment in the case *Prosegur/Blindados del Norte*,[27] the Supreme Court also stated that courts cannot substitute the discretionary content of the decision of the Government. However, this does not mean that discretion can be understood to be of an absolute nature, since in principle the validity of decisions subjecting mergers to conditions does not exclude the analysis of each of the conditions imposed to verify their conformity with the law.

Some other judgments reinforce the discretionary nature of governmental decisions on economic concentrations, though at the same time there is the underlying notion that judges are empowered to review the meta-legal criteria used by the Government by comparing them to factual reality so that the Government does not trespass the limits of rationality and it does not invoke discretion to act in an arbitrary way.[28]

---

26 Decision of 9 June 2000.

27 Decision of 2 April 2002.

28 Decision of the Supreme Court of 29 March 2004 (*Sociedad Azucarera Ebro Agrícola* case). See further, on the attitude of the Supreme Court towards governmental decisions on economic concentration issues, Trillo Torres (2007).

## 5.2 *Tetra Laval* in the case law of the Supreme Court

*Tetra Laval* has been referred to in two competition cases before the Supreme Court, but only in the, both dissenting, opinions issued by the minority of the judges. The judgments adopted by the majority of the Court do not mention the case. These judgments concern the *Sogecable/Vía Digital* case, and the *Endesa/Gas Natural* case. These will be discussed in the following section.

### 5.2.1 *The Sogecable/Vía Digital* case

The first case in which *Tetra Laval* plays a role deals with the merger of the two existing Digital Television Platforms (*Sogecable* and *Vía Digital*). On 29 November 2002 the Spanish Government allowed the concentration to proceed, but it was subject to ten conditions related to the market for the broadcasting of football events and to 24 conditions related to other broadcasting markets.

The decision of the Government was appealed by competitors, but the Supreme Court upheld the decision.[29] The Supreme Court stated that the appellants argue that the governmental solution is not the appropriate one, since its conditions are inefficient to compensate for the restrictive effects of the concentration on competition, and that therefore the proper decision would have been to reject the concentration. Against that statement the Court noted that it falls to the Government to evaluate the competitive circumstances in view of the produced reports within the file.

*Tetra Laval,* intentionally or unintentionally, assumes that, in principle, companies enjoy the right to merge and that the opposition of the Commission must be understood as an exception on grounds of the defence of the rights of other companies and of the protection of competition, so that the powers of the Commission to prohibit an economic concentration must be subject to a restrictive interpretation. This is also the position of the Spanish Supreme Court in the *Sogecable/Vía Digital* case, in which the Court held that subjecting the concentration to conditions is less restrictive of the freedom of enterprise than prohibiting the concentration.

In the view of the Supreme Court, a prohibition of a concentration can only be adopted when it is impossible to compensate the restrictive effects on competition by means of the imposition of conditions. However, the criteria to evaluate when this impossibility exists lie in the area of discretion for the Government. Also, it is the Government's choice as to which conditions it should impose when it finds there are indeed options to compensate the restrictive effects on competition, so that the Government can make the choice it thinks is the

[29] Decisions of the Supreme Court of 7 and 29 November 2005. The same conclusions are contained in the Decision of the Supreme Court of 3 October 2006 (in a similar appeal against the concentration between *Vía Digital* and *Sogecable*).

most appropriate to reach the aims of merger control. It is therefore a subjective consideration where the criteria of the Government overrule the particular opinion of appellants, which cannot be reviewed by courts other than by means of the mechanisms established by the legal order for the control of discretion. In any case, courts cannot substitute the discretionary content of the decision, as article 72 of the Judicial Review Act 1998 states.

In this judgment the Supreme Court refers to the judgments in the *Prosegur/Blindados del Norte* and *Unión Radio* cases, which were discussed in section 5.1. A considerable part of the judgment in the *Vía Digital/Sogecable* case is devoted to verifying whether the conditions imposed by the Government are sufficient to compensate for the restrictive effects on competition. Also, the judgment holds that those conditions are capable of maintaining the existing level of competition, for if the Government had tried to create more competition than existed before, it would have violated the right to freedom of enterprise of the companies involved in the concentration.

In one of the two dissenting opinions attached to the decision we read a reference to *Tetra Laval*:

> 'The majority of the Chamber leans to two general arguments which, in my view, are not entirely correct. The first one refers to the intensity of the judicial review of governmental decisions in concentration cases, particularly those aspects of the decision related to the conditions for approval. Although the majority and minority positions are not so distant as they may seem (as is also the case in the academic debate on the limits of judicial review of administrative discretion), the criteria, in accordance with Spanish Law, to judicially review discretion are stricter than simply checking whether discretion has been exercised in a manner that is arbitrary, irrational or grounded on a manifest error, as stated in the decision from which I dissent. Limiting the control of administrative discretion to those factors would mean, in my opinion, a backward movement in relation with previous decisions, from the last decades, of the Supreme Court. It is true that the reference to those factors is in the line of what the Court of First Instance of the EU has traditionally upheld in concentration cases, some of those judgments having been referred to by the judgment, but it does not take into account, on the one hand, the switch that the Court concerned recently made and the ECJ reinforced by making a much more profound analysis of the content of each decision which included the identification of errors. For this purpose, it is sufficient to read the judgment of 15 February 2005, by which the ECJ rejects the appeal of the Commission against the judgment of the Court of First Instance, adopted on 25 October 2002, Tetra Laval/Commission (T-5/02), by which it had renounced Decision no 2004/124/CE of 30 October 2001 related to concentration (COMP/M. 2416 Tetra Laval/Sidel). Against the position of the Commission, the judgment of the ECJ states that '*Whilst the Court recognises that the Commission has a margin of discretion with regard to economic matters, that does not mean that the Community Courts must refrain from reviewing the Commission's interpretation of information*

> *of an economic nature. Not only must the Community Courts, inter alia, establish whether the evidence relied on is factually accurate, reliable and consistent but also whether that evidence contains all the information which must be taken into account in order to assess a complex situation and whether it is capable of substantiating the conclusions drawn from it. Such a review is all the more necessary in the case of a prospective analysis required when examining a planned merger with conglomerate effect.'* On the other hand, I do not think that the existing parallel between the community judicial review and that of national courts must be translated into a decrease of the level of control already exercised by those national courts on national administrative decisions: parameters used by national courts to review administrative decisions, either of a discretionary nature or not, ought not to be equalised (in this case to a lower level of review), only because in EU law exists, or has existed, a more or less wide scope for the application of the deference principle in relation with decisions of the European administrative authority' (*authors translation*).[30]

The dissenting judge, therefore, holds that although the difference between his opinion and that of the majority of the court should not be overstated, there is an argument in the *Tetra Laval* judgment for a more intensive review than the Supreme Court is willing to undertake.

### 5.2.2 The *Endesa/Gas Natural* case

On 5 September 2005, the biggest Spanish Gas utility (*Gas Natural*) made a takeover bid for the biggest Spanish Electricity utility (*Endesa*), which was immediately considered by the former to be a hostile bid. This move set off the legal mechanisms of the Spanish legal order to deal with mergers of energy companies in three main areas, namely the security of energy supply, the protection of competition within energy markets and the transparency of the financial markets. While all those mechanisms were being developed, the German energy giant *E.On* made a takeover bid for *Endesa* on 20 February 2006, at a more attractive price for shareholders than the offer of *Gas Natural*. The bid of *E.On* caused a controversy between the European Commission and the Spanish Government with regard to the conditions the latter imposed upon *E.On* on grounds of the security of energy supply. Actually, the ECJ has recently condemned the Kingdom of Spain for not having withdrawn the conditions imposed upon *E.On*.[31] At the end of this complex story, neither *Gas Natural* nor *E.On* was successful in their purpose, but instead *Endesa* was taken over by both the Italian ENEL and the Spanish company *ACCIONA*. In the view of the Spanish Commission for Energy, the takeover could be approved by the Government, but would be subject to many conditions, including a far-reaching divestiture programme, whereas the TDC (the Tribunal for the Defence of Competition)

[30] See further, López de Castro García-Morato (2003) pp. 348-449.

[31] Case C-196/07 *Commission* v. *Spain* (OJ C 107, 26.04.08, p. 9).

expressed as its opinion that the takeover should be prohibited by the Government. The Spanish Government eventually authorised the takeover to proceed, subject to a number of conditions, which were not as strict as those proposed by the Energy Commission.

*Endesa* appealed against the governmental decision to allow the takeover-bid to proceed before the Spanish Supreme Court, and asked for an interim suspension of the bid. The Court awarded this suspension, but with a remarkable division of opinions among the judges-members of the panel; around half of them were in favour, the others were against. For a number of reasons, the interim suspension of the takeover meant the failure of the bid, as is always the case in concentrations procedures, due to a number of specificities of the Spanish judicial system; the remarkable slowness of it being the most relevant one.

In accordance with Spanish law, appeals against administrative acts in principle do not suspend the efficacy (or legal force) of the act, so that it can be enforced. The main statutory ground for awarding an interim judicial suspension of an administrative decision is the *periculum in mora*, that is the risk that if no interim suspension is awarded, the future judicial decision in favour of the applicant would be worthless. However, courts do also apply further verification, which is the analysis of the *prima facie* merits of the application for judicial review (*fumus boni iuris*); in other words, they check whether the arguments of the applicant might succeed, but only on first impression. However, in dealing with applications for interim relief courts are specifically asked by law not to make any statement on the substance of the case, that is, not to prejudge the case. Obviously, in doing this second check, there is a clear risk that courts get into the core of the decision and that is, in my view, what happened with the interim suspension of the takeover of *Gas Natural* over *Endesa*.

By means of a Judicial Resolution of the Spanish Supreme Court of 28 April 2006, the Court awarded Endesa the interim suspension it had asked for. The relevance of this Resolution is that the Court showed a strong readiness to analyse the decision of the Government. The arguments used by the Court, including the lack of competition in energy markets, and the actual inability of the conditions imposed by the Government to really compensate the restrictive effects on competition, clearly showed that the Court went beyond what is expected from a court in dealing with an application for judicial interim relief. On the other hand, the court said that if an interim suspension was not awarded at that moment, the reverse of the takeover, if the future final decision were issued in favour of the applicant (*Endesa*), would not be possible. Undoubtedly, the Court showed that it was ready to go to the substance of the governmental decision, in the line of *Tetra Laval*.

It must be noted that *Tetra Laval* quashed a decision of the Commission prohibiting a concentration, but that in this case the Spanish Supreme Court awarded interim relief with regard to (in practical terms, *quashed*) a decision of the Spanish Government which would allow the concentration to proceed. In my view, the intensity of the judicial review should be stronger in the first case (prohibition decisions) than in the second case (decisions to allow the concentration), since the fundamental constitutional right of freedom of enterprise is involved.

In fact, the *Tetra Laval* case is referred to in the Judical Resolution rewarding interim measures, of the Spanish Supreme Court of 28 April 2006. However, the reference can not be found in the text of the majority of judges, but in a dissenting opinion.[32] As part of a very detailed and fundamental dissenting opinion, the President of the Section made the following statement:

> 'With regard to the conglomerate effect, produced by the interaction of markets, as a consequence of the management of assets, which is different from the mere relation between assets within the organisation of the company, it must be taken into account, firstly, that authors almost unanimously consider that such a conglomerate effect does not automatically emerge against competition in all cases, and that is why, in this area, the analysis of the conglomerate effect must be done in accordance with European jurisprudence, taking into account the circumstances which, allegedly, will produce such negative effects, and must be analysed in a precise way, based on solid evidence (Decisions of the Court of First Instance, *Tetra Laval B* v. *Commission*, T-502, *Asunto* T-5/02 and T-342/99 *Airtours* v. *Commission*)' *(authors translation)*.[33]

This reference, however, seems limited to the assessment of the conglomerate effect, and does not seem to imply a less intensive review of the merger than undertaken by the Supreme Court itself. The Supreme Court itself indeed also showed that it is willing to undertake an intensive review, even in a case of interim measures, concerning a decision in which the concentration is allowed to proceed, which seems in accordance with the review of the Court of Justice in *Tetra Laval*.

## 6 Judicial review within the context of the new Defence of Competition Act 2007

As already noted, the new Defence of Competition Act 2007 may open the door for an even more substantive review of decisions on competition issues. The new regulation of the control of economic concentrations includes, firstly, a clarification and extension of the concept of concentration for the purposes of control, establishing a simplified procedure for operations less likely to affect competition. Secondly, the new Act maintains the system of mandatory notification with suspending effect, but envisages the possible revocation of the obligation to suspend the execution of the concentration at any

[32] In fact, the reference can be found in the dissenting opinion of the President of the Section for Judicial Review, who was in favour of dismissing the application of *Endesa* for interim relief.

[33] See further, Del Guayo (2007) pp. 1123-1127, and Del Guayo (2006).

time in the course of the proceedings. Thirdly, the treatment of takeover bids is aligned with Community treatment, so that the obligation of suspension shall only affect the exercise of the voting rights inherent in their titles and not the possibility of launching the bid. And fourthly, the new Act strengthens the participation of the CNC (the National Commission for Competition) in the control of concentrations, it limits the government's role in it, and it specifies the criteria of substantive assessment that will guide the decisions of both the CNC and the Government. With regard to the criteria of substantive assessment, the Act clearly separates those that will guide the decision-making process of the CNC, focusing on the maintenance of effective competition in the markets, from those on which government intervention may be based, related to the protection of the general interest of society.

Consequently, on the one hand, the elements that the CNC will assess are clarified with systematisation of, amongst others, those elements that have been considered to date from the reports of the former SDC (the Service for the Defence of Competition) and of the TDC (the Tribunal for the Defence of Competition), but with a clarification of the treatment of business efficiencies and maintenance of the assessment of the co-operative aspects or of the restrictions on competition accessory to concentrations. On the other hand, the criteria of substantive assessment are indicated, which will guide a contrary decision of the Council of Ministers, including a non-exhaustive list of specific criteria.

It is now for the CNC to adopt a final decision. At first instance, and within a first file, the CNC may authorise the concentration to proceed or to subordinate it to the fulfilment of certain commitments proposed by the notifying parties. If the CNC thinks that the concentration can create obstacles for the maintenance of competition in the market, it may open a second file and, at second instance, decide to prohibit the concentration to proceed, or to subordinate it to the fulfilment of certain commitments proposed by the notifying parties, or to subordinate it to conditions. When the CNC decides to prohibit a concentration, or to subordinate it to conditions, the Ministry for Economy may decide to refer the case to the Council of Ministers. The Council of Ministers may confirm the decision of the CNC or decide to authorise the concentration with or without further conditions. This decision must be duly justified on the basis of reasons of general interest other than protecting competition, in accordance with the provisions of the Act. These reasons are enumerated as being the following: a) defence and national security; b) protection of public security or public health; c) free movement of goods and services within the national territory; d) environmental protection; e) promotion of technological research and development; and f) guarantee of adequate maintenance of the objectives of sectoral regulation.

Decisions of the President and of the Council of the CNC may be appealed to the Judicial Review Section of the *Audiencia Nacional*, which is a central Court located in Madrid, whose judgment, in turn, may be appealed to the Judicial Review Section of the Spanish Supreme Court. It must be noted that the seventeen Spanish Autonomous Communities may establish their own authorities for the defence of competition within the territorial limits of each Community, whose decisions may be appealed to the Judicial Review Section of the High Court of the Community.[34]

The new Act seeks to limit the scope of discretion with respect to awarding or denying the authorisation to proceed with an economic concentration. It will also help courts to properly review decisions in this area, but problems will still emerge regarding the interpretation of a number of concepts, since, for example, the concept of national security is undoubtedly a vague one.[35]

## 7 Concluding remarks

The influence of *Tetra Laval* on Spanish Courts can only be assessed after the true meaning of said judgment has been clarified within the context of the jurisprudence of both the CFI and the ECJ, since it is sometimes difficult to determine whether *Tetra Laval* is a starting point or a finishing line. If *Tetra Laval* reveals no more than a stricter exercise of the traditional review, based on the traditional tests used by the EU courts, in particular the manifest error test, it would be fair to say that Spanish courts are already further ahead than the ECJ in pursuing that trend. However, if *Tetra Laval* is understood to have meant a more intensive review of a decision of the European Commission, so that as a result there is a substitution of the appreciation of economic facts of the European Commission by the appreciation of the Courts themselves, then *Tetra Laval* could hardly have any influence in Spanish courts, since it would clash with some constitutional exigencies and with the principles contained in the doctrine of the Spanish Supreme Court. In a case by case analysis, however, one may find judgments of the Supreme Court which might surpass what is the traditional understanding of the review of public discretion.

There are increasing signals of the willingness of the Spanish judiciary to review the core of governmental decisions on economic issues, including competition decisions, but this trend cannot be attributed only to judgments such as *Tetra Laval*, but mainly to a number of idiosyncratic characteristics of the Spanish legal order. These characteristics are, on the one hand, the progressive development of a number of key constitutional provisions, which have resulted in a more pro-active attitude of judges towards administrative and governmental decisions; on the other hand, recent legislation on judicial review provides for renewed foundations for substantial review of governmental decisions by means of a better understanding of what *political decisions* mean. Importantly, whenever constitutional rights are involved in a public decision, this fosters a more substantial review. This trend, however, will have to face three main limits. First, the technical character of decisions on the economy, involving a particu-

[34] Specific legislation has already been passed by the Autonomous Communities of Andalucía, Aragon, and Castille and Leon.

[35] See further, Soriano (2007).

lar expertise, which judges lack and which they are not asked to have, creates a presumption of correctness of decisions taken by specialised governmental or administrative bodies. Second, the Spanish legal order allocates discretionary powers on the economy to public authorities, such as the various Public Administrations and the Government itself, and not to judges, whose own discretion can not substitute the discretion of said authorities. Third, it is for the Government to design and implement policies, such as economic policy, and the review of the appropriateness of said policies by judges should be banned. In this regard it is worth mentioning that the Spanish Judge of the European Court of First Instance, in an express reference to *Tetra Laval*, has said that there is a *red line* which the Court cannot cross when reviewing decisions of the European Commission on economic concentration cases, so that the Court must limit itself to judge whether the appreciation of the European Commission is plausible and not whether other appreciations are equally possible.[36]

[36] García-Valdecasas y Fernández (2007) p. 211.

## Bibliography

ALONSO GARCÍA (2008)

R. Alonso García, L. Moral Soriano, and C. Plaza Martín, 'EU Rights and Discretion as Reflected in Spanish Public Law' in S. Prechal and B. van Roermund (eds), *The Coherence of EU Law. The search for Unity in Divergent Concepts* (Oxford University Press, Oxford 2008)

CALVIÑO (2007)

N. Calviño, 'La revisión judicial en materia de concentraciones y el análisis económico' in S. Martínez Lage and A. Petitbò Juan (eds), *El derecho de la competencia y los jueces* (Marcial Pons, Madrid 2007)

DEL GUAYO (2007)

I. del Guayo, 'Energy Law in Spain' in M. Roggenkamp, C. Redgwell, I. del Guayo, and A. Ronne (eds), *Energy Law in Europe. National, EU and International Regulation* (Oxford University Press, Oxford 2007)

DEL GUAYO (2006)

I. del Guayo, J. López, L. Hancher, *Competencia y regulación. Un análisis de la OPA de Gas Natural sobre Endesa* (Marcial Pons, Madrid 2006)

GARCÍA – VALDECASAS (2007)

R. García-Valdecasas y Fernández, 'El estándar de control judicial en materia de concentraciones' in S. Martínez Lage and A. Petitbò Juan (eds), *El derecho de la competencia y los jueces* (Marcial Pons, Madrid 2007)

LÓPEZ DE CASTRO GARCÍA-MORATO (2003)

L. López de Castro García-Morato and G. Ariño Ortiz, *La competencia en sectores regulados. Regulación empresarial y mercado de empresas* (Comares, Granada 2003)

SORIANO GARCÍA (2007)

J. E. Soriano García, *La defensa de la competencia en España* (IUSTEL, Madrid 2007)

TRILLO TORRES (2007)

R. Trillo Torres, 'Revisión judicial de autorizaciones y prohibiciones en material de concentraciones' in S. Martínez Lage and A. Petitbò Juan (eds), *El derecho de la competencia y los jueces* (Marcial Pons, Madrid 2007)

CHAPTER 12

# Judicial Review in Economic Regulation and Competition Law in Sweden

E. Edwardsson

## 1 Introduction

When answering the question of what impact European law, in particular, what impact the *Tetra Laval* case, has had on the standard of judicial review in Sweden, one must bear in mind that the procedures for reviewing competition law-cases, as well as the general system of judicial control of administrative decisions applied in Sweden, differ from those in most EU member states.[1] The administrative courts in Sweden traditionally have the power to conduct an intense review.[2] Administrative courts may determine the suitability or reasonableness of an administrative authority's decision. An administrative court that finds the decision of an administrative body inadequate generally has the power to make a new decision itself. In doing so, the court has the same power as does the administrative authority.[3] There are also other administrative courts in Europe that have these powers.[4] In Sweden however, this is a power which all administrative courts *normally* have. To put it differently: For a Swedish administrative court it is the main rule to decide on the suitability of an authority's decision. For the court to limit itself to the question of legality only is the exception. As a consequence the normal standard of review, for example, in electronic communication cases, is a full review.

Over the years, European law, specifically, the European Convention of Human Rights (ECHR), has had a significant impact on the judicial review system in Sweden. Due to the principle of procedural autonomy and to the fact that judicial review as exercised by the European Community courts so far has been less intense than in Swedish courts, the impact of EU law has not been particularly strong. However, it could be that the question of how the judicial review of the complicated decisions of competition authorities and regulatory agencies is best carried out may prove to be a key to renewed discussion in Sweden of the appropriate standard of judicial review. Moreover, the Swedish

1 In Swedish legal commentary, Hans Ragnemalm has suggested that there are three different models of judicial review. First, there is the 'Anglo-Saxon model', in which civil courts supervise public authorities, and second is the 'continental model', in which judicial review is carried out by separate administrative courts. In both models the standard of review is, from a Swedish perspective, perceived to be marginal. Sweden (and Finland, which basically uses the same model) is recognised as using an identifiable third model, in which the administrative courts intensely review decisions made by administrative authorities and regularly have the power to replace an authority's decision with its own, Ragnemalm (2007) pp. 142–143; see also Smith (1999) p. 296.

2 Smith (2006) p. 214.

3 Ragnemalm (1991) pp. 237–238. Smith points out that courts in other European countries, regardless of how the court systems are organised, generally do not have the same powers as those that are vested in Swedish courts, which include the power to change the decision of an administrative authority. He also points out that Sweden's approach is quite distinct, even in comparison with those of neighbouring countries such as Denmark and Norway, Smith (2006) p. 211, 217.

4 See the contribution of C. Graham in this book, where it is described that the CAT under the Competition Act 1998 can make any decision which the OFT itself could have made.

experience of an intense standard of review might also be of interest at the European level.

Regarding competition, Sweden is one of a minority of EU Member States in which the National Competition Authority (*Konkurrensverket*) cannot make a binding decision regarding competition law infringements on its own. Rather, it must initiate proceedings against an undertaking at the Stockholm District Court, which is a civil or general court.

As the Swedish system is clearly different from those of most EU Member States, especially concerning the judicial review of economic regulations, a few pages will be devoted, not only to the characteristics of the Swedish system of judicial review, but also to its historical background.

## 2 Judicial review in Sweden: a different approach

### 2.1 The constitutional justification

Administrative authorities in Sweden, as in most other countries, are parts of a hierarchy. An authority is subordinate to a superior authority and ultimately to the Government in its entirety.[5] When deciding on a particular matter, however, the constitution provides that the authority is strictly independent.[6] According to article 11:7 of the Instrument of Government (*Regeringsformen*), no authority, neither Parliament nor any other decision-making body, may interfere with a decision made by an authority in a particular case or when the authority is applying the law.

As it is not possible for a higher authority to interfere with the decision-making process of a lower authority, it was deemed necessary to allow appeals from the lower authority to the superior. The superior authorities deal with both regular administrative tasks and reviewing decisions made by lower authorities.[7] It was therefore considered indispensable that the higher authority should have all the decision-making power of the lower authority. Consequently, a tradition developed through the centuries in which administrative decisions could be appealed to a superior authority possessing the competence to review the case fully. Appeal to a court could, of course, have been another alternative, but

5 The Swedish Government, like the EU Commission, acts collectively. A minister is head of a ministry, but not of the authorities subordinate to the ministry. Authorities such as the Swedish National Competition Authority (*Konkurrensverket*) or the Post and Telecom Agency (*Post- och telestyrelsen*), the regulatory agency for mail and telecom matters, have their own general directors. They are not subordinate to the Ministry of Enterprise, Energy and Communications (*Näringsdepartementet*).

6 Four legal acts form the Swedish Constitution; the only important one for the questions discussed here is the Instrument of Government, see Ragnemalm (1991) pp. 11, 24–26.

7 Ragnemalm (1991) pp. 209–210.

traditionally the higher instance was a superior authority.[8] Swedish administrative courts have partly been created for reasons of legal certainty, but also for the practical reason of relieving the administration (including the Government) of the burden of reviewing individual administrative decisions.[9]

## 2.2 The influence of the ECHR

With the creation in 1971 of the 'lowest' administrative courts, the county courts (of which there are 23 today), it was increasingly prescribed by statute that administrative decisions could be appealed to an administrative court rather than a superior authority.[10] Without explicit legislative support, however, decisions were still to be appealed to a superior authority.

It follows from article 6 of the ECHR that administrative appeal concerning civil rights by a superior authority is not sufficient; appeal must be made to a court. In the 1980s it became clear that the Swedish model for reviewing administrative decisions concerning civil rights fell short of the standards of the European Court of Human Rights (ECHR) in Strasbourg, as Sweden was found to be in breach of the ECHR in a number of cases. It was assumed in Sweden that 'civil' rights could be given quite a narrow interpretation. As the European court in Strasbourg saw it differently, the Swedish system of judicial review had been called into question and some reforms were necessary. Since 1998, all administrative decisions – including those to which the ECHR is not applicable – are appealed to an administrative court at the lowest level, namely, the County Administrative Court. There is a possibility to appeal the County Administrative Court's decision to one of the four Administrative Courts of Appeal and ultimately to the Supreme Administrative Court (*Regeringsrätten*), provided that leave to appeal is granted.

However, the general shift from appealing to a superior authority to appealing to an administrative court did not mean that the full review model was abandoned. As a result, in Sweden, judicial review (*förvaltningsbesvär, lämplighetprövning*), or 'administrative–judicial review' (a term Ragnemalm has suggested), encompasses the full review of questions of law, as well as questions of facts and reasonableness.[11] An upheld appeal can result in a new decision if

8 Before 1971 there were only two administrative courts in Sweden, *Regeringsrätten* and *Kammarrätten*. *Regeringsrätten* literally means 'government court'. *Regeringsrätten* is the Swedish Supreme Administrative Court. It was founded in 1909 and its task was to rule on appeals concerning administrative decisions, appeals that previously had been handled by the government itself. The oldest administrative court, however, is *Kammarrätten* (the Court Chamber) in Stockholm. In 1695 this court was created as a separate branch of the Chamber (*Kammarkollegiet*). Today *Kammarrätten* in Stockholm is one of four Administrative Courts of Appeal.

9 Sjöberg (2005) pp. 291–292, 302. Sjöberg indicates that the 'practical' reason was the more important of the two.

10 Sjöberg (2005) p. 301.

11 Ragnemalm (1991) pp. 210, 237–238.

the higher instance finds it suitable, in which case the court will have the same powers as the authority that made the original decision. That is why the intense review, in which the court can substitute its own decision for that of the authority, is the normal standard of review of administrative decisions in Sweden.[12]

### 2.3 Other types of judicial review

Not all administrative decisions will be reviewed via an administrative–judicial review process, however, with its intense standard of review. There are other types of review in Sweden, in cases in which the review only is allowed to concern the question of legality. The first example is the review that the administrative courts will perform after a 'municipal appeal'.[13] Such a municipal appeal is referred to as assessment of legality (*'laglighetsprövning'*) and can treat decisions made by municipal bodies under the terms of the Local Government Act (SFS 1991:900).[14] The court hierarchy is the same as in administrative–judicial reviews appeals (i.e., County Administrative Court, Administrative Court of Appeal, and the Supreme Court of Administration). Judicial review in municipal appeals is limited only to the question of the legality of the decision. An upheld appeal can only quash the original decision, not replace it with a new court decision.

The second type of appeal is regulated in the Law (2006:304) on Legal Review of certain Government's Decisions (*Rättsprövningslagen*). Legal Review (*rättsprövning*) concerns the legality of decisions made by the Government, and was a reform introduced in response to the ECHR requirement regarding effective judicial protection.[15] Government decisions that affect an individual's civil rights can on application be reviewed by the Supreme Administrative Court, and the review will be limited to the question of the legality of the Government's decision.[16] The court can quash the original decision, but, unsurprisingly, not replace it with its own.

When carrying out legal review the Supreme Administrative Court has stated that it will assess whether the facts and evidence have been correctly evaluated, whether the authority making the decision has taken due account of the constitutional principles of objectivity, impartiality, and equality, and whether the limits of the Government's discretion have been respected.[17] Essentially, in

---

12 Reichel (2006) p. 327. It seems as though the Swedish system with full judicial review can be explained primarily by tradition. Smith has implied that the actual lack of debate on these issues in itself can explain why Sweden has an alternative system, Smith (2006) pp. 214, 216.

13 Ragnemalm (1991) p. 210. The municipalities represent the local level of government in Sweden. Their independence from the state is laid down in the constitution.

14 Ragnemalm (1991) pp. 238–239.

15 Originally Legal Review of Certain Government's Decisions was introduced under law (1988:205). The act has now been replaced by law (2006:304).

16 Ragnemalm (2007) pp. 191–192.

17 Smith (2006) p. 216, with reference to case RÅ 1989 ref. 95.

cases of legal review of Government' decisions, the Supreme Administrative Court will apply a standard of review that is quite close to the standard used by the European Courts in the *Tetra Laval* case.[18]

### 2.4 The main form of judicial review – administrative-judicial review

Legal assessment under the Local Government Act and Legal Review of Certain Government's Decisions, however, are applied in a minority of the administrative appeal cases. The most important form of judicial review in Sweden is still the administrative–judicial appeal – which in Swedish is called *lämplighetsprövning*.

Limiting court power to reviewing the legality of the decisions of administrative bodies can be perceived as a consequence of the division of powers between courts and administrative authorities. The role of the judiciary is thus limited to the question of legality in the majority of the EU countries.[19] Of course, the idea of Montesquieu to separate powers has had an immense impact also on the Swedish constitution. Ragnemalm, however, refers to the Swedish constitutional model as one of the separation of functions, rather than of the separation of powers.[20] The first sentence of the Instrument of Government is *'All offentlig makt i Sverige utgår från folket'* (Instrument of Government 1:1), meaning 'All public power in Sweden emanates from the people'. Sweden has no constitutional court and there is scepticism regarding the idea of giving judges the power to exercise authority over Parliamentary decisions.[21]

The Swedish model of judicial review has been called into question and criticized.[22] So far the criticism has not resulted in serious discussion of the appropriateness of the Swedish system.[23] However, questions have been asked concerning whether the administrative courts of the first instance really have the competence to hear appeals of the decisions of qualified authorities.[24] The Norwegian Scholar Eivind Smith has also pointed out that the intense standard of judicial review gives courts in Sweden a comparatively stronger position vis-à-vis administrative authorities, than in other European countries.[25] Another point made by Smith is that where the legislation leaves little room for discretion,

---

18 Marcusson (1992) pp 131-135; Smith (2006) p. 217.

19 Smith (2006) p. 211.

20 Ragnemalm (1991) pp. 16–17. Smith points out that Sweden clearly deviates from other European countries in including courts and administrative authorities in the same chapter of the Instrument of Government, Smith (2006) pp. 225–226.

21 Smith (1999) pp. 290, 301.

22 Smith (2006) pp. 211, 213.

23 Sjöberg (2005) p. 303; Smith (2006) p. 211.

24 Strömberg (2005) p. 343.

25 Smith (2006) p. 215.

Swedish administrative courts are likely applying the same standards of judicial review as do other European courts.[26]

## 3 Competent courts and judicial control

### 3.1 The Swedish court structure

There are two kinds of courts in Sweden – general courts and administrative courts. In both cases they exist at three levels. The general courts of appeal, of which there are six, consider appeals from the general district courts, which form the lowest level in the general court system. The highest general court is the Supreme Court, which considers cases only after leave to appeal has been granted. Such dispensation is granted only if the case involves an important issue of law.[27] General courts use the Code (1942:740) of Judicial Procedure for both civil and criminal cases.

The lowest administrative court level is that of the County Courts, which hear appeals against decisions made by administrative authorities. If the next level – the Administrative Courts of Appeal – is to hear a case, a leave to appeal must be granted in the majority of cases (an important exception is tax law). The highest level is the Supreme Administrative Court. All the administrative courts use the Administrative Court Procedure Act (*Förvaltningsprocesslagen*) (SFS 1971:291) to guide the proceedings.

Apart from these courts, there are also a few 'special courts', the jurisdictions of which are limited to specific areas of law, such as labour law, which is dealt with by the Labour Court. The Market Court (*Marknadsdomstolen*) is a specialised court that handles cases related to the Competition Act. In a competition case, the Market Court is the highest court of appeal. The Market Court consists of a Chair, a Vice Chair, and five special members. The Chair, Vice Chair, and one special member must be lawyers with experience as judges; the other special members are experts in economics.

### 3.2 The competent authorities and the review of their decisions

The authority in charge of applying the enacted electronic communication directives is the Post and Telecom Agency (PTA). This administrative body is domiciled in Stockholm and its task is to monitor the electronic communications and postal sectors. The relevant legislation is the Electronic Communications Act (*lag om elektronisk kommunikation*) (2003:389).

Decisions under the Act may be appealed to the County Administrative Court in Stockholm (*Länsrätten i Stockholm*). Since a reform in 2007, the last

[26] Smith (2006) p. 221.

[27] Ragnemalm (1991) p. 44.

instance will be the Administrative Court of Appeal in Stockholm; not the Supreme Administrative Court.[28] Appeals will be heard if the Administrative Court of Appeal grants leave to appeal. The above Administrative Court Procedure Act will be used, with its full review standard. However, due to a change in the Electronic Communication act decided in 2007, some deviations have been made on the procedural rules to be used in electronic communication cases.[29] For example if the appellant wants to put forward new circumstances and evidence at the county administrative court there are certain limitations (Electronic Communication Act 8:24).

The competent authority in competition law is the National (Swedish) Competition Authority (NCA) (*Konkurrensverket*, Sw.). The NCA applies Articles 81 and 82 of the EC-treaty as well as the Swedish Competition Act (2008:579) which from 1 November 2008 has replaced the former act (1993:20). Under the new Competition Act as well as under the former, the most important questions of infringements of the Competition Act or of fines cannot be made by the NCA itself. Instead fines will be imposed by the Stockholm City Court on the petition of the NCA.[30] A case will be heard after the National Competition Authority has initiated proceedings against one or several undertakings. The decision of the court can be appealed to the Market Court. The Market Court is a specialised court and its procedures are regulated in law (1970:417) on the Market Court (*lag (1970:417 om marknadsdomstol)*. Since 1 November 2008 leave to appeal must be granted by the Market Court.

## 3.3 Principles of procedure, discretion and burden of proof

The questions of procedural principles, discretion, standard of judicial review, and burden of proof must be discussed in relation to the two kinds of court systems.

### 3.3.1 Judicial review in electronic communication cases

According to the Instrument of Government, Section 1:9, in their activities, all public authorities and courts must maintain objectivity and

[28] Interestingly enough one of the reasons to the recent reduction of the number of appeal instances from three to two was that the PTA's decisions were considered to be appealed unusually often. One might ask if the responsibility for the courts to make a full review of these complicated matters has in itself led to drawn-out proceedings. Any undertaking that made an appeal could stop the enforcement of PTA's decisions for a considerable time.

[29] See Law Bill 'A more effective Electronic Communications Act', Govt. Bill 2006/07:119 from 31 May 2007.

[30] There is, however, a number of more limited decisions by the NCA, such as orders or withdrawal from an application for group exemption. Such decisions can be appealed to and reviewed directly by the Market Court, which will be the first and last instance.

impartiality.[31] In economic regulation matters, the Post and Telecoms Agency in some cases is involved in a two-party process and in other cases has the role of 'prosecuting' individual undertakings.[32] In the latter, authorities are responsible for matters being investigated in a satisfactory way.[33] When two or more undertakings with conflicting interests are involved, the guiding principle for an authority such as the PTA will be more of a negotiating nature. The parties will be responsible for producing factual evidence and the PTA will have a more neutral role.

Decisions by the PTA will be reviewed by the administrative courts and according to the Swedish tradition explained above, there will be a full review where the courts can, for example, quash the decision and send it back to the PTA for a new decision or alter the PTA's decision in a way the court finds suitable. It follows from Section 8 of the Administrative Court Procedure Act that it is for the court to ensure that a case is as well investigated as its nature requires and then to make the correct decision. This is called the principle of investigation (*officialprövningsprincipen*). Here there can be said to exist a certain discretion on the court's side, meaning that it is up to the court to decide if it will be convinced whether the decision from the PTA is correct or not. It can also be claimed that it flows from the official principle that Swedish administrative courts must *ex officio* engage in questions not presented to it by the parties, also due to Section 8 of the Administrative Court Procedure Act.[34] However, as the process will be between two parties – the PTA on one side and one or more undertakings on the other, the court's responsibility to see that the case is properly investigated, is relaxed.[35] The relaxation of the court's responsibility adds perhaps further to the responsibility of the PTA.

One basic principle in Swedish Administrative Law is that the one who makes an allegation or accusation, has the burden of proof. Consequently, the PTA has the burden of proof to convince the courts that it has a solid legal ground for its decisions and also for other matters of law or of facts.

### 3.3.2 Judicial review in competition law cases

As mentioned before, the NCA, unlike many other national competition authorities, does not have the power to decide on financial penalties for infringing competition rules. A governmental committee with the task to investigate whether a change on this point would be preferable came to the

31 Ragnemalm (1991) p. 159.

32 Ragnemalm (1991) p. 158.

33 Ragnemalm (1991) p. 178.

34 Andersson (1998) p. 815, Reichel (2006) pp. 322, 325-331.

35 Lavin (1989) p. 77.

conclusion that the present model of judicial review of competition cases works relatively well and will not be changed.[36]

Whether or not it has to do with the system of judicial review of competition cases in Sweden, there has been criticism regarding the fact that the NCA is less successful in court than other European competition authorities and that the litigation is far too drawn-out a procedure. In some cases the court procedures have taken nearly five years. It is hoped that the solution to this problem lies in a more active formal and material procedural leadership on the side of the courts.

Also in competition law cases the above mentioned official principle will be used, as such cases will be handled as contentious cases.[37] This means that the court is responsible to see to the case being investigated in the proper manner.[38] Parallel to the judicial review regarding electronic communication, the court's own responsibility to have the matter properly investigated can be said to stand for a kind of discretion on the side of the court. But the intensity of the review is also in the case of competition law a full review.

As the NCA must take matters to court and there claim that a competition law infringement has taken place, it has the burden of proof for its allegations. In concentration matters the involved undertakings have the burden of proof when it concerns the question whether the concentration will contribute to enhanced efficiency. It is not a task for the NCA to prove that.

### 3.3.3 Conclusion

The model of judicial review in Sweden has the effect that competition matters are dealt with by the general courts and a specialised court of appeal, whereas judicial review in economic regulation is carried out by the administrative courts. In both cases there is a very limited, not to say non-existent, influence by European law concerning the standard of judicial review.

---

36 Swedish Government Official Report 2006:99, *A new Competition Act* (SOU 2006:99 En ny konkurrenslag, p. 30. In this report there is, on page 315, an explicit reference to the case C-12/03 P, *Tetra Laval.* It is said that one reason put forward for giving the NCA the decision-making power on fines, could be that the proponents would like to see a similar legal situation as within EU Law where 'the courts seem to accept that the EU Commission has a certain degree of discretion'. The report continues to say that such a development is not desirable because of reasons of legal certainty.

37 Lavin (1989) p. 77.

38 Lavin (1989) p. 76.

## 4 The case law: lack of landmark cases

If the task is to find Swedish court cases where the C-12/03 P *Tetra Laval* case can be said to have an influence on the standard of judicial review carried out by Swedish courts, this is not likely to be successful.[39]

### 4.1 Electronic communications, an example

*Dispute settlement between TeliaSonera and Itesco AB*

To illustrate the abovementioned statement with just one example from electronic communication law, I refer to a case concerning a dispute settlement between the former de facto monopolist *TeliaSonera* (formerly Telia AB) and the company *Itesco*. The PTA decided on certain obligations on behalf of *TeliaSonera*.[40] Those obligations were partly quashed, partly upheld and partly changed in substance by the County Administrative Court, which is just one of many examples where administrative courts do not hesitate to make new decisions.[41] Later the Administrative Court of Appeal upheld the lower court's decision[42] and the case did not get leave to appeal to the Supreme Administrative Court.[43]

The review that the County Administrative Court carries out is detailed, both concerning law and facts, as can be expected according to the principles of judicial review applied in Sweden.

### 4.2 Competition law

Since October 2002, the Market Court has decided on 16 cases on the Competition Act (SFS 1993:20). In none of these cases an explicit reference to the *Tetra Laval* case was made.

In June 2000 the NCA initiated proceedings in the case MD 2005:7 before the Stockholm City Court against five petroleum companies (Norsk Hydro, OK-Q8, Preem Petroleum, Swedish Shell and Statoil). The NCA applied for a 68

39 The relevant period of time to investigate is from February 2005 or with a greater level of ambition, from October 2002, when the CFI decided the Case T-80/02 *Tetra Laval* v. *Commission* [2002] ECR II-4519. As the probability to find an explicit or implicit reference in Swedish case law is so small, the author has settled with searching for an explicit reference to the case *Tetra Laval* in the judgments (of which there are none). The question whether European Law affects or can affect the Swedish standard of review in the opposite direction, that is to shift the intensity of the review from a full review to a more marginal review, is extremely interesting, but it was not possible to investigate this within the limits of this paper.

40 Decision in Case 04-13249 from 11 May 2005.

41 Case 12790-05 from 4 May 2007.

42 Case 3757-07 from 28 December 2007.

43 Decision in Case 514-08 from 16 May 2008.

million Euros fine.[44] The NCA later lowered this to 42 million Euros. The fine rewarded by the Stockholm City Court was 5,3 million Euros, which the Market Court later raised to 11,7 million Euros. The NCA was of the opinion that the undertakings were involved in an agreement or a concerted practice regarding the withdrawal of rebates and on the maximum rebates according to different categories of customers. The undertakings admitted to have met and to some extent to have exchanged information, but denied any agreement or concerted practice contrary to Section 6 of the Competition Act (1993:20).[45] The Stockholm City Court found that there had been an agreement on the reduction of rebates, but only regarding certain categories of customers. The Market Court was not of the opinion that there had been an agreement, but instead found proof of concerted practice. Both the Stockholm City Court and the Market Court made an intense review of the claim put forward by the NCA, in full accordance with Swedish Law.

Regarding concentration decisions only one Swedish case has been decided upon by the Market Court and that was in 1998, several years before the *Tetra Laval* case. In this case, MD 1998:10 (the *Optiroc* case), the NCA failed to convince the Market Court that competition could be seriously harmed if the merger between two undertakings in the construction sector would be allowed. The Market Court did not explicitly mention the standard of proof, but it can be assumed that the NCA failed to prove its allegation that competition would be seriously harmed.

## 5 Concluding remarks: the impact of the *Tetra Laval* case

In the *Tetra Laval* case, the ECJ stated that European Community courts could review the EU Commission's evidence regarding economic matters. Ensuring that evidence is factually accurate, reliable, and consistent and contains all the information needed is something that is also done in Sweden in the normal process of judicial review. A major difference is that Swedish administrative courts can replace its own decision for that of the authority. The normal standard of review thus is a full review.

As Swedish courts apply an intense standard of review in 'internal' cases before administrative courts, it must follow from the European equality principle that the same standard must be applied in cases regarding electronic communication and competition law.

Interestingly enough, however, even in the few instances in which Swedish judicial review is less intense – the case of municipal appeal and legal review

44 Simonsson/Öberg, have published a well written and very critical article on the case in Svensk Juristtidning, Simonsson (2006) pp. 24-42.

45 The Market Court considered, due to circumstances in the case, that the agreement did not affect the trade between Member States, a point of view that has been criticised by Simonsson/Öberg (2006) pp. 27-30.

of certain government's decisions mentioned above – questions of whether the facts are accurate and reliable can still be examined. Even here the Swedish system of judicial review comes close to the actual standard of the *Tetra Laval* case.

In competition law, the intense review standard follows from the fact that the NCA has to bring cases concerning fines to a general court. The NCA has the burden of proof for its allegation and the courts the responsibility to have the matter properly investigated.

Either way, as the standard of review in Sweden has been relatively intense all along; there is little likelihood that the *Tetra Laval* case can have an impact on Swedish courts. In Sweden there is practically no debate on problems regarding legal certainty in competition law or economic regulation. But there is another debate – on how efficient the NCA and the PTA really are when it comes to the enforcement of these important pieces of market oriented legislation.

## Bibliography


ANDERSSON (1998)
T. Andersson, 'EG-rätten och den svenska processrätten' *Juridisk tidskrift* [1989-99/4] pp. 807-817

BEJSTAM (2005)
L. Bejstam, 'I förvaltningslagens gränsland' in *i Festskrift till Hans Ragnemalm*, (Juristförlaget, Lund 2005)

LAVIN (1989)
R. Lavin, 'Civilprocessen och förvaltningsprocessen – en jämförelse' *Juridisk tidskrift* [1989-99] pp. 70-88

MARCUSSON (1992)
L. Marcusson, 'Laglighets- och lämplighetsprövning en titt i backspegeln och framåt' *Förvaltningsrättslig Tidskrift* häfte nr 1-3/1992, pp. 121-138.

RAGNEMALM (1991)
H. Ragnemalm, *'Administrative Justice in Sweden'* (Juristfo rlaget, Stockholm 1991)

RAGNEMALM (2007)
H. Ragnemalm, *'Förvaltningsprocessrättens grunder'* (LiberForlag, Stockholm 2007)

REICHEL (2006)
J. Reichel, *'God förvaltning i EU och Sverige'* (Jure, Stockholm 2006)

REICHEL (2007)
J. Reichel, 'Svenska myndigheter som EU-myndigheter' *Juridisk tidskrift, Jubileumsskrift [2007]* pp. 103–112

SIMONSSON (2006)
I. Simonsson, 'Bensinkartelldomen MD 2005:7 – fördragsstridig tillämpning av EG:s konkurrensrätt?' [2006/91] *Svensk Juristtidning* pp. 23-42

SJÖBERG (2005)
M. Sjöberg, *'Den långa vägen till en generell regel om domstolsprövning av förvaltningsbeslut'* (Jurist-förlaget, Lund 2005)

SMITH (1999)
E. Smith, 'On the Formation and Development of Constitutional Jurisdiction in a Democratic Society' in *Festskrift till Fredrik Sterzel*, (Iustus förlag, Uppsala 1999)

SMITH (2006)
E. Smith, 'Juger l'administration cést aussi administer. Om förvaltningen och dess domare i Sverige' in L. Marcusson *'God förvaltning – ideal och praktik.'* (Iustus, Uppsala 2006)

STRÖMBERG (1999)
H. Strömberg, 'Förvaltningsrättsskipning i omdaning – en återblick på tre decenniers reformarbete' (Uppsala 1999)

CHAPTER 13

# Judicial Review of the Decisions of the Competition Authorities and the Economic Regulators in the UK

C. Graham

## 1 Introduction[1]

The starting point for this paper was the question of what influence the European Court of Justice's judgment in *Tetra Laval* v. *Commission*[2] has had on judicial review of decisions taken by the competition authorities and economic regulators in the UK. Although the initial question was answered quite easily, as *Tetra Laval* appears to have been cited once only by the Competition Appeal Tribunal (CAT), and then in relation to the standard of proof that the competition authority should meet, this led to other issues.[3] One such issue was whether a different approach applies to the decisions of competition authorities as opposed to economic regulators. Both are agencies which are independent from government in their decision-making and attempt to apply specialist economic expertise in their decisions; whereas judicial review decisions with respect to competition authorities are taken by the CAT, and, with respect to economic regulators, by the High Court. Having examined this, it became apparent that the approach applied by the CAT in relation to its exercise of the judicial review function is very similar to that expounded by the ECJ in *Tetra Laval*. Therefore, it is worth asking how this might have come about.

In order to understand this issue properly this contribution first provides some definitions and descriptions of basic terms used in the UK (see below). Secondly, it describes the decision-making powers of the UK competition authorities, the various routes to challenge their decisions, primarily before the CAT, and the approach taken by the CAT in hearing appeals or reviewing such decisions. Thirdly, it explains the decision-making powers of the economic regulators, the routes available to challenge their decisions, primarily through the High Court via an action for judicial review, and the approach taken by the High Court to such challenges. Fourthly, it compares the approach of the UK and EU judicial bodies and offers some conclusions.

*UK terminology*

Judicial review in the UK is part of the inherent jurisdiction of the High Court and is based on common law decisions. There is no statutory basis for the exercise of this jurisdiction, except as regards procedural matters. The influence of European law on administrative law appears confined to two areas: cases where the courts are involved in the application of European Community law and human rights cases, where the Human Rights Act 1998 compels reference to Strasbourg jurisprudence. The function of judicial review proceedings is to

---

1 My particular thanks go to Adam Scott, TD, for his very helpful comments on this paper. I have also benefited from the help and advice of Saskia Lavrijssen, Aidan Robertson, Marcus Clements and the Ofgem Library. All mistakes and opinions are of course my own. This paper was written before the CAT judgments in *British Sky Broadcasting* v. *Competition Commission* and *Tesco* v. *Competition Commission* were delivered.

2 Case C-13/03 *Commission* v. *Tetra Laval* [2005] ECR I-1113.

3 See *Hutchison 3G (UK)* v. *Office of Communications* [2005] CAT 39.

control the *legality* of actions by public authorities and this is typically contrasted with control of the *merits* of a decision, which would be done through an appeal process. An appeal in the UK must have a statutory basis and the grounds for the appeal, and other matters, will be set out in the statute. Provisions for appeal in statutes may vary from a full appeal on the merits to an appeal limited to issues of legality.

A discretionary decision is where the decision-maker has a *power* to make a decision but is not under a *duty* to make a decision, although there is a duty to consider whether or not to exercise the power. Discretionary decisions therefore connote that the public authority has some choice about what decision to take.

Intensity of review in the UK relates to discretionary decisions, because it tends to be assumed by courts that matters of law or legal interpretation have right or wrong answers and that the courts are the final arbiters of such issues.[4] The intensity of review that will be applied will vary depending on the context of the case but it is difficult to go beyond listing contextual factors that the court will take into account.[5] It is clear that the intensity of review will be at its highest when the human rights issues are affected by the decision of a public authority; this is sometimes referred to as 'anxious scrutiny'.[6] Even at the most intense end of the spectrum, a UK court will not make a decision on the 'merits' of the case, that is, whether or not the decision is right or wrong. It will always maintain that it is making a decision on legality. At the other extreme there may be issues of economic policy or technical expertise where the courts exercise very limited scrutiny, although they will check that there is a factual basis for the decision which is supported by adequate reasoning, although seemingly without probing too deeply into the reasoning. Between these two extremes a variety of factors may come into play, perhaps most importantly the nature of the issue and the inherent probability of the conclusions by the public agency. Thus, for example, the determination of the turnover of a company is an issue more susceptible to judicial review than the question of whether an incumbent company is earning monopoly rents or how joint costs should be allocated.[7]

Within UK law, the *burden of proof* refers to which party in a proceeding, typically adversarial, is required to prove the requisite facts or arguments to make their case. The *standard of proof* refers to the issue of how difficult it is to prove a point or case. In criminal matters, the standard is normally said to be 'beyond reasonable doubt', while in civil matters, it is normally said to be 'on the balance of probabilities', which can be considered as above 50%. When enforcing competition law or imposing regulatory penalties in the UK, the burden of proof is clearly on the public authorities to show a breach of the prohibitions but the standard of proof is somewhere above the civil standard and below the criminal

4 Although this is not always the case, see: *R* v. *Monopolies and Mergers Commission ex parte South Yorkshire Transport* [1993] 1 All ER 289.

5 Vajda (2005) provide a useful list at 6-049 to 6-56.

6 *R* v. *Ministry of Defence ex parte Smith* [1996] QB 517.

7 See *Telecom Corporation of New Zealand* v. *Clear Communications* [1994] CLC 1312.

standard. When it comes to regulatory action which does not involve imposing a penalty there is, strictly speaking, no burden of proof on the public authorities, but the decision must have a factual basis which can be proven to the appropriate standard, which will vary depending on the context. So, for example, in merger cases, the Competition Commission (CC) states that in order for it to reach an adverse result it must have an expectation, that is, that something is more likely than not, that there will be a substantial lessening of competition.[8] As Vajda and Gregory have pointed out, the standard of proof will tend to be determined by the court's view as to the appropriate level of intensity of review.[9]

## 2 Setting the scene

Before beginning with this discussion, four long term themes can be highlighted which underpin developments in the UK. Taking them in historical order, the first has been the development of independent agencies responsible for the regulation of particular industries, primarily consequent on the privatisation of certain nationalised industries, although not necessarily.[10] The clearest exception to this has been the creation of the Postal Services Commission (PSC) to regulate the Royal Mail, which has remained in government ownership. Although there are some historical precedents, notably the Civil Aviation Authority and the regulation of the rail industry for part of the nineteenth century, these developments have been seen within political science literature as part of a wider and longer term trend, towards the creation of something that is referred to as the 'regulatory state'.[11] This refers to a number of developments, but some of the key elements are an increasing reliance on market mechanisms which are policed by agencies acting independently of elected politicians and make decisions on the basis of their specialised expertise. The role of governments is therefore more constrained but the agencies may be given a limited brief and will be hedged round with various checks and balances, such as consultation requirements, while an important constraint in principle is the need to act within their legal powers, something which is controlled by the courts. This reliance on independent agencies is challenging in the UK, where the central means of accountability have traditionally been political, rather than judicial and one of the issues has been how to create a coherent system of accountability for these new institutions. Internally to government much effort has been devoted to the Better Regulation initiative, although this is not directly relevant

---

8 Competition Commission *Mergers Reference Guidance* (2004) para. 1.19.

9 Competition Commission *Mergers Reference Guidance* (2004) para. 6-048.

10 For the purposes of this paper the economic regulators are: Office of Communications (Ofcom), Office of Gas and Electricity Markets (Ofgem), Office of Water Services (Ofwat), Office of Rail Regulation and PSC.

11 Moran (2003).

to independent regulatory agencies and the competition authorities.[12] As regards challenging the decisions of these bodies, a piecemeal system remains in place, despite complaints from the industries concerned and one which can be contrasted with the reform of the tribunal system which has just been undertaken.[13]

Related to this broader development is the second theme, namely the transformation of UK competition law roughly in the period 1998 to 2002, although the first discussion of reform arose around 1988, marked by the Competition Act 1998 and the Enterprise Act 2002. Prior to this point, the UK had a unique system for dealing with anti-competitive agreements and abuse of a dominant position as well as a system of merger control where there were substantial amounts of political involvement, a high level of discretion and a distinct lack of transparency. The Competition Act 1998 brought the UK system for the control of anti-competitive agreements and abuse of dominant position into line with EC law introducing for the first time a prohibition in domestic law which was virtually identical to Articles 81 and 82 EC. The Enterprise Act 2002 reformed the system of merger control and the system for the investigation of particular markets by removing most of the scope for political intervention and leaving decision-making to independent agencies while also limiting those agencies to consideration of competition questions, rather than wider public interest criteria. An important difference between the two pieces of legislation is that the Competition Act was deliberately aimed at bringing the UK system into line with the EC system, whereas this was not an aim of the Enterprise Act. Indeed, two aspects of the Enterprise Act, market investigations and the criminalisation of certain cartel activities, have no counterpart in EC competition law. As we shall see, these differences have affected the mechanisms of judicial control that have been created.

The third theme that underpins this contribution is changes in the courts' approach to the judicial review jurisdiction. Judicial review in the UK is based on the common law, not on statute, and the approach that should be taken to it, as a matter of principle, has been a matter of fierce academic debate.[14] Leaving aside this theoretical debate, it has become clear in the last decade or so, that the role of the courts in reviewing executive and legislative action has changed dramatically. This is particularly notable through the introduction of the Human Rights Act 1998 which allows the UK courts to scrutinise the activities of the executive, and indeed the legislature, for their compatibility with the requirements of the European Convention on Human Rights. In general this seems to have resulted in more intervention by the courts and the development of certain principles, such as proportionality, which were not present in the common law. The human rights case law has not been directly relevant in

12 See http://www.berr.gov.uk/bre/about/page44014.html (Accessed 2 June 2008).

13 See House of Lords Select Committee on the Constitution *The Regulatory State: Ensuring its Accountability* (2004 HL 68-I), Chapter 11 for criticisms of the appeal process and the Tribunals Courts and Enforcement Act 2007 for the reform of tribunals.

14 See, for example, Craig (2001) p. 763, Forsyth (2003) pp. 286-307, Allan (2004) pp. 563-583.

the review of decisions of economic regulators or the competition authorities, although in principle such issues could arise. The question is whether or not the more activist approach of the courts in this area will spill over into another area, given that it is the same judges hearing the cases, or whether a distinction can be maintained. For example, it is the case that proportionality, as a ground of review, is only relevant in cases under the Human Rights Act and cases involving European Community law, but, outside these two areas, the traditional approach of the common law, based on the *Wednesbury* principles of unreasonableness, should apply.[15]

The Human Rights Act and its related case law has been of significant influence in relation to the design of institutions and procedures in relation to the competition authorities and this brings us to the fourth, and final, theme; the question of European influences on the development of UK administrative law. The most obvious influence has been in the role of the CAT as the body which hears appeals against decisions by the Office of Fair Trading (OFT) for breaches of the Competition Act. The CAT, as we shall see, is an independent judicial body which hears appeals on the merits and can make any decision that the OFT has made, which thus makes the decision-making process compatible with Article 6 ECHR. It avoids the criticisms that have been levelled at the combination of functions within the European Commission on Article 6 grounds, even though the OFT has a similar combination of functions, because it is clear that the procedure as a whole meets the Article 6 criteria, something which was less obvious in relation to the EC arrangements. In addition, the OFT, and other authorities, have taken some pains to create procedures which are compliant with Article 6, and any UK principles of judicial review, in order to try and ensure that challenges focus on the substance of decisions, rather than the procedure by which they were taken. As for the broader question of the influence of EC law on the development of UK administrative law, we shall see that it is not obvious that there has been any such influence, although in relation to the substance of competition law there is meant to be consistency between UK and EC law and this may have provided an unarticulated bridge to come to the same conclusions.

## 3 Enforcing competition law

For our purposes, the enforcement of UK competition law can be divided into the enforcement of the prohibitions against anti-competitive agreements and abuse of dominant position and the provisions on merger control and market investigations. The prohibitions against anti-competitive agreements and abuse of dominant position are contained in Articles 81 and 82 of the EC Treaty and, at a domestic level, mirrored in sections 2 and 18 of the

15 See *R (on the application of Mabanaft)* v. *Secretary of State for Trade and Industry* [2008] EWHC 1052 Admin Court.

Competition Act, commonly referred to, respectively, as the Chapter I and Chapter II prohibitions. Enforcement of these prohibitions is the responsibility of the OFT *and* the economic regulators. In other words, the economic regulators have concurrent powers with the OFT to enforce the prohibitions and this power is separate from the other powers that they have in relation to economic regulation.[16] When utilising these powers the OFT and the economic regulators decide whether or not to investigate a matter, and then, after an investigation, whether or not there has been a breach of the prohibitions and, if there is, what penalty should be imposed.[17]

The position in relation to merger control is, however, different. There is no prohibition against mergers and no compulsory notification process. Instead, the OFT has the responsibility to examine qualifying mergers which come to its attention and if it believes that the merger may be expected to result in a substantial lessening of competition (SLC) within any market or markets in the UK for goods or services, it shall make a reference to the Competition Commission (CC).[18] There are certain exceptions to this duty and three situations where the OFT has discretion ('may') not to make a reference.[19]

The CC conducts a new, in-depth inquiry into the merger and is required to decide whether the creation of that situation may be expected to result in a substantial lessening of competition within any market or markets in the United Kingdom for goods or services.[20] If this is the case, the CC considers first whether it should take action to remedy the SLC and also whether it should recommend that others, for example, government departments or regulatory agencies, should take action. The CC is required to have regard to achieving as comprehensive a solution as is reasonable and practicable for the SLC and any adverse effects resulting from it.[21]

A similar structure exists in relation to market investigations. Here the OFT may make a reference to the CC where it has reasonable grounds for suspecting that any feature or combination of features of a market for goods or services prevents, restricts or distorts competition in the supply of goods or services.[22]

---

16 Generally see Department of Trade and Industry *Concurrent Competition Powers in Sectoral Regulation* (2006) available at: http://www.berr.gov.uk/files/file29454.pdf (accessed 2 June 2008). Although between January 2001 and September 2005, there were no findings by the regulators of infringement of the competition legislation: ibid at para. 5.1.

17 For example, Ofgem fined National Grid £41.6 million for abusing its dominant position for the supply of domestic-sized gas meters. See Ofgem *Investigation into National Grid (formerly known as Transco)* (Case CA98/STG/06) 21 February 2008.

18 S. 33 (1) Enterprise Act 2002 (EA).

19 EA ss. 2293) and 33 (3).

20 SS. 35 and 36 Enterprise Act 2002.

21 EA s. 35 (4) 36 (3).

22 EA s. 131(1). A feature of the market is defined as meaning any structural characteristics of the market, any conduct by one or more persons in relation to the goods or services in the market or any conduct by the customers of suppliers of goods or services: EA s. 131 (2).

When an issue is referred to the CC, it is required to decide whether any feature or combination of features, of each relevant market prevents, restricts or distorts competition in connection with the supply or acquisition of any goods or services in the United Kingdom or a part of the United Kingdom.[23] This is referred to as an adverse effect on competition (AEC). If, after investigation, the CC decides that there is an adverse effect on competition, then it is under a duty to decide whether it should take action to remedy the adverse effect on competition or recommend others to take action to remedy it.[24]

In order to remedy an adverse effect on competition, the CC has powers to accept legally binding undertakings[25] from any persons that it considers appropriate, normally those who have been party to the investigation.[26] If undertakings cannot be agreed, or are not considered to be appropriate, the CC has the power to make final orders, effectively the equivalent of delegated legislation.[27] The CC has wide powers to prohibit certain types of conduct, such as withholding supply or price discrimination, power to regulate prices, a power to order the divestiture and break-up of a company and power to require companies to provide information.[28] Although these are extensive powers, they are narrower than the power to accept final undertakings, which is in practice limited only by the willingness of parties to agree to accept and be bound by undertakings.

There are some important differences between the procedures described above. A breach of the prohibitions results in a penalty for past conduct and is considered as something akin to a criminal conviction or prosecution, at least in the UK.[29] The monetary penalties which may be imposed can be quite severe, with a maximum penalty of ten percent of annual turnover capable of being imposed. By contrast, merger control is based on the competition authorities' view of what the future consequences of a merger are likely to be and the worst that can happen is that a merger can be prohibited, with the consequent disruption to corporate plans. Market investigations do not allow the CC to penalise undertakings subject to such investigations for their past conduct. Indeed, for the purposes of Regulation 1/2003, the CC is not a designated competition authority. The remedies that the CC may impose are directed towards the future conduct of the parties in the market concerned. These may have important implications for a firm's particular business model. For example, the CC has provisionally proposed that the British Airports Authority should sell two of its

23 EA s. 134 (1).

24 EA ss. 134 (2) and 138.

25 'Undertaking' here means, roughly, a legally binding promise by a person to do or not do something, that is, they have undertaken to act in a particular way. The use of this word, in the context of remedies, needs to be distinguished from its use in Articles 81 and 82 EC, where the reference is to entities carrying on an economic activity.

26 EA s. 159.

27 EA s. 161.

28 EA Schedule 8.

29 See *Napp Pharmaceuticals* v. *Director General of Fair Trading* [2001] CAT 1 at para 93.

three London airports,[30] and may reduce its profitability in the future. However, this is a different matter from finding a breach of one of the prohibitions.

## 4 Challenging the decisions of the competition authorities

These differences between the two modes of enforcement are reflected in the different criteria for challenging decisions under the two procedures. Decisions made by the OFT, the economic regulators or the CC under either the Competition Act or the Enterprise Act are challengeable before the Competition Appeal Tribunal (CAT), a judicial body which was specially created to deal with competition matters. Cases before the CAT are heard by a panel of three, whose Chair is a judge or senior lawyer, with equivalent status to a High Court judge.[31] The other two panel members have expertise in law or related fields, such as economics or accountancy. It is thus a specialised competition court, appeals from it going to the Court of Appeal on a point of law.

Challenges to decisions that the prohibitions under Articles 81 and 82 EC or that Chapters I and II of the Competition Act have been breached, the imposition of penalties and decisions cancelling block or parallel exemptions as well as withdrawing the benefit of a Commission Regulation taken by the OFT and the economic regulators may be subject to an appeal to the CAT.[32] The CAT is directed to determine such an appeal on the merits, by reference to the grounds of appeal. The CAT is allowed to confirm or set aside the decision which is the subject of the appeal, or any part of it, and may remit the matter to the OFT, impose or revoke, or vary the amount of a penalty, give such directions, or take such other steps as the OFT could itself have given or taken, or make any other decision which the OFT could itself have made. Even if it confirms the decision, it may still set aside a finding of fact made by the OFT, for example, that a firm is in a dominant position.[33]

We should note as well section 60 of the Competition Act which says:

> '(2) At any time when the court determines a question arising under this Part, it must act ... with a view to securing that there is no inconsistency between—

---

[30] Competition Commission News Release 20 August 2008. Although BAA is proposing to sell one of its airports, it has mounted a strong attack to the CC's conclusions: response for BAA Ltd to Provisional Findings (2008) available at: http://www.competition-commission.org.uk/inquiries/ref2007/airports/responses_baa_provisional_findings.htm.

[31] The first President of the CAT, and thus responsible for hearing the majority of the cases, was Sir Christopher Bellamy, who had previously been a judge of the CFI. The current President is Sir Gerald Barling, who is a Justice of the Chancery Division of the High Court.

[32] S. Barling, who is a Justice of the Chancery Division of the High Court. Competition Act 1998.

[33] Schedule 8, para 3 Competition Act 1998. This is one of the grounds of appeal in *National Grid* v. *Gas and Electricity Markets Authority*, currently before the CAT.

(a) the principles applied, and decision reached, by the court in determining that question; and

(b) the principles laid down by the Treaty and the European Court, and any relevant decision of that Court, as applicable at that time in determining any corresponding question arising in Community law.'

By contrast, any decisions taken by the OFT, CC or the Secretary of State under the Enterprise Act provisions relating to mergers or market investigations may also be appealed to the CAT but these are to be determined on the same principles as would be applied by a court in an action for judicial review.[34] The CAT has the power to dismiss the appeal or quash the decision, in whole or in part, and may refer the decision back to the decision-maker.

The competition authorities may not wish to undertake a full scale investigation, under either the Competition or the Enterprise Act, if the matter can be resolved otherwise. The legislation allows them to accept commitments either to meet the competition concerns which have arisen in an investigation under the Competition Act or in place of making a merger or market reference.[35] The OFT has utilised this procedure in a number of cases, as has Ofcom, the communications regulator, in relation to BT, the UK's incumbent telecommunications provider, as part of its strategic review of telecommunications markets. These decisions may be challenged before the CAT on judicial review grounds.[36]

Thus the same judicial body has to apply two different standards in relation to appeals, depending on what sort of decision has been challenged. The CAT has made it clear in the case of *Freeserve.com* that when the appeal is on the merits, the CAT's function is not limited to applying the principles of judicial review nor to the heads of review contained in Article 230 EC.[37] Regardless of whether there is a finding of an infringement, or non-infringement, an appeal on the merits means that the CAT may decide whether or not the OFT or an economic regulator has made an error of fact or law, an error of appraisal or of procedure, or whether the matter has been sufficiently investigated.[38] The CAT has said that a convenient check list of points for an appellant was: that the decision is incorrect or, at the least, insufficient, from the point of view of (i) the reasons given; (ii) the facts and analysis relied on; (iii) the law applied; (iv) the investigation undertaken; or (v) the procedure followed.[39]

The CAT went on to emphasise in *Freeserve.com* that it was an appellate tribunal and that if it felt the OFT was incorrectly informed, it should in general remit the matter to the OFT to decide again, rather than make its own decision. Even so, in the *Burgess* case, the CAT set aside the OFT's decision that there had

[34] Ss. 120 and 179 Enterprise Act 2002.

[35] Competition Act s. 31A, EA ss. 73 and 154.

[36] Competition Act ss. 46 and 47, EA ss. 120 and 179.

[37] *Freeserve.com* v. *Director General of Communications* [2003] CAT 15, at para. 106.

[38] *Freeserve.com* v. *Director General of Communications* at para. 110.

[39] *Freeserve.com* v. *Director General of Communications* at para. 114.

been no abuse of a dominant position and decided that there had been such an abuse, a refusal to supply, without remitting the matter back to the OFT.[40] In this case, the CAT set out the view that it should, if necessary, take its own decision rather than remit if (i) it has or can obtain all the necessary material (ii) the requirements of procedural fairness are respected and (iii) the course the Tribunal proposes to take is desirable from the point of view of the need for expedition and saving costs.[41]

## 5 Challenging the decisions of the economic regulators

The first thing to be aware of is that the economic regulators have a variety of powers which have been granted to them by statute. As mentioned above, they enjoy concurrent powers under competition law with the OFT and in the exercise of these powers they are subject to an appeal to the CAT in the same way as discussed above. Leaving these powers aside, the central part of economic regulation in the UK resides in the licence which is granted to companies and which allows them to operate in each industry. The licence[42] contains the terms and conditions under which a company is entitled to operate. The level of detail varies from industry to industry and also depends on the complexity of the condition. So, for example, the price control conditions for the water and sewerage companies are highly complex, whilst the provisions relating to consumer complaints are much simpler. The job of the economic regulators in relation to the licence conditions is twofold: first, they are responsible for policing the licences and ensuring that the companies obey the licences and, secondly, they are responsible for keeping the licence conditions under review and amending them to take account of changing conditions in the industry. The regulators do not, however, have a unilateral power to amend the licences; in general terms they can only amend a licence if the licensee, or a specified majority of licensees in the case of standard licences, agree to the amendment. If the regulator is unable to obtain such agreement, their only recourse is to make a reference to the CC which will decide whether or not the amendment is necessary.[43] CC decisions on this matter are subject to judicial review in the High Court. Given that this is a relatively long process, requiring the regulator to commit substantial resources to make their case before the CC, and there is no guarantee that the CC will accept the regulator's case, it has only been utilised on three occasions.[44]

Enforcement of the licence conditions through the statutory procedure is hedged around with procedural protections, although it allows the regulators

40 *M.E. Burgess* v. *Office of Fair Trading* [2005] CAT 25. See also *Floe Telecom* v. *Ofcom* [2005] CAT 14.

41 *Freeserve.com* v. *Director General of Communications* at para. 132.

42 Which may be an individual or a standard licence.

43 See Water Industry Act 1991 ss. 13-14.

44 Competition Commission *Mobile Phone Charges* (2003), Competition Commission *Electricity Generators* (2001), Competition Commission *Chatline and Message Services* (1989).

to give directions to the company in breach. Also, since 2000, the regulators have the power to impose monetary penalties on companies which are in breach of their licence conditions. A separate appeal procedure to the High Court is provided to challenge the imposition of penalties.[45] When an enforcement decision is taken via this route, the legislation provides for a route of challenge to the High Court and allows the licence holder to challenge the decision on the basis that it was not within the powers of the regulator or that the correct procedure has not been followed, as long as this is done within forty-two days.[46] This is equivalent to a challenge using the traditional grounds of judicial review but, so far as the author is aware, this procedure has never been used.

Inevitably, there are certain exceptions to the picture painted here. The first is telecommunications regulation, which was changed by the Communications Act 2003 in part in order to implement the relevant EC Directives on telecommunications. Therefore, rather than there being a system of licences, there is a system of conditions which are imposed on all telecommunications providers, which are policed by Ofcom. Ofcom has the power to set, modify and revoke these conditions, some of which are general, and others may be applied to specific people or classes of people, notably if Ofcom decides that a telecommunications provider has significant market power.[47] These conditions may be imposed without the agreement of the providers and without a reference to the CC.[48] Article 4 of the framework Directive for electronic communications provides that there should be an appeal against decisions of the regulatory body and that this appeal should ensure that the merits of the case are taken into account and this has been implemented through an appeal to the CAT,[49] except for price control issues which are referred to the CC for a determination.[50] The determination of the CC on price control matters is binding on the CAT. Appeals under section 192 are to be decided on the merits and in accordance with the grounds of appeal and must include a decision on what action, if any, it is appropriate for Ofcom to take in relation to the subject matter of the appeal.

---

45 See s. 36 Postal Services Act 2000, discussed in *Royal Mail Group* v. *Postal Services Commission* [2007] EWHC 1205 Admin., Electricity Act 1989 s, 27E, Gas Act 1986 s. 30E, Railways Act 1993 s. 57F. The Regulatory Enforcement and Sanctions Bill provides for greater availability of civil penalties but any appeal against such penalties is likely to be to the new Upper Tribunal established under the Tribunals, Courts and Enforcement Act 2007.

46 See Electricity Act 1989 s. 27, Water Industry Act 1991 s. 21.

47 Communications Act 2003 s. 45.

48 Communications Act 2003 ss. 46-48.

49 Directive 2002/21/EC on a common regulatory framework for electronic communications networks and services OJ L 108, 24.4.2002, p.33. Communications Act 2003 s. 192.

50 The parties may dispute the principles applied in price control, the methods for determining the control, the data used and what the provisions should be, including the level of the price control: Competition Appeal Tribunal (Amendment and Communications Act Appeals) Rules 2004 Rule 3.

The decision under appeal must be sent back to Ofcom with such directions as the CAT considers appropriate for it to resolve the case in hand.[51]

A second exception exists in relation to the water industry as price control determinations by the Office of Water Service (Ofwat) may be challenged by the companies through making a reference to the CC which is provided for within their licences, rather than the legislation. This is a provision which has only been utilised rarely by the water companies and they have not had much success at challenging Ofwat's decisions on price control matters.[52] A third exception exists in relation to the various codes in the gas and electricity industries which govern matters such as use of the system, connection, energy balancing and other issues. There is a complex procedure for consultation within the industry leading to an expert panel which makes a recommendation to Ofgem.[53] Ofgem has the final decision on whether or not to modify the Code but its decision on this issue is appealable, on the basis of the merits of the decision, to the CC under ss. 173 to 177 of the Energy Act 2004.[54]

Two points can be made about these arrangements. First, it has been argued that one of the aims of the original privatisation legislation was to ensure that disputes about decisions by the economic regulators were kept out of the courts and the structure for licence modification was designed with that objective in mind.[55] If this is true, it does seem to have been successful as there have been very few cases arriving in the courts. Secondly, leaving aside Ofcom and price control matters in water, the route to challenge an economic regulator's decision is through judicial review, rather than an appeal on the merits to a specialist tribunal.

## 6 Judicial review of decisions of economic regulators

Judicial review is an investigation into the legality of a decision and in the UK, there are often said to be three main headings: illegality, procedural impropriety and irrationality.[56] These grounds are similar, but not identical to those listed in Article 230 EC, so it can roughly be said that a similar role is envisaged for the UK and European Community courts when undertaking review of decisions by public authorities. Within this contribution, our interest in judicial review is not on the first two grounds of review, illegality and procedural impropriety, as these are well established grounds where there is no

51 S. 195 Communications Act 2003.

52 Price control matters for airports are also decided by the CC.

53 Formally called the Gas and Electricity Markets Authority but known as the Office of Gas and Electricity Markets (Ofgem).

54 See Bates (2008) pp. 99-113.

55 Foster (1992).

56 Lord Diplock in *Council of Civil Service Unions* v. *Minister for the Civil Service* [1985] AC 374. Vajda (2005) have a more detailed list.

controversy that, if they are established, it is appropriate for a court to intervene. In relation to judicial review of regulatory decisions, there are a number of cases over the years where decisions have been overturned on these grounds.[57] The key ground for our purposes is irrationality, which can be seen as equating to misuse of powers. The starting point for consideration of this doctrine is the rather old case of *Associated Provincial Picture House* v. *Wednesbury Corporation* where Lord Greene, MR put the principle this way:

> 'The court is entitled to investigate the action of the [public] authority with a view to seeing whether they have taken into account matters which they ought not to take into account, or, conversely, have refused to take into account or neglected to take into account matters which they ought to take into account. Once that question is answered in favour of the [public] authority, it may be still possible to say that, although the [public] authority have kept within the four corners of the matters which they ought to consider, they have nevertheless come to a conclusion so unreasonable that no reasonable authority could ever have come to it. In such a case, again, I think the court can interfere.'[58]

Quite what this means has been a matter of controversy, and academic and judicial opinion has been very critical of the test.[59] In addition, the courts' approach to applying *Wednesbury* in particular cases has fluctuated between very limited intervention to more intrusive review,[60] although without ever really explaining their rationale in a coherent manner. Clayton and Galy have recently argued that the question of irrationality may be answered in two different ways: either that the conclusion itself is unsustainable or that the reasoning process itself was logically flawed.[61] The sustainability of a conclusion depends on whether or not a decision is within a range of reasonable responses for a public authority, which they see as more intensive scrutiny than a traditional *Wednesbury* approach. They go on to make the point that the context of the decision under challenge is always vital and there is a spectrum of control ranging from anxious scrutiny, involving human rights issues, to issues of economic policy or resource allocation where the court will be more reluctant to intervene. In the context of judicial review of the decisions of an economic regulator, we shall see that the courts have been reluctant to scrutinise these decisions too intensively and have tended to see them as decisions which relate to issues within the regulator's expertise.

---

57 See Graham (2000) Ch. 4 for examples. *Royal Mail Group* v. *Consumer Council for Postal Services* [2007] EWCA Civ 167 (interpretation of statutory scheme).

58 [1947] 2 All ER 680. 'public' substituted for 'local' in this quote.

59 See *R (ABCIFER)* v. *Secretary of State for Defence* [2003] QB 1397 at paras. 34-7.

60 Compare *Nottinghamshire County Council* v. *Secretary of State for the Environment* [1986] AC 240 (very limited scrutiny) with *Wheeler* v. *Leicester City Council* [1985] AC 1054 (more intensive scrutiny).

61 Clayton (2007) pp. 210-18.

The discussion that follows, concentrates on decisions taken since 2003, which raise the *Wednesbury* issue, of which there are very few.[62]

One of the more controversial was the *T-Mobile* case,[63] which involved a challenge to the recommendations of the CC on an inquiry into mobile phone call termination charges. The inquiry had come about because of a reference from the Director General of Telecommunications (DGT) and the CC had decided that the termination charges exceeded the CC's assessment of a fair charge and had recommended a price cap which was implemented by the DGT, albeit for a very short period. This was a very complicated case, partly because it involved transitional arrangements from one regime to another, but there was also an attempt to challenge the CC's recommendations on the grounds of rationality. These challenges were dismissed by Moses, J (as he then was) as going to the merits of the decision, rather than being based on irrationality. The CC's report was heavily criticised by consultants employed by the mobile phone operators, who asserted that judicial review could not deal with poor analysis hidden in a lengthy, 1500 pages long, report from an expert body. The consultants hypothesised that a more expert body, such as the CAT, might have come to a different decision.[64] This view seems to gain some support from the recent decision of the CAT on Ofcom's determination of certain disputes over call termination charges, where the CAT overturned Ofcom's decision, albeit in the context of appeals under s. 192 Communications Act 2003, in other words, on the merits of the matter.[65]

In *London and Continental* v. *Rail Regulator*[66] there was a dispute between the owners of St Pancras station and the Regulator over the terms of an access agreement that the Regulator had imposed to compensate one of the train companies that used the station for its losses while the terminal was being reconstructed in order to accommodate the Eurostar. Here the judge, Moses, J (as he then was) made the point that the Rail Regulator was required to exercise its powers in the national public interest and, in so doing, was not constrained by the wishes of any party. The Rail Regulator was better placed than a court to make an overall assessment of what was in the interests of the rail network as a whole and this explained the limited scope of intervention that the court had in this area. The judge then went on to cite passages from Lightman, J in *R* v. *Director General of Telecommunications ex parte Cellcom and others*[67]where he said:

---

62 For discussion of decisions before then see Robertson (2007) pp. 553-562.

63 *R on the application of T-Mobile (UK )* v. *Competition Commission* [2003] EWHC 1566 Admin.

64 Walker (2003).

65 *T-Mobile (UK) and others* v. *Office of Communications* [2008] CAT 12. See further *T-Mobile (UK) and others* v. *Office of Communications* [2008] CAT 19.

66 [2003] EWHC 2607 Admin.

67 [1999] ECC 314 at para. 26. Also cited with approval in *R on the application of Wildman* v. *Office of Communications* [2005] EWHC 1573 Admin.

> 'Where the Act has conferred the decision-making function on the Director, it is for him, and him alone, to consider the economic arguments, weigh the compelling considerations and arrive at a judgment. The applicants have no right of appeal; in these judicial review proceedings so long as he directs himself correctly in law, his decision may only be challenged on *Wednesbury* grounds. The court must be astute to avoid the danger of substituting its views for the decision-maker and of contradicting (as in this case) a conscientious decision-maker acting in good faith and with knowledge of all the facts. If (as I have stated) the court should be very slow to impugn decisions of fact made by an expert and experienced decision-maker, it must surely be even slower to impugn his educated prophesises and predictions for the future.'

In conclusion the judge felt that the role of the courts in constraining the Regulator's exercise of his decision-making power in this context was small. That this was the correct approach to take in these areas was confirmed in a later case where a challenge to the Office of Rail Regulation's view that the variable track access charge was the best available measure of cost that is directly incurred, was rejected, citing Moses J's views in support.[68]

There have been a number of challenges to decisions of Ofgem, in a variety of different contexts. In the *Exoteric* case,[69] there was a challenge to Ofgem's decision not to take enforcement action, after the receipt of complaints by Exoteric, in relation to gas connection services provided by Transco, the network operator, but instead to conduct an industry wide investigation. The judge summarised the essence of the dispute as whether Ofgem could reasonably disagree with Exoteric's contention that the result of its survey were representative across the whole of the connections market and the best evidence that would ever be available. Ofgem was entitled to disagree because the quotations were a tiny percentage of the connections business and because the bad relations between the two companies suggested that their relationship was atypical of the industry. The judge concluded by saying, 'These are judicial review proceedings. This is not a Court of Appeal from Ofgem's decision on the merits. It is an expert body, upon which Parliament has deliberately conferred a broad discretionary area of judgment. Its judgment that investigation rather than immediate enforcement was appropriate was well within the bounds of that broad discretion.'[70]

In the *ScottishPower* case,[71] there was a challenge to the new method used for calculating charges for the use of the transmission system in Great Britain. The effect of the new system was that the Scottish generators would pay substan-

68 *Great North Eastern Railway* v. *Office of Rail Regulation* [2006] EWHC 1942 Admin at para. 39.

69 *R (on the application of Exoteric Gas Solutions Ltd)* v. *Gas & Electricity Market Authority (OFGEM)* [2003] EWHC 2072.

70 *R (on the application of Exoteric Gas Solutions Ltd)* v. *Gas & Electricity Market Authority (OFGEM)* [2003] EWHC 2072 at para. 83.

71 *ScottishPower Energy Management Ltd* v. *Gas and Electricity Markets Authority* [2005] EWHC 2324.

tially more in transmission charges than their English and Welsh competitors. Although substantial submissions were made about the intensity of review which should be conducted by the court, this issue was not addressed because, even applying the highest intensity of review which had been argued for (and it is not explained what this is), the judge found that there was no legal basis to uphold the challenge on the specific points.

Most recently in *Royal Mail Group* v. *Postal Services Commission*,[72] the Postal Services Commission (PSC) imposed a fine of £ 9.6 million on Royal Mail for breach of its licence conditions, relating to mail integrity, i.e., lost post. The basis of the calculation was that half of the lost volume was attributable to the licence breaches. In its statement of policy on imposing penalties, PSC said that they would endeavour to ensure that decisions were soundly based in fact. PSC did not receive information from Royal Mail and tried to carry out some benchmarking, but this was of limited value. Pill, LJ, in the Court of Appeal, acknowledged that a very broad discretion was placed on the PSC when exercising its statutory duties and that it had used its best endeavours to ensure that its decision was soundly based in fact:

> 'What [the PSC] has done, as an expert tribunal familiar with postal services and their problems, is to consider the nature, seriousness and length of the breaches of condition and to assess their likely consequences in a situation in which the possibility of losses from other causes, some the fault of Royal Mail and others beyond their control, must be kept in mind. In making its assessment, [the PSC] has not had the benefit of full co-operation by Royal Mail, (...) , notwithstanding the requirement in its licence to collect and analyse statistics to achieve the purpose of minimising loss.'

It should be evident from the discussion above that the High Court has adopted a deferential standard of review in relation to decisions of economic regulators and that it is not obvious that this has been influenced by any European Community case law. The High Court does not subject the regulator's reasons to detailed scrutiny, nor is there a searching examination of the evidence base. So, in this context, *Wednesbury* offers only limited scrutiny.

### 6.1 *Tetra Laval* in the CAT

Before examining the CAT's approach to its judicial review jurisdiction, we should discuss the one case where *Tetra Laval* was addressed at some length, namely *Hutchison*.[73] Here Hutchison had appealed against a decision of Ofcom, using s. 192 of the Communications Act 2003, that is, an appeal on the merits, that they had significant market power in the market for wholesale voice call termination. It was argued on behalf of Hutchison that there

---

[72] (CA) [2008] EWCA Civ 33.

[73] *Hutchison 3G (UK)* v. *Office of Communications* [2005] CAT 39.

was a high burden of proof on a regulator making such a decision, with counsel relying on the *Tetra Laval* decision, which had been decided three months before the main hearing in this case, in support of this proposition. The CAT were not prepared to accept this argument, pointing out that *Tetra Laval* was concerned with a conglomerate merger and predictions about the possible future behaviour of the merged entity. Ofcom was deciding instead that Hutchison had significant market power now, not at any point in the future. The CAT took the view that the evidence had to be looked at and properly assessed and Ofcom needed to prove what needed to be proved to the appropriate level of proof. There had to be proper evidence that there was significant market power in the market, the evidence did not have to achieve a high degree of weight.[74] However, although rejecting this submission, the CAT carried out a careful examination of the reasons and evidence underlying Ofcom's determination and came to the conclusion that the determination was flawed because Ofcom had not carried out a full assessment of the extent to which BT had countervailing buyer power.[75] The CAT therefore remitted the decision back to Ofcom to reconsider the determination of significant market power taking into account the extent to which BT had countervailing buyer power.[76]

## 6.2 Judicial review in the CAT

The CAT's first attempt to explain what it understood by the ordinary principles of judicial review came in the *IBA Health* case, which was a case where the OFT's decision *not* to refer a merger to the CC was challenged by a third party competitor. The central issue revolved around the correct interpretation of the OFT's duty, but the CAT also addressed the issue of the principles of judicial review. The CAT did not find it entirely easy to apply this duty and pointed out that the principles of judicial review varied according to the context of the case. One of the important parts of this context was that the CAT was a specialist tribunal so they were not persuaded that cases such as *Cellcom* and *London and Continental* could be read across into this area. They also pointed out that there were a variety of decisions which could potentially be reviewed, ranging from national security issues to calculations of turnover to remedial matters. The present case they thought was not really about challenging the exercise of a discretion but about the interpretation of the statute.

The case was appealed to the Court of Appeal,[77] which upheld the decision but had a different reasoning on the substance of the matter. On the issue of the scope of judicial review, the CAT's approach was criticised by Carnwath LJ,[78]

74 *Hutchison 3G (UK)* v. *Office of Communications* [2005] CAT 39 para. 34.

75 *Hutchison 3G (UK)* v. *Office of Communications* [2005] CAT 39 para. 145.

76 Ofcom decided again that Hutchison had significant market power but this time the conclusion was upheld by the CAT: *Hutchison 3G (UK)* v. *Office of Communications* [2008] CAT 11.

77 *Office of Fair Trading* v. *IBA Health* [2004] 4 All ER 1103.

78 *Office of Fair Trading* v. *IBA Health* [2004] 4 All ER 1103 at paras. 88-101.

who said that they could usefully have started by looking at some of the text-books in the area! Overall, Carnwath LJ thought that the principles of judicial review are flexible enough to be adapted to the specific statutory context. He emphasised that the intensity of review under the *Wednesbury* standard varied depending on the context, from cases which depended essentially on political judgment, where there was a low intensity of review, to cases involving fundamental human rights where review is stricter. Another factor in his view was whether the issue was properly one within the province of the court or tribunal and here he contrasted cases involving procedural impropriety with issues of administrative or political judgement. In the case in question, Carnwath LJ felt that there was no doubt that the court was entitled to inquire into whether or not there was sufficient material to support the OFT's belief. This was a question which was wholly suitable for a court to resolve and involved no question of policy or political judgement.

Since this decision, the CAT has been reluctant to discuss the issue of its approach to judicial review in any depth. The clearest statement came in *Unichem* v. *OFT*[79] where it held:

> 'the Tribunal has jurisdiction, acting in a supervisory rather than appellate capacity, to determine whether the OFT's conclusions are adequately supported by evidence, that the facts have been properly found, that all material factual considerations have been taken into account, and that material facts have not been omitted.'

Subsequently in *Somerfield* v. *Competition Commission* the CAT simply adopted this statement as a starting point,[80] while in *Co-Operative Group* v. *Office of Fair Trading* it was slightly more expansive, putting the test thus:

> 'It considers whether the OFT has directed itself properly in law; whether the OFT has called its attention to the matters it is bound to consider; whether the OFT has excluded from its consideration matters which are irrelevant to that which it has to consider and whether the decision to which it has come is one which is reasonable in this sense: that it is, or can be, supported with good reasons and is a decision which a reasonable authority might reasonably reach.' [81]

We should contrast the last phrase, 'a decision which a reasonable authority might reasonably reach' with the original formulation in the *Wednesbury* case of 'a conclusion so unreasonable that no reasonable authority could ever have come to it' which, although it sounds like more intensive review, is probably a similar standard. More difficult is the comment in *Unichem* that the CAT has the jurisdiction to determine whether or not the OFT's conclusions are 'adequately

79 [2005] CAT 8 at para. 174.

80 [2006] CAT 4 paras. 55-7.

81 [2007] CAT 24 at para. 91.

supported by evidence'. Typically, it would be said that judicial review is available where there is no evidence to support factual findings made or they are plainly untenable or if the decision-maker is shown to have misunderstood or been ignorant of an established and relevant fact but the reference to adequacy suggests a higher level of review than is traditional under domestic case law.[82] It may be that the reference to adequacy is a reference to the CAT examining the reasons underlying the decision, as in *Co-Operative Group*, in order to see that they are logical and coherent, but this does suggest a more intensive standard of review than is engaged in as regards the economic regulators by the High Court.[83]

If, however, there is an argument that the CAT's approach to judicial review takes it further than domestic law, it is worth returning to the original premise of this contribution: a comparison of the approach of the CAT to that of the ECJ in *Tetra Laval*, which is illustrated in the table below:

| *Tetra Laval* | *Unichem* v. *OFT* |
|---|---|
| •establish whether the evidence relied on is factually accurate, reliable and consistent but also | •whether the OFT's conclusions are adequately supported by evidence, |
| •whether that evidence contains all the information which must be taken into account in order to assess a complex situation and | •that the facts have been properly found, |
| •whether it is capable of substantiating the conclusions drawn from it. | •that all material factual considerations have been taken into account, and |
| | •that material facts have not been omitted. |

This demonstrates, rather neatly, that the tests are, if not identical, very similar. We should also note that although the CAT is reviewing legality in all these cases, there is a very careful check on the reasoning process of the competition authorities, perhaps most noticeably for our purposes in the *Somerfield* case where the CAT looks very closely at the reasoning and the basis for it in the CC's decision on remedies.

## 7 Conclusions

As we can see from the discussion above, the main discussion of *Tetra Laval* was in the *Hutchison* case, where the issue it was used for was not the intensity or grounds of review, but rather the burden of proof that rested on the regulator. In the field of merger control, the case is only mentioned in

82 Lord Bingham in *Begum* v. *Tower Hamlets* [2003] 2 AC 430 at 439.

83 Although compare *R* v. *(on the application of Medway Council)* v. *Secretary of State for Transport* [2002] EWHC 2516 Admin where it was accepted that the Secretary of State did not have adequate reasons for his decision which was therefore irrational.

*Somerfield* where the CC submitted that the standard of review should not be that applied in *Tetra Laval*, but the CAT made no explicit response to this submission. It is probably true though, with the first President of the CAT having come from the CFI, he would have been aware of the case law.[84] The position that the CAT has reached does seem to be in advance of the High Court as regards review of factual matters, although this is not an area of great clarity.[85]

It seems, therefore, that the standard of review in the CAT is more intensive than has been the case in judicial review procedures with respect to decisions of economic regulators. The point was put neatly by counsel in *British Sky Broadcasting* v. *Competition Commission* when they submitted that:

> '... whereas under s.120(4) [Enterprise Act 2002] this Tribunal is obliged to apply the same principles as would be applied by a court on an application for judicial review, they are not obliged by statute or otherwise to apply them in the same way.'[86]

This is, however, a central point of contention between the parties in this case[87] and it is possible that the CAT will reject this submission or not deal with the point explicitly but exercise a more intensive scrutiny than the High Court would in a judicial review application. If the CAT does continue to exercise more intensive scrutiny, this would seem to be because it is a specialist competition tribunal, with experience of appeals on the merits or because the issues raised before it in cases so far have been the sort of issues that are more susceptible to judicial determination. It may also be related to a court's assessment of the inherent plausibility of the factual finding at issue.[88] The issues which have arisen in the judicial review of decisions by economic regulators have looked, by contrast, much less like issues susceptible to determination by a court. The recent challenges in *Tesco* v. *Competition Commission* and *British Sky Broadcasting* v. *Competition Commission* do go further than previous cases because the substance of the decision is being challenged. It will be interesting to see exactly what approach to the intensity of review, and indeed issues on the standard of proof, is taken by the CAT.

---

84 There is an Association of European Competition Law Judges who meet regularly to discuss, among other things, cases in their countries and at European Community level.

85 See Craig (2004) pp. 788-807.

86 *British Sky Broadcasting* v. *Competition Commission* [2008] CAT 35, Transcript of first day hearing at p. 5.

87 See Transcript of second day hearing at pp. 9-13 and 40-5.

88 A point made by Vajda (2005) at para. 6-052.

## Bibliography


ALLAN (2004)

T. R. S. Allan, 'Legislative Supremacy and Legislative Intent: A Reply to Professor Craig' [2004/24] *Oxford Journal of Legal Studies* pp. 563-583

BATES (2008)

A. Bates, 'Intensity of Review: The Approach of the Competition Commission in Energy Code Modification Appeals' [2008]*Competition Law Journal* pp. 99-113

CLAYTON (2007)

R. Clayton, QC and K. Galy, 'Shifting Standards of Review' [2007] *Judicial Review* pp. 210-18

CRAIG (2001)

P. Craig and N. Bamforth, 'Constitutional Analysis, Constitutional Principle and Judicial Review' [2001] *Public Law* pp. 763-780

CRAIG (2004)

P. Craig, 'Judicial review, appeal and factual error' [2004] *Public Law* pp. 788-807

FORSYTH (2003)

C. Forsyth and M. Elliott, 'The Legitimacy of Judicial Review' [2003] *Public Law* pp. 286-307.

FOSTER (1992)

C. Foster, *Privatization, Public Ownership and the Regulation of Natural Monopoly* (Oxford 1992)

GRAHAM (2000)

C. Graham, *Regulating Public Utilities* (Hart Publishing, Oxford 2000)

MORAN (2003)

M. Moran, *The British Regulatory State* (Oxford University Press, Oxford 2003)

ROBERTSON (2007)

A. Robertson, M. Lester and S. Love, 'Judicial review in the UK of competition and state aid decisions: Part 1' [2007/10] *European Competition Law Review* pp. 553-562.

VAJDA (2005)

C. Vajda, QC and J. Gregory in T. Ward and K. Smith (eds), *Competition Litigation in the UK* (London 2005)

WALKER (2003)

M. Walker, 'Mobile phone charges inquiry and judicial review. A worrying failure of analysis' *NYP, but given at BIICL Practitioner Workshop 16 September 2003.*

CHAPTER 14

# European and National Standards of Review: Differentiation or Convergence

S. Lavrijssen, A. Gerbrandy, O. Essens

On the basis of the contributions preceding this Chapter and the discussions during the conference, this concluding synthesis aims to find some answers and formulate suggestions concerning the sub-questions and the central question of this book. The structure of this synthesis reflects the order of the sub-questions as presented in the introductory chapter. These sub-questions were the following:

- How should the *Tetra Laval* standard of the ECJ be interpreted?
- Is this standard binding on the national courts?
- What are the standards of review and standards of proof applied by national courts when reviewing decisions of national competition authorities and national regulatory authorities?
- What is the influence of European law on the national standards of review and the national standards of proof? Have the national courts applied the *Tetra Laval* standard or a similar standard in practice?
- What are the reasons for the presence or absence of a European legal influence on the national standards of review and standards of proof?
- Are there many differences between the standards of review and standards of proof applied by the national courts of the different Member States?
- Should there be more convergence between the standards of review and the standards of proof applied by the national courts of the different Member States and should there be more convergence between the European and national standards?
- Should the *Tetra Laval* standard play a role in the convergence of national standards of review and standards of proof in competition law and economic regulation cases and if so, how?

In this concluding Chapter we will gather up several threads, discuss remaining questions, and will attempt to see through the looking glass and beyond judicial review in *Tetra Laval*.

## 1 The interpretation and practical meaning of *Tetra Laval*

### 1.1 Judicial review under Article 230 EC

In order to understand the meaning of the *Tetra Laval* judgment of the ECJ, first the scope of legal review of administrative decisions by the European courts on the basis of Article 230 EC should be recalled. In this respect, the contribution of Judge Arjen Meij elucidates that the action under Article 230 EC was initially modelled after the *'recours pour excès de pouvoir'* before the French *Conseil d'État*. This is, also in the European courts, conceived as a *'recours objectif'*, the main purpose of which is to review the legality of the act (*'contentieux de la légalité'*) in order to either uphold this act or remove it wholly or partially from what is called the 'objective legal order' through its annulment *erga omnes* (Meij). It is not the task for the European courts to pronounce themselves on the merits of a case, let alone to take over the role of the administration by adopting a new decision. This concerns a '*full* jurisdiction' in that it covers review of the establishment of facts,[1] the assessment of these facts and the legal interpretation. This full jurisdiction is, however, limited to *legality* review. This means that when there is a discretionary power for the Commission – discretion in the assessment of facts – this part is *remotely* (or *marginally*) reviewed. To review discretionary power fully would mean a review on the *merits* (see below). It should be noted, however, that the European courts, like most national courts, have *unlimited* jurisdiction ('*contentieux de pleine jurisdiction*') in relation to the review of fines (Article 229 EC). Of course, this unlimited jurisdiction relating to fines also stems from article 6 of the European Convention of Human Rights. The difference, then, between full jurisdiction (legality review) and unlimited jurisdiction is that in the latter the courts are not only asked to review the legality of the decision but also its expediency.

In cases concerning complex economic, legal or scientific assessments, the European courts will only *remotely* or *marginally* review the discretion of the Commission with regard to the appraisal of economic data and the conclusions to be drawn from this appraisal.[2] This is in clear contrast to full review – a review of the facts, the assessment and the interpretation – which is the most common starting point for the European courts in judicial review. There is no review on the merits in the application of discretion. The courts will not review whether the appraisal of the Commission was correct; they will review whether the relevant procedural rules have been complied with, whether the statement of reasons for the decision is adequate, whether the facts have been accurately stated and whether there has been any manifest error of appraisal or a misuse of powers. Schimmel and Widdershoven clarify that the ground of review of 'manifest error of assessment', denotes the situation where an error is evident and grave enough so as to preclude any 'potential concurrence' between the established facts on the one hand, and the conclusion drawn from these facts on the other.

### 1.1.1 Types and standards of review

In general, there are several distinctions to be made in types and standards of review that may be helpful as basic principles when comparing the different concepts of review as used by the national courts and the possible influence of the *Tetra Laval* judgment on them. All review relates to the three classical threads of substantive judicial decision-making: the finding of facts, the assessment of these facts (in relation to the legal provision that is applied) and

1 Though, of course, the review of the ECJ in appeal is limited to questions of law.

2 The notion of discretion will be explained in section 3.3.2.

the interpretation of the legal provision that is applicable.[3] Review in administrative law also covers the procedural aspects of the decision-making at the level of the authority.

The *standard* of review could then be distinguished in *full* or *comprehensive* review as contrasted with *remote* or *marginal* review. *Legality* review as contrasted with review on the *merits* are both *types* of review. The standard of full review means that the court can substitute its findings for that of the authority; the standard of marginal review implies more distance between the court and the authority and leaves the ultimate finding and assessment of the facts in the hands of the authority. Neither standard necessarily implies that the court will have the power to decide the case itself after quashing a decision instead of referring it back to the authority.

The point of departure is that the type of review called 'legality review' is a full review, unless the authority that took the decision has discretionary power. This discretionary power classically relates only to the assessment of facts. When there is such power, the legality review moves back from being a full review, and will move toward marginal review. This is in contrast to the type of review called 'review on the merits', which implies a standard of full review even regarding the discretionary assessment of facts. With regard to both types of review it should be borne in mind that the courts will hold final authority on interpretation of the law; to say what the law is and what the law means is the ultimate power of the judiciary. 'Unlimited review', the third type of review, finally, implies not only review of the legality and the merits of the (part of) the decision of the authority but also of its *expediency*.

Usually, and logically, it would follow that unlimited review holds with it the power for the court not only to quash the decision and substitute its own findings for that of the authority, but also to actually decide the case itself, in the sense that the case is not referred back to the authority to decide: For instance the court can decide on the level of the fine itself. The same is usually true for a review on the merits, but this power is not necessarily granted and if granted the court will not always make use of it. Legality review, at least at the level of the Community Court, means that the court does not have this power. However, to complicate matters, some national courts that are limited to legality review, may – in certain circumstances – take a new decision themselves.

### 1.2 *Tetra Laval*: a more intensive application of the legality review?

With the above-mentioned situation regarding the standard of review of the European Courts in mind, the question can be raised as to how the *Tetra Laval* judgment should be interpreted. Some of the authors in this book argue that the CFI has subjected the factual assessment by the Commission to a more rigorous examination than before (Zwart, Lavrijssen). Others, including

[3] Of course, this is a simplification. However, it is very useful as a model.

judges of the CFI, are of the opinion, that the CFI has not applied a new, more intensive standard of review. The latter view holds that the CFI has simply specified more exactly than before the actions that the standard of review and the standard of proof under Article 230 EC require from the Commission (Meij).[4]

The contributions in this book and the discussions during the conference show that there is still much controversy as to the question whether the European courts have intensified the scope of review of Commission decisions implying a margin of discretion with regard to the assessment of economic matters. In this respect Del Guayo raises the question whether *Tetra Laval* can be understood as a full deployment, or the logical consequence, of the traditional review based on the manifest error test or, on the contrary, as a review of the appreciation of economic facts or even further as an evaluation of the appropriateness of the decisions of the European Commission.

We do not aim to take a definitive position with regard to the intensity of review exercised by the CFI in Article 230 EC actions. We would like to make three observations, however. First, in the formal legal sense, it is clear that the European courts do not apply a more intensive standard of review than they did before. Nevertheless, it can be argued that by specifying more exactly and transparently what is required from the Commission in terms of the standard of proof, the courts *de facto* subject the Commission's economic assessment to a more intensive scrutiny, in the sense that the discretionary room for the Commission has decreased, albeit still without the Court substituting its opinion for that of the Commission.

Secondly, although the European courts subject the Commission's decisions to a legality review, the exact application of this type of review may differ depending on the circumstances of the case, such as the nature and the scope of the margin of discretion and the type of decision (an authorisation or an infringement decision). The margin of discretion can be wider or narrower in scope, and this would mean that the area in which discretion is still granted (and at least formally, a standard of marginal review should be applied) will differ between the different types of decisions.

Thirdly, the position of the contributors to this book on the intensity of review in Article 230 EC actions and the *Tetra Laval* judgment depends also on the perspective from which the standard of review is assessed. This perspective is informed by national circumstances. For instance, in France the Paris Court of Appeal is the primary venue for challenging decisions of the Competition Council. This Court has traditionally been placed under the duty to painstakingly scrutinise the Competition Council's decisions and has the duty to replace or reform the Council's decisions with its own (Petit and Rabeux). From this perspective, Petit and Rabeux take the view that in *Tetra Laval* the ECJ defined a more traditional, arguably remote, standard of review. However, from a Dutch perspective, the standard of review applied by the ECJ in *Tetra Laval* can be seen as a more intensive one in comparison to the traditional marginal reasonable-

[4] Vesterdorf 2003, p. 136-144.

ness review to which Dutch administrative courts subject administrative decisions implying a significant margin of discretion (Lavrijssen). According to the latter test the courts merely establish whether or not the authority concerned acted reasonably.

### 1.3 The *Tetra Laval* standard; analytical clarifications

Instead of taking a definitive position on the intensity of review in Article 230 EC actions in merger control and competition law, which may fluctuate depending on the circumstances of the case, we propose that it is useful to analyse the practical consequences of the *Tetra Laval* judgment. The question is whether the judgment brings with it either a higher standard of scrutiny than before, or a high standard of scrutiny as compared to national standards, when the European and national courts review administrative decisions based on complex economic appraisals. The contributions of Meij and of Schimmel and Widdershoven analyse this in a very enlightening way. Both contributions emphasise that the application of the *Tetra Laval* standard is by no means unique for the area of competition law. The European courts apply a similar standard in other areas of European law, in which the European Commission has to take decisions on the basis of complex economic, technical or scientific appraisals implying a margin of appreciation or in areas in which the Community Institutions are granted more far-reaching discretionary powers to make policy decisions, such as in the area of public health policy or counterterrorism policy.[5]

Schimmel and Widdershoven laud the fact that the ECJ made it explicitly clear in *Tetra Laval* that the intensity of judicial control will vary according to the stage of the administrative fact-finding process under review. The Courts differentiate between the review of the establishment of the facts on the one hand and the review of the subsequent appraisal of those facts on the other hand. In their application of what Schimmel and Widdershoven call the two-staged review, the CFI and the ECJ will fully scrutinise the correctness of the established facts, but they will by contrast only marginally check whether the ensuing appraisal stage meets the appropriate standard of soundness in that they will search this stage exclusively for manifest errors of assessment.

In their contribution, Schimmel and Widdershoven clarify how the establishment stage and the appraisal stage may be distinguished from a theoretical point of view and which tools the European courts have at their disposal to review the different stages. Although this explanation is very useful for a good comprehension of the way the European courts review decisions of the European Commission, their approach faces practical limits. As recognized by the authors, in practice the distinction between the establishment stage and the appraisal stage is not always easy to make as these two stages are closely intertwined. Things are further complicated by the fact, that the European courts may adopt

---

5 See for a discussion of the concept of discretion section 3.3.2.

two seemingly opposing views where a legal provision uses open-ended notions the content of which still needs to be clarified (Meij). In this respect Meij considers that on the one hand the ECJ may well think that the legal provision leaves discretion to the administrative body as to the policy to be developed on its basis. On the other hand, the Court, ultimately responsible for the interpretation of the Treaty and the law derived from it (Article 220 EC), will be led, as the case law advances, to progressively set out the precise legal content of that provision, such as it has done in the case law in relation to Article 82 EC. This will necessarily increase the role of the European courts.

## 2 Legal consequences for the national courts

One of the questions raised in this book is whether the *Tetra Laval* standard is legally binding on the national courts on the basis of Article 10 EC when reviewing administrative decisions that apply European law. It follows from case law of the ECJ that as long as the standard of review and the standard of proof have not been harmonised by European law, the principle of the procedural autonomy prevails (Schimmel and Widdershoven).[6] This implies that the standard of review and the burden of proof are determined on the basis of national procedural law, provided that the principles of equivalence and effectiveness are respected (Ottow). Of course, in competition law this means that the standard of review as laid down in *Tetra Lava,* is not legally binding. This is evidenced for one by the one-stop shop principle in merger control which precludes the direct application of the EC merger control substantive test and procedural framework to national mergers not having a Community dimension. For another, even in the decentralised application of Articles 81 and 82 EC, as required by Regulation 1/2003, harmonisation of a standard of proof for competition decisions is not required.

Where European law does harmonise the standard of review and the standard of proof, the European standard prevails. In this respect Article 4 of the Framework Directive may serve as an example (see also Lavrijssen and Schimmel and Widdershoven).[7] This Article stipulates:

> 'Member States shall ensure that effective mechanisms exist at national level under which any user or undertaking providing electronic communications networks/and or services who is affected by a decision of a national regulatory authority has the right of appeal against the decision to an appeal body that is independent of the parties involved (..). Member States shall ensure that the

---

6 Case C-120/97 *Upjohn II* [1999] ECR I-223 and Case C-55/06 *Arcor* [2008] ECR I-2931.

7 Directive 2002/21/EC of the European Parliament and of the Council of 7 March 2002 on a Common Regulatory Framework for Electronic Communications Networks and Services (Framework Directive), OJ 2003 L 108/33.

> merits of the case are duly taken into account and there is an effective appeal mechanism (...).'.

There is some confusion about the correct interpretation of this provision (Lavrijssen). The English language version of the Framework Directive implies that the competent appeals bodies should fully review the merits of the case, which means that they may, if necessary, substitute the NRA's assessment. The Dutch language version of the same provision is less far-reaching, as it states 'that the facts of the case should be duly taken into account'. As argued by Schimmel and Widdershoven, if the ECJ would be asked to give guidance as to the correct interpretation and application of Article 4 of the Framework Directive, the ECJ could use the *Tetra Laval* standard as a source of inspiration for setting out the manner in which the national courts 'can duly take into account the merits of the case'. If this would be the case, the *Tetra Laval* standard would become binding on national courts in the area of electronic communications, but only through the extra step taken by the ECJ in expressly providing so.

As the European Commission and national competition authorities have parallel competences to enforce Articles 81 and 82 EC and closely co-operate in the application of these articles on the basis of Regulation 1/2003, Schimmel and Widdershoven argue that a similar development may occur in the area of competition law.[8] In their view, in the current system of enforcement, the principle of equality would be violated if decisions taken by the Commission are subjected to a different standard of review than in similar cases decided by the national competition authorities. However, as held previously, Regulation 1/2003 does not explicitly harmonise the standard of review to be applied by the national courts when reviewing decisions of the national competition authorities applying Articles 81 and 82 EC. Furthermore, this point of view can be debated as the application of a standard of review for *national* cases is one step removed from the standard of review in decentralised application of European Competition law. However, the point that national courts may well be unable to apply two different sets of standards to review a mixed case of national and European competition law, is well taken,[9] though it should be recalled that most national cases of competition law only concern national law.

The Dutch *T-Mobile* case may illustrate the point: in this case the Dutch Trade and Industry Appeals Tribunal (*CBB*) submitted a preliminary ruling to the ECJ, raising the interesting question whether the principle of procedural autonomy also applies in case of the direct application of European competition law by a national competition authority relating to rules on the *burden* of proof.[10] The recent judgment of the ECJ in this case provides more clarity on the question to what extent the principle of procedural autonomy applies to the enforcement of the Articles 81 and 82 EC by the national competition authorities, as the

---

8 Regulation 1/2003/EC, OJ 2003 L 1/1.

9 See on 'two sets of rules' in general Van Gerven 1995, p. 700; and also Temple Lang 2000, p. 262.

10 CBB, 31 December 2007, AWB 06/657, *Mobiele Operators*, LJN: BC1396.

ECJ holds that an EC-presumption of proof also applies in decentralised enforcement of EC competition law. If extended, this might come to mean that also the standard of review should be re-evaluated.[11]

## 3 Comparative approach: the standards of review and proof as applied by national courts

### 3.1 A variety of legal systems

Although national courts are not obliged to apply the *Tetra Laval* standard in the absence of European rules harmonising the standard of review, they may nevertheless voluntarily draw inspiration from this standard. This section will analyse which standards of review are applied by the national courts of the seven Member States that are covered in this book. In this section the influence of European law in competition law and economic regulation cases will be assessed. As we will only deal with seven out of 27 Member States, there is no claim of a complete overview of these developments. Nevertheless, by choosing the seven jurisdictions we have tried to reflect on the variety of systems of legal review, particularly in the area of competition law and economic regulation, within the EU. Compare, for example, France, a founding Member State, with its traditional '*recours pour excès de pouvoir*' to review administrative decisions by the Council of State, with Germany, also a founding Member State, but with a profoundly different view of the role of administrative courts: a strong constitutional tradition and intensive judicial review. In Hungary, a relatively new Member State, and Italy, another founding Member State, both systems revolve around administrative legality review. In the Netherlands, very much in contrast to for example Germany, there is a rather weak constitutional tradition, whereas in Spain the constitutional tradition is strong and revolves around the important concepts of political acts and administrative acts. Sweden, is a proponent of the Scandinavian tradition, in which alternatives to 'classical' legality review have been important, and where administrative review is – in contrast to for example France – a full review, in which decisions can be substituted by the courts. The United Kingdom with an administrative law tradition which is much younger than some continental systems of judicial review, has experienced major changes to its administrative law system after accession to the EU. Now it has a system that provides a mix of legality review and appeal on the merits. Some of the states mentioned have specialised courts for competition law and economic regulation, such as the Netherlands, Sweden and the United Kingdom; some do not. Some of these courts have non-lawyers as court members, as is possible in the United Kingdom; most do not. If anything, this – very short – overview adds to the existing picture in administrative law that the gen-

11 Case C-8/08 *T-Mobile* n.y.r.

eral systems of review in administrative law differ considerably. The same holds true for competition law and economic regulation.

By analysing how the national courts apply the standard of review in practice in these seven Member states, we can provide some indication on the similarities and differences between the functioning of the legal systems in the EU Member States for at least a part of European-influenced economic law. As the national courts of the chosen Member States operate in different constitutional and legal contexts, this section will first set out the constraints on this comparative approach and its purpose (section 3.2). After that, we will deal in a comparative manner with the main concepts that are related to judicial review (section 3.3). Subsequently, we will analyse how national courts review the decisions of national competition authorities and national regulatory authorities in practice (section 3.4) and the influence of European law thereon (section 3.5).

### 3.2 Constraints

The exercise of comparing the functioning of the legal review by the national courts in competition law and economic regulation cases in seven Member States is faced with several constraints:

- the systems of legal review by the national courts function in different constitutional, legal and cultural contexts;
- there is a variety of designs of the national systems for the legal review of the decisions of competition authorities and national regulatory authorities by the national courts (see section 3.1);
- within the Member States themselves, decisions of national authorities may be subject to different legal review procedures, depending on the type of the decision taken – e.g. an authorisation or an infringement decision – and the authority involved – e.g. a competition authority or a national regulatory authority – and the nature of the discretion of the authorities;
- moreover, the application of a certain standard of review may not only differ depending on the circumstances of the case but also on the expertise of the authorities and the expertise and attitude of the judges;
- within the different jurisdictions, the concepts that are related to judicial review are characterised by different terminology and may have different meanings;
- the national courts of the different Member States apply different standards of review in similar cases;
- it seems a general attribute that judges hardly motivate their choice of a certain standard of review and the way they apply it;
- finally, judges do not always do what they say they do.

Some of these constraints are general issues that make comparison problematic. The fact, for example that judges seem not to motivate their choice, or do not always do what they say they do – for example, in applying a certain standard of review – seems universal.[12] Other constraints more directly concern the issues under debate, for example the aspect that the concepts or standards of review are different. However, although the concepts or standards may seem different at first sight, upon closer examination there are many similarities. It is not the level of terminology that is under discussion, but their application. Indeed, their application may in practice lead to very similar, and, at the very least, comparable results in the sense that the results can be meaningfully compared. Therefore, taking into account the above-mentioned constraints, the purpose of this comparative exercise is to analyse, on the basis of a careful examination of national landmark cases, how the different systems, concepts and standards work in practice. The aim of this practical approach is to find out about the similarities and differences between the functioning of the different systems of legal review by the national courts and the impact of European law, in an area of European administrative law.

## 3.3 Concepts

### 3.3.1 Judicial review

One of the main concepts in this book is the concept of 'judicial review'. This concept is a source of confusion. In this project it signifies the review of administrative actions by a court of law; that is, actions – usually decisions – taken by an administrative authority.[13] Judicial review is part of the democratic rule of law, as it forms part of the separation of powers and a system of checks and balances.

To clarify matters, let us start by pointing out that the concept of 'judicial review' may be used in a strict sense, which might be called the 'traditional' sense, and in a broad sense. The meaning of the 'traditional' concept of judicial review can be seen in the manner in which it is used in the UK. There, the concept refers to the type of legal review which aims to control the *legality* of actions by public authorities (legality review). For judicial legality review in the UK, there are often said to be three main *grounds* of review: illegality, procedural impropriety and irrationality (Graham). Upon closer examination these grounds of review are similar (but not identical) to the grounds of legality review as exercised by the European, Italian, Dutch, Spanish, Hungarian and French administrative courts.

In other systems (Germany, Sweden, France), it seems that the concept of judicial review may also be used in a broad sense: judicial review then does not only relate to legality review, but refers to a general review of administrative

---

[12] See e.g. Sunstein 2008.

[13] Judicial review can also denote the review of legislation. However, in this book judicial review of legislative acts is not the primary focus.

action by the national courts, including both a traditional legality review and an appeal on the merits (Petit and Rabeux, Edwardsson, and Terhechte).

### 3.3.2 Discretion

Related to the concept of judicial review is the notion of 'discretion'. In case an administrative decision is adopted through the exercise of discretion by the administrative authority, the courts are inclined to review this in a remote or marginal manner (see sections 1.1 and 3.3.3).

Discretion is a classical but very complex notion that may cover different types of leeway that the administrative authorities may be able to dispose of.[14] Moreover, the concept is not always consistently applied by the European and national courts. Although different terms are used within the seven jurisdictions that are the subject of study in this book, it follows from the description of the different systems that, in general, two types of discretion may be distinguished.

The first type of discretion can be denoted as *policy* or *proper* discretion.[15] This type of discretion refers to the power of administrative authorities to make policy choices (Graham, Caranta and Marchetti, Meij, Schimmel and Widdershoven, Lavrijssen, Terhechte). Schimmel and Widdershoven clarify that in the event of policy discretion the institution concerned is empowered to define the actual criteria by which a decision is reached. The classical example of policy discretion in EC competition law used to be the application of the criteria of Article 81, paragraph 3 EC. An example that is still current is the policy discretion of the Commission in deciding whether or not to investigate a competition complaint. Policy discretion implies that a decision-maker has the power to take a specific decision or not and/or the power to decide on the type of decision to be adopted; there is no obligation that prescribes a specific decision, such as an enforcement decision, to be taken (Graham and Lavrijssen). In this context especially the country report regarding Spain is interesting, in the sense that in this system the Constitution explicitly awards the Government the role of deploying its own policies, including economic policies, by which it chooses from a number of political options. In principle, these choices cannot be overturned by the judiciary when reviewing decisions of the Government, although the Spanish legal order has evolved in the sense that even political choices can be reviewed on some grounds, such as the protection of human rights (Del Guayo). This is in contrast with other systems, in which policy-related discretion has been developed, usually by the judiciary itself. Policy discretion, as recognised by the courts, is a logical corollary to the doctrine of separation of powers: if it is for the administration to decide, then it should not be for the judiciary to over-

---

14 See generally, for example, Gil Ibanez 1999.

15 See also: Bailey 2003, p. 845-888; Bailey 2004, p. 1327-1360, Bailey 2007, p. 101-139; Odudu 2002, p. 17-25; Hofman 2003, p. 114-131.

rule such a decision where the administration had freedom in reaching that very decision.

The second type of discretion can be denoted as 'a margin of appreciation' or technical discretion.[16] This type of discretion refers to the situation where an administrative institution has some leeway in assessing the facts it has gathered to reach a decision. In European law this relates to the leeway of the Commission when performing a complex economic, technical or scientific assessment within a framework of set (ambiguous) legal criteria that may play a role in the decision-making process. A well-known example of this type of discretion in European competition law is the discretion in assessing complex economic facts in Article 81 EC proceedings. Although the concepts differ in their precise implications – and we do not wish to belittle the practical consequences of these different implications – it can be seen that such a type of discretion is recognised in many systems of administrative law. In Italy, for example, it has been recognised that the application of open-ended and/or ambiguous legal and, especially, factual words and phrases, referring to complex facts, may imply an authority's technical discretion (Caranta and Marchetti). In the Netherlands this type of discretion is denoted as '*beoordelingsvrijheid*' (Lavrijssen). In Germany the similar concept of '*Beurteilungsspielraum*' refers to a special margin of discretion while interpreting open-textured norms ('*Unbestimmter Rechtsbegriff*' (Terhechte). In Spain, the Constitution distinguishes the role of the Government in deploying its own policies (political acts) from the concept of discretion, and discretion then relates to this second form of leeway. The Government and the public administration enjoy discretion, whenever it is so stated by an Act of Parliament. From the Spanish perspective the concept of discretion is closely linked to the notion of undefined legal concepts and the doctrine of the margin of appraisal (Del Guayo). Unlike the political choices, the exercise of the latter type of discretion may be subject to a wide judicial review. This review includes not only a review of the legality of decisions, but also a check whether or not discretion has been exercised within the limits established by the relevant Act of Parliament, and, in any case, whether or not it has turned into arbitrariness.

### 3.3.3 Standards of review

In his contribution, Zwart highlights that in every jurisdiction, both national and international, courts and administrative authorities are faced with similar tensions caused by two aspects of the concept of the separation of powers, or the institutional balance, which may conflict in any given case. On the one hand, the concept of separation of powers implies that administrative authorities should remain within the territory assigned to them by the law, in particular by the constitution. The courts have the duty to review the lawfulness of administrative acts to ensure that the authorities will not act *ultra vires* their constitutional remit. On the other hand, the concept of separation of powers also

[16] See Bailey 2007; Odudu 2002.

guarantees the agency's freedom to act within the territory assigned to it by the constitution. This guarantee sets limits to what the courts can do when reviewing agency action; the courts are not supposed to substitute their own decisions for those of the administrative authorities nor second-guess their findings (Zwart).

According to Zwart the bipolarity created by the seemingly contradictory need for review and the need for agency autonomy is evidenced by two opposing tests or standards that the courts have used in approaching the review of administrative action, i.e. comprehensive (full) review and remote (marginal) review. These two standards are also used by the European courts and the national courts that are analysed in this book. As we stated above, these two standards of review can be used within the context of a legality review. A review on the merits will necessarily be linked to a full review. Both the European courts and the national courts subject decisions of the Commission or of the national authorities to at least a legality review. As will be discussed below, in some jurisdictions (part of) the administrative decisions may be subject to an appeal on the merits.

As said, in applying legality review the courts may apply a comprehensive (full) test. This seems to be the starting point for most systems. Usually the full test will be remote (or marginal) for some aspects of the decision: generally, within the context of legality review, the European and national courts fully review the establishment of the facts, the interpretation of the law and the compliance with the relevant procedures. They may evaluate whether the findings of the authority were correct with regard to these matters and they may substitute the agency's findings with their own. However, to the extent that the authorities dispose of discretion, the courts apply a marginal review within the context of the legality review. A marginal review implies that the courts do not review whether the exercise of discretion was correct. They review whether the decision is 'outrageous' or 'patently unreasonable', or whether the decision is outside the reasonable modes of action.

A marginal test can be applied with greater or lesser deference towards the original decision-maker. For instance, the traditional test to review discretion in judicial review proceedings in the UK is *'Wednesbury unreasonableness'* (Zwart and Graham). In the *Wednesbury* case itself *'Wednesbury unreasonableness'* was used in a very restricted sense; courts can only interfere if a decision 'is so unreasonable that no reasonable authority could ever have come to it'.[17] In his contribution Graham clarifies that in practice courts may also review whether or not a decision is within a range of reasonable responses for a public authority, which can be seen as more intensive scrutiny than a traditional *Wednesbury* approach.[18] As the application of the *Wednesbury* test will vary according to the circumstances of the cases, the context of the decision under review is vital. There is a spectrum of control ranging from intensive scrutiny, involving

[17] [1948] 1 KB 223.

[18] See also Clayton and Galy 2007, pp. 210-218.

human rights issues, to issues of economic policy or resource allocation where the courts will be more reluctant to intervene.

A marginal test comparable to *Wednesbury unreasonableness* was also introduced by courts in other jurisdictions (Zwart). Although this test is denoted by different terminology, in essence it allows the courts to review the 'patent unreasonableness' or 'reasonableness' of discretionary acts. For example, the European courts check whether there is a 'manifest error of assessment', referring to the situation wherein an error is evident and grave enough so as to preclude any 'potential concurrence' between the established facts on the one hand, and the conclusion drawn from these facts on the other. This European standard that is applied in Article 230 EC actions was inspired by the standard of *'erreur manifeste d'appreciation'* applied by the French Council of State in the *'recours pour excès de pouvoir'*. Also the Italian (*'eccesso di potere'*), Spanish ('arbitrariness'), Dutch ('reasonableness') and Hungarian ('reasonableness') standards for the review of discretion are similar to *Wednesbury unreasonableness*. Like in the UK, the marginal test can be applied in other jurisdictions with lesser or greater deference towards the original decision-maker, depending on the circumstances of the case. For instance, when administrative authorities enjoy a significant degree of discretion, which may especially be the case in the event of policy discretion, the courts may review the exercise of discretion more remotely than when there is limited technical discretion in assessing a set of complicated economic facts (see section 3.4).

### 3.3.4 Appeal on the merits

It should be recalled that not all decisions of competition authorities and economic regulators are subject to a legality review. In some jurisdictions (part of) these decisions may be subject to an appeal on the merits, implying a full review of the exercise of discretion and the possibility for the court to substitute the administrative authority's findings with its own. A well known example can be found in the system in the UK. There, the Competition Appeal Tribunal (CAT) hears appeals on the merits against decisions by the Office of Fair Trading (OFT) and economic regulators for breaches of the Competition Act and Articles 81 and 82 EC. The CAT – the court – can take any decision that the OFT – the authority – could have taken itself. In contrast, regulatory decisions of economic regulators which are not related to breaches of competition law are generally subject to judicial review proceedings. However, as a consequence of Article 4 of the Framework Directive for electronic communications, the CAT also hears appeals on the merits against regulatory decisions of the Office of Communications with regard to the designation and regulation of market parties having 'significant market power' (Graham). It is interesting to note that in contrast to many other Member States, in Sweden it is the *general* rule that administrative courts may determine the suitability or reasonableness of an administrative authority's decision. An administrative court that finds the decision of an administrative body inadequate has the *general* power to take a new decision itself. In doing so, the court holds the same powers as the administrative authority (Edwardsson). In this respect the situation in France should also be noted. Here, the administrative court (Council of State) is in theory the natural venue for actions against national administrative authorities. Although generally the Council of State applies a marginal review ('*contrôle restraint*') where the administrative authority enjoys discretionary power, there has been an interesting development. Over the years, the administrative court's legal monopoly has been significantly curtailed and in practice the civil Paris Court of Appeal has become the primary venue for challenging decisions of the Competition Council, as well as dispute settlement decisions of National Regulatory Authorities. The Paris Court of Appeal subjects the decisions concerned to a review on the merits and has not only the power, but the *duty* to replace (or reform) the authority's decision with its own decision to terminate the dispute (Petit and Rabeux). Traditionally, also in Germany the decisions of the national competition authority and the Federal Network Agency are subject to an appeal on the merits. At first glance, it seems the relevant laws empower the competent administrative or civil courts to fully review all dimensions of the authorities' decisions. However, a closer look at the current situation in Germany reveals that the system is apparently trying to change. Especially in the field of economic regulation, some courts have established a wide discretion for the Federal Network Agency (Terhechte).

## 3.4 The application of standards of review in practice

As administrative authorities dispose generally of more leeway when exercising policy discretion, including the power to define the criteria by which a decision should be reached, than in the case of technical discretion, it would seem logical that the European and national courts will exercise a more marginal review in the event of policy discretion. In this regard it can also be noted that the assessment of complex facts (technical discretion) often is closely intertwined with the establishment of the facts and the interpretation of the law in relation to those facts. As these different stages of the review process may be difficult to distinguish in practice, the courts may be more inclined to consider that elements of complex factual assessments are more properly contained in the sphere of a less marginal review than the court would exercise when reviewing decisions involving policy discretion. In this respect, the judgment of the UK Court of Appeal in the *IBA Health* case is illustrative, where it considered that there was no doubt that the court was entitled to inquire into whether or not there was sufficient evidence to support the Office of Fair Trading's belief that the legal conditions for a referral of a merger to the Competition Commission were not met (Graham).[19]

---

19 *Office of Fair Trading* v. *IBA Health* [2004] 4 All ER 1103.

From the above it follows that national courts do not necessarily review decisions involving technical assessments only marginally. For example, also in France the Council of State has usually considered that most complex economic assessments in the field of competition law constitute factual, objective issues, over which – disputably – the deciding authority enjoys in fact little discretionary power (Petit and Rabeux). Lavrijssen also illustrates that the District Court of Rotterdam and the Trade and Industry Appeals Tribunal (*CBB*) commonly engage in an intensive review of decisions by the competition authority concerning the application of Articles 81 and 82 EC. The District Court has at times substituted its own assessment for that of the authority, a practice condoned by the CBB on appeal.

In this respect the situation in Italy must also be noted. Caranta and Marchetti discuss that in Italy it is possible to discern *different* standards of review with regard to the review of technical appraisals. Particularly if the statutory language provides for technical factual analysis and the administrative agency has specific institutional expertise in the matter, a weak judicial review (based on grounds of legality) could be justified. By contrast, if the administrative authority does not have specific expertise and the statute provides for complex assessments of a technical nature, a *de novo* (strong) review will generally be accorded. Therefore, the question of whether the court could be entitled to substitute its own construction for that of the administration in decisions involving complex technical appraisals seems to depend on the technical expertise of the *administrative authority*. This is interesting, because in other jurisdictions it seems that the question of whether the court can substitute its own views in complex technical matters may depend on the technical expertise of the court *itself*, as is the case in the United Kingdom, for example.

However, Caranta and Marchetti note that the Italian case law is still in flux and that scholary opinions diverge sharply. Illustrative for this ambiguity are the *Jet Fuel* cases as decided by the *Consiglio di Stato*. In these cases the appeals and cross appeals lodged by the market parties concerned were heard by panels (consisting of five *Consiglieri*, including the President), each having a slightly different composition, and the drafting of the judgments was entrusted to different *Consiglieri*. Although all panels in the different judgments rejected the appeals, they show remarkable differences with regard to the question of intensity of review of antitrust decisions. For instance, one *Consigliere* stressed that the Antitrust Authority disposed of wide margins of technical discretion and that therefore the judicial review should be confined to a legality review along the lines of '*eccesso di potere*', with insufficient and inconsistent reasoning as the foremost ground of review. In this view, any incursion upon the merits of the decision is to be excluded. But other *Consiglieri* subject the Antitrust Authority's decision to a very probing analysis. In the latter view the court may reconsider the technical choices and impose its own reading of 'indeterminate legal concepts'. In other words, there is no reason to distinguish between soft review and intensive review. In this regard the *Consigliere* responsible for one of the judgments considers that judicial review should be intense, complete and effective, the only limit being the impossibility to take the decision in the place of the competent administrative authority. On the basis of an analysis of several other important cases, Caranta and Marchetti conclude that the picture is one of confusion as to what exactly is the standard of judicial review applied by the administrative courts in reviewing decisions by the Italian Antitrust authority.

In his contribution regarding Spain, Del Guayo discusses that there has always been a degree of reluctance on the side of the Spanish courts not only to quash administrative decisions on economic issues, but also to review the core of the decision on grounds related to, on the one hand, the technical discretion which is involved in such decisions, a discretion they cannot substitute with their own, and, on the other hand, the fact that the decisions have been adopted in the light of reports produced by specialised bodies. As mentioned in para. 3.3.2, there exists a strong sense of the political realm in Spain, in which the courts traditionally do not tread. However, in several merger cases the Spanish Supreme Court has demonstrated that it will subject the economic assessments in merger cases to a more intensive scrutiny, albeit without substituting the administrative authority's opinion. In a Judicial Resolution, for instance, the Spanish Supreme Court awarded *Endesa*, the biggest Spanish electricity utility, an interim suspension of the go-ahead decision by the government regarding a takeover by *Gas Natural*.[20] The Supreme Court showed a strong readiness to analyse the decision of the government. The arguments that were used, including the lack of competition in the energy markets and the inability of the conditions imposed by the Government to really compensate the restrictive effects on competition, clearly showed that the Supreme Court went beyond what is expected from a court in dealing with an application for judicial interim relief. In the opinion of Del Guayo, the Court undoubtedly showed that it was ready to go into the substance of the governmental decision, in line with the *Tetra Laval* judgment.

Cseres and Langer show that in Hungary most, if not all, judgments rendered in the field of the cartel prohibition and the prohibition on the abuse of dominance display a striking degree of judicial deference to the (economic) assessments made by the Hungarian Antitrust Authority and accordingly do not go beyond a marginal review which hinges on verifying whether the authority has made a manifest error of appraisal. Yet in the field of merger control the Budapest Municipal Court seems to be willing to depart from this. Illustrative is the acquisition of *Népszabadság Rt.* by *B.V. Tabora*, a member of the Swiss *Ringier Group*, which is active in the newspaper market in many European countries. On appeal, the Budapest Municipal Court annulled the decision of the Antitrust Authority to prohibit the merger on the basis of a full review of the economic evidence supporting the decision, but adopted a more remote review with regard to the application of the portfolio-theory of competitive harm. Therefore, the Court accepted *as fact* that the portfolio-effect on the market for dailies

[20] Judicial Resolution of the Supreme Court of 28 April 2006, *Endesa*.

strengthened a dominant position and thus had detrimental effects on competition. Surprisingly, the Court nonetheless reviewed whether the economic analysis, the facts and the evidence convincingly characterised the claimed detrimental effects. It considered: 'The Court emphasises that it does not question the appraisal of the authority, but has examined the disclosed facts and circumstances that were taken into account in the [GVH's] assessment. Furthermore, it has disclosed the blatantly unreasonable conclusions and dismissed the incorrect facts (i.e. lack of supply side substitution) and substituted them for facts based on the available data.' If anything, this case also shows how difficult it is to make a strict distinction between the review of the establishment of the facts and the subsequent assessment of those facts. Cseres and Langer submit that the approach adopted by the Hungarian court is arguably in line with the principles of judicial review laid down in the *Tetra Laval* ruling, even though it was handed down on 23 September 2004.

The developments in the aforementioned Member States show the tendency of national courts to fully, or at least more intensively, review the exercise of (technical) discretion in a legality review in certain circumstances.

Developments in Germany, on the contrary, show that the competent courts have remotely reviewed the exercise of discretion by the Federal Network Agency in the context of an appeal on the merits (Terhechte). In 2007 the Federal Administrative Court of Germany (*Bundesverwaltungsgericht*) affirmed in a landmark decision a more restrictive approach regarding its burden of proof concerning discretionary decisions launched by the Federal Network Agency.[21] According to Terhechte, the court delivered a very new approach towards the doctrine of discretion in German administrative law. Because of the lack of clarity of the legal provision and the very complex dimensions of the concrete decision of the agency, it is not possible for courts to review all aspects of such decisions. According to the judgment, courts can only review, first, whether all relevant interests of the parties involved were properly investigated, secondly, whether all relevant facts of the case were explored, thirdly, whether all relevant matters were considered in the case, and, finally, that no arguments were taken into consideration which had or have no connection to the case. The judgment has stirred a heated academic debate on the meaning of the judgment. Some scholars proclaim that a new doctrine of 'Regulatory Discretion' should be established, implying that decisions or part of decisions based on complex economic assessments should not be subject to judicial review or the judicial review should at least be restricted.

[21] Bundesverwaltungsgericht (Federal Administrative Court of Germany), Case 6 C 42.06 of (28. November 2007), Deutsches Verwaltungsblatt (DVBl.) 2008, 659; the judgment is available online at http://www.bundesverwaltungsgericht.de. See also the review of the judgment by Thorsten Attendorn, 'Das Bundesverwaltungsgericht, die Bundesnetzagentur und die Sinnenprüfung – planerische Gestaltungsfreiräume bei der Zugangsanordnung nach § 21 TKG?' , *Deutsches Verwaltungsblatt (DVBl.)* 2008, p. 1408 et seq.

Unlike the developments in Germany, in Sweden there are no indications that the legal review of administrative action within the context of an appeal on the merits is exercised in a less intensive way, nor is there a lively academic debate on the (lowering of the) standard of review (Edwardsson).

### 3.5 Influence of EC law

#### 3.5.1 Little influence of EC law

When organising the conference that lies at the basis of this book, it was expected that the *Tetra Laval* case (and subsequent cases) would have quite an impact on the national standards of review; as is well-known the standard of review in this case was extensively discussed at the European level, and it seemed logical to assume that this impact would reverberate throughout judicial Europe. It was this academic interest that led the organisers to embark on the project of which this book is the conclusion. It came therefore as quite a surprise that, as can be concluded from the contributions of this book, in general there is *little* influence of EC law, and the *Tetra Laval* standard in particular, on the standard of review applied by the national courts when reviewing decisions of national competition authorities and national regulatory authorities that apply European law or national competition law. Only in the Netherlands and in Italy administrative courts have referred explicitly or implicitly to relevant case law of the European courts in order to justify or specify the applicable standard of review in a certain case. However, the national courts give little or no explanation as to why they draw inspiration from the relevant European cases and to what extent these cases are relevant for the standards of review applied.[22]

In the Italian *Consip* case the *Consiglio di Stato* again used the case law of the European courts as the necessary yardstick for judicial review of antitrust decisions at national level.[23] According to the *Consiglio di Stato* this is even more relevant after the entry into force of Regulation 1/2003 on the application of the Articles 81 and 82 EC. The *Consiglio di Stato* then recalls that European courts are ready to verify whether the rules on procedure and of the statement of reasons have been complied with, whether the facts have been accurately stated and whether there has been any manifest error of appraisal or misuse if powers. The court admits that the European courts have at times given a very probing look at the Commission's antitrust decisions, but it maintains that the judicial review as performed by the Italian courts is no less stringent. However, as remarked above (section 3.4), more recent Italian case law shows there is still a lot of controversy as to the theoretical underpinnings and the practical applica-

22 Even among the authors of this synthesis opinions differ on whether or not the Trade and Industry Appeals Tribunal does or does not rely on *Tetra Laval* in its judgments. It is clear that it does not do so explicitly, but compare Lavrijssen's contribution in this volume with Gerbrandy 2009.

23 Cons. St., Sez. VI, 2 Marzo 2004, n. 926, *Buoni pasto, Urbanistica e appalti*, 2004, 817, note by S. Mirate, Autorità antitrust e controllo giurisdizionale sulle valutazioni techniche.

tion of the judicial review tasks. The more recent European cases, such as *Tetra Laval*, even if they are a possible source of inspiration for some of the trends discernible in the Italian case law, are not openly discussed in the judgments handed down by the administrative courts (Caranta and Marchetti).

In Spain *dissenting* judges of the Spanish Supreme Court referred to the *Tetra Laval* standard in two merger cases. But the judgments adopted by the majority of the Supreme Court do not mention the case (Del Guayo).

Several reasons can be identified to explain the limited influence of European law on the standards of review applied by the national courts. First, it should be recalled that in most cases, with the exception of the application of the electronic communications directives, there is no harmonisation of the standard of review. This means that the principle of procedural autonomy prevails (see section 2).

Secondly, constitutional reasons may prevent the national courts from applying a European standard of review. Petit and Rabeux emphasise that certain endogenous features of the French court system appear manifestly incongruous with the principles enshrined in *Tetra Laval*. Of particular importance is the fact that the intrusive standard of review applied by the Paris Court of Appeal is consubstantial to the constitutionally protected right of appeal. Any lowering of the Paris Court of Appeal's standard of judicial review could thus entail a violation of the French constitution. Also in Sweden and Germany there are constitutional justifications for the intensive review of administrative decisions conducted by the Swedish and German administrative courts (Edwardsson, Terhechte). This means that the general national legal culture may block a spontaneous spill-over effect from the European courts to the national courts.

Thirdly, there may be a culture within the specific courts not to look at the case law of the European courts. Del Guayo, for instance, argues that Spanish courts do not refer often to decisions of the EC, due partially to the fact that Spain is a relatively young member of the EU. Cseres and Langer also raise the question as to why the Hungarian courts do not refer to or rely on European law more often. They argue that as there is a high degree of convergence between national Hungarian substantive competition rules and the European competition law provisions it could reasonably be expected that the enforcement of these closely aligned rules follow the guidelines provided by the European Courts. But this is, in fact, not the case. Cseres and Langer submit that one possible explanation for this could be that, unlike the national competition authorities that actively participate in the European Competition Network, national courts are still more embedded in their national legal system and focus more on national legal rules and jurisprudence.

In following this line of reasoning, one might expect that the influence of the European standard of review would be greater in national legal cultures that mirror closely the legal culture of the European Community Courts. Very generally speaking, one would thus expect direct influence in, for example, the founding Member States more readily than in the new Member States, and more directly in the system on which the European administrative law system was built – mainly the French system – than in others. But his is not necessarily reflected in the judgments of the national courts. It must also be noted that this argument may be reversed: if the national judicial culture is comparable to the Community judicial culture, it is not necessary to refer to European judgments explicitly, since the standards of review are comparable to begin with (see section 3.5.2). Furthermore, if *this* line is followed, it could be expected that in the new Member States, where the alliance with European law is more recent, explicit references would be made. As the example of Hungary shows, however, this is not necessarily the case in practice.

There may be another interesting theme here that revolves around the role of case law in the common law system and the continental – civil – law systems. As the role of precedents is, theoretically at least, much larger in the common law system, it might perhaps be expected that explicit reference to case law – including case law of the Court of Justice – would be more generally available. In traditional civil law courts referring to case law including that of the Court of Justice has only recently been adopted as an explicitly-mentioned line of reasoning – also as a result of the influence of the European Court of Human Rights;[24] referring to and following a standard of review laid down by another court could be more or less reasonably expected. However, as with the assumption made above for Hungary, this assumption is also not confirmed in practice. It is unclear whether this may be caused by the view of the national judiciary on its autonomy, for example, even in the light of European influence, or whether perhaps a more general national scepticism which may exist in some Member States could be at the root. What is clear is that, in practice, many elements may shape the attitude of the judiciary on influences from outside the national legal system. The authors of this synthesis sincerely regret that these themes, relating to the roles legal culture and national culture could play in explaining why a national court would (or would not) rely on European case law and a European standard of review, cannot be disentangled here.[25] In this respect further research could and perhaps should be undertaken.

### 3.5.2 Possible convergence between European and national standards of review

The fact that we have identified no significant explicit influence of European law on the standards of review applied by the national courts in competition law and economic regulation cases does not automatically justify the conclusion that there are enormous differences between the standards of review applied by national courts. Nor does it mean that the influence of the European standard of review is nonexistent: it might only be less apparent than is evident at first glance. Although there is a significant difference between

24 Koopmans 1999.

25 On this issue see, among others, Ewald 1995, p. 489-510 and Teubner 2000

the systems for legal review that allow an appeal on the merits – present in the UK, France, Germany and Sweden – and the *Tetra Laval* standard, upon closer examination it turns out that national courts exercise the legality review in competition law cases in a similar way as the European courts do in *Tetra Laval*, which arguably amounts to a more intensive application of the legality review (section 1.2).

For instance, in his contribution Graham compares in detail the standard of review as applied by the ECJ in *Tetra Laval* with the standard of review applied by the Competition Appeal Tribunal (CAT) in judicial review proceedings with regard to merger decisions of the Office of Fair Trading. He concludes that the tests are, if not identical, very similar. It seems therefore that the standard of review applied by the CAT in judicial review proceedings concerning competition law cases is more intensive than has been the case in judicial review procedures with respect to decisions of economic regulators that were decided by the High Court.

Also in Spain, Hungary, Italy and the Netherlands, there are examples of competition law cases, where the competent administrative courts apply the standard of review in a legality review in a similar way as the ECJ in *Tetra Laval* (see also section 3.4). In Germany, the decisions of the national competition authority and the Federal Network Agency are subject to a full review within the context of an appeal on the merits. One could submit that the way the German courts apply the standard of review may also converge towards the *Tetra Laval* standard, as there seems to be a tendency to review the exercise of discretion in a more remote way. As mentioned by Terhechte, the German example could mark the boundaries of the tendency of a more intensive application of the legality review. Because of the special characteristics of legislation in the field of economic regulation and competition it is, of course, not possible to review every interpretation of the vague and open-textured rules as well as it is not possible to review all dimensions of the economic assessments in these special fields.

To answer the question whether or not the *Tetra Laval* case of the Court of Justice has actually influenced the national standards of review, however, even though it is not explicitly mentioned in national court cases, further (empirical) research should be undertaken.[26]

## 4 Concluding remarks

Contrary to what one might expect, upon closer examination of the way the standards of review are applied in practice, there are striking similarities between the way the European courts exercise the legality review in Article 230 EC actions and the way the national courts do this in national judicial review proceedings. It might be concluded that the above-mentioned developments indicate a tendency of spontaneous convergence between the

26 See, for the Netherlands, A. Gerbrandy 2009.

manner of legality review by the European and national courts. But it is not necessarily so that there is only a top-down influence by the European standards on the national standards. It seems that this tendency can partly be explained by internal factors. For instance, Del Guayo attributes the increasing willingness of the Spanish judiciary to review the core of administrative decisions on economic issues, including competition decisions, mainly to a number of idiosyncratic characteristics of the Spanish legal order, such as the progressive development of a number of key constitutional provisions, which have resulted in a more proactive attitude of the judiciary towards administrative and governmental decisions. Importantly, whenever constitutional rights are involved in a public decision, this fosters a more substantial review.

It should be recalled that even if the European legal principle of procedural autonomy prevails in the absence of European harmonisation, national courts do not operate in isolation. On the basis of Article 10 EC, all national courts have to safeguard the right to effective legal protection, which is part of the common legal tradition of the EU Member States and enshrined in the European Convention on Human Rights. It is argued that the last-mentioned right entails an obligation for national courts to refrain from a very marginal review of national administrative decisions that execute European law. In any event the courts should have a careful look at the facts, reasoning and assessment of the facts, albeit without substituting the opinion of the administrative authority with their own. Moreover, the judges that are members of the European courts all have experience as judges in national courts. This means that national experiences and attitudes with regard to the application of the standard of review in judicial review proceedings may find their way to influence the application of the European standard of review in 230 EC actions. In its turn, this European standard of review may further influence the application of the national standards of review by the national courts. This process of cross-fertilisation between European and national standards of review may be further stimulated in the situation that European law requires close co-operation between the European Commission and national authorities in the application of European law, such as in the case of the enforcement of Articles 81 and 82 EC. Schimmel and Widdershoven have argued that in these type of cases it would be justified that administrative decisions are subjected to the same standard of review, irrespective by which authority (national or European) a certain decision was adopted.

In each case the European and national courts will have to walk the tightrope between the right to effective legal protection and the need for efficient and effective (multi-level) decision-making processes by the administrative authorities. It is submitted that the *Tetra Laval* standard may be a good starting point in finding this balance. This standard provides transparency with regard to the different stages of the review process; the establishment stage, which is subject to a full review, and the assessment stage, which is subject to a more restrained review. By applying this two-stage approach the courts may serve as catalysts to ensure that decision-making procedures are proper, that the evidential basis is of high quality, encompassing all relevant facts and that the reasoning with regard to the assessment of the facts is logical, coherent and consistent. This enables the European and national courts to review carefully whether all conflicting interests are weighed in a proportionate way, but without substituting the opinion of the competent bodies with their own.[27]

When the *Tetra Laval* standard is adopted as a starting point, it can be envisioned as a consolidation of the developments in the Member States as set out in this book. The success in walking the tight rope between effective legal protection and efficient and effective decision-making will, finally, depend on the national context – the constitutional, legal and judicial culture – which will add its own elements to the exercise of this standard.

[27] Scott and Sturm 2007, pp. 565-594.

## Bibliography


BAILEY (2003)

D. Bailey 2003, 'Standard of Proof in EC Merger Proceedings: A Common Law Perspective', [2003] *Common Market Law Review* 40, no. 4, pp. 845-888.

BAILEY (2004)

D. Bailey, 'Scoope of Judicial Review under article 81 EC', [2004] *Common Market Law Review* 41, no. 5, pp. 1327-1360.

BAILEY (2007)

D. Bailey, 'Damages Actions under the EC Merger Regulation', [2007] *Common Market Law Review* 44, no. 1, pp. 101-139.

CLAYTON (2007)

R. Clayton, QC and K. Galy, 'Shifting Standards of Review', [2007] *Judicial Review*, pp. 210-21

EWALD (1995)

W. Ewald,, 'Comparative Jurisprudence (II): The logic of legal transplants', [1995] *Am.J.Comp. L.* 43: pp. 489-510.

GERBRANDY (2009)

A. Gerbrandy, *Convergentie in het mededingingsrecht. De invloed van het EG-recht op materiële toepassing, toegang, bewijs en toetsing bij de Nederlandse mededingingsbestuursrechter, bezien in het licht van effectieve rechtsbescherming*, (Boom Juridische Uitgevers, Den Haag 2009)

GERVEN, VAN (1995)

W. van Gerven, 'Bridging the Gap between Community and National law: Towards a Principle of Homogeneity in the Field of Legal Remedies?' [1995] *Common Market Law Review* no. 3, p. 700

GIL IBANEZ (1999)

A.J. Gil Ibanez, *The Administrative Supervision and Enforcement of EC Law: Powers, Procedures and Limits* (Hart Publishing, Oxford, 1999)

HOFMAN (2003)

H.C.H. Hofman, 'Good Governance in European Merger Control: Due Process and Checks and Balances under Review', *European Competition Law Review* 24, no. 3, pp. 114-131.

KOOPMANS (1999)

T. Koopmans, *Drie typen van rechtsvinding* (G.J. Wiarda): Nabeschouwing (W.E.J. Tjeenk Willink, Zwolle 1999)

ODUDU (2002)

O. Odudu, 'Article 81(3), Discretion and Direct Effect, [2002] *European Competition Law Review* 23, no. 1, pp. 17-25.

SCOTT (2007)

J. Scott & S. Sturm, 'Courts as Catalysts; Re-thinking the Judicial Role in New Governance', [2007] *Columbia Journal of European Law* , no 3, pp. 565-594.

SUNSTEIN (2008)
C.R. Sunstein, *Beyond Judicial Minimalism*, Harvard Public Law Working Paper, no. 08-40, 2008.

TEMPLE LANG (2000)
J. Temple Lang, 'The Principle of Effective Protection of Community Law Rights', in D. O'Keeffe (ed.), *Judicial Review in European Union Law*, Liber Amicorum Lord Slynn of Hadley (Kluwer Law International, The Hague/London/Boston 2000)

TEUBER (2000)
G. Teubner, 'Legal Irritants: Good Faith in British Law or How Unifying Law Ends up in New Divergences', in: F. Snyder (ed.), *The Europeanisation of Law: the Legal Effects of European Integration*, (Hart Publishing, Oxford/Portland Oregon) pp. 243-268

VESTERDORF (2003)
B. Vesterdorf, 'Certain Reflections on Recent Judgments Reviewing Commission Merger Control Decisions', in: M. Hoskins & W. Robinson (eds), *A True European: Essays for judge David Edward* (Hart Publishing, Oxford 2003), p. 136-144.

# Cases

**European Court of Justice**

**Opinion AG**



**Court of First Instance**

**The Netherlands**

*CBB*



*District Court Rotterdam*

# Contributors

*Roberto Caranta*
Professor of Administrative Law, University of Torino, Italy

*Kati Cseres*
Associate Professor of European Law, Europa Instituut, University of Amsterdam, the Netherlands

*Iñigo del Guayo*
Professor of Administrative Law, University of Almería, Spain

*Eva Edwardsson*
Juris Doktor, University of Uppsala

*Oda Essens*
Lecturer of Economic Public Law, Europa Instituut, Utrecht University, the Netherlands

*Anna Gerbrandy*
Lecturer of Economic Public Law, Europa Instituut, Utrecht University, the Netherlands

*Cosmo Graham*
Professor of Law, School of Law, University of Leicester, United Kingdom

*Jurian Langer*
Senior lawyer, Ministry of Foreign Affairs, The Hague, the Netherlands

*Saskia Lavrijssen*
Senior lecturer of Economic Public Law, Europa Instituut, Utrecht University, the Netherlands

*Barbara Marchetti*
Professor of Administrative Law, University of Trento, Italy

*Arjen Meij*
Judge at the Court of First Instance of the EC and Wiarda Professor of Law, Faculty of Law, Utrecht University, the Netherlands

*Annetje Ottow*
Professor of Economic Public Law, Europa Instituut, Utrecht University, the Netherlands

*Nicolas Petit*
Lecturer in Competition Law and Economics, University of Liege, Belgium, co-director of the Institute for European Legal Studies; Associate, Howrey LLP, Brussels

*Sacha Prechal*
Professor of European Law, Europa Instituut, Utrecht University, the Netherlands

*Louise Rabeux*
Associate, Howrey LLP, Brussels

*Matthieu Schimmel*
Having obtained a Master's degree in European Law at Utrecht University, Mathieu Schimmel is currently enrolled in a Master of Public Affairs programme at Sciences Po Paris

*Joerg Terhechte*
Dr. iur., Assistant Professor of Law at the Institute for European Law, Hamburg University School of Law, Germany

*Rob Widdershoven*
Professor of European Administrative Law, Utrecht University, the Netherlands

*Tom Zwart*
Professor of Law, Utrecht University, and Director of the Dutch School of Human Rights Research